the differing views of individual Justices are closely studied. But the book brings out clearly the logical consistency that has in fact marked the Court's major decisions. Never dodging the difficult issues, but carefully sifting each case in nontechnical language, the author moves surely toward conclusions that will be illuminating to all with an interest in the American political scene.

ABOUT THE AUTHOR

"Dr. BERNARD SCHWARTZ has achieved recognition as one of the nation's leading legal scholars and teachers. The late Arthur T. Vanderbilt, Chief Justice of the New Jersey Supreme Court, who had taught the young Schwartz at New York University, helped him to persuade Harvard University to waive its seven-year study requirement for entering the graduate law school. If they turned down Mr. Schwartz, the jurist wrote Harvard authorities, they would be repeating the mistake they had made nearly 200 years earlier in refusing another bright law student, Alexander Hamilton.

"There is no denying that New York University's homegrown legal light is a man with bounce and brilliance. Dr. Schwartz has been director of the university's Institute of Comparative Law since its inception in 1953. He is internationally known for his lucid studies in comparative administrative law — American, French, and British. His latest, and perhaps most widely acclaimed, book is *The Supreme Court: Constitutional Revolution in Retrospect.*" — *The New York Times*

THE
SUPREME COURT

CONSTITUTIONAL REVOLUTION
IN RETROSPECT

BERNARD SCHWARTZ

PROFESSOR OF LAW
DIRECTOR OF THE INSTITUTE OF COMPARATIVE LAW
NEW YORK UNIVERSITY SCHOOL OF LAW

THE RONALD PRESS COMPANY   •   NEW YORK

Library of Congress Catalog Card Number: 57–9302

PRINTED IN THE UNITED STATES OF AMERICA

PREFACE

Ever since de Tocqueville, men have emphasized the primordial role of the judge in American society. For it has become almost a commonplace that the courts—and particularly the Supreme Court —are the fulcrum upon which our institutions turn. And it follows from this that a real understanding of our system and how it operates is impossible without some knowledge of the manner in which the Supreme Court has exercised its constitutional role.

One for whom the *United States Supreme Court Reports* constitute his staple reading cannot help but note the extent to which he has been joined by others who have become concerned with the work of the highest tribunal. Contemporary interest in the Supreme Court appears, indeed, to be at an almost all-time high. Throughout the country, there is the keenest desire to learn more about the institution which, all have come to see, plays such a vital part in our polity.

At the same time, it cannot be gainsaid that there has been, during the past generation, a profound change in the manner in which Americans have tended to regard their highest judicial institution. Until recently, the attitude of Americans toward the Supreme Court recalled with singular fidelity that with which, according to Burke, Englishmen of a century and a half ago should have looked upon the institutions of their country: "We ought to understand it according to our measure; and to venerate where we are not able to understand." Yet, if to our grandfathers and our fathers the functioning of the Supreme Court was a sacred mystery of American statesmanship, in our own day the pendulum has swung to the opposite extreme. Veneration has, all too often, given way to vituperation, and the high tribunal has been the subject of more than its share of purely partisan censure and attack.

To be sure, no governmental institution in a democratic society should be above and beyond criticism. Criticism to be fruitful, however, should be based upon understanding. In the case of the Supreme Court, there has been all too little comprehension. Nor have there been many attempts by lawyers familiar with the Court

iii

to explain what that tribunal has done except to those, who, like themselves, are specialists in the law. But, if one thing is clear, in a country such as ours, it is that the work of the Supreme Court is too significant to be the domain of a relatively few legal specialists. War, according to the famous aphorism, is too important a matter to be left to the generals. American constitutional law is similarly too significant to be left only to the lawyers and law professors.

This book has been written upon the assumption that the constitutional law dispensed by the Supreme Court is more than the private preserve of the legal profession. As such, it has sought to deal with all the important areas of the Court's work, while at the same time seeking to avoid the arid pedantry all too often characteristic of the legal treatise. It is, of course, true that much of the Court's work has concerned technical legal subjects that can hardly be presented with all the fluency of popular fiction. Yet even these matters need not be obscured, as they all too often are, in the technical vacuum of overwordy legal language. Even they can be presented in readable fashion and in a manner that makes clear their significance to the nonlawyer interested in the functioning of his country's political system. That, at least, is the faith that has led to the writing of this book.

Of especial significance to one concerned with the Supreme Court is the manner in which that tribunal's role has altered in recent years. In 1937, there occurred a veritable revolution in the Court's jurisprudence. This has affected the course of our constitutional law more than has generally been realized. It is this constitutional revolution, now some twenty years old, that has served as the central theme of this book. In all the important areas of the Court's work, the changed role of the Court has had its effects. The areas themselves constitute the stuff of American public law and political life. Here, we shall be dealing with the Court's relationship to the other departments of the Government, its position as the arbiter of federalism, its role as guardian of the Bill of Rights, and, of particular moment in a society dominated by international conflict and tension, the manner in which the Court's work has been affected by war and cold war. We will see that, despite aberrations, notably by certain Justices, the Court's decisions have followed logical patterns, consistent with the bases of the constitutional revolution of 1937. This, it is believed, is the most important factor to be noted. Despite claims to the contrary, the Supreme Court *has* carried forward the institutional development of our public law and has done so in accordance with the logical consistency required in any matured legal system.

A work like the present cannot, if it is to be faithful to its purpose, be mere panegyric. This is perhaps the most painful part of authorship for one to whom constitutional law is more than a mere vocation. Still, just as an omelet is impossible without some breaking of eggs, so is an account of the working of any human institution without some censure. Judges are, it is true, only men; but so are those who write about them. To denigrate either the Supreme Court as an institution or any of its individual members is the last thing intended by the present writer. On the contrary, as Chief Justice Stone aptly stated: "I have no patience with the complaint that criticism of judicial action involves any lack of respect for the courts. Where the courts deal, as ours do, with great public questions, the only protection against unwise decisions, and even judicial usurpation, is careful scrutiny of their action and fearless comment upon it."

Bernard Schwartz

New York
    April, 1957

CONTENTS

THE
SUPREME COURT

1

THE COURT AND CONSTITUTIONAL REVOLUTION

On the north and south walls of the Supreme Court Chamber in Washington are carved two marble panels depicting processions of historical lawgivers. Of the eighteen figures on the panels only one is there because of his work as a judge, and he is the one American represented: John Marshall. This is more than mere coincidence, for it sharply illustrates a basic difference between the making of law in the United States and in other countries. The great lawgivers in other systems have been mighty monarchs, of the type of Hammurabi and Justinian, divinely inspired prophets like Moses, philosophers such as Confucius, or scholars like Hugo Grotius and Blackstone. We in the United States have certainly had our share of the last two types of lawgiver—particularly among the men who drew up the organic documents upon which our present polity is based. Significantly enough, however, it is not a Jefferson nor a Madison who is depicted as *the* American lawgiver, but the great Chief Justice who, more than any one man, has left his imprint upon the development of our constitutional law.

John Marshall may be represented as the American lawgiver par excellence, because it is he, more than anyone else, who represents for us the voice of the Federal Supreme Court. It was Marshall who established the role of the highest Court as the authoritative expounder of the Constitution, and it has been, in consequence, the Court, more even than the draftsmen of the Constitution, that has been the lawgiver in the American system. The organic instrument drawn up in 1787 lays down only the framework of our governmental system. One who looks merely to the language of the constitutional text will obtain but a partial and distorted picture

3

of the actual working of our polity. That this is true is obvious if one considers the brevity of the constitutional document, with its seven thousand words more or less. Compared with the succinctness of this basic text, the bulk of Supreme Court materials is immense. According to a recent estimate,[1] the highest tribunal has decided well over four thousand cases involving questions of constitutional interpretation, with the result that at least fifty thousand pages of the *United States Supreme Court Reports* are devoted to constitutional law topics. The suggestion that the Constitution contains in embryo the entirety of this mass of constitutional law confronts the will to believe with a well-nigh impossible test.[2]

Nor is it accurate to think of the work of the Supreme Court as mere exegesis of a fundamental text. A picture of American constitutional law as only a mechanical process, akin to the judicial construction of a contract or a will, though true sometimes, is at variance with reality in the great majority of instances. The most important cases in our constitutional law have stemmed from a handful of brief phrases in the organic document, particularly the grant of Congressional power "To regulate Commerce . . . among the several States" and the prohibition against the deprivation of "life, liberty, or property, without due process of law." In giving meaning to these general phrases (which have constituted the heart of constitutional-law litigation), the Supreme Court has been left almost completely at large. Furnished with no guide, beyond the broad language of the text, the Court has been able to give meaning to the phrases in question in accordance with its own policy considerations in specific cases—and, in this field, not even entirely subject to the normal necessity of keeping the corpus of the law internally consistent.

It is true, in the phrase of a leading Supreme Court historian, that, however the Court may interpret the provisions of the Constitution, it is still the Constitution which is the law and not the decisions of the Court. Yet, in most cases of consequence, the constitutional language is not so precise as to make its application automatic; even in supposedly simple cases, the Supreme Court presents anything but the aspect of a judicial "slot machine." On the contrary, as Charles Evans Hughes once so candidly remarked, "We are under a Constitution, but the Constitution is what the judges say it is." The Federal Constitution is not a self-executing document. The *ought* laid down in 1787 must run the gauntlet of judicial interpretation before it attains the practical status of an *is*. This is, in a sense, true of all legislation; but it is especially true of a constitution whose terms must, of necessity, be less specific and detailed than those of an ordinary law. Thus, a constitution must, in practice, be what the judges say it is.

Need for Judicial Review

The power peremptorily to define the Constitution is what makes the work of the Supreme Court of such consequence. Indeed, it is not going too far to say that because of it the Court is unique among contemporary governmental institutions. To it alone, in the last analysis, is assigned the function of guarding the ark of the Constitution. Through the exercise of its constitutional role, the Court has wielded power far beyond that assumed by any other judicial tribunal. "In no other nation on earth," caustically declares a recent critic, "does a group of judges hold the sweeping political power—the privilege in practice, not just in theory, of saying the last governmental word—that is held by the nine U.S. Supreme Court Justices." [4]

Authority such as that exercised by our highest Court is not inherent in the nature of judicial power. In truth, as the experience of other countries amply demonstrates, the judiciary is normally the weakest of the branches of government. "The judiciary," wrote Alexander Hamilton in the *Federalist Papers,* "is beyond comparison the weakest of the three departments of power. . . . [It] has no influence over either the sword or the purse; no direction either of the strength or the wealth of the society; and can take no active resolution whatever. It may truly be said to have neither FORCE nor WILL, but merely judgment."

Despite the inherent weakness of its original position, the Supreme Court has managed successfully to assert its power as authoritative expounder of the Constitution. Though it possesses neither the sword of the executive nor the purse of the legislature, its judgments are normally adhered to without question by those who direct the strength and the wealth of the society. As an acute English observer put it, with reference to the Court's invalidation of President Truman's action in the celebrated *Steel-Seizure* case: *

All observers of the American scene should have noted, with respect, the most impressive fact. This is that the Supreme Court, although it does not possess and never has possessed any means of enforcing its decisions, has once more brought to heel the mighty: the President, the union, the industry, and Congress. All that was needed to produce this effect was the knowledge that the Court had seen and was ready to do its constitutional duty. [5]

* *Infra,* pp. 62-81.

That the Supreme Court has been accorded such deference, despite its dependence upon the political branches of government for enforcement of its decisions, has been due to the universal recognition among Americans that a system such as ours, based upon a written constitution, can hardly be effective in practice without an authoritative judicial arbiter of constitutional issues. Addressing the court in the *Five Knight's* case (one of the great State Trials of Stuart England), the attorney general of Charles I asked, "Shall any say, The King cannot do this? No, we may only say, He will not do this." [6] It was precisely to ensure that, in our system, we would be able to say, "The State *cannot* do this" that we enacted a written constitution containing basic limitations upon the powers of government. Of what avail would such limitations be, however, if there were no legal machinery to enforce them? Without such machinery, our present system would be no more effective than that set up under the Articles of Confederation adopted after the Revolution. To avoid the weaknesses which had rendered the Confederation futile, the Constitution must incorporate, the men of 1787 well knew, "a coercive principle"—the only question, as one of the Founders expressed it, was whether it should be "a coercion of law, or a coercion of arms." [7] The provision of effective "coercion of law" for enforcement of the Constitution has been the uniquely American contribution to the science of government. For the ineffectiveness of other constitutions, whose violations could be censured only by the threat or the exercise of revolutionary force, we have substituted the institution of review by the Supreme Court of the constitutionality of exercises of governmental power. Whatever one may think of the way in which their authority has been exercised by different Courts, the securing of a sanction short of force for our constitutional rights certainly represents a basic forward step in constitutional history.

It is in recognition of the above that, in the words of the most famous of *Commentaries* upon our Constitution, "The universal sense of America has decided, that in the last resort the judiciary must decide upon the constitutionality of the acts and laws of the general and state governments, so far as they are capable of being made the subject of judicial controversy." [8] A constitution that cannot be enforced by the courts contains but empty words. It is judicial enforcement alone that makes the provisions of the Constitution more than mere maxims of political morality. Unless the courts can intervene in cases where they are violated, the principle of supremacy of the fundamental law becomes but as "sounding brass or a tinkling cymbal." A constitution is only a paper instrument if the restrictions contained in it cannot be given effect by the courts. As a congressman eloquently exclaimed over a hundred and fifty years ago:

How vain is a paper restriction if it confers neither power nor right. Of what importance is to say, Congress are prohibited from doing certain acts, if no legitimate authority exists in the country to decide whether an act done *is* a prohibited act? Do gentlemen perceive the consequences which would follow from establishing the principle that Congress have the exclusive right to decide on their own powers? This principle admitted, does any Constitution remain? Does not the power of the Legislature become absolute and omnipotent? Can you talk to them of transgressing their powers, when no one has a right to judge of those powers but themselves? [9]

The Court and Conservatism

Impressive though the role of the Supreme Court may seem in the constitutional scheme of things, its basic support is not in the Court's constitutional position, which, as Hamilton noted, is inherently a weak one in comparison with that of the executive and legislative branches, but in the acceptance by public opinion of the Court's role as guardian of the Constitution. In a representative, democratic government, writes one of our leading state judges, the power of the judiciary depends largely on its reputation for independence, integrity, and wisdom.[10] The Supreme Court has been able to maintain its role as the ultimate expounder of constitutional law only because it has, by and large, continued to maintain its reputation in these respects in the public eye.

That the Court itself has recognized the basic weakness of its position unless it is supported by public sentiment was seen acutely the better part of a century ago by James Bryce. "The Supreme Court," said he, "feels the touch of public opinion. Opinion is stronger in America than anywhere else in the world, and judges are only men. To yield a little may be prudent, for the tree that cannot bend to the blast may be broken." [11] When the Court's place in public esteem has tended to go down and there has been genuine danger of its losing its status, it has sooner or later remolded its jurisprudence to accord with public demands.

But, though there is thus a real relationship between the work of the highest tribunal and public opinion, that relationship can by no means be as direct as it is where the work of the political departments of government is concerned. Mr. Dooley notwithstanding, the Supreme Court does not immediately follow the election returns.

The actual effect of public sentiment upon the Court is not too difficult to determine if one bears constantly in mind Bryce's truism that judges are only men. And, because of the manner in which judges are chosen and their length of tenure, they are men of the prior generation. The Supreme Court is almost never a really contemporary institution.[12] The operation of life tenure in the Court, as against elections at short intervals of the Congress, usually keeps the average viewpoint of the two institutions a generation apart. The Court is consequently the check of a preceding generation on the present one. That being the case, it is hardly surprising that there is at times a gap between the desires of public opinion and the decisions of the Supreme Court. The judges of that tribunal are, to be sure, only men, who, like their fellows, normally seek to keep in tune with the common sentiment of the community. Yet they are men whose roots are more in the past than are those of most others in public life. Looking at the problems of the present through the distorting lenses of the experience of their generation, they may naturally be slower to accept drastic changes than those in the political departments.

Nor is the judicial lag in this respect necessarily an undesirable element in the working of our governmental system. The Constitution itself, it should not be forgotten, is a check of preceding generations upon the present one. Its limitations often serve as what may seem to be undue restraints upon the popular will at a given time. But that is the very essence of constitutionalism. It is the peculiar purpose of a written constitution to classify certain things as legal fundamentals; these fundamentals may not be changed except by the slow and cumbersome process of amendment. The people themselves have decided, in constitutional convention assembled, to limit themselves and future generations in the exercise of the sovereign power which they would otherwise possess in a representative democracy. And it is precisely these limitations from prior generations that enable those subject to governmental authority to appeal from the people drunk to the people sober in periods of excitement and hysteria. The Constitution is essentially a conservative check upon the present by the past.

If the limitations contained in the Constitution are to be given full effect, their enforcement must not be controlled by every shift in popular whims. A conservative institution which bends slowly is alone suited to serve as the enforcing organ. The function of interpreting the Constitution was conferred upon a Supreme Court intended to be such a basically conservative organ. That the Court may lag behind popular sentiment as expressed in the legislative and executive branches is exactly what was intended.

Judicial lag must not, all the same, serve to prevent the law from adapting itself to meet changed external conditions. It is even more true of constitutional law than of other branches of the law that it must be stable and yet it cannot stand still. According to Justice Cardozo, the power of precedent, when analyzed, is the power of the beaten track.[13] But judicial respect for precedent must not preclude the ability of the courts to strike out onto new paths to cope with novel situations. Had Anglo-American courts not constantly recognized this, our law would never have progressed from the system suitable for Norman and Angevin society in which it had its roots. In law, as in life, stagnation means atrophy.

The Supreme Court itself has, of course, recognized that there may be legitimate need for change in the field of constitutional law. The decisions of yesterday may prove so out of line with the needs of today that they should be discarded even by a conservative body normally wedded to precedent. In such cases, the Court should bow to the lessons of experience and recognize that the process of trial and error, so fruitful in the natural sciences, is appropriate also in the judicial function.[14] As early as 1851, the Court expressed the view that it would overrule its earlier decisions when it was convinced they were erroneous.[15] \As the Court itself stated in 1944,

when convinced of former error, this Court has never felt constrained to follow precedent. In constitutional questions, where correction depends upon amendment and not upon legislative action this Court throughout its history has freely exercised its power to reexamine the basis of its constitutional decisions. This has long been accepted practice, and this practice has continued to this day.[16]

We are thus left with the following picture of the Nation's highest Court: That tribunal is, as it must be, an essentially conservative body. Though not unresponsive to public sentiment, it tends often to lag behind the immediate demands of public opinion. At the same time, as the Court itself has recognized, constitutional law must not prove too slow in adapting itself to basic political, economic, and social changes. We must never forget, in the words of one of the great opinions of Chief Justice John Marshall, that "it is a *constitution* we are expounding" [17]—a living instrument that must be construed so as to meet the practical necessities of present-day government.

\What happens, nevertheless, if the inherent conservatism of the Supreme Court and its lag behind public opinion (both, we have seen, a necessary part of the highest judicial institution) lead it unduly to obstruct legal changes deemed essential to cope with novel needs? When the cleavage between the old order, represented by the Court, and the new, represented by an Administration with novel programs and policies, is particularly sharp, must there not inevitably result a thwarting of the popular will by judges wedded to constitutional precedents unsuited to modern demands? In such a case, there may well be a frustration of effective government by representative democracy, unless the Court remakes its law to accord with the legitimate claims of contemporary government./

The Court and the New Deal

Perhaps the outstanding example in our constitutional history of judicial lag in operation occurred during the Supreme Court's reception of the legislative measures of the New Deal. In the three years beginning with the October, 1933 term (i.e., from the latter part of 1933 to the middle of 1936), the Court held acts of the Congress unconstitutional in twelve decisions. These decisions, in the apt characterization of Robert H. Jackson, who had helped argue many of them, all but nullified the New Deal [18] (or at least many of its most important measures).

The Court's invalidation of the heart of the New Deal program demonstrates in a striking manner the way in which the Supreme Court had come to interpret its constitutional role. Without a doubt, the outstanding aspect of the American constitutional system has been the doctrine of judicial supremacy under which the highest Court functions as the supreme arbiter of the constitutionality of legislation. No feature in our government has awakened so much curiosity in foreign minds, caused so much discussion, been so criticized, and been more frequently misunderstood, than the duties of the Supreme Court in enforcing the Constitution. Under the doctrine of judicial supremacy, it has been the Court that has determined conflicts between acts of government and the Constitution, and it has done so through the technical forms of the lawsuit. These lawsuits have been the chief instrument of power in our system. Struggles over power that in Europe call forth regiments of troops, in this country call forth battalions of lawyers.[19]

Government by lawsuit [20] in operation is nowhere better illustrated than in the cases in which the New Deal legislation was at issue before the highest Court. Thus, on June 5, 1933, the Congress passed a joint resolution banning so-called "gold clauses" (which purported to give obligees a right to require payment of obligations to them only in gold) from all existing contracts of public and private debt. Under the resolution, all such contracts must "be discharged upon payment, dollar for dollar, in any coin or currency which at the time of payment is legal tender." The resolution was intended to prevent creditors protected by "gold clauses" from gaining a windfall under an act authorizing devaluation of the gold content of the dollar up to 50 per cent. In *Norman v. Baltimore & Ohio R. Co.*,[21] the holder of a railroad bond bearing an interest coupon payable in gold, of face value of $22.50, which had been issued before the gold content of the dollar had been lowered, brought suit for $38.10 in payment after devaluation, but the Court held that he was required to accept the face value of the coupon in the devalued dollars. It has been estimated that gold clauses of the type annulled by the Congressional resolution were contained in public and private contracts worth about one hundred billion dollars. The question of the validity of the resolution was consequently a matter of life and death to the whole economy. Upon it turned the whole power of the Federal Government to fix a national monetary policy. Yet it was in an ordinary contract action between private parties over a mere difference of $15.60 that the vital constitutional issue was decided. Here, indeed, was government by lawsuit with a vengeance!

In the *Gold Clause* case, the power of the Government was upheld, albeit by only a bare majority of the Court. It was, however, in similar lawsuits that much of the New Deal program was nullified. A judgment in a lawsuit negated the National Industrial Recovery Act—in many ways the most important of the early New Deal regulatory measures. Another lawsuit ended the Agricultural Adjustment Act—the major New Deal law designed to deal with the depressed condition of agriculture. Still other lawsuits struck down federal measures providing for railroad pensions, regulation of the bituminous coal industry, municipal bankruptcy relief, and farm debtors' relief. All in all, government by lawsuit during 1934–36 did much to render ineffective government by the elected representatives of the people.

It was not alone the invalidation by the Court of the New Deal measures that was of significance, but, even more so, the manner in which the decrees of invalidity were delivered. Speaking in 1928 of Supreme Court decisions setting aside statutes enacted by the Congress, Chief Justice Hughes asserted that few of these cases had been of great importance in shaping the course of the Nation.[22]

The same clearly could not be said of the 1934–36 decisions of the Court nullifying the New Deal measures. As far as the measures annulled themselves were concerned, even their proponents had to concede that many of them were imperfectly conceived and crudely executed.[23] There is little doubt that they were subject to legitimate constitutional attack. Had the Court in its decisions confined itself to these limited constitutional issues, at the same time leaving the way open for the Congress to remedy the defects by tighter draftsmanship, it would hardly have been subjected to such bitter controversy.

But the Court deliberately did not choose the more prudent course. To paraphrase Justice Jackson,[24] in striking at the New Deal legislation, the Court allowed its language to run riot. It sought to engraft its own nineteenth-century laissez-faire philosophy into the Constitution. In invalidating the National Industrial Recovery Act,[25] the Court did not limit itself to criticism of the obviously objectionable features of that law; the rationale of its decision was, instead, so broad that it struck at all national efforts to maintain fair industrial and labor standards. Similarly, in overthrowing the Agricultural Adjustment Act,[26] the Court cast doubt upon all federal aid to agriculture, as well as upon any extensive use of the Congressional power to tax and spend in order to promote the general welfare. And the Court's action in this respect came to its culmination just before the 1936 election, when it declared that there was no power in either states or Nation to enact a minimum-wage law.[27] In the words of a contemporary critic, "The Court not merely challenged the policies of the New Deal but erected judicial barriers to the reasonable exercise of legislative powers, both state and national, to meet the urgent needs of a twentieth-century community."[28]

In the decisions of the Supreme Court invalidating the New Deal legislation, we have, without a doubt, the apogee of the doctrine of judicial supremacy. That doctrine itself, it should be noted, did not come into being full grown upon the establishment of the Republic. Although the doctrine was first enunciated in the celebrated case of *Marbury v. Madison*[29] in 1803, it remained quiescent for the better part of a century. It was not until the latter part of the nineteenth century that judicial review came to play a really significant part in our governmental system, for it was in the post-Civil War era that the Court began to exercise freely its authority as arbiter of the validity of laws. Thus, while in the first seventy years of the Republic, only two laws of the Congress were declared invalid by the highest tribunal, in the next seventy years, some fifty-eight such laws were invalidated, and these figures do not include the New Deal period, when the Court's power was asserted with even greater persistency. But it was not merely, or even primarily, the frequency with which the Court exercised its authority to declare federal laws unconstitutional that caused the difficulty. It was, rather, the manner in which the Court interpreted its role under the doctrine of judicial supremacy.

Under the classic decision of John Marshall in *Marbury v. Madison*, the Supreme Court was clearly established as the ultimate arbiter of the constitutionality of laws in our system. According to the great Chief Justice there,

if a law be in opposition to the constitution; if both the law and the constitution apply to a particular case, so that the court must either decide that case conformably to the law, disregarding the constitution; or conformably to the constitution, disregarding the law; the court must determine which of these conflicting rules governs the case. This is of the very essence of judicial duty.[30]

Under this theory, the authority to declare constitutionality flows naturally and necessarily from the judicial duty to determine the law.

In Marshall's theory of review, the judicial role, though vital, was not unrestrained. The primary responsibility for government was in the elected representatives of the people. If the latter clearly transgressed the limits of the powers delegated to them by the Constitution, the courts would, of course, intervene; but, for mere Congressional abuse of power there was to be no judicial remedy. In the words of *Gibbons v. Ogden*,[31] one of the most famous of Marshall opinions:

The wisdom and the discretion of Congress, their identity with the people, and the influence which their constituents possess at elections, are, in this, as in many other instances, as that, for example, of declaring war, the sole restraints on which they have relied, to secure them from its abuse. They are the restraints on which the people must often rely solely, in all representative governments.

By the time of the New Deal, however, the highest Court had abandoned this restrained approach to its function of judicial review and had come instead to conceive of itself as the Supreme Censor of all legislation. The case which perhaps best illustrates the new approach of the Court in cases involving review of the validity of legislative action is *Lochner v. New York*,[32] in which the constitutionality of a New York statute fixing maximum hours for bakers furnished the issue. In holding the statute invalid, Justice

Peckham, speaking for the majority of the Court, stated the question
to be determined in this class of case as follows:

In every case that comes before this court, . . . where legislation of this
character is concerned and where the protection of the Federal Constitution is sought, the question necessarily arises: Is this a fair, reasonable
and appropriate exercise of the police power of the State, or is it an
unreasonable, unnecessary and arbitrary interference with the right of
the individual to his personal liberty or to enter into those contracts in
relation to labor which may seem to him appropriate or necessary for
the support of himself and his family? [33]

In applying a test as vague and indefinite as the above—i.e., is
the statute unreasonable, unnecessary, and arbitrary?—the Court
was, in effect, determining upon its own judgment whether particular legislation was desirable. The Court thus came virtually to exercise the functions of a "super-legislature," [34] to be what Harold J.
Laski termed "a third chamber in the United States." [35] The Supreme Court Justices, like senators or representatives, cast their
votes for or against a law on the basis of whether they thought such
law was desirable. In a lecture to law students some years ago,
Justice Harlan (the grandfather of the present Justice of that name)
was so candid as to declare, "I want to say to you young gentlemen
that if we don't like an act of Congress, we don't have much trouble
to find grounds for declaring it unconstitutional." [36]
     Though the Court, even in the heyday of judicial supremacy, con-
tinually asserted that it was not, like the legislature itself, concerned
with the wisdom and policy of legislation, the manner in which
it actually acted belied its assertion. This was particularly true of
the period when the New Deal statutes were invalidated. According to Justice McReynolds in 1934, "plainly . . . this Court must
have regard to the wisdom of the enactment. At least, we must
inquire concerning its purpose and decide whether . . . the end is
legitimate, and the means appropriate." [37] In accordance with
this frank avowal by one of the most outspoken of its members,
the 1934–36 Supreme Court was, in practice, using its power to
review the wisdom of much of the New Deal legislation before it.
The due process clause, declares one of Justice Holmes's noted
dissenting opinions, "does not enact Mr. Herbert Spencer's Social
Statics." [38] It was, all the same, most difficult for judges whose
formative years occurred when Spencer was generally considered
a second Book of Revelations not to look with hostility upon laws
which did violence to Spencerian dogmas. It was all too easy for
them to assume that the Constitution itself was intended to give

them carte blanche to embody their economic and moral beliefs in its prohibitions.[39]

ᛗTo the majority of the Court that nullified the New Deal legislation, it was the duty of each individual Justice to determine for himself the desirability of challenged legislation⁄ Though expressing formal compliance with the principle that any rational doubts must be resolved in favor of the constitutionality of legislation, the 1934–36 Court majority went on to ask: "But whose doubts, and by whom resolved?" [40] And they went on unequivocally to answer that it was for the conscience of each individual judge to resolve these matters. As Justice Sutherland (in many ways the most able member of the 1934–36 Court majority) put it:

The oath which he takes as a judge is not a composite oath, but an individual one. And in passing upon the validity of a statute, he discharges a duty imposed upon *him*, which cannot be consummated justly by an automatic acceptance of the views of others which have neither convinced, nor created a reasonable doubt in, his mind.[41]

The judge cannot subordinate his own personal convictions in determining the validity of a law; indeed, for him to attempt to do so, was, in the view of the 1934–36 Court, for him to lose "faith with his oath [and] his judicial and moral independence." [42]

ᛗWhat restraint, if any, was there upon the Supreme Court under this theory of its functioning? Said Justice Sutherland, in answer to this query, "The check upon the judge is that imposed by his oath of office, by the Constitution and by his own conscientious and informed convictions; and since he has the duty to make up his own mind and adjudge accordingly, it is hard to see how there could be any other restraint." [43] In effect, of course, this meant that there was, in reality, no practical check upon abuses by the Supreme Court of its reviewing power⁄ As it was pungently put by Justice Stone, in dissenting from the Court's nullification of one of the most important New Deal measures, "while unconstitutional exercise of power by the executive and legislative branches of the government is subject to judicial restraint, the only check upon our own exercise of power is our own sense of self-restraint." [44] ᛗThe lack of effective external restraints upon the Court was what made the decisions of the 1934–36 Court particularly galling to those who thought that they rested upon an unduly narrow and outmoded interpretation of the Constitution⁄ In cases involving the Federal Constitution, the position of the Supreme Court is unique in contemporary legal systems. In such cases, as a practical matter, the Court itself alone can correct its own errors; in only two cases has the process of constitutional amendment been successfully employed to correct decisions of the Supreme Court. It was this which once led a noted law teacher to suggest that counsel arguing constitutional cases before the Court ought to address the Justices, not as "Your Honors," but as "Your Lordships." The Supreme Court had become the American counterpart of the House of Lords, sitting as an upper legislative chamber, before that body's powers were curtailed in 1911. Well could men say of the highest tribunal in 1936 that, under its decisions, they could discover hardly any limit but the sky to the authority claimed by the Court to nullify any law which might happen to strike a majority of the Justices as undesirable.[45]

Constitutional Revolution, Ltd.

In political, as in natural, science, extremes beget extremes. Action which moves too far in one direction ultimately provokes an equivalent reaction in the opposite direction. Even an institution as august as the United States Supreme Court cannot escape the law of the pendulum. If, in the generation before 1937, the Court construed the doctrine of judicial supremacy so as to give itself the virtual powers of a super-legislature, in the twenty years since that time, the Court's authority vis-à-vis the Congress has all but atrophied.

Early in 1937, there took place the remarkable reversal in the Supreme Court's attitude toward the New Deal program. Before that time, as has been stressed, the Court rendered twelve decisions declaring invalid legislative measures of the New Deal; starting in March, 1937, that tribunal upheld every New Deal law presented to it, including some that were basically similar to earlier statutes which it had nullified. It is, in fact, hardly too far-fetched to assert that, in 1937, there took place a veritable revolution in the jurisprudence of the Supreme Court—a revolution which has been appropriately characterized as "Constitutional Revolution, Ltd." [46]

It is all too facile to state that the 1937 change in the high Court's jurisprudence was only a direct protective response to President Roosevelt's Court Reorganization Plan—to assert, as did so many contemporary wags, that "a switch in time saved Nine." It would be idle to deny that the furor over the President's proposal did have repercussions within the marble halls of the Supreme Court building. The members of the Court are not demigods far above the sweaty crowd; they are, to refer again to Bryce's truism, only men. As such, it is hardly surprising that they were intimately concerned with a proposal that affected so directly the institution of which they were a part. This was especially true of Chief Justice Hughes, who did not hesitate to play an active role in the struggle to defeat the President's "Court-packing" plan. There is little doubt that the Chief Justice helped persuade a majority of the Court to liberalize its case law, in order to help preserve that tribunal in all its institutional strength. As President Roosevelt himself expressed it, "It would be a little naïve to refuse to recognize some connection between these 1937 decisions and the Supreme Court fight."[47] In truth, the new decisions of the Court, in F.D.R.'s own words, "did more than anything else to bring about the defeat of the [Court Reorganization] plan in the halls of Congress."[48] It was surely not unnatural of the Justices to reconstrue the law so as to help bring about this result.

At the same time, it would be wholly to misconceive the nature of the Supreme Court and its manner of operation as a judicial tribunal to assume that the 1937 change in jurisprudence was solely the result of a cause and effect relationship to the President's "Court-packing" plan. In actuality, the pre-1937 decisions of the Court which so greatly restricted the powers of the National Government were based upon a wholly outmoded conception of the proper role of the State. Even at the time of the previously mentioned *Lochner* case, Justice Holmes, dissenting, could assert, "This case is decided upon an economic theory which a large part of the country does not entertain."[49] By the time of the New Deal, that theory, though still persisted in by a bare majority of the Supreme Court, had been expressly repudiated by the people and by the President and the Congress whom they had voted into office. The Court's conception of the proper constitutional role of government may well have been sound when it was first formulated in the 1890's. It was utterly inconsistent with an era which demanded ever-expanding governmental authority. It could, as a practical matter, be maintained only when the exercise of State power was dominated by the concept of laissez faire. "Leviathan hath two swords: war and justice," stated Hobbes in a famous passage. The need effectively to deal with the great economic crisis of the early 1930's had, nevertheless, made it plain that the armory of the State had to include much more than these two elementary weapons. Before the New Deal, government was chiefly negative; its main task, apart from defense, was to support the status quo and maintain some semblance of fair play while private interests asserted themselves freely. Under the Roosevelt Administration, government became positive in a new sense.

Before then, the State acted only as policeman, soldier, and judge. Since 1933, the State has had to act also as doctor, nurse, insurance-supplier, house-builder, chemist, power-supplier, town-planner, pensions-distributor, economic controller, benefactor of labor and agriculture, and in a whole host of other capacities. For the State effectively to execute the manifold functions which economic and social exigencies required it to assume, it had to intervene in social and economic affairs upon a national scale. Governmental action limited to the local level could hardly prove efficacious where problems national in scope had to be dealt with.

For the Supreme Court, Canute-like, to attempt to hold back indefinitely the waves of ever-increasing governmental authority was for it to set itself an impossible task. "Looking back," declared Justice Roberts (the man whose switch is, more than anything else, said to have "saved the Nine" in 1937) in 1951, "it is difficult to see how the Court could have resisted the popular urge for uniform standards throughout the country—for what in effect was a unified economy." [50] The laissez-faire doctrine, upon which the operation of American government had been essentially based since the founding of the Republic, had by then proved inadequate to meet pressing economic problems. The national economy could be resuscitated only by extended federal intervention. For the Government in Washington to be able to exercise regulatory authority upon the necessary national scale, it was essential that the Supreme Court liberalize its construction of the Constitution. To quote Justice Roberts again:

An insistence by the Court on holding federal power to what seemed its appropriate orbit when the Constitution was adopted might have resulted in even more radical changes in our dual structure than those which have been gradually accomplished through the extension of the limited jurisdiction conferred on the federal government. [51]

That the Supreme Court would ultimately recognize the inevitable was itself inevitable. Benjamin Nathan Cardozo has shown how the results reached in cases like the 1934–36 decisions we have been discussing were due to the judicial choice of starting points:

A problem in the choice of methods lay back of the problem of law, and determined its solution. On the one hand, the right of property, as it was known to the fathers of the republic, was posited as permanent and absolute. Impairment was not to be suffered except within narrow limits of history and precedent. No experiment was to be made along new lines of social betterment. The image was a perfect sphere. The least dent or abrasion was a subtraction from its essence. Given such premises, the conclusion is inevitable. The statute becomes an illegitimate assault upon rights assured to the individual against the encroachments of society. The method of logic . . . is at work in all its plentitude.[52]

By 1937, it had become clear that not logic alone, based upon outmoded starting points, had become the instrument of advance. Even judges whose logos had been based upon Spencerian dogma (or at least a majority of them) had come to see that the philosophy upon which they had based their decisions had been left behind by the changed needs of a new era. "The meaning of the Constitution does not change with the ebb and flow of economic events," plaintively declared a member of the 1934–36 Court majority, after the Court had begun its historic shift.[53] But, though the words of the basic document have remained essentially what they were in 1787, the Court itself has come to recognize that the proper interpretation of that instrument does change to meet the new demands imposed by changed external conditions. The Constitution must be capable of adaptation to needs that were wholly unforeseen by the Founding Fathers; else, it is less a document intended to endure through the ages than a governmental suicide-pact.

The 1937 reversal in the jurisprudence of the Supreme Court reflected changes in legal ideology common to the entire American legal profession. The extreme individualist philosophy upon which the Justices had been nurtured has been shaken to its foundations during the present century. If Spencerian laissez faire gave way on the bench to the judicial pragmatism of Justice Holmes, it was only because a similar movement had taken place in the country as a whole. That there was a lag between the change in the country and the change in the Court cannot, of course, be denied. Such a lag, as has been mentioned, appears to be inherent in the functioning of any judicial tribunal which is compelled by changing external conditions to make fundamental modifications in its case law. As has been stressed, this is a necessary aspect of the American system of judicial review. It is true that it may, at times, constitute a great danger of the system: the basic conservatism of the Court may make it difficult for its members to make the necessary accommodation before it is too late.

In 1937, the danger referred to was averted by the Court's reversal in jurisprudence. And, even then, it should be noted, a hard core of the 1934–36 majority utterly refused to alter its views—which shows how narrow the actual margin of change was in the Court. In reality, it was the recognition by two Justices (primarily Roberts and, to a lesser extent, Hughes) of the need for increased national governmental power that made for the switch-over in the high tribunal. "Years ago," wrote an eminent professor of constitutional law of the Court of the mid-thirties, "that learned lawyer John Selden in talking of 'Council' observed: 'They talk (but blasphemously enough) that the Holy Ghost is President of their General Councils when the truth is, the odd Man is still the Holy Ghost.' " [54] It was the conversion of "odd men" Roberts and Hughes that made the constitutional revolution of 1937 possible.

301 U.S.

Narrow though the margin for change may have been, there is little doubt that there was a real conversion among the new majority of the Supreme Court and that its effects well justify the characterization of "constitutional revolution." It is usually overlooked that the Court decisions first signalling the reversal in its jurisprudence were, in all probability, reached before the President had even announced his Court Reorganization Plan. On March 29, 1937, the Chief Justice announced a decision upholding a state minimum-wage law basically similar to that which the Court had held to be beyond the power of both states and Nation to enact only nine months before.[55] According to one who sat at the Government counsel table that day, "the spectacle of the Court that day frankly and completely reversing itself and striking down its opinion but a few months old was a moment never to be forgotten." [56] Yet, though the Court's confession of error was announced a month after the President's proposal, the case itself appears to have been decided in conference among the Justices about a month before the "Court-packing" plan was made public. The circumstantial evidence available to us on this point strongly bears out the statement made some years later by Chief Justice Hughes to his authorized biographer: "The President's proposal had not the slightest effect on our decision." [57] The decision marking the first drastic change in its 1934–36 case law had not been influenced by the Roosevelt plan, because it had actually been made within the Court before the publication of the President's proposal.[58] (All of which tends to bear out the view that the Court's jurisprudence was ripe for reversal and that such reversal would have occurred even without the pressure of the "Court-packing" plan.)

March 29, 1937, as already indicated, saw the upholding of a state minimum-wage law. Though not directly concerned with national power, the Court did expressly overrule a 1923 precedent [59] denying Congressional authority to fix wages; hence, the decision was a substantial step forward from the point of view of advocates of increased national power. On the same day, the Court dealt squarely with federal statutes similar to several annulled in the 1934–36 period. This time the Court upheld laws providing for farm debtors' relief,[60] collective bargaining in the Nation's railroads,[61] and a penalizing tax on firearms analogous to that which it had struck down under the Agricultural Adjustment Act.[62] Well could a leading New Dealer chortle, "What a day! To labor, minimum-wage laws and collective bargaining; to farmers, relief in bankruptcy; to law enforcement, the firearms control. The Court was on the march!"[63]

These cases, in Volume 300 of the *Supreme Court Reports,* were to prove but the prelude to an even more drastic revolution in constitutional jurisprudence. To demonstrate the extent of the judicial revolution, one has, to use the method stated by Edward S. Corwin, only to "turn to Volume 301 of the *United States Supreme Court Reports,* a volume which has a single counterpart in the Court's annals. I mean Volume 11 of Peters's *Reports,* wherein is recorded the somewhat lesser revolution in our constitutional law precisely 100 years earlier, which followed upon Taney's succession to Marshall."[64]

On page 1 of 301 U.S., there is printed the April 12, 1937 decision of the Court in the great case of *National Labor Relations Board v. Jones & Laughlin Steel Corp.* In it, the constitutionality of the National Labor Relations Act of 1935 was upheld. Robert H. Jackson termed the decision there the most far-reaching victory ever won on behalf of labor in the Supreme Court.[65] This was no overstatement, for the 1935 Act was the Magna Carta of the American labor movement. It guaranteed the right of employees to organize collectively in unions and made it an unfair labor practice prohibited by law for employers to interfere with such right or to refuse to bargain collectively with the representatives chosen by their employees. The act was intended to apply to industries throughout the Nation, to those engaged in production and manufacture as well as to those engaged in commerce, literally speaking. But this appeared to bring it directly in conflict with important Supreme Court decisions drastically limiting the scope of the Federal Government's authority over interstate commerce,* including some of the decisions of the 1934–36 period on which the ink was scarcely dry. This was particularly true of the Court's decision nullifying the National Industrial Recovery Act, which had denied power in the Congress to regulate local business activities, even though they affected interstate commerce. In the *Jones & Laughlin* case, these precedents

* *Infra,* pp. 30-32.

were not followed; "These cases," laconically stated the Court, "are not controlling here." [66]   Instead, the Court gave the federal power over interstate commerce its maximum sweep. Mines, mills, and factories, whose activities had formerly been decided to be "local," and hence immune from federal regulation, were now held to affect interstate commerce directly enough to justify Congressional control. There is little doubt that, as the dissenting Justices in *Jones & Laughlin* protested, the Congress in the Labor Act exercised a power of control over purely local industry beyond anything theretofore deemed permissible. Indeed, as the dissenters accurately stated, in characterizing the effect of the Court's reinterpretation of the commerce power, "Almost anything—marriage, birth, death— may in some fashion affect commerce." [67]

The *Jones & Laughlin* case was followed some six weeks later by three equally significant decisions, also printed in Volume 301 of the *Supreme Court Reports,* upholding the constitutionality of one of the most important of the New Deal innovations, the Social Security Act of 1935. That law, which for the first time brought the Federal Government extensively into the field of social insurance, had been held unconstitutional by the Circuit Court of Appeals for the First Circuit. The Supreme Court, however, in a precedent-making opinion by Justice Cardozo, reversed that tribunal, holding that the scheme of old-age benefits provided for by the federal law did not contravene any constitutional prohibition.[68]   In so doing, the Court gave the broadest possible scope to the Congressional power to tax and spend for the general welfare, even though its reasoning on this point was inconsistent with its 1936 decision invalidating the Agricultural Adjustment Act. In addition, the Court upheld the unemployment compensation schemes established under the Social Security Act.[69]   The decisions sustaining that law put an end to fears that unemployment insurance and old-age benefit laws might prove to be beyond the power of either states or Nation, as minimum-wage regulation had been held to be under the pre-1937 Court. Henceforth the United States was not to be the one great nation powerless to adopt such measures.

These decisions in 301 U.S. formed the heart of the constitutional revolution of 1937. Breaking with its previous jurisprudence, the Supreme Court upheld the authority of the Federal Government to regulate the entire economy under its commerce power and to use its power to tax and spend to set up comprehensive schemes of social insurance. And, it should be noted, in the light of later criticisms of the Court, whose members were subsequently appointed by President Roosevelt, because of its claimed cavalier discard of established precedents, the cases in 301 U.S. were decided before a single Roosevelt-appointed Justice took his seat upon the bench. The most important of the old precedents which so restricted the scope of governmental authority were repudiated by the identical Court which had previously invoked them.   There was no change in the Court's personnel until after it provided new precedents that served as a basis for much that the new judges were later to decide.

Judicial Self-Restraint

The decisions rendered by the highest tribunal in 1937 can be characterized as constituting a constitutional revolution not just because they recognized in the Federal Government significant substantive powers that had theretofore been denied.   Even more important, perhaps, to one concerned with the workings of the Supreme Court is the fact that they inaugurated a drastic shift in the balance that had previously existed between the Court and the other branches of the Government.   The pre-1937 interpretation of the doctrine of judicial supremacy had been dominated by the primacy of the Supreme Court, culminating, as we have seen, in the Court's review of the desirability of early New Deal legislation.   Since 1937, the Court has receded to a much more subdued position.

Where the Court prior to 1937 set itself up as Supreme Censor of the wisdom of challenged legislation, it has, since that time, more or less adopted the view formerly expressed in dissent by Justice Holmes as to what its function should be vis-à-vis the legislature. The Holmesian viewpoint was pithily expressed in his comment to Justice Stone: "About seventy-five years ago I learnt that I was not God.   And so, when the people . . . want to do something I can't find anything in the Constitution expressly forbidding them to do, I say, whether I like it or not, 'Goddammit, let 'em do it!'" [70]

In this comment is expressed the essence of the self-restraint which prevails among the present Supreme Court.   Unless the statute at issue patently violates an express constitutional provision, it will be upheld.   Clearly, under this approach, there is no place for the "super-legislature" conception of the Court's role that prevailed prior to 1937.   Instead, the Court is now controlled by the conviction that it is an awesome thing to strike down an act of the elected representatives of the people, and that its power to do so should not be exercised save where the occasion is clear beyond fair debate. [71] As Justice Holmes expressed it in a celebrated dissent, a statute should not be held invalid "unless it can be said that a rational and fair man necessarily would admit that the statute proposed would infringe fundamental principles as they have been understood by the traditions of our people and our law." [72]

In the Holmesian view, the test to be applied is whether a reasonable legislator—the Congressional version of the "reasonable man"—could have adopted a law like that at issue. Is the statute as applied so clearly arbitrary or capricious that legislators acting reasonably could not have believed it to be necessary or appropriate for the public welfare? [73] Under the approach of the pre-1937 Court, the test was whether the Court itself thought the statute was desirable. Now the Court looks only to see whether there was a rational basis for the challenged legislative action. Under the pre-1937 approach, the desirability of a statute was determined as an objective fact by the Court on its own independent judgment. Today a more subjective test is applied—could rational legislators have regarded the statute as a reasonable method of reaching the desired result? [74] In the words of Justice Frankfurter:

It can never be emphasized too much that one's own opinion about the wisdom or evil of a law should be excluded altogether when one is doing one's duty on the bench. The only opinion of our own even looking in that direction that is material is our opinion whether legislators could in reason have enacted such a law.[75]

Revolution in Retrospect

Writing as a contemporary who participated at the Government counsel table in the 1937 cases that have been discussed, Robert H. Jackson noted acutely that the new decisions of the Court did not necessarily establish immutably the constitutional law of the future:

No doubt another day will find one of its tasks to be correction of mistakes that time will reveal in this structure in which we now take pride. Our innovations will then have become the established order, and only fanatics underestimate the power of an established order. As one who knows well the workmen and the work of this generation, I bespeak the right of the future to undo our work when it no longer serves acceptably.[76]

It is now some twenty years since the constitutional revolution of 1937. The constitutional doctrines enunciated by the Supreme Court then, particularly that of judicial self-restraint, have become the established order in the Court today. Already there are complaints that this order, like the pre-1937 one that preceded it, is in need of correction. At the same time, the extent of the fundamental change brought about by the highest tribunal is still not generally grasped. In well-nigh every aspect of constitutional law, the law today differs greatly from that enunciated and applied by the pre-1937 Court. And these basic changes have persisted despite comparatively minor fluctuations within the Court upon which public attention has been focused.

Twenty years may be a brief span in the life of an institution like the United States Supreme Court. It is, however, long enough for the work of the tribunal during that time to be analyzed with some depth. It is certainly long enough to enable us to judge, with something of the calm perspective of hindsight, the effects of the constitutional revolution of 1937 upon the subsequent work of the high Court. The purpose of this book will be to present an analysis of the different aspects of the work of the Court during the past twenty years, with emphasis upon the extent to which the Court has changed our constitutional law since 1937. Such an analysis should, it is felt, be of more than mere academic concern to Americans interested in understanding the actual functioning of our governmental system. For it is no exaggeration to say that the Supreme Court is the fulcrum upon which our constitutional institutions turn. The interpretation of the Constitution by the Court plays a vital part in American history—and this is true not only of legal history in the narrow sense. It may be going too far to say that the history of this country could be written in terms of leading Supreme Court decisions. But it is certainly true that a study of American history that did not consider them would be incomplete and distorted.

2

THE CONGRESS

In the three years just prior to 1937, the Supreme Court nullified exercises of legislative power by the Congress twelve times, and the statutes involved included, as we have seen, the most important measures enacted under the New Deal's program to meet the problems presented by economic depression. In the twenty years since 1937, the Court has declared invalid only three federal statutes, and not one of these three laws was a legislative measure of great significance.

These comparative figures, perhaps better than anything else, illustrate what we have already noted to be the outstanding feature of the constitutional revolution of the past two decades, namely, the change in the relationship of the highest tribunal to exercises of Congressional power. Before 1937, the most striking aspect of the American governmental system by far—that which most struck foreign observers with awe and amazement—was the frequency with which the Supreme Court interposed its power to negate acts of the duly elected representatives of the people. Shortly after the Court upheld, by a bare majority only, the power of the Congress to devalue the dollar in the already discussed *Gold Clause* case,* Robert H. Jackson (himself afterwards a member of the supreme bench) was asked by Swedish lawyers and bankers how we could allow within one of a majority of the members of our Court to hold that the Nation lacked power to change its monetary policy: "Why, anyway, should lawyer-judges be supreme over the national parliament, the President, the Treasury, and the whole government in a matter so vital to economic life?"[1] In a similar vein, the leading French study of review of the constitutionality of laws by our Supreme Court published during the pre-1937 period was entitled *Government by Judiciary*.[2]

Whatever else one may say of our governmental system during the past twenty years, it certainly can no longer be characterized as

* *Supra,* p. 11.

"government by the judiciary." The Supreme Court of 1937–57
has been dominated by the conviction that its authority to annul
acts of the Congress is one that should be exercised reluctantly and
only when a patent transgression of the Constitution leaves the
judge no choice. As we saw in the last chapter, the Court no longer
determines on its own judgment the wisdom and desirability of
challenged legislation. It decides only, following the approach
earlier urged by Justice Holmes, whether a rational legislator could
have adopted the statute at issue.* As Justice Frankfurter has put
the present view, responsibility for legislation lies with the legislature, answerable as it is directly to the people, and the Court's only
and very narrow function is to determine whether within the broad
grant of authority vested in the legislature it has exercised a judgment for which reasonable justification can be offered.[3]

A Court which applies this approach in determining the constitutionality of Congressional acts should, as a practical matter, not
invalidate such acts very often, for there is almost always at least
some "reasonable justification" for a law. It is therefore hardly surprising that so few federal statutes have been held invalid in the past
two decades. To the post-1937 Supreme Court, the Congress,
charged with all of the legislative powers granted by the Constitution, is entitled to its own choice among all rationally permissible
opinions as to what the Constitution allows. To set aside the enactments of such a body, representing in the legislative field the ultimate sovereign, should be a solemn, unusual, and painful act.[4]

At the same time, it cannot be gainsaid that the past generation
has been a period of the most intense legislative activity. In the
1920's, the growing point of our law still lay in the courts, rather
than in legislation. "We are governed by our judges and not by our
legislatures," wrote a North Dakota judge in 1924. "It is our judges
who formulate our public policies and our basic law."[5] All of this
has been completely changed. In the 1930's, the instrument of reform was legislation; and legislation there was, unprecedented in
volume and importance. A century earlier, a similar development
had taken place in Britain. Prodded by the Philippics of Jeremy
Bentham, whose writings make our current diatribes seem bland
and amiable,[6] the Parliament consciously used its legislative power
to regulate what were deemed to be harmful aspects of the economic, social, and political system and to remold much of the ar-
chaism of the judge-made law. Statute law was the great weapon
in the Benthamite armory; for the first time, legislation, rather than
case law, became the instrument of advance in the common law.

* *Supra,* pp. 23-24.

Starting with the New Deal laws, Benthamism came to the United States—and with a vengeance. Regulation from Washington has become a commonplace of the American system; it is now almost trite to point out how the operations of the National Government have come to guard and control the average citizen from the cradle to the grave.

In contemporary America, as in Benthamite Britain, the great instrument of government intervention has been statute law enacted by the national legislature. More and more, acts of the Congress have been asserting its control over matters formerly deemed to be beyond the scope of federal governmental authority. But, as has already been emphasized, these magnifications of national authority have not met with any check from the tribunal that, in our system, was designed to hold the constitutional balance. On the contrary, the growth in Congressional pretensions to power has been accompanied by a drastic decline in the Supreme Court as a restraining organ. The consequence has, not unnaturally, been a decided trend in our system in the direction of federal predominance. In governmental, as in physical, science, power abhors a vacuum. It is hardly surprising, therefore, that Congressional assertions of authority have rushed in to fill the space left vacant by post-1937 judicial abnegation. Nor can it be denied that the resultant increase in the authority of the Federal Government has meant a basic shift in our constitutional center of gravity. Their fear of inordinate governmental authority led the draftsmen of the Constitution to emphasize the division of political power as its predominant characteristic. Power was parceled out between the Nation and the states. The authority reserved to the latter was to check the overaggrandizement of that vested in the center. \The growth of Congressional authority in the past two decades has, however, basically altered the balance between states and Nation. Intervention by Washington in matters that were formerly deemed to be purely within local competence has, indeed, become so frequent that many wonder whether the states are not doomed to become mere vestigial survivals of a formerly flourishing federal system./

Commerce Power: Pre-1937 Views

Most of the Congressional power to enact regulatory laws stems from a brief clause in Article I, section 8 of the Constitution. Under it, the Congress is vested with the authority "To regulate Commerce with foreign Nations, and among the several States, and with the Indian Tribes." This clause is, as a member of the highest Court has put it, "the fount and origin of vast power"; [7] it is, in fact, the direct source of the most important powers which the National Government exercises in time of peace. Until relatively recently, nevertheless, in a system based upon the laissez-faire conception of government, the Congressional authority under the commerce clause remained largely in repose. In fact, the overwhelming proportion of the 1,400 or so cases which the Supreme Court decided under the clause before 1900 involved state legislation which was claimed unconstitutionally to curtail interstate commerce.[8] For a century then, there was, the highest Court itself has said,[9] little occasion for the affirmative exercise of the Congressional commerce power, and the influence of the commerce clause on American life and law was a negative one. It is thus that the word "commerce," as designating the thing to be protected against state interference, came to dominate the clause, while the word "regulate" remained in the background.[10]

But, if the federal sovereign was a legislator who slumbered during the first hundred years of our history, it has more than made up for this by its subsequent spate of activity. Starting with the Interstate Commerce Act of 1887 and the Sherman Anti-Trust Act of 1890—the two pioneer regulatory laws based upon the federal commerce power—the Congress has more and more been exercising legislative authority under its power to regulate commerce. This has been particularly true of the period since Franklin D. Roosevelt's first election to the Presidency. In the quarter century since that time, the federal statute book has become filled with a whole host of regulatory laws enacted under the Congressional commerce power.

What is the scope of the authority given to the Congress under the commerce clause? The first cases in point arose when John Marshall was Chief Justice, and it was without a doubt he, with his firm belief that the Constitution must be construed so as to make a strong National Government possible, who led the Court to look favorably upon federal legislative authority over commerce. At the beginning, the Supreme Court informed us in 1942,[11] Chief Justice Marshall described the federal commerce power with a breadth never yet exceeded. In the great case of *Gibbons v. Ogden*,[12] Marshall defined commerce as intercourse, a conception broad enough to include within its scope all business dealings. Even Justice Johnson, the first Jeffersonian appointed to the Marshall Court and, as such, inclined toward a far less sanguine view of the scope of federal authority than his Chief, concurred in construing commerce most broadly in a separate opinion which he delivered in the case.

Commerce, in its simplest signification, means an exchange of goods; but in the advancement of society, labor, transportation, intelligence, care, and various mediums of exchange, become commodities, and enter into commerce; . . . the nation which could not legislate over these subjects, would not possess power to regulate commerce.[13]

Having given such a broad construction to the noun *commerce* (which determines the subjects to which Congressional power extends), the Marshall Court proceeded to take an equally liberal view of the meaning of the verb *regulate* (which determines the type of authority that the Congress can exert). "What is this power?" asked Marshall in his *Gibbons v. Ogden* opinion.

It is the power to regulate; that is, to prescribe the rule by which commerce is to be governed. This power, like all others vested in congress is complete in itself, may be exercised to its utmost extent, and acknowledges no limitations, other than are prescribed in the constitution. . . . If, as has always been understood, the sovereignty of congress, though limited to specified objects, is plenary as to those objects, the power over commerce with foreign nations, and among the several states, is vested in congress as absolutely as it would be in a single government.[14]

Or, as it was more succinctly stated in Justice Johnson's concurring opinion, "The power of a sovereign state over commerce . . . amounts to nothing more than a power to limit and restrain it at pleasure." [15]

After Marshall's time, the Supreme Court tended greatly to limit the broad scope which he had given to the Congressional commerce power. The trend in this direction began almost as soon as Andrew Jackson appointed Chief Justice Taney as Marshall's successor in 1835; it attained its zenith in the 1934–36 decisions of the highest tribunal invalidating the legislative measures of the New Deal.

John Marshall, we saw, gave a broad construction both to the term "commerce" and to the Congressional power to "regulate." The post-Marshall Court restricted the meaning of both of these commerce-clause terms. In the first place, the Court withdrew from the conception of commerce a large part of the economic activity of the Nation. Of especial significance in this respect were a series of decisions holding that production or manufacturing was not commerce subject to Congressional authority, even though such production or manufacturing was undertaken with the intent that the products should be transported across state lines.[16] According to the Court's new notion, which prevailed from the post-Marshall period all the way to 1937, production itself was a purely local act divorced from the flow of interstate commerce and hence subject only to state regulation. And, in the Court's theory, the same came to be true of mining [17] and agriculture. [18] These, too, were purely local events, not part of the interstate commerce subject to federal control, even where the end result was the shipment of the mineral or farm products to other states. In the view of the Court, as it developed to its peak in the pre-1937 period, it made no difference that the manufacture, or mining, or agriculture—what it considered the purely local activity—had an effect upon interstate commerce, unless the effect was so immediate that the Court considered it to be "direct."

What this restricted conception of the commerce that Congress could reach meant in practice is shown dramatically by one of the most significant of the New Deal cases in the pre-1937 Supreme Court. In *Carter v. Carter Coal Co.,*[19] the Court had before it an act regulating the bituminous coal industry by price-fixing, proscription of unfair trade practices, and prescription of labor conditions. In declaring this act, and particularly its labor provisions, invalid, the majority of the Court relied directly upon the narrowed notion of commerce already referred to. Justice Sutherland's opinion rests upon the proposition that mere manufacturing or mining does not constitute commerce: "The local character of mining, of manufacturing and of crop growing is a fact, and remains a fact, whatever may be done with the products." [20] The effect of the labor provisions of the challenged law, said the Court, primarily falls upon production, not upon commerce. Commerce was said to be a thing apart from the relation of employer and employee, which in all producing occupations was purely local in character. Nor, in the Court's view, did it make any difference that labor practices in the gigantic coal industry clearly had an effect upon interstate commerce. To the Court, this effect was not "direct" enough; the direct effect was upon production and, then, the production itself affected commerce. The evils at which the law was directed, declared the Court majority, were all local evils over which the Federal Government had no legislative control: "Such effect as they may have upon commerce, however extensive it may be, is secondary and indirect. An increase in the greatness of the effect adds to its importance. It does not alter its character." [21]

The reasoning of the *Carter* case just discussed had been previously applied by the Court to nullify the two most important measures of the New Deal—the National Industrial Recovery Act and the Agricultural Adjustment Act. The NIRA was held beyond the reach of Congressional power as applied to small wholesale poultry dealers in Brooklyn. [22] The business done by them was purely local in character, even though the poultry handled by them came from outside the state. And, under the approach already mentioned, it did not make any difference that there was some effect upon interstate commerce by the business being regulated. Similarly, in holding the AAA unconstitutional,[23] the Court had relied upon the proposition that agriculture, like manufacturing or mining, is not commerce and hence is immune from federal control. In both cases, the restricted post-Marshall meaning of the term "commerce" had been used to deny to the Congress authority over the most vital aspects of the national economy.

But the pre-1937 Supreme Court went even further in restricting the broad scope which the Marshall Court had given to the Congressional commerce power. In addition to narrowing the connotation of "commerce," the Court moved sharply away from the meaning Marshall had given to the verb "regulate" in the constitutional clause. To Marshall and his associates, it will be recalled, the power to regulate was the complete power to control; even Justice Johnson, the otherwise staunch Jeffersonian, had recognized that the power to regulate commerce was the "power to limit and restrain it at pleasure." * Under the Marshall-Johnson view, it seems clear that the power of Congress to regulate was one which might be exercised for any reason. The sole question for the Court was whether what was at issue was actually a regulation of commerce; if it was, it was valid under the plenary Congressional power, regardless of the motives which had called forth the exercise of such power. Here, too, the post-Marshall Court differed. In its view, the fact that regulation of commerce was involved did not necessarily conclude the case. The Court had to determine also whether the end for which the Congress had exerted its commerce power was itself one toward which Congressional authority could lawfully be directed.

The classic case to illustrate this limitation of the term "regulate" in the commerce clause by the Court in the century following the death of John Marshall is *Hammer v. Dagenhart*,[24] usually known as the *Child Labor* case, which became one of the *causes célèbres* of our constitutional law. It involved the constitutionality of a federal statute which prohibited the transportation in interstate commerce of goods made in factories that employed children under a specified age. This law clearly purported to be limited to the confines of the express power of the Congress to regulate interstate commerce. But there is no doubt that, though it did not in its terms seek to interfere with local production or manufacturing, the real purpose of

---

* *Supra,* p. 30.

the Congress in enacting the statute was to suppress child labor in this country. Denied its interstate market, child labor could not continue upon a widespread scale.

To the majority of the Court, the Congressional purpose rendered the law at issue invalid. By its enactment of the statute, the federal legislature was seeking primarily to regulate the manner in which manufacturing was carried on; such manufacturing, we have seen, under the restricted meaning of the Court, was not commerce which could be reached by Congressional authority. "In our view," reads the *Child Labor* case opinion, "the necessary effect of this act is, by means of a prohibition against the movement in interstate commerce of ordinary commercial commodities, to regulate the hours of labor of children in factories and mines within the States, a purely state authority." [25] The Congress could not, in other words, even by an act whose terms were specifically limited to the regulation of interstate commerce, use its commerce power to exert regulatory authority over matters like manufacturing which were not, within the Court's narrow notion, commerce.

The restrictive interpretation of the commerce power in the decisions just discussed was catastrophic in its consequences upon effective governmental regulation. Elimination of manufacturing, mining, and agriculture from the reach of the commerce clause rendered the Congress powerless to deal with problems in those fields however pressing they might become. And so, as Justice Jackson stated, in characterizing the effect of the *Carter Coal Co.* decision, "a national government that has power, through the Federal Trade Commission, to prohibit the giving of prizes with penny candy shipped by the manufacturer from one state to another, was powerless to deal with the causes of critical stoppages in the gigantic bituminous coal industry." [26] Similarly, under the *Child Labor* case, the Federal Congress was precluded from taking effective action against the products of child labor.

It is true that the Court's decisions in the cases discussed did not affect the authority of the states to control production within their own boundaries. But state power must necessarily end at the state limits and is hardly competent to cope with modern economic activity which so often extends over more than one state. In addition, regulation limited to that exerted by the states must, of necessity, vary from state to state. State control cannot in most cases have the uniform character necessary for efficacious economic regulation. If a national industry like bituminous coal production or a practice like child labor is effectively to be regulated, it must be by regulation that is national in character. Under the cases we have discussed, nevertheless, such national regulation was precluded. In effect, then, the result of the restricted conception of the commerce clause taken by the post-Marshall Court was to prevent effectual economic regulation in this country.

Almost needless to say, the recession from the Marshall conception fitted in perfectly with the laissez-faire theory of governmental function that dominated political and economic thinking for almost a century after the death of the great Chief Justice. To bar federal intervention, as the Supreme Court did in these cases, was all but to exclude the possibility of any effective regulation in them. This was, of course, exactly what was demanded by the advocates of laissez faire; for, to them, the economic system could function efficiently only if it was permitted to operate free from governmental interference. The Supreme Court's narrow notion of the commerce power was a necessary complement of laissez faire. That is why it was one of the foremost casualties of the constitutional revolution of 1937; the decisions of that year marked the beginning of a significant return to the commerce-clause jurisprudence of John Marshall.

Back to Marshall

Critics of the Supreme Court have urged that its recent jurisprudence has vested unprecedented powers in the Federal Government, thus completely upsetting the equilibrium between states and Nation that prior Courts were so careful to maintain. It cannot be denied that this criticism is valid if one looks only at the precedents of the half-century or so prior to 1937; some of the decisions after that time, to paraphrase one attorney, discarded "the precedents of fifty years without even the decency of funeral obsequies." [27] Yet, as we have just seen, the precedents of the pre-1937 period had themselves been based upon a repudiation of earlier precedents. The Court itself had ignored the broad holdings of the John Marshall Court in adopting its restrictive interpretation of the Congressional commerce power.

According to a contemporary analysis by Robert H. Jackson, the post-1937 decisions of the Supreme Court marked a "retreat to the Constitution" [28] by the highest tribunal. This view may express too sanguine an opinion of the Court's new decisions; but, resting as these decisions did upon a broad construction of the commerce clause, they certainly did, at the least, mark a return by the Court to the Marshall conception of the Congressional commerce power.

This can be seen from the *Jones & Laughlin* decision,[29] already dealt with in Chapter 1, and there termed the landmark case of the constitutional revolution of 1937.* In *Jones & Laughlin,* the Court upheld the constitutionality of the National Labor Relations Act of 1935, under which the Congress had enacted a comprehensive scheme for the regulation of labor relations in the American economy. The difficulty in the case arose from the fact that the company being regulated was engaged only in the business of manufacturing iron and steel. Under the narrow interpretation which had been given to the commerce clause only the year before in the *Carter Coal Co.* case, such manufacturing was not commerce and hence not subject to Congressional control. Nor, under the *Carter* approach, we have seen, did it make any difference that the company being regulated was an industrial giant whose operations clearly had an effect upon interstate commerce. Such effect could not, in the *Carter* view, give the Congress authority over purely local production. It is not surprising that the lower court held that the Labor Act lay beyond the range of federal power. Indeed, considering the Supreme Court's resolute language in *Carter,* it is somewhat surprising that it should have even permitted argument on the point. Yet, not only was extensive argument allowed, but the Court itself, in its decision, completely abandoned its previous restrictive approach to the meaning of commerce and returned to the broad sweep which John Marshall had given to the term more than a century earlier.

The company regulated in the *Jones & Laughlin* case relied directly upon the decisions holding that manufacturing in itself was not commerce, arguing that because of them the industrial relations and activities in its manufacturing department were not subject to federal regulation. Chief Justice Hughes, in a masterful opinion for the majority of the Court stated, however, that the fact that the employees here concerned were engaged in production was not determinative: "The close and intimate effect which brings the subject within the reach of federal power may be due to activities in relation to productive industry although the industry when separately viewed is local." [30] In the present case, there is no doubt—any more than there was in a case like *Carter v. Carter Coal Co.*—that the production regulated affected interstate commerce. But here the Court declared that, in view of the company's far-flung activities, it would be idle to say that such effect was only indirect:

When industries organize themselves on a national scale, making their relation to interstate commerce the dominant factor in their activities, how can it be maintained that their industrial labor relations constitute

* *Supra,* p. 21.

a forbidden field into which Congress may not enter when it is necessary to protect interstate commerce from the paralyzing consequences of industrial war? [31]

The *Jones & Laughlin* rationale, as already emphasized, rests upon a repudiation of the limited connotation of commerce upon which decisions like that in the *Carter Coal Co.* case had been based. *Carter* had declared that production was not commerce; *Jones & Laughlin* held production to be subject to Congressional regulation under the commerce power. *Carter* had found immaterial the evils which had induced the Congress to act and their effect upon interstate commerce, declaring that, extensive though such effect might be, it was only secondary and indirect; *Jones & Laughlin* was fully cognizant of the catastrophic effect which industrial strife could have upon interstate commerce, and asserted categorically that such effect could not be dismissed as only indirect.

The *Jones & Laughlin* decision marks a definite break with the pre-1937 Court's imposition of restrictions upon the scope of the term "commerce"; under it, as just pointed out, manufacturing as such is not automatically excluded from the reach of the commerce power. Later cases extend the *Jones & Laughlin* approach to mining and agriculture. In 1940, the Court upheld a new Congressional act regulating the bituminous coal industry, similar in many ways to that which had been annulled in the *Carter Coal Co.* case. This time there was no doubt that coal mining was not considered immune from the commerce power. "The regulatory provisions," reads the Court's opinion, "are clearly within the power of Congress under the commerce clause of the Constitution . . . . Congress under the commerce clause is not impotent to deal with what it may consider to be dire consequences of laissez-faire." [32] Similarly, in 1939, the Court held valid the Agricultural Adjustment Act of 1938, whose basic features were not unlike those of the law of the same name condemned in 1936.[33] It is true that the Court did not expressly find that agriculture came within the definition of commerce, which omission led a lower federal court as late as 1954 to declare that "agriculture is not commerce" and hence "federal regulation of agriculture invades the reserved rights of the states." [34] The Supreme Court itself quickly laid to rest this ghost of the first *AAA* case, declaring categorically in 1955 that the regulation of agriculture was within the federal commerce power.[35]

Having removed the post-Marshall restrictions upon the meaning of commerce, the highest Court then proceeded, in the period after 1937, to return to the great Chief Justice's view of the Congressional power to *regulate* under the commerce clause as a complete one. That power, said Chief Justice Hughes in his *Jones & Laughlin* opinion, is plenary and may be exerted to foster, protect, control, and restrain commerce.[36] That being the case, it seems clear that there has been no room in the post-1937 Court for a case like the decision, already discussed, in *Hammer v. Dagenhart*,[*] which invalidated an admitted regulation of interstate commerce because the Congressional purpose had been to regulate indirectly local economic activities which were beyond the reach of the federal commerce power. After decisions in 1938 [37] and 1939 [38] eroding the constitutional basis of *Hammer v. Dagenhart*, the Court in 1941 expressly overruled that case. This occurred in *United States v. Darby*,[39] where the legality of the Fair Labor Standards Act of 1938 was at issue. That law provides for the fixing of minimum wages and maximum hours by a federal agency. It prohibits the shipment in interstate commerce of goods manufactured by employees whose wages are less than the prescribed minimum or whose hours of work are more than the prescribed maximum. As such, it was not unlike the law at issue in *Hammer v. Dagenhart*, which had prohibited the transportation in interstate commerce of goods produced by child labor. In its *Darby* decision, nonetheless, the Court refused to follow the reasoning of the *Child Labor* case: "The reasoning and conclusion of the Court's opinion there cannot be reconciled with the conclusion which we have reached, that the power of Congress under the Commerce Clause is plenary to exclude any article from interstate commerce subject only to the specific prohibitions of the Constitution." [40]

The *Darby* Court was, of course, aware that the motive and purpose of the Congressional prohibition at issue were to make effective the legislative policy of eliminating substandard labor conditions by closing the markets of interstate commerce to goods produced under such conditions. In this sense, the effect of the challenged law was clearly a regulation of the wages and hours of those engaged in what had formerly been held to be only local production and manufacturing. But the whole point about the *Darby* decision is that, under it, the end toward which a Congressional exercise of regulatory power over commerce is directed is irrelevant. According to Justice Stone's opinion for a now unanimous Court, "The motive and purpose of a regulation of interstate commerce are matters for the legislative judgment upon the exercise of which the Constitution places no restriction and over which the courts are given no control." [41] Thus the Court definitely disowned the *Child Labor* case thesis that the motive of the prohibition or its effect to

[*] *Supra*, pp. 32-33.

control in some measure the production within the states of the
article excluded from commerce could operate to deprive the Congressional regulation of its constitutional validity. Instead the
Court relied directly upon the Marshall definition of the power to
regulate commerce as the power "to prescribe the rule by which
commerce is governed." [42] "Whatever their motive and purpose,"
declared the *Darby* opinion, "regulations of commerce which do not
infringe some constitutional prohibition are within the plenary
power conferred on Congress by the Commerce Clause." [43] Thus
had the wheel of constitutional construction swung full circle in the
century after the death of John Marshall.

Beyond Marshall

The post-1937 decisions of the highest bench just discussed did,
without any doubt, represent a sharp break with what had gone before in Supreme Court jurisprudence. All the same, it is unwarranted to describe them, as contemporary critics did, as constituting
a radical and unprecedented extension of Congressional authority.
The cases we have analyzed indicate only a return to the Marshall
meaning of the commerce clause; both the noun *commerce* and the
verb *regulate* in that clause have been given back the sweeping construction that they had at the time of the great Chief Justice. That
being the case, the decisions discussed can hardly be characterized
as subversive underminings of the federal structure erected by the
Founding Fathers. Marshall himself was a staunch conservative,
personally familiar with the intent of the men of 1787. A Court
that restores his view of a basic constitutional provision is not moving the Ship of State from its settled mooring. Even Justice Johnson—normally the constant Jeffersonian—could, it will be recalled,*
join in the Marshall construction of the commerce clause without
feeling it did violence to his basic beliefs.

But the Supreme Court has not been content merely to return to
the Marshallian conception of the commerce power. In a whole
series of more recent decisions, it has gone beyond John Marshall in
expanding Congressional authority under the commerce clause. Indeed, even Marshall himself—faithful federalist though he was—
could hardly have conceived of the extent to which the commerce
power has become distended in the past decade and a half. "No
political dreamer," asserted Marshall in one of his most celebrated
opinions, "was ever wild enough to think of breaking down the lines

* *Supra,* pp. 29-30.

which separate the states and of compounding the American people into one common mass." [44] Certainly, the more recent jurisprudence of the Supreme Court does not go so far as to destroy federalism as a flourishing system. Yet, that it constitutes an important step in that direction cannot be denied.

The Court has gone far beyond even John Marshall's broad conception of the commerce power by carrying the test of effect upon commerce to its logical extreme. In the *Jones & Laughlin* case, we saw, it was held that the iron and steel company's manufacturing activities were subject to Congressional control because they had a clear effect upon interstate commerce; nor, in the Court's view there, could such effect be dismissed as merely indirect. The company regulated in *Jones & Laughlin* was an industrial giant whose activities, without any doubt, had a substantial impact upon interstate commerce. In later cases, however, the Court has applied the *Jones & Laughlin* reasoning to much smaller companies. In a 1939 decision,[45] the Court held expressly that the operation of the commerce power does not depend on any particular volume of commerce affected. The smallness of the volume of commerce affected in the particular case, said Justice Stone, is without significance. The test, in other words, is whether the economic activity being regulated affects interstate commerce; if it does, it is subject to the Congressional commerce power regardless of the actual degree of such effect.

The only difficulty with this test is that, under contemporary conditions, the economic system is so interconnected in its parts that there are few, if any, even purely local business activities which may not have at least some repercussions upon commerce which extends beyond state lines. Too broad a view of what constitutes a consequential effect upon commerce would, in Justice Cardozo's apt language, obliterate the distinction between what is national and what is local in the field of commerce: "Motion at the outer rim is communicated perceptibly, though minutely, to recording instruments at the center. A society such as ours is an elastic medium which transmits all tremors throughout its territory." [46] In a complex modern society, there is such interdependence of its members that the activities of most of them are necessary to the activities of most others. One may wonder, all the same, whether that should be made the basis of the coverage of the commerce clause. If it is, there is practically no economic activity in this country that is not subject to Congressional control. By a "house-that-Jack-built" chain of causation, there is brought within the sweep of the com-

merce power every stage of economic activity—even the ultimate
causa causarum which results in the production of goods for commerce.[47]

The scope of the commerce power under the Supreme Court's
present application of the "effect on interstate commerce" approach
is well seen from two 1942 decisions. The first of these upheld the
constitutionality of Congressional regulation of the price of milk
produced and sold entirely within the state of Illinois. And this
despite the fact that federal power under the commerce clause appears clearly to be limited to the regulation of interstate commerce
alone. In the case under discussion, the Court justified the regulation at issue because the intrastate milk being regulated was sold in
competition with milk transported from outside the state. According to Chief Justice Stone, "the marketing of a local product in competition with that of a like commodity moving interstate may so
interfere with interstate commerce or its regulation as to afford a
basis for Congressional regulation of the intrastate activity." [48]
Here, too, it is the fact that there is effect upon interstate commerce
that furnishes the occasion for the exertion of federal authority.
But, if that is true, it is hard to see what form of intrastate activity
cannot be reached by the Congress. At the present time, all local
commerce competes to some extent with commerce from beyond
the state and, under the decision just dealt with, all such local commerce is in consequence within the scope of federal power.

The second 1942 decision referred to—*Wickard v. Filburn* [49]—
sustained an even deeper penetration by the Congress into purely
local activities. The Agricultural Adjustment Act of 1938 extends
the federal regulation of agricultural production to produce not intended in any part for commerce but wholly for consumption on the
producer's farm. In other words, as Justice Douglas has recently
described it, wheat consumed on the farm and never reaching any
conventional market was subject to penalties if grown on acreage
in excess of that allowed to the producer concerned: "Wheat that
was eaten by chickens or pigs or consumed by the farmer at his table
was treated the same as wheat sent into the vast stream of commerce reaching the nation's grain markets." [50] In upholding this
federal regulation of the home-consumed agricultural product which
never saw the light of commerce, the Supreme Court asserted that
a home-consumed product like wheat has a substantial effect upon
the price and market conditions for wheat. Though never mar-
keted, it supplies a need of the grower which otherwise would be
met by purchases in the commercial market. In this sense, said the
Court, home-grown wheat competes with wheat in commerce. And

this, of course, brings *Wickard v. Filburn* within the principle of the first 1942 decision discussed above. As the opinion of Justice Jackson put it:

Even if appellee's activity be local and though it may not be regarded as commerce, it may still, whatever its nature, be reached by Congress if it exerts a substantial economic effect on interstate commerce, this irrespective of whether such effect is what might at some earlier time have been defined as "direct" or "indirect." . . . Congress may properly have considered that wheat consumed on the farm where grown, if wholly outside the scheme of regulation, would have a substantial effect in defeating and obstructing its purpose to stimulate trade therein at increased prices.[51]

With the Court's decision in *Wickard v. Filburn,* a climax is reached in the recent broadening of the Congressional commerce power. Under the doctrine of that case, federal authority may be exerted over purely local transactions, though they themselves are not commercial in character. Even so, under the Court's reasoning, they have sufficient effect upon commerce to furnish the occasion for the exercise of Congressional power. But, following this approach, it is difficult to see what aspect of economic activity within the states cannot be subjected to federal authority. If it is the existence of effect on interstate commerce, however slight or indirect, that is now the test, there are really no limitations other than Congressional self-restraint upon the federal commerce power. Thus, under Supreme Court decisions, Congressional regulatory authority now extends to employees engaged in the maintenance and operation of a building in which goods for interstate commerce are produced; [52] to the employees of a window-cleaning company that cleans windows of people engaged in interstate commerce; [53] to a local newspaper with a limited circulation; [54] and to a local gas and electric company whose product is entirely generated and sold within the confines of a single state.[55] These activities all appear clearly to have been local in nature. Congressional action with regard to them was nonetheless sustained because of the Court's opinion that they might have some effect, tenuous though it might be, on interstate commerce. According to a prophetic passage by Chief Justice Hughes in 1935:

If the commerce clause were construed to reach all enterprises and transactions which could be said to have an . . . effect upon interstate commerce, the federal authority would embrace practically all the activities of the people and the authority of the State over its domestic concerns would exist only by sufferance of the federal government.[56]

Yet this is precisely what *has* happened under the Supreme Court decisions that have just been discussed.

Insurance and Navigation

As early as 1878, the highest Court recognized that the Congressional commerce power is not a static concept. The powers granted by the commerce clause, declared Chief Justice Waite at that time,

are not confined to the instrumentalities of commerce . . . known or in use when the Constitution was adopted, but they keep pace with the progress of the country, and adapt themselves to the new developments of times and circumstances. They extend from the horse with its rider to the stage-coach, from the sailing-vessel to the steamboat, from the coach and the steamboat to the railroad, and from the railroad to the telegraph, as these new agencies are successively brought into use to meet the demands of increasing population and wealth. They were intended for the government of the business to which they relate, at all times and under all circumstances.[57]

Few will deny that the scope of the commerce power must alter to meet changed external conditions. At the same time, modifications should not be imposed by the judiciary, in cavalier disregard of an accumulated mass of precedents, when there is no real need for change and no indication that the Congress itself desires it. It is one thing for the highest Court to abandon unjustified restrictions upon the commerce clause in the face of legislative desires to exercise authority at least as wide as that which had been conceded by John Marshall. It is quite another for that tribunal gratuitously to confer upon the Congress, in disruption of existing state regulatory schemes, exclusive authority that it had never sought.

A celebrated instance where the post-1937 Court rushed in where Congress feared to tread was its 1944 decision holding that insurance constituted commerce and was consequently, when conducted across state lines, subject to exclusive Congressional control under the commerce clause.[58] What made this decision a drastic one was the fact that, seventy-five years earlier, the Court had held that insurance was not commerce and was, as such, subject only to state regulation.[59] Relying upon the 1869 decision and the unbroken line of cases following its doctrine, the states had established an elaborate structure of regulation and taxation of the insurance business; "on the rationalization that insurance was not commerce, yet was business affected with a vast public interest, the states developed

comprehensive regulatory and taxing systems." [60] It was this existing structure of regulation and taxation that the Court was upsetting by its insurance decision, at least so far as interstate insurance
(by far the great bulk of the business) was concerned. And for
what purpose was this radical result reached? The Congress had
never indicated dissatisfaction with existing state laws or a desire
to appropriate the regulation of insurance for itself. Indeed, so
far from desiring to exercise authority in this field, the Congress,
within less than a year after the Supreme Court's 1944 decision,
passed a law expressly authorizing state regulation and taxation of
insurance. As the Court itself later conceded, with regard to this
law, "Obviously Congress' purpose was broadly to give support to
the existing and future state systems for regulating and taxing the
business of insurance." [61]

Even though abstract logic, in the light of the Court's already-
discussed magnification of the commerce clause, may support the
drastic course taken by the Court majority in its 1944 decision, the
common-sense wisdom of the situation, in the words of a dissenting
Justice, seems opposed.[62] The immediate and practical effect of the
Court's decision was to withdraw from the states (with whom such
regulation was a successful going concern) the regulation of insurance and to confer it on the Congress, which had adopted no legislative policy and evolved no scheme of regulation with respect to
insurance. These consequences should have stayed reversal of a
long-established doctrine, not unsound in principle and not plainly
inconsistent with accepted Supreme Court doctrine, which prom-
ised so little of advantage and so much of harm.[63] It is hard not to
agree with the conclusion of Justice Jackson's dissent:

To use my office, at a time like this, and with so little justification in
necessity, to dislocate the functions and revenues of the states and to
catapult Congress into immediate and undivided responsibility for supervision of the nation's insurance business is more than I can reconcile
with my view of the function of this Court in our Society.[64]

That the dire consequences foreseen by the dissenters did not come
to pass is due only to the fact that, as already mentioned, the Congress passed a law repudiating the Supreme Court's decision, by
relinquishing jurisdiction over insurance to the states.

Whether justified or not, the Court's 1944 insurance decision
was based upon the extent to which the business of insurance had
changed in the seventy-five years since that business had been held
not to constitute commerce. The modern insurance business had

grown so greatly as to hold what the Court termed a commanding position in the trade and commerce of our Nation. This, in the Court's view, necessitated a drastically altered construction of the commerce clause with regard to it.

Another field where the post-1937 Court has drastically expanded the scope of federal power because of changes in the field itself caused by modern technological developments is that of the regulation of navigable waterways. Here, too, the authority of Congress arises from the commerce clause. A river is a highway for travel between states—at least, it could be such, if it were navigable.[65] And that is why Chief Justice Marshall, in *Gibbons v. Ogden*,[66] declared that the Congressional power under the commerce clause extends to the navigable streams of the Nation. But, under present-day conditions, a river may be much more than a highway; it may also be a vital source of hydroelectric power, and that whether it is navigable or not. In addition, a river may often be a source of danger to the surrounding countryside; flood control consequently becomes a subject of proper governmental concern.

In Marshall's time and for a century thereafter, the Congressional power over waterways could without difficulty be limited to streams which were, in fact, navigable, for it was only with regard to them that commerce could be carried on. More recently, however, the highest Court has abandoned the requirement that, to be subject to the commerce clause, a stream must be "navigable in fact." In *United States v. Appalachian Power Co.*,[67] decided at the end of 1940, two lower courts had found as a fact that the New River in Virginia was not navigable; upon that finding, those courts had held that the Federal Government had no authority to prevent the defendant company from constructing and putting into operation a hydroelectric dam in the river. The Supreme Court reversed, declaring that the test of navigability was not whether the river in its natural state could be used as a waterway. Its possible availability for navigation, said the Court, must also be considered: "A waterway, otherwise suitable for navigation, is not barred from that classification merely because artificial aids must make the highway suitable for use before commercial navigation may be undertaken." [68] In other words, for federal jurisdiction under the commerce clause to attach, it is not necessary that the stream concerned be navigable; it is enough that it might some day be rendered navigable. Thus, as Justice Douglas has recently explained it,[69] a stream may not in fact be navigable at present; yet, if it can be made so, it is in the federal domain.

The Court has gone even further in upholding federal regulatory power in the field of flood control. Congressional control over our waters, said the Court in the *Appalachian Power* case, is not limited to control for navigation. Federal "authority is as broad as the needs of commerce." [70] Water power development is stated to be a by-product of the general use of rivers for commerce and, as such, subject to commerce control. And flood protection and watershed development are likewise parts of commerce control. In a 1941 case, the state of Oklahoma sought to restrain the construction of a federal dam and reservoir upon one of its rivers, asserting that the river in question was not navigable. The dam at issue was part of a comprehensive scheme for controlling floods in the Mississippi River through reservoir control of its tributaries, of which the Oklahoma river was one. The Court, in refusing to prohibit the federal project, declared that, if flood control of the Mississippi were to be successful, some control of its tributaries, whether navigable or not, was necessary. The power of flood control, reads the opinion of Justice Douglas, "extends to the tributaries of navigable streams. For, just as control over the non-navigable parts of a river may be essential or desirable in the interests of the navigable portions, so may the key to flood control on a navigable stream be found in whole or in part in flood control on its tributaries." [71]

In a more recent comment, Justice Douglas has stated that the cases on Congressional control of navigable waterways "show, perhaps as well as the history of any other constitutional principle, how the changing needs of oncoming generations have their impact on law, how old precepts are put to new and greater uses, as social, economic, engineering, and political wisdom increase." [72] That may well be true. Some may wonder, all the same, whether it was necessary for the Court so completely to disregard the accumulated wisdom of earlier days in this field. The decisions of the pre-1937 Court limited the commerce power to navigable streams. This left substantial jurisdiction to the states. Under the *Appalachian Power* case, this state authority is all but eliminated; under its test, almost all streams in this country are subject to exclusive Congressional control. As Justice Roberts aptly pointed out in dissent in *Appalachian Power:*

If this test be adopted, then every creek in every state of the Union which has enough water, when conserved by dams and locks or chanelled by wing dams and sluices, to float a boat drawing two feet of water, may be pronounced navigable because, by the expenditure of some enormous sum, such a project would be possible of execution. . . . If this criterion be the correct one, it is not seen how any stream can be found not to be navigable.[73]

Certainly, under the Supreme Court's new doctrine, the plenary control of the Federal Government over waterways and the hydro-electric power derived from them is pushed to its widest possible extent. And this, of course, means the virtual elimination of the states from this important field of regulatory activity. Truly, to use Justice Douglas' meet phrase,[74] the power of Congress over navigable streams has evolved to a point never dreamed of by Chief Justice Marshall.

Back to 1787?

Recent researchers into our constitutional history have asserted that the Founding Fathers intended the commerce clause to have an even broader sweep than that attributed to it by John Marshall. According to them, indeed, it is all but impossible for us today to sense fully the broad meaning which was given to the term *commerce* when the Constitution was written:

The Eighteenth Century did not separate by artificial lines aspects of a culture which are inseparable. It had no lexicon of legalisms extracted from the law reports in which judicial usage lies in a world apart from the ordinary affairs of life. Commerce was then more than we imply now by business or industry. It was a name for the economic order, the domain of political economy, the realm of a comprehensive public policy. It is a word which makes trades, activities and interests an instrument in the culture of the people. If trust was to repose in parchment, it was the only word which could catch up into a single comprehensive term all activities directly affecting the wealth of the nation.[75]

If this view is correct, then the framers of our organic document intended "commerce" to mean any gainful activity. And, these same scholars say, "among the several States" meant, to the draftsmen of the Constitution, among the people of this country. If this was their meaning, the power of the Congress was intended to extend, not only to gainful activities extending across state lines, but to all the internal commerce of the Nation as well. Under this analysis, a member of the highest Court has said:

Congress could enter fields seldom dreamed of up to this time. Under [this] view, Congress would have the power to pass a uniform Negotiable Instruments Act applicable to all commercial transactions in the nation, whether or not interstate, a Uniform Sales Act covering all sales, both local and interstate, and a Uniform Corporation Law requiring the incorporation even of the corner grocery store that neither buys nor sells in interstate commerce.[76]

Yet this is precisely the compass of the commerce clause that the present Supreme Court has enunciated. The recent decisions of that tribunal that have been discussed extend the reach of the Congressional commerce power to all gainful activities among the people of this country and, under cases like *Wickard v. Filburn,*[*] whether or not such activities actually extend across state lines. But, if this is true, are not the extreme recent decisions that give a hitherto unprecedented scope to federal authority justified as a return to the meaning which the commerce clause had to the men of 1787 themselves?

Even if it be assumed, without conceding, that the recent researchers referred to are correct in their interpretation of the literal meaning of the words used in the commerce clause at the time the Constitution was adopted (and, it must be emphasized, most constitutional historians would not agree with their view), it does not necessarily follow that such assumption must support the recent Supreme Court jurisprudence on the commerce clause. The present writer does not, of course, intend to go so far as a noted Harvard law professor who used to warn his class in constitutional law each year against reading the Constitution, asserting that to do so would be apt to "confuse their minds." At the same time, it must be recognized that the Constitution and what it means today are scarcely comprehended in the few thousand words that make up the organic instrument of 1787. The Constitution, it constantly bears repeating, is a document that must be read with the gloss of over a century and a half of constitutional history. It is true also of a Constitution that "The letter killeth"; it can hardly serve as a living instrument of government if read in a purely literal vacuum.

It is not, to be sure, contended that the meaning which words used in the Constitution may have had in the common parlance of the late eighteenth century is lightly to be dismissed; certainly the construction which the Founding Fathers may have actually given to a constitutional provision is entitled to the greatest respect. That does not mean, nevertheless, that such construction must be conclusive in resolving the constitutional problems of our own day. This is particularly true when problems which the Founders could not have foreseen are before us for solution.

The men of 1787 were certainly aware of the need for restrictions upon government. Having just fought a revolution against what they considered excessive governmental authority, one of their primary concerns was to ensure against the possibility of

[*] *Supra,* pp. 40-41.

similar excesses in the constitutional structure they were establishing. All the same, there is no doubt that the problem of controlling governmental authority is far more vital now than it was when able gentlemen in knee breeches, lace, and three-cornered hats burned midnight candles in Philadelphia and wrote the Constitution. If the reader had lived then, he would hardly have been aware of the existence of the National Government. Today, such existence is the predominant fact in our polity. The Congress now exerts more regulatory authority than would have even appeared possible to contemporaries of King George III.

Expansion of federal power, canalized within banks to keep it from overflowing, is not inconsistent with our constitutional structure; so staunch a constitutionalist as John Marshall, we saw, favored a broad view of Congressional authority. To construe such authority as unlimited is, however, incompatible with the proper functioning of federalism. If the states are to continue as operating governmental entities, all power must not be concentrated in Washington. Unabated continuation of the trend toward federal aggrandizement must inevitably result in the substitution of a unitarian form of government for that established under the Constitution, even though the federal form remains as a vestigial survival. If the Founding Fathers really did intend such to be the eventual form of American government, it is pertinent to ask why they bothered to provide for a federal system, in which all powers not granted to the Nation were reserved to the states. It is the question of the maintenance of federalism itself that is raised by the removal of all effective barriers to Congressional authority. And, it is relevant to note, a country of continental extent such as ours has never been effectively governed save by a federal system or a despotism. If ours is to remain a federal system, it is for the Supreme Court, as for other governmental organs, to ensure that the interpenetrations of modern society do not wipe out state lines. As Justice Frankfurter has well stated,

It is not for us to make inroads upon our federal system either by indifference to its maintenance or excessive regard for the unifying forces of modern technology. Scholastic reasoning may prove that no activity is isolated within the boundaries of a single State, but that cannot justify absorption of legislative power by the United States over every activity.[77]

Taxing and Spending Power

To complete our picture of the expansion of federal authority under the post-1937 jurisprudence of the Supreme Court, attention should be paid to the Congressional taxing and spending power. Under Article I, section 8, of the Constitution, "The Congress shall have Power To lay and collect Taxes, Duties, Imposts and Excises, to pay the Debts and provide for the common Defence and general Welfare of the United States."

What is included in the power of the Congress to provide for the general welfare? Some have argued that it is an independent grant of authority, and not a mere qualification of the taxing power. The constitutional phraseology, it is said, was intended as a comprehensive grant of authority to the Congress to take any action which might promote the general welfare of the country. This extreme position has not been followed. As it was expressed by the first, and perhaps still the greatest, of *Commentaries* on the Constitution—that by Justice Joseph Story over a century ago—to accept such a view would be to create,

a general authority in congress to pass all laws, which they may deem for the common defence or general welfare. Under such circumstances, the constitution would practically create an unlimited national government. The enumerated powers would tend to embarrassment and confusion; since they would only give rise to doubts, as to the true extent of the general power, or of the enumerated powers.[78]

The view of the general welfare clause that has prevailed is that stated by Thomas Jefferson: "the laying of taxes is the *power*, and the general welfare the *purpose* for which the power is to be exercised. . . . [The Congress] are not *to do anything they please* to provide for the general welfare, but only to *lay taxes* for that purpose." [79] The general welfare clause is, in other words, not an independent grant of power, but a qualification of the taxing power.

Yet even looked at in this way, the general welfare clause appears to confer tremendous powers upon the Government in Washington. If the Congress may impose taxes to promote the general welfare, it means, because of the broadness of the term used, that its taxing authority is practically unlimited. Its power to impose taxes is consequently not limited to imposition for the purpose of securing revenue. And its power of expenditure would certainly seem to be as broad as its authority to tax.

In the *Federalist*, there is a sharp debate between Madison and Hamilton on the scope of the power to tax and spend for the general welfare. Madison contended that the power should be regarded as merely incidental to the remaining powers of the Congress; in his view, the power to tax and spend must be confined to the enumerated legislative fields committed to the Congress.

Hamilton, on the other hand, adopted the literal, broad meaning of the constitutional language; he maintained that the general welfare clause confers a power separate and distinct from those later enumerated and is not restricted in meaning by the grant of them.[80] In the Hamiltonian interpretation, the taxing and spending power is not limited by the direct grants of legislative power found in the Constitution.

The pre-1937 Supreme Court, despite its express disclaimer of intention to do so,[81] appears to have adopted the more limited Madisonian view in its decision nullifying the Agricultural Adjustment Act of 1933. That law, one of the most important regulatory measures of the early New Deal, was based entirely upon the taxing and spending power. It sought to eliminate overproduction of farm products by furnishing the farmer with sufficient inducement for curtailing his production. Under the act, a processing tax was levied upon different agricultural commodities, and the proceeds from this tax were used to compensate farmers who agreed beforehand to raise less or none of such commodities. It seems obvious that the prime purpose of this exercise of the power to tax was the regulation of agricultural production, rather than the securing of revenue. It was for this reason that the law in question was held unconstitutional in 1936 by the Supreme Court. The act, said the Court, attempted to regulate local production under the guise of an exercise of the taxing power:

If the act before us is a proper exercise of the federal taxing power, evidently the regulation of all industry throughout the United States may be accomplished by similar exercises of the same power. It would be possible to exact money from one branch of an industry and pay it to another branch in every field of activity which lies within the province of the states. The mere threat of such a procedure might well induce the surrender of rights and the compliance with federal regulation as the price of continuance in business.[82]

In the opinion of the majority of the Court, the taxing and spending power could not be used to accomplish regulation of agricultural production, which (under the Court's view at that time) was beyond the scope of the Congressional commerce power.

The Court's AAA opinion shows clearly why the power to tax and spend for the general welfare can be of such significance. The power to tax, reads one of the most celebrated statements by Chief Justice John Marshall, involves the power to destroy.[83] But the power to tax may also involve, as a law like the AAA shows, the power to regulate. If any tax may be imposed that promotes the general welfare, exercise of the taxing power is not limited to the securing of revenue. The taxing power may also serve as the basis for federal regulation, with the imposition of taxes serving as the sanction behind the regulatory scheme. As the Court put it in the portion of its *AAA* opinion already quoted, the regulation of every field of activity (even those that may lie within the province of the states) may be accomplished by exercises of the taxing power.

Under the post-1937 decisions of the highest tribunal, the limitation imposed on the taxing power by the *AAA* case has been eliminated. The Agricultural Adjustment Act of 1938, which differed only in details from that held invalid in 1936, was, we have already seen,* sustained in 1939. The motive of the Congress in exerting its power, said the Court then, is irrelevant to the validity of its legislation.[84] In other decisions, the Court has refused to invalidate taxes merely because their primary purpose was regulation, not revenue. A tax, in the Court's present view, is not any the less a tax because it has a regulatory effect; [85] a tax does not cease to be valid merely because it regulates, discourages, or even definitely deters the activities taxed.[86] And the Court has indicated unequivocally that it is for the Congress, not for it, to determine whether particular exercises of the power to tax and spend will actually promote the general welfare. In Justice Cardozo's language in a leading 1937 case:

The line must still be drawn between one welfare and another, between particular and general. Where this shall be placed cannot be known through a formula in advance of the event. There is a middle ground or certainly a penumbra in which discretion is at large. The discretion, however, is not confided to the courts. The discretion belongs to Congress.[87]

But the Court has gone even further in repudiating the 1936 *AAA* decision. In 1950, it stated categorically that a tax statute does not fall because it touches on activities which Congress might not otherwise regulate.[88] What this means in terms of present-day Congressional regulatory power is well shown by the 1953 decision of the Court in *United States v. Kahriger*.[89] At issue in it was the constitutionality of the so-called gambler's occupational tax law, enacted by the Congress in 1951. That law, which Justice Frankfurter characterized in 1955 as "a spurious use of the taxing power as a means of facilitating prosecution of federal offenses," [90] levied a tax of fifty dollars per year upon persons engaged in the business

* *Supra*, p. 36.

of accepting wagers, and required such persons to register with the
Federal Collector of Internal Revenue their names, addresses, and
places of business. Though ostensibly a revenue measure, the
primary purpose of the wagering tax law appears clearly to have
been to aid in the suppression of gambling. To quote from Justice
Frankfurter's dissent in the *Kahriger* case:

The context of the circumstances which brought forth this enactment—
sensationally exploited disclosures regarding gambling in big cities and
small, the relation of this gambling to corrupt politics, the impatient
public response to these disclosures, the feeling of ineptitude or paralysis
on the part of local law-enforcing agencies—emphatically supports what
was revealed on the floor of Congress, namely that what was formally
a means of revenue for the Federal Government was essentially an effort
to check if not to stamp out professional gambling.[91]

The law in question was intended to place the professional gambler
on the horns of a legal dilemma. If he were not to register and pay
the tax required by the law, he would commit a federal offense for
which he could be punished criminally. On the other hand, if he
were to come forward to register and, in effect, confess that he
was engaged in the business of gambling, he would lay himself open
to prosecution by local law-enforcement authorities, for there are
antigambling laws on most state statute books. The act at issue,
in the words of one member of the Supreme Court, "creates a
squeezing device contrived to put a man in federal prison if he
refuses to confess himself into a state prison as a violator of state
gambling laws."[92]

Although the object of the wagering tax law was thus the regulation of professional gambling rather than the securing of revenue,
it was held by the Court that this did not render it unconstitutional.
"A federal excise tax does not cease to be valid," said its opinion,
"merely because it discourages or deters the activities taxed. Nor
is the tax invalid merely because the revenue obtained is negligible.
. . . The instant tax has a regulatory effect. But regardless of its
regulatory effect, the wagering tax produces revenue."[93] Or, to put
it another way, the Court will not go behind what is formally a
revenue measure to determine whether the raising of revenue is, in
actuality, its primary purpose. The fact that the taxing power is
used as an instrument of regulation does not, in the present view
of the Supreme Court, affect the validity of its exercise: "It is
axiomatic that the power of Congress to tax is extensive and falls
with crushing effect on businesses deemed unessential or inimical
to the public welfare. . . . As is well known, the constitutional restraints on taxing are few."[94]

Under a decision like that in the *Kahriger* case, just discussed, the Federal Congress is provided with a ready means in its power to tax of asserting authority over matters that were formerly deemed to be wholly within the competence of the states. We can take the regulation of professional gambling, at issue in *Kahriger,* as a good example. Such regulation would appear to fall within the reserved powers of the states, at least where purely local gambling is involved. And, even under the expanded concept of the national commerce power which, we have seen, now dominates the jurisprudence of the Supreme Court, it is doubtful whether such local gambling can be considered to have any effect upon interstate commerce so as to be subject to federal regulatory authority. Yet, by framing its regulatory law in the form of a nominal taxing measure, the Congress is, under the *Kahriger* decision, enabled to make what might otherwise be an inadmissible intrusion into a domain of legislation reserved for the states. Clearly, as Justice Frankfurter pointed out in his *Kahriger* dissent, the Court's decision there gravely affects the balance of powers within the federal system:

To allow what otherwise is excluded from congressional authority to be brought within it by casting legislation in the form of a revenue measure could . . . offer an easy way for the legislative imagination to control "any one of the great number of subjects of public interest, jurisdiction of which the States have never parted with. . . ."[95]

Investigatory Power

It is perhaps characteristic of the way in which constitutional problems have been popularly presented that public attention in recent years has been focused, not on the landmark decisions so drastically expanding federal legislative authority already discussed in this chapter, but on a Congressional power that is, after all, only ancillary to the power to make laws, namely, the Congressional power of investigation. Significant though the use, and even the abuse, of investigatory power by the Congress in the last decade or so may have been, to one interested in an over-all picture of constitutional development in that time, they cannot begin to compare in consequence with the magnification of Congressional law-making authority, sanctioned by the highest Court, that has altered so profoundly the balance of our federal system.

This is not to deny the importance of the Congressional power of investigation; the indispensable informing function of Congress, in the words of a 1953 Supreme Court opinion, is not to be minimized.[96] Certainly, the power of inquiry is an essential auxiliary

to the legislative functions of the Congress. As the Court itself
recognized in the leading case upholding Congressional investigatory authority (its 1927 decision in *McGrain v. Daugherty*), "A
legislative body cannot legislate wisely or effectively in the absence
of information respecting the conditions which the legislation is
intended to affect or change; and where the legislative body does
not itself possess the requisite information—which not infrequently
is true—recourse must be had to others who do possess it." [97] It is
by use of its investigatory power that the Congress obtains the
information needed to enable it properly to perform its functions.
It is, indeed, not too much to say that, under contemporary conditions, investigating committees have become, in large part, the eyes
and ears of the Congress. "Without the power to investigate," as
Chief Justice Warren recently put it, "Congress could be seriously
handicapped in its efforts to exercise its constitutional function
wisely and effectively." [98]

At the same time, some recent exercises of investigatory authority
by Congressional committees have given rise to expressions of
legitimate anxiety. In Justice Frankfurter's words, "we would have
to be that 'blind' Court, against which Mr. Chief Justice Taft
admonished in a famous passage, . . . that does not see what
'[a]ll others can see and understand' not to know that there is wide
concern, both in and out of Congress, over some aspects of the
exercise of the congressional power of investigation." [99] Yet, even
if we concede, as we must, what is now common knowledge, that
there have been abuses within the Congress of investigatory power,
that does not, in any way, answer the cardinal question of what
the proper remedy is for the removal of such abuses.

It is hardly surprising that the present Supreme Court, wedded
as it has been to the doctrine of judicial restraint in the face of
Congressional exertions of power, has indicated that the primary
remedy against investigative abuses is with the Congress itself or,
ultimately, with the people to whom that body is responsible.
"Courts," the highest tribunal stated in 1951, "are not the place for
such controversies. Self-discipline and the voters must be the ultimate reliance for discouraging or correcting such abuses." [100] The
late Justice Jackson went even further. Though emphasizing that
he did not want to be understood as approving the use that Congressional committees had at times made of their power, he went
on to declare, in a 1949 opinion, "I think it would be an unwarranted act of judicial usurpation to strip Congress of its investigatory power, or to assume for the courts the function of supervising
congressional committees. I should . . . leave the responsibility

for the behavior of its committees squarely on the shoulders of Congress." [101]

It is significant that, despite claimed abuses by the House of Representatives Committee on Un-American Activities, Senator McCarthy, and others of their ilk, the Supreme Court has not found any exercise of Congressional investigatory authority to exceed the constitutional limits upon legislative power. In truth, the extreme reluctance (some might say timidity) of the Court to intervene in this field is well shown by the fact that, in the most important and controversial cases on investigatory power decided by the lower federal courts in recent years, the highest tribunal exercised its discretionary power to refuse even to review those cases, thus upholding the lower court decisions (all of which had sustained the validity of Congressional committee action) by the bare denial of certiorari.

In the cases where the Court has seen fit to pass upon exercises of Congressional investigatory power, it has been astute to avoid the important constitutional issues presented. Perhaps the best known of these cases is *United States v. Rumely*,[102] decided early in 1953. It arose out of a resolution of the House of Representatives establishing a select committee to investigate "lobbying activities." Respondent Rumely was the secretary of an organization charged with lobbying which, among other activities, engaged in the sale of books and other literature of a political nature. He refused to disclose to the House select committee the names of those who made bulk purchases of these books for further distribution. He was convicted under the statute providing criminal penalties for refusal to give testimony or to produce relevant papers "upon any matter" under Congressional inquiry. In his defense, Rumely raised the broadest constitutional issues. He urged that investigation, even by the Congress, into the affairs of a publishing organization like his was an interference with freedom of speech and the press forbidden by the First Amendment. This posed directly a constitutional issue never answered by the highest Court—that of the extent to which the Congressional investigatory power is limited by the First Amendment. Nor, despite the clearness of the challenge, did the Court answer, or even deal with, this question in the *Rumely* case. In this field of legislative power particularly, said Justice Frankfurter, the Court must tread warily and avoid constitutional issues if their resolution is not inescapably necessary for the decision of the case before it. Here, according to the learned judge, choice was left to the Court. The House, says he, had meant to authorize its select committee only to investigate lobbying in its "commonly accepted sense," that is, "representations made directly to the Congress, its members, or its committees." [103] That being the case, the committee had acted beyond its authority in investigating the selling of books by Rumely's organization. Since it is a basic principle that a Congressional committee is wholly a creature of the resolution setting it up and cannot act *ultra vires* that instrument, it follows that Rumely's conviction had to be reversed.

It should be pointed out that the entire membership of the Court has not concurred in what they consider this overcautious approach to the question of the proper exercise of legislative investigatory authority. In the *Rumely* case itself, Justices Douglas and Black urged that the basic constitutional issue be decided and that it be declared that investigation into the sale of books by a publisher, such as that at issue, clearly contravened the First Amendment. As Justice Douglas has more recently stated his view, Congressional investigatory "power, being derived from the Constitution, rises no higher than its source, and even in its limited sphere exists only insofar as it is congenial to other constitutional rights and guarantees." [104]

To the present writer, it is not the Douglas-Black view that is important to one interested in the actual state of Supreme Court jurisprudence, but the overriding fact that a majority of the present Court has not as yet upheld any constitutional challenge to Congressional investigatory activities. It is true that the Court did, in the oft-cited 1880 case of *Kilbourn v. Thompson*,[105] invalidate an investigation by a committee of the House of Representatives, on the ground that it bore no relation to any contemplated exercise of law-making power. More recent cases indicate that that decision must now be regarded with caution. Thus, the Court in 1953 referred to "The loose language of *Kilbourn v. Thompson*, . . . the weighty criticism to which it has been subjected, . . . the inroads that have been made upon that case by later cases." [106] To the extent that its decisions thus far are a criterion, a majority of the highest Court appears to be of the view that there are few, if any, constitutional restrictions of consequence upon the permissible scope of Congressional inquiries.

Nor is the Supreme Court's abstinence in this field necessarily to be deplored. The power of investigation is, as all recognize, an essential incident of the legislative function. The Congress, like the Parliament in Britain, should be looked upon as a great public forum for the ventilation of popular grievances. The elected representatives of the people, more directly responsible to the citizenry

than any other organ of government, should not be closely restricted by the courts in their efforts to bring to light anything
that they feel should be subjected to public scrutiny. As Woodrow
Wilson aptly expressed it:

Unless Congress have and use every means of acquainting itself with the
acts and the disposition of the administrative agents of the government,
the country must be helpless to learn how it is being served; and unless
Congress both scrutinize these things and sift them by every form of
discussion, the country must remain in embarrassing, crippling ignorance
of the very affairs which it is most important that it should understand
and direct. The informing function of Congress should be preferred
even to its legislative function.[107]

These may be strong words, particularly in the light of what
we have learned since Wilson's day of possible misuses of Congressional investigatory authority. The fact that it may be abused
does not, however, bear on the existence and scope of investigatory
power, for the same is true of the law-making power of the Congress and, indeed, of all governmental power. And, more pertinent
for our present purposes, it does not justify the courts in setting
themselves up as censors of what is, after all, the internal functioning of a coordinate branch of government. "We would not be
understood . . ." stated the Supreme Court in 1950, "as expressing
either approval or disapproval of those practices [of Congressional
committees]. But the remedy, if any is needed, is certainly not to
destroy the effective operation of all committees, which is the necessary result if they cannot compel the disclosure of facts." [108]

Judges vs. Legislators

The years since the first inauguration of Franklin Roosevelt have
been ones of unprecedented federal legislative activity. During
them, a plethora of Congressional acts have found their way into
the federal statute book. Prompted by the need to deal with the
exigencies of a disastrous economic crisis, a global conflict, and the
tensions of a "cold war" period, the Congress has more and more
intervened in matters that were formerly deemed outside legislative competence. Since the adoption by the Supreme Court in
1937 of its present restrained attitude toward exertions of federal
legislative power, not one Congressional act of consequence has
been invalidated by the high tribunal. The major regulatory measures of the later New Deal, the important more recent assertions
of federal control over the economic and social system, the unprecedented regimentation to meet the needs of world war, the

drastic restrictions upon person and property that have accompanied our efforts to attain security in the tensions of the postwar period— all of these have been sustained by the Supreme Court.

In fact, as already pointed out, in the twenty years since the high Court assumed its more subdued position vis-à-vis the Congress, in only three cases have federal laws been declared unconstitutional. The first of these cases is *Tot v. United States*,[109] a 1943 decision holding invalid a section of the Federal Firearms Act establishing a presumption of violation of the law based on a prior conviction and possession of a firearm. According to the Court there, the mere possession of a pistol coupled with conviction of a prior crime is no evidence at all that the possessor of the pistol has acquired it in violation of the federal law; there is thus no rational connection between the facts proved and that presumed. and the presumption must fall. The second post-1937 case annulling a federal statute is *United States v. Lovett*,[110] a 1946 decision dealing with a provision in an appropriations act directing that no salary should be paid to three named federal employees out of moneys appropriated. In the Court's view, this law was really a legislative punishment of the three employees without judicial trial; this amounted to a bill of attainder expressly prohibited by the Constitution. The last of the three cases referred to is more recent. It is the 1955 decision of the Court in *Toth v. Quarles*,[111] which concerned a section of the Uniform Code of Military Justice authorizing the trial by court martial of ex-servicemen for any offense, punishable by at least five years of imprisonment, committed while in service, unless the offense was also punishable in a civil court. This provision was held to violate the right of civilians to a trial by jury in an ordinary court under the Bill of Rights.

Important though these three cases may have been to those concerned, none of them involved a major Congressional measure. While the three laws referred to were invalidated, the Court was sustaining all the extensions of Congressional authority already discussed in this chapter. It may, nevertheless, be said that there is a basic difference between the three cases of unconstitutionality and those upholding recent federal laws. The statutes upheld which have been discussed in this chapter all involved exercises of Congressional authority over different aspects of the economic system. In them, it was the right of property that was being regulated. In the three cases of unconstitutionality, on the other hand, it was personal rights that were at issue. This, it has been said, indicates a different attitude on the part of the present Court where questions of personal right are concerned. In such cases, perhaps, the Court abandons its deferential posture toward the Congress. It must be conceded that there has been strong support within the Supreme Court itself in recent years for so differentiating between the personal and property right cases. At the same time, it should be noted that even so far as personal rights are concerned, the *Tot, Lovett,* and *Toth* cases involved relatively minor statutes. While the Court invalidated these laws, it was upholding all of the major restrictions upon personal rights which the Congress felt were necessitated by the demands of war and the dangers of subversion in a "cold war" period. Even insofar as personal rights are concerned, we shall see,* the basic tenet of the Court is still that of deference toward the federal legislature.

What seems to differentiate the cases of unconstitutionality is the fact that, in two of them, there was a clear violation of an express constitutional provision, while in the third, the legislator had, in the Court's view, exceeded the bounds of reason. In the *Lovett* and *Toth* cases, the Congress had contravened specific constitutional prohibitions, in the one case against the infliction by the Congress of punishment against particular individuals without a judicial trial, in the other against depriving civilians tried for crimes of the safeguards of the criminal law. However deferential the judge may be toward the legislator, he must, if he is to keep faith with his oath of office, draw the line at a direct violation of an express constitutional prohibition. In *Tot v. United States,* the Court found that there was no rational connection at all between the facts proved and the presumption of law violation established by the Congress. In such a case, even under the Holmesian view of judicial self-restraint which the Court has adopted, the legislative act must be set aside. Though the Court now looks only to see whether rational legislators could have regarded the statute as a reasonable method of reaching the desired result, still the statute must fall where, as in the *Tot* case, there is found to be no rational basis for the legislative action.

The corollary of what has just been said is that where a challenged law neither contravenes a specific constitutional prohibition nor is lacking in a rational basis, it must be upheld; hence the mere handful of Congressional acts held invalid by the highest Court in the twenty years since it relinquished its position as the Supreme Censor of all legislation.

But if judicial self-restraint has become the keystone of Supreme Court jurisprudence in the past two decades, it has itself come more and more to be questioned as the "be all and end all" of the

* *Infra,* pp. 239-318.

judicial function. Particularly in the field of civil liberties, it is urged by some, the highest tribunal should play a more active role in holding the Congress within the confines of the Constitution.

The innovations of 1937 have now become the established order and, to requote Justice Jackson,* only fanatics will underestimate the power of an established order. Similarly, none should underestimate the attraction to many of being able to denigrate an established order. Yet the fact that an order has become established does not necessarily mean that it should be changed. Progress does not always consist of innovations; established doctrine that works satisfactorily is better built upon than repudiated merely for the sake of change.

Few students of the Supreme Court seriously claim today that the proper role for such a tribunal is that performed by the pre-1937 Court. Judicial supremacy in the saddle is no longer desired even by those who criticize the "inactivism" of the post-1937 Court. In a system such as ours, it is surely for the elected representatives of the people to have the primary responsibility of government. Judicial review, though of course an essential institution in a system governed by written restrictions upon government, is basically an undemocratic institution. Judges appointed for life are removed from the democratic pressures that are exerted upon the political departments. The high Court is, one of its own members has candidly conceded, an inherently oligarchic body.[112] That being the case, it seems essential that the Court does not try again to serve as the supplanter of the legislative judgment and sit in judgment upon the right or wrong of a challenged measure: "In the day-to-day working of our democracy it is vital that the power of the non-democratic organ of our Government be exercised with rigorous self-restraint." [113]

Still, it will be said, legislators are capable of great abuses; it is the responsibility of the Court to protect the people against such abuses. This utterly misconceives the function of a tribunal like the Supreme Court. In the words of a great constitutional lawyer of half a century ago, "if it be true that the holders of legislative power are careless or evil, yet the constitutional duty of the court remains untouched; it cannot rightly attempt to protect the people, by undertaking a function not its own." [114] Constitutionality is not synonymous with wisdom; it is not for the Court to nullify an expression of legislative will merely because the law enacted to give effect to that will is deemed socially undesirable. When Justice Holmes wrote that "it must be remembered that legislatures are

* *Supra*, p. 24.

ultimate guardians of the liberties and welfare of the people in quite as great a degree as the courts," [115] he went to the very heart of the democratic conception of our society.[116] If the highest Court is not to return to its pre-1937 position of a "super-legislature," it must be keen to avoid the all too easy transition from disapproval of what is undesirable to condemnation as unconstitutional. Abnegation rather than activism remains the proper posture for a judicial tribunal to assume toward the elected representatives of the people.

3

THE PRESIDENT

In 1637, one John Hampden was prosecuted for failing to pay a tax assessed by a decree of Charles I. The tax in question was part of a general levy imposed to obtain funds for the navy. Though the king had acted without the consent of Parliament, his action was based upon what he claimed was his absolute prerogative to do what he thought necessary for the good of the realm. This prerogative was said to be a power "innate in the person of an absolute king, and in the persons of the kings of England"; it was "the majestical right, and power of a free monarch." [1]

On April 8, 1952, President Truman issued an executive order directing the Secretary of Commerce to seize and operate the plants and facilities of the Nation's steel industry. The President had acted in order to head off a steel strike that was to have begun the next day. The seizure, he declared, was necessary in order to ensure the continued availability of steel and to avoid the adverse effects upon national defense and the economy which a steel stoppage would entail. "A work stoppage," proclaimed the President's order, "would immediately jeopardize and imperil our national defense and the defense of those joined with us in resisting aggression, and would add to the continuing danger of our soldiers, sailors, and airmen engaged in combat in the field." In order to avert these dangers "it is necessary that the United States take possession of and operate the plants, facilities, and other property of the said companies."

President Truman, like his royal predecessor three centuries earlier, had been motivated by his conception of what was necessitated by the public interest, but, like Charles I, the President, too, had acted without any authorization from the legislature. And the claims of Government counsel in seeking to have the courts uphold the President's action were, in many ways, but a modern echo of those made for the Crown in John Hampden's case. This can be seen clearly from the following colloquy, taken from the official transcript, between Mr. Baldridge, the Assistant Attorney General

62

who argued for the Government, and the district judge before whom the *Steel-Seizure* case was heard:

The Court: So you contend the Executive has unlimited power in time of an emergency?

Mr. Baldridge: He has the power to take such action as is necessary to meet the emergency.

The Court: If the emergency is great, it is unlimited, is it?

Mr. Baldridge: I suppose if you carry it to its logical conclusion, that is true. . . .

The Court: Then, as I understand it, you claim that in time of emergency the Executive has this great power.

Mr. Baldridge: That is correct.

The Court: And that the Executive determines the emergencies and the Courts cannot even review whether it is an emergency.

Mr. Baldridge: That is correct.

The extreme nature of the Government's position in the steel case is perhaps even better illustrated by another portion of the argument:

The Court: So, when the sovereign people adopted the Constitution, it enumerated the powers set up in the Constitution, but limited the powers of the Congress and limited the powers of the judiciary, but it did not limit the powers of the Executive. Is that what you say?

Mr. Baldridge: That is the way we read Article II of the Constitution.

In 1637, the court upheld the king's prerogative in what is usually known as the *Ship-Money* case.[2] The extent to which the judges of the time went in upholding the royal claim can be seen from the list of concrete powers said by one of them to be included in the Crown's prerogative. According to Justice Crawley, the powers possessed by the king included the following: To "give laws to his subjects"; "To make peace and war"; "To create supreme magistrates"; "That the last appeal be to the king"; "To pardon offences"; "To coin money"; "To have allegiance, fealty, and homage," and "To impose taxes without common consent in parliament."[3] Truly, under such a view of royal authority, could counsel for the Crown, in another of the great State Trials of the early seventeenth century, refer to "that *absoluta potestas* that a sovereign hath, by which a king commands."[4]

In 1952, the Supreme Court rejected the claim that the President of the United States possessed a comparable absolute prerogative and nullified his steel-seizure order.[5] "The example of such unlimited executive power that must have most impressed the forefathers," declared Justice Jackson in a concurring opinion there, "was the prerogative exercised by George III, and the description of its evils in the Declaration of Independence leads me to doubt that they were creating their new Executive in his image." [6] Thus, the claim for which Charles I lost his life and James II his throne was rejected when put forth on behalf of a representative product of the sturdy democratic traditions of the Mississippi Valley.[7] Though it may be absurd to see a would-be Stuart tyrant in the Presidential pretensions of 1952, that does not affect the importance of judicial rejection of such pretensions: "The accretion of dangerous power does not come in a day. It does come, however slowly, from the generative force of unchecked disregard of the restrictions that fence in even the most disinterested assertion of authority." [8]

The President and the Court

The judges in Stuart England were really in no position to cast doubt on the legality of royal assertions of authority. "The courts of justice," to quote the judgment of a famous English historian, "did not consist of men conscientiously impartial between the king and the subject; some corrupt with hope of promotion, many more fearful of removal, or awe-struck by the frowns of power." [9]

Those who built the American constitutional structure were well aware that judges of this type could not be counted on to perform the high functions imposed upon them by our organic instrument. Indeed, the subservience of the royal judges to George III was one of the grievances that helped bring on the Revolution. "He has made Judges dependent on his Will alone," reads the ninth specification of the Declaration of Independence, "for the tenure of their offices, and the amount and payment of their salaries." The Founding Fathers were careful to ensure that such a complaint could not be articulated in the governmental system they were creating:

To that end, they set apart a body of men, who were to be the depositories of law, who by their disciplined training and character and by withdrawal from the usual temptations of private interest may reasonably be expected to be "as free, impartial, and independent as the lot of humanity will admit." So strongly were the framers of the Constitution bent on securing a reign of law that they endowed the judicial office with extraordinary safeguards and prestige.[10]

To eliminate the possibility that American judges might emulate those who decided the case of *Ship-Money* in favor of governmental pretensions, the Framers clearly and specifically provided the conditions for complete judicial independence. "The Judges," reads Article III of the Constitution, "both of the supreme and inferior

Courts, shall hold their Offices during good Behaviour, and shall, at stated Times, receive for their Services, a Compensation, which shall not be diminished during their Continuance in Office." Life tenure and a salary which could not be lowered by the political departments were intended to enable the judges, in the words of a great Chief Justice, to uphold and maintain constitutional guarantees "free from every influence, direct or indirect, that might by possibility in times of political excitement warp their judgments." [11] The President might appoint the judges of the federal courts; but, once appointed, they could act without fear or favor, with what the highest Court has termed "that independence of action and judgment which is essential to the maintenance of the guaranties, limitations and pervading principles of the Constitution and to the administration of justice without respect to persons." [12]

The constitutional provisions protecting federal judges have enabled them throughout our history to maintain an attitude of independence toward the Chief Executive such as seventeenth-century English courts could never successfully assert against their Stuart masters. Not that this has necessarily prevented Presidents from seeking to control the judiciary. From the time of Jefferson, at the very beginning of our history, to that of Franklin D. Roosevelt, almost a century and a half later, there have been Presidential attempts at subverting judicial independence. And, if the courts have thus far emerged unscathed from these efforts, their margin of escape has at times been a narrow one. Yet the significant fact is that the Supreme Court *has* been able thus far successfully to weather all the executive assaults against it. As Justice Jackson pointed out shortly before his death,

The Court has been sharply attacked by Presidents Jefferson, Jackson, Lincoln, and both Roosevelts. Yet no substantial sentiment exists for any curtailment of the Court's powers. Even President Roosevelt in the bitterest conflict with judicial powers in our history suggested only changes in the Court's composition, none in its constitutional prerogatives.[13]

Having been, in Alexander Hamilton's words,[14] afforded a better prospect of independence than were any previous judges, our courts have never had to act as mere rubber stamps of executive fiat. The Constitution sets bounds upon executive, as upon legislative, action; in the one case, as in the other, it is for the courts to determine whether, in cases presented to them for decision, those bounds have been exceeded. " 'A government of laws and not of men' was the rejection in positive terms of rule by fiat. . . . Every act of government may be challenged by an appeal to law, as finally pronounced by this Court," declared a member of the highest Court in 1947.[15] If this principle is to be maintained as a basic one in our constitutional system, it must embrace all governmental acts, including those of the executive. The President alone cannot, consistently with the theory of our polity, be *legibus solutus*—above the law, as was the emperor in imperial Roman law.

It will, however, be objected that to subject the President to judicial control is to violate the separation of powers. As the head of a coordinate branch of government, it will be said, the President must remain master in his own house; our Constitution requires executive independence of the judiciary as much as it requires judicial independence of the executive. "But," in Thomas Jefferson's crucial question, "would the Executive be independent of the judiciary if he were subject to the *Commands* of the latter?" [16]

The Supreme Court itself answered Jefferson's question in the negative in the post-Civil War case of *Mississippi v. Johnson.*[17] That case involved an action against President Johnson to enjoin him from enforcing the Reconstruction Acts, on the ground that they were unconstitutional. The Court held that such an action could not be maintained. "We are fully satisfied," reads the opinion of Chief Justice Chase, "that this court has no jurisdiction of a bill to enjoin the President in the performance of his official duties; and that no such bill ought to be received by us." [18] The Court's decision was based squarely on the separation of powers doctrine: "The Congress is the legislative department of the government; the President is the executive department. Neither can be restrained in its action by the judicial department." [19] For the Court to attempt to control Presidential action would, in this view, amount to undue interference by the judiciary with the workings of a coordinate, independent branch of the Government.

Mississippi v. Johnson prevents the courts from issuing an injunction directly against the President. The Court there agreed with Jefferson that the Chief Executive ought not to be subject to the immediate *commands* of the judiciary. The holding that the President himself cannot be enjoined does not, all the same, necessarily mean that the legality of Presidential action is not at all subject to judicial review. If it meant that, it would place Presidential action beyond any judicial control—which would, in effect, make such action free from control by law. It is to pervert the separation of powers doctrine to say that the Supreme Court interferes unduly in the operations of another department when it reviews the legality of Presidential action. The essence of judicial power is the application of the law in cases presented to the Court for decision. The fact that the legality of executive action happens to be at issue in a given case does not mean that a court, in deciding that case, is exercising other than purely judicial power. "From their own experience and their deep reading in history," a member of the high Court eloquently informs us, "the Founders knew that Law alone saves a society from being rent by internecine strife or ruled by mere brute power however described." [20] No one in our system, no matter how exalted his public office or how righteous his motive, can be above appeal to law, as finally pronounced by the Supreme Court. This principle must apply to all governmental acts, whether done by the humblest official or the President of the Republic. If you make just one exception to the rule of law, you cannot tell where it will lead you. To make a single exception is to take the fatal first step toward the totalitarian doctrine that the State is above every rule of law.

The proper approach in cases involving acts of the head of the executive was enunciated almost three centuries ago by an eminent English Chief Justice. Said Lord Hale at that time,

though the King, in case of such acts done contrary to the directive power of the law, is not subject to the coercive power of the law in respect of the sacredness and sublimity of his person, the instruments and ministers that are the immediate actors of such unlawful things are subject to the coercive power of the law, for the Kings act in such cases being void doth not justify or defend the instruments. This is one of the principal reasons of the maxim in law, that the King can do no wrong, for if it be wrong and contrary to the law, it is not the act of the King but of the minister or instrument that puts it in execution and consequently such minister is liable to the coercion of the law and to make satisfaction.[21]

Under Lord Hale's view, the Chief Executive—be he king or President—is responsible to the law, and this responsibility is enforceable legally by the courts against the inferior instruments through whom the chief acts. Since, in practice, the Chief Executive always acts through subordinate officials—he is never the immediate actor in the execution of his own decrees—the legality of his acts can be tested in the courts without any need formally to hold him subject to the coercive power of the law. The subordinate alone is summoned before the bar of justice; but it is the act of the chief that is really at issue. Thus the legality of action of the Chief Executive can be determined without the need for any formal violation of the separation of powers.

Within the past decade, what is essentially the approach of Lord

Hale has been adopted by the Supreme Court in this country to enable it to overcome the doctrine that acts of the head of the executive cannot be reviewed judicially. The basic step in this direction was taken in a 1948 decision, *Williams v. Fanning*,[22] which did not involve an act of the President at all, but only that of the Postmaster General. In the case referred to, the Court held that the Postmaster General was not an indispensable party in an action to enjoin a local postmaster from carrying out the provisions of an order not to deliver mail to plaintiff, though all that the postmaster was actually doing was to carry out the orders of his department head. Even though the challenged order is that of the department head, said the Court, that is immaterial if the decree which is entered will effectively grant the relief desired by expending itself on the subordinate official who is before the court. The decree in order to be effective need not require the department head to do a single thing.

If the doctrine of *Williams v. Fanning* is applied to acts of the President, it leads substantially to the approach advocated so many years ago by Lord Hale. The President, like the Postmaster General, acts entirely through subordinate officials. Under *Williams v. Fanning*, the instruments through whom the President acts can be restrained from executing illegal Presidential orders. In such a case, too, the court's decree will effectively grant the relief desired by expending itself on the immediate actor who is before the court. The Lord Hale—*Williams v. Fanning* approach enables the courts to review the legality of acts of the President, without the need for formally ordering the Chief Executive to do, or to refrain from doing, anything.

It was basically this approach which enabled the Supreme Court to review the legality of President Truman's steel-seizure order in 1952. That order, it will be recalled, directed the Secretary of Commerce to seize the Nation's steel mills. It would have availed the steel companies nothing to seek to have the courts restrain the President from persisting in his illegal order; *Mississippi v. Johnson* debars the judiciary from issuing direct commands to the Chief Executive. But there is no such immunity in a Presidential subordinate like the Secretary of Commerce, who was, in this case, the instrument for the execution of the President's order. An action to restrain the Secretary from enforcing the order would require the court before whom it was brought to determine whether the order itself was legal and the court's decision could expend itself on the Secretary, without any need formally to summon the President before the bar of justice. This is exactly what was done in the *Steel-*

Seizure case, where the steel companies tested the validity of the seizure of their property by an action to restrain Secretary of Commerce Sawyer from carrying out the President's order directing seizure. The Secretary set up, in defense, the claim that the federal courts were without power to negate action of the President, relying upon cases like *Mississippi v. Johnson*. But, said Judge Pine, in his now-famous opinion in the district court,

. . . in this case the President has not been sued. Charles Sawyer is the defendant, and the Supreme Court has held on many occasions that officers of the Executive Branch of the Government may be enjoined when their conduct is unauthorized by statute. . . . There is no doubt, therefore, that the defendant is subject to an injunction, and the President not only is not a party but he is not an indispensable party to this action, as held in Williams v. Fanning.[23]

In upholding Judge Pine's decision, the majority of the Supreme Court clearly appears to have agreed with his opinion on this point. Indeed, the only mention of the issue is in the dissenting opinion of Chief Justice Vinson and he states merely "we assume that defendant Charles Sawyer is not immune from judicial restraint and that plaintiffs are entitled to equitable relief if we find that the Executive Order under which defendant acts is unconstitutional." [24]

In some ways, the most important aspect of the *Steel-Seizure* case is its rejection of the claim that acts of the President are immune from judicial review. Not one member of the highest Court (in a case in which, we shall see, seven separate opinions were delivered) questioned the propriety of testing the legality of the President's order in the injunction suit against the Secretary of Commerce.

The notion that the action of the Chief Executive is free from judicial scrutiny of the type to which all other government acts are subject in our system is inconsistent with the whole concept of constitutionalism. "No man . . . is so high that he is above the law," declares a classic expression of the Court. "All the officers of the government, from the highest to the lowest, are creatures of the law, and are bound to obey it." [25] To assert that the President alone should not be subject to this duty is to advance an argument as untenable today as when it was cast in the language of the Plantagenets, the Tudors, and the Stuarts.[26] If that position were deemed valid, the fiat of the President, and not the Constitution, would be the supreme law of the land. There is no such avenue of escape from the rule of law.[27] Presidential action must not be proof of its own legality; nor must the *ipse dixit* of the President be conclusive that his action was justified. To claim, as once did James I, that the prerogative of the Chief Executive is "no subject for the tongue of a lawyer" is a heresy wholly inconsistent with the essence of our constitutional structure.

Emergency Power and Steel Seizure

On September 7, 1942, President Franklin D. Roosevelt sent a message to the Congress demanding the immediate repeal of certain provisions of the Emergency Price Control Act of that year. The message declared,

In the event that the Congress should fail to act, and act adequately, I shall accept the responsibility, and I will act. At the same time that prices are stabilized, wages can and will be stabilized also. This I will do. The President has the powers, under the Constitution . . . , to take measures necessary to avert a disaster which would interfere with the winning of the war.[28]

Congressional compliance with the President's demand rendered unnecessary an effort on his part to amend the Price Control Act. But that in no way alters the extent of President Roosevelt's far-reaching claim. In effect, he was asserting in himself the power to repeal an act of Congress, despite the fact that it is the Congress alone that is entrusted with all of the legislative powers granted by the Constitution. This extraordinary assertion may be characterized as a claim of power to suspend the Constitution, and, moreover, to suspend it as to its most important feature—the division of power between the President and the Congress.[29] In Franklin Roosevelt's view, his authority was based upon his responsibility as Chief Executive to take any measures that might be necessary to deal with an emergency facing the country. His claim in this respect was not a new one, though it had never before been so blatantly urged by an incumbent of the chief magistracy. F.D.R.'s 1942 message really carries to its logical extreme the so-called "stewardship" theory of the Presidency, expounded almost half a century earlier by the first Roosevelt in the White House. "My view," wrote Theodore Roosevelt in his *Autobiography*, "was that [the President] was a steward of the people bound actively and affirmatively to do all he could for the people. . . . I declined to adopt the view that what was imperatively necessary for the Nation could not be done by the President unless he could find some specific authorization to do it." [30]

The first Roosevelt wrote of Presidential power in the halcyon days of the pre-First World War era; his views at that time were more a matter of theory than practice. The second Roosevelt enunciated his broad conception of authority in the midst of global war. He put T.R.'s theory into practice, but, as is usually the case in wartime, his extreme assertions were left virtually unchallenged. It fell to F.D.R.'s successor to assert, in his turn, the same wide range of Presidential power in his seizure of the steel industry. But this time, as is well known, the Presidential claim was put to the constitutional test and was found wanting by the highest Court of the land.

Two things are clear from the Supreme Court's decision in the *Steel-Seizure* case. The first is that, as already emphasized, the legality of the President's action was clearly subject to judicial review. The second is that the President's steel-seizure order was held invalid by a majority of the Court. The actual grounds of decision and their meaning for the future are, at the same time, much more debatable. And this is due largely to the manner in which the Court announced its decision in the case. For a judicial tribunal to speak with certainty in deciding an important case, it is essential that it speak with a single voice. But this is precisely what was not done in the *Steel-Seizure* case. Almost at the outset there, Justice Frankfurter expressly rejected the notion that the basic principle of the Court's decision should be pronounced by a united tribunal. According to him, even though the individual Justices' "differences in attitude toward this principle may be merely differences in emphasis and nuance, they can hardly be reflected by a single opinion for the Court. Individual expression of views in reaching a common result is therefore important." [31] In the *Steel-Seizure* case, the decision of the Court was announced and explained in an "opinion of the Court" delivered by Justice Black. In addition, true to Justice Frankfurter's quoted statement, each of the six Justices who made up the majority of the Court saw fit to deliver a distinct opinion articulating his own individual views of the relevant principles in the case, and there was also a separate opinion rendered for the three dissenting Justices. It is not unfair to say that no two of these opinions deal with the case in exactly the same way. And, though four members of the majority are listed as concurring with Justice Black in his "opinion of the Court," their separate accompanying opinions whittle their concurrence in some instances to the vanishing point. The diversity in opinion expressed among the Justices tends to destroy much of the force of their holding that the President's order was invalid. "What is the law of the case?" is the natural query of the lawyer after an important Supreme Court case. It must be admitted that it cannot be answered with full certainty after the prolixity of the *Steel-Seizure* decision. It may be, as John Winthrop expressed it in 1644, that "Judges are Gods upon earth," [32] but a pantheon that speaks with seven inconsistent voices hardly inspires the listener with the feeling of divine certainty.

The problem just referred to would not arise at all had the majority members of the Court seen fit to concur silently in Justice Black's opinion. It, like the decision of Judge Pine in the district court which it affirmed, involved an unequivocal rejection of the Rooseveltian doctrine of Presidential emergency power upon which President Truman had apparently acted. According to counsel for the Government, a strike disrupting steel production for even a brief period would have so endangered the well-being and safety of the Nation that the President had "inherent power" to do what he had done—power asserted to be "supported by the Constitution, by historical precedent, and by court decisions." This, as has already been pointed out, was to repeat the Stuart claim three centuries earlier of executive prerogative to take any measures deemed necessary for the well-being and safety of the realm. Justice Black, however, denied that the President had any such prerogative to exercise what amounted to law-making authority: "In the framework of our Constitution, the President's power to see that the laws are faithfully executed refutes the idea that he is to be a lawmaker. . . . The Founders of this Nation entrusted the lawmaking power to the Congress alone in both good and bad times." [33] The President, in Justice Black's opinion, had no authority, either as Chief Executive or Commander in Chief, to take possession of private property in order to keep labor disputes from stopping production: "This is a job for the Nation's lawmakers." [34]

Judge Pine, in the district court, had been even more blunt. Referring to the provisions of the Constitution vesting authority in the President, he declared:

Neither singly nor in the aggregate do they grant the President, expressly or impliedly, . . . the "residuum of power" or "inherent" power which authorizes him, as defendant claims, to take such action as he may deem to be necessary, including seizure of plaintiffs' properties, whenever in his opinion an emergency exists requiring him to do so in the public interest.[35]

Justice Black did not, it is true, go quite so far in rejecting the Presidential pretensions. His opinion appears to be based upon the proposition that the President cannot act without Congressional authorization in an area where Congress can clothe him with authority to act. In this case, since the Congress could have permitted the seizure of private property for public use, the President lacked the power to seize the steel mills without statutory authorization. Yet, it is obvious that, in substance, Justice Black is here rejecting, almost as fully as did Judge Pine, the Rooseveltian doctrine of Presidential emergency power. In all areas where Congress can legislate, states the Black opinion, the President cannot take action legislative in nature without Congressional authorization. This is, of course, a complete judicial repudiation of Franklin Roosevelt's assertion that he could alter a statute enacted by the Congress, if his view of public necessity required it, and even of Theodore Roosevelt's claim that the President could do what he deemed imperatively necessary for the Nation without specific authorization. Under Justice Black's view, there is no power in the President alone to deal with emergency: if the Presidential act is one which the Congress could have empowered him to do, then, in the absence of a Congressional grant of authority, he cannot do it on the plea alone that an emergency requires it.

Concurring Opinions

Justice Black's rejection of the claim of inherent power in the President to deal with emergency as he deems fit was based upon his interpretation of the basic doctrine of the separation of powers. It has been said by one commentator that Black's statement of that doctrine, "in its rigor and naïveté, is probably without precedent in Supreme Court history." [36] This characterization is certainly too extreme, but it seems clear that Justice Black's colleagues on the majority of the Court (with the probable exception of Justice Douglas) felt that his opinion greatly oversimplified the issues in the case. As Justice Frankfurter put it, "the considerations relevant to the legal enforcement of the principle of separation of powers seem to me more complicated and flexible than may appear from what Mr. Justice Black has written." [37]

Though only one member of the six-man Court majority expressly disaffirmed concurrence in the reasoning of Justice Black's opinion,[38] each of the other majority Justices, as already pointed out, filed separate opinions which are not on all fours with Justice Black's "opinion of the Court" in which they had theoretically joined. In Justice Black's opinion, the issue of inherent Presidential power to seize private property to meet the needs of emergency is met head-on. To Justice Black, the *Steel-Seizure* case was a simple one of Presidential action in the absence of either a Congressional grant or denial of authority, thus presenting squarely for decision the question of whether the President had inherent authority to act as he did. With the likely exception of Justice Douglas, the other majority Justices, in their concurring opinions, indicated their views that the issue was not thus baldly presented. On the contrary, as Justice Frankfurter stated at the outset of his opinion, "We must . . . put to one side consideration of what powers the President would have had if there had been no legislation whatever bearing on the authority asserted by the seizure." [39] In the view of the four majority Justices referred to, the Presidential seizure was incompatible with the expressed (or at least the implied) will of the Congress.

The conflict between the President's action and the Congressional will arose out of the provision by the Congress in the Taft-Hartley Act of 1947 of a procedure alternative to seizure, which the President could have followed to deal with the threat of a steel strike. Taft-Hartley includes provisions adopted for the purpose of dealing with nation-wide strikes. They establish a procedure whereby the President may appoint a board of inquiry and, thereafter, in proper cases, seek relief by injunction from a district court for an eighty-day period against a threatened work stoppage. The President can invoke that procedure whenever, in his opinion, "a threatened or actual strike . . . affecting an entire industry . . . will, if permitted to occur or to continue, imperil the national health or safety." At the time when the Taft-Hartley Act was passed, the Congress specifically rejected a proposal to empower the President to seize any "plant, mine, or facility" in which a threatened work stoppage would, in his judgment, "imperil the public health or security." Instead, the act directed the President, in the event of a strike not being settled during the eighty-day injunction period, to submit to Congress "a full and comprehensive report . . . together with such recommendations as he may see fit to make for consideration and appropriate action."

To the four majority Justices already referred to, the Congress, by these Taft-Hartley Act provisions, had exercised its power in opposition to the exercise of any executive seizure authority. Congress, in the words of one of them, "has expressed its will to withhold this power from the President as though it had said so in so many words." [40] The Taft-Hartley provisions, said Justice Burton, "distinguish this emergency from one in which Congress takes no action and outlines no governmental policy. In the case before us, Congress authorized a procedure which the President declined to follow." [41] Justice Clark's concurrence (the only one among the majority which expressly disclaims adherence to the opinion of Justice Black) is even clearer on this point. Where Congress has laid down specific procedures to deal with the emergency confronting the President, stated that judge, he must follow those procedures: "I cannot sustain the seizure in question because here . . . Congress had prescribed methods to be followed by the President in meeting the emergency at hand." [42]

There is little doubt that the evident belief expressed by at least four of the majority Justices that the President's order was incompatible with the will of the Congress blurs the force of Justice Black's clear repudiation of the claims of Presidential prerogative in his "opinion of the Court" in the *Steel-Seizure* case. Indeed, of the four Justices referred to, only one (Justice Burton) goes so far as to state expressly his agreement with Justice Black's view that the President had no inherent constitutional power to seize private property without Congressional authorization in the circumstances of the case. The other three Justices appeared to assume that, in the absence of Congressional restrictions, such as those imposed here by the Taft-Hartley Act, the President does possess inherent power to deal with national emergencies. Recognition of such authority in the Chief Executive is clearest in the opinion of Justice Clark, who asserts expressly that "the Constitution does grant to the President extensive authority in times of grave and imperative national emergency. In fact, to my thinking, such a grant may well be necessary to the very existence of the Constitution itself." [43] Justice Jackson, though more hesitant, appeared also to embrace this view and Justice Frankfurter, who explicitly disavowed any intention to consider the President's inherent powers, said nothing inconsistent with it. It thus turns out that only three of the Justices (Black, Douglas, and Burton) clearly rejected the notion of inherent authority in the President to seize the steel industry in the absence of Congressional authorization. The three dissenting Justices, led by Chief Justice Vinson, were, of course, firm adherents of the broad view of Presidential authority. Of the remaining Justices, at least one (Clark) and probably Jackson as well would have upheld the President if no policy contrary to seizure had been expressed by the Congress. It consequently appears that at least four, and probably five, of the Justices expressed attachment to the view that the President has power himself to deal with what he deems the demands of emergency. The only difficulty with this analysis is that Justice Jackson did not state any express disapproval of the "opinion of the Court" announced by Justice Black, despite the inconsistency between that opinion and some of the views expressed in his own concurrence. Certainly, as already pointed out, the profusion of individualistic opinions delivered in the *Steel-Seizure* case makes it difficult for commentators to assess the precise impact of that case.

Judicial Restraint and Steel Seizure

How does the resolution by the Supreme Court of the *Steel-Seizure* case comport with the doctrine of judicial self-restraint that, as already emphasized, has dominated the jurisprudence of the highest tribunal since 1937? At first glance, the invalidation of the President's seizure order seems inconsistent with the deference which the Court has shown toward the political departments in the past twenty years; in the words of one observer, "The doctrine of judicial self-restraint vigorously applied in this situation would call for upholding the President's action if at all possible." [44]

To the four members of the Court majority who saw the President's seizure order to be directly contrary to the will of the Congress, as expressed in a law like the Taft-Hartley Act, the steel case was not one which involved only the question of whether the Court should defer to the President's action. On the contrary, the Court here, in Justice Frankfurter's phrase, had "to intervene in determining where authority lies as between the democratic forces in our scheme of government." [45] In the steel case, the Court was acting, not as the overseer of the Chief Executive, but as holder of the constitutional balance between the two political branches of government, to both of which the Court, under its post-1937 doctrine, owed deference. In such a situation, to which branch should the Court yield? Where power to seize private property for public use (clearly within the legislative authority of the Congress) is involved, it seems that the supremacy of the Congressional policy is the only principle consistent with a polity in which all legislative powers have been vested in the Congress. "A statute derogatory to the prerogative," declared one of the king's judges in the *Ship-Money* case, "doth not bind the king." [46] The whole system of Anglo-American public law since the final expulsion of the Stuarts has, however, been based upon the repudiation of this theory. Even if the President possesses inherent powers over the internal economy of the country in certain instances, when the Congress intervenes and provides by statute that such powers are to be exercised in a particular manner and subject to the limitations and provisions contained in the statute, they can only be so exercised. Otherwise, what use would there be in imposing statutory limitations, if the President could at his pleasure disregard them and fall back on his inherent powers?

The opinion of Justice Black (as well as Justice Douglas' full concurrence in it) cannot, to be sure, be reconciled so readily with the doctrine of judicial self-restraint. Yet, in the Black-Douglas view, too, the case presented a conflict between Presidential and Congressional authority. According to Justice Black's opinion, the President's order encroached upon a domain purely within legislative competence; in such a case, the Chief Executive could not act without Congressional authorization. In these circumstances, the question for Justices Black and Douglas was not, no more than it was for the other majority Justices, one of whether the Court should defer to the President, but whether the trespass by one of the political branches upon the area reserved by the Constitution to the other should be upheld. Here, again, under the Court's post-1937 doctrine, deference was owing to both branches, so that judicial self-restraint alone could not resolve the case. In the Black-Douglas view, the case came down to one of a claimed unwritten prerogative inherent in executive power as against the express delegation of legislative authority in the premises to the Congress. In a case of that type, it was the duty of the Court to uphold the specific as against the general power. Particularly is this true when one bears in mind the experience which the Founders had had with blendings of executive and legislative power—experience which led them definitively to reject such a political arrangement. As Justice Douglas puts it, "We could not sanction the seizures and condemnations of the steel plants in this case without reading Article II as giving the President not only the power to execute the laws but to make some. Such a step would most assuredly alter the pattern of the Constitution." [47] Even judges more closely wedded to the doctrine of judicial self-restraint than Messrs. Black and Douglas (in many ways the most activist members of the post-1937 Court) might well invalidate the President's action in these circumstances.

Emergency Power Today

Where stands now the inherent power of the President to deal with emergencies, in the light of the Supreme Court's decision in the *Steel-Seizure* case? As already pointed out, at least two of the majority Justices there, as well as the three dissenters, expressed the opinion that the President does have extensive emergency power, even in the absence of specific Congressional authorization. That the President does, in fact, possess some inherent authority himself to cope with sudden emergencies confronting the Nation is clear in our constitutional system. Even the majority Justices who did not expressly admit the existence of any such executive power (including even Black and Douglas) could, it is believed, not deny that there exists in the President some residuum of such emergency power. Would any of the Justices deny to the President the authority to act on his own in circumstances such as those which confronted Abraham Lincoln after the fall of Fort Sumter? As Justice Burton put it in the steel case, it is only under the circumstances presented that the President had no inherent power to act as he did: "The present situation is not comparable to that of an imminent invasion or threatened attack. We do not face the issue of what might be the President's constitutional power to meet such catastrophic situations."[48] Nor, according to the same learned judge, was there an issue here of a command "addressed by the President, as Commander-in-Chief, to a mobilized nation waging, or imminently threatened with, total war."[49] If these situations did arise, it is to be doubted that any judge would deny inherent power in the President to deal with them. If an atom bomb were dropped on Washington, New York, and our other principal cities, who would deny that the branch of government endowed with the force of politically organized society could take whatever measures were deemed necessary?[50]

If the President does possess such emergency power, despite the *Steel-Seizure* decision, are we not back to the law of the *Ship-Money* case, under which the Chief Executive may take whatever action he deems necessary for the safety of the country? There are, however, two substantial differences between the law of executive emergency power today and that of Stuart England. In the first place, as already pointed out, the prerogative which his judges recognized in Charles I was not subject to any legislative restriction; a statute derogatory to his prerogative did not bind the king. Today, on the contrary, as the *Steel-Seizure* case itself shows clearly, whatever prerogative the President may possess is subject to Congressional restraints. Presidential inherent power must yield before a law of the Congress. Any action of the President of the type involved in the steel case is always subject to revision and disallowance by the legislature. This is a substantial check upon executive prerogative that was lacking in the time of Charles I. Whatever prerogative may be conceded in the President today, it is wholly subject to the legislative power exercised, in our system, by the elected representatives of the people.

Just as important in differentiating the law today from that of three centuries ago is the fact that, unlike the judges of Charles I, our courts no longer recognize the executive as the conclusive judge of the existence of emergency. The importance of this limitation was acutely seen by counsel for John Hampden in the *Ship-Money* case. According to him, there was a basic distinction between "necessity, and leaving the king judge of the necessity; that in judgment so to do it, is all one as to leave it to him arbitrarily, if he will." [51] To give the executive the power to act in emergency and to "have no judge but himself of the occasion and proportion" [52] is, in effect, to vest the executive with the sovereign power in the Constitution. If we admit such sovereign power, we shall, paraphrasing Lord Coke's famous phrase,[53] weaken the foundation of law, and then the building must needs fall; the Constitution is such a fellow that he will have no sovereign.

Though we may recognize, as we must in some cases, that the President possesses inherent power to take measures necessary to deal with pressing emergencies facing the Nation, that does not mean that the President must have the last word on the question of whether the particular occasion justifies the use of his extraordinary power. On the contrary, if we leave the President the sole judge of the necessity, we vest him with the same arbitrary power that the *Ship-Money* case recognized in Charles I. Even if there is inherent emergency power in the Chief Executive, it must be subject to the fundamental limitation that there is in fact an emergency and the measures taken must be *necessary* to meet that emergency. In the words of Chief Justice Taney, still apt though uttered over a century ago, "in all of these cases the danger must be immediate and impending; or the necessity urgent for the public service, such as will not admit of delay. . . . It is the emergency that gives the right, and the emergency must be shown to exist before the taking can be justified." [54] Necessity is an objective standard by which Presidential action can be justified. Under it, wholly arbitrary action, where there is no real emergency or where the steps taken bear no relation to the emergency they are ostensibly calculated to meet, can be condemned. The test of necessity may also serve as a guide to limit the duration of Presidential emergency power; where the emergency has ended, so also must the extraordinary measures taken to meet it cease.[55]

It is in this test of necessity and the fact that it can be applied by the courts that our law of executive emergency power today diverges sharply from that enunciated by the Stuart judges in the *Ship-Money* case. To the argument made in that case that the king might abuse his power and act where there was no real emergency, the judges answered, "so pious and just a king will never pretend a danger, if it were not *re vera*." [56] Three subsequent centuries of constitutional history have taught us that confidence in the good faith of the governmental actor is irrelevant in any consideration of the extent of governmental power. It is only by subjecting governmental power to the control of the impersonal forces of the law that we can be certain such power will not be abused.

This does not mean a renaissance of the high Court as the Supreme Censor of Presidential emergency power. It may be feared that judicial scrutiny in this field will enable the courts to substitute their judgment for that of the Chief Executive on the question of the necessity of challenged action. But no one proposes either a substitution or an appeal from the President to the courts. The judicial function here is to prevent arbitrary executive action, taken under the guise of emergency power. At the same time, it is not for the Court to substitute its judgment for that of the President on the factual question of whether the necessities of emergency really justified his action. The essentials of the judicial function are preserved when it is determined that there was a rational basis for the President's action. The proper judicial approach is that followed by the Court in an important wartime case: "Our investigation here does not go beyond the inquiry whether, in the light of all the relevant circumstances preceding and attending their promulgation, the challenged orders . . . afforded a reasonable basis for the action taken." [57] In a case of this type, it is enough that there was a rational basis for the exercise of emergency power. Whether the Court itself would necessarily have taken the same action, had it been in the President's shoes, is irrelevant. Under this test, sufficient scope is given to the executive to enable grave national emergencies to be dealt with. At the same time, the President is not the final judge. Measures that are manifestly arbitrary—those that bear no reasonable relation to the necessities of the situation—can thus be condemned. Judicial control to this extent is of fundamental importance, if even Presidential prerogative is to be exercised in some subordination to law.

Valuable though it may doubtless be, judicial control based upon only the rational basis test, administered by a Court which is a firm adherent of the doctrine of judicial self-restraint, seems hardly enough by itself to preserve us against inordinate exercises of executive emergency power. For every *Steel-Seizure* case, where the judges draw a line beyond which the President cannot advance, there is a mass of executive practice by strong Chief Executives like Franklin Roosevelt, whose extreme assertions of Presidential prerogative prevailed in fact, if not in law. This is not to deny the importance of judicial review in this field, but only to concede the inadequacies of judicial power by itself to appraise or control the realistic balance of power in our polity. As Justice Jackson stated in the *Steel-Seizure* case, "If not good law, there was worldly wisdom in the maxim attributed to Napoleon that 'The tools belong to the man who can use them.' We may say that power to legislate for emergencies belongs in the hands of Congress, but only Congress itself can prevent power from slipping through its fingers." [58]   In the field of emergency power, the authority of the Court must be supplemented by that of the Congress. It is for that body to exercise the power which it clearly possesses under the steel decision and restrict executive emergency power within reasonable limits. It is particularly important that the President's authority to deal with foreseeable contingencies such as war be canalized in advance within statutory banks to keep it from overflowing. Otherwise, the onset of emergency will leave the Chief Executive wholly at large; no Supreme Court decision delivered years earlier will prevent him from acting as he deems necessary to meet the emergency. No matter what the Court may say about the overriding power of the Congress in these cases, only Congress itself can keep its power from slipping through its fingers. In other words, as a recent commentary states it, the real lesson of the *Steel-Seizure* case is that, "just as nature abhors a vacuum, so does an age of emergency. Let Congress see to it, then, that no such vacuum occurs. The best escape from presidential autocracy in the age we inhabit is not, in short, judicial review, which can supply only a vacuum, but timely legislation." [59]

Foreign Affairs

Under the *Steel-Seizure* case, as has been emphasized, the legality of President Truman's order was clearly subject to judicial review. Indeed, we have seen, the approach of the highest Court in that case enables it to reach the legality of all Presidential acts, without any need for it to commit a formal violation of the separation of powers by directly ordering the Chief Executive to do, or to refrain from doing, anything. It should, however, be noted that the Presidential power exercised in the steel case touched the internal economy of the country. It was, in Justice Jackson's meet characterization, turned inward, not because of rebellion, but because of a lawful economic struggle between industry and labor.[60]   In such a case, the Court might well scrutinize with care the legality of the President's order. A different case is presented where Presidential power is turned against the outside world for the security of our society. When the Chief Executive acts in such a way, the Court will indulge the widest latitude of interpretation to sustain his authority.

Our Constitution assigns a unique role (unique, that is, in a system of representative democracy) to the President in the field of external affairs. "The President," declared John Marshall in a noted debate in the House of Representatives before his appointment to judicial office, "is the sole organ of the nation in its external relations, and its sole representative with foreign nations. . . . He possesses the whole Executive power. He holds and directs the force of the nation. Of consequence, any act to be performed by the force of the nation is to be performed through him." [61] Marshall's dictum has today become a commonplace.[62] The Supreme Court itself has in recent years fully recognized its validity. On December 21, 1936, the Court, in the words of a leading Government lawyer,[63] made a Christmas present to the President of a power over foreign affairs even larger than the Government had really contended for. Declares the Court's opinion, in the case referred to:

In this vast external realm, with its important, complicated, delicate and manifold problems, the President alone has the power to speak or listen as a representative of the nation. He *makes* treaties with the advice and consent of the Senate; but he alone negotiates. Into the field of negotiation the Senate cannot intrude; and Congress itself is powerless to invade it.[64]

More than this, the Court went so far as to state that the President's powers of external sovereignty did not depend upon the affirmative grants of the Constitution. The power adequately to conduct external affairs, if it had never been mentioned in the Constitution, would have vested in the President as a necessary concomitant of national executive power.

From almost the beginning of the Republic, the Supreme Court has adopted a hands-off policy so far as executive action in the field of foreign affairs is concerned. The Court has designedly abjured authority in the external sphere because of its feeling that the exercise of judicial power is peculiarly inappropriate with regard to it. The conduct of foreign relations, declared the highest tribunal as early as 1796, involves "considerations of policy, considerations of extreme magnitude, and certainly entirely incompetent to the examination and decision of a Court of Justice." [65] Ever since, the Court has recognized a basic difference between its review power over executive action touching domestic or internal affairs and that touching foreign or external affairs. A case like that of steel seizure shows that the high Court can and will review the legality of Presidential action having impact directly within our borders. Where such impact is external, on the other hand, abnegation has been the constant judicial theme. The conduct of our foreign relations, stated the Court in 1918, is committed by the Constitution to the Chief Executive "and the propriety of what may be done in the exercise of this political power is not subject to judicial inquiry or decision." [66]

The Supreme Court since 1937 has consistently adhered to the view that exercises of Presidential authority in the field of foreign affairs are immune from judicial review. In fact, it has been the post-1937 Court that has delivered perhaps the strongest judicial statement in support of abstinence by the courts in the field of external relations. Almost a decade ago the Court stated:

The President, both as Commander-in-Chief and as the Nation's organ for foreign affairs, has available intelligence services whose reports are not and ought not to be published to the world. It would be intolerable that courts, without the relevant information, should review and perhaps nullify actions of the Executive taken on information properly held secret. Nor can courts sit in camera in order to be taken into executive confidences. But even if courts could require full disclosure, the very nature of executive decisions as to foreign policy is political, not judicial. Such decisions are wholly confided by our Constitution to the political departments of the government, Executive and Legislative. They are delicate, complex, and involve large elements of prophecy. They are and should be undertaken only by those directly responsible to the people whose welfare they advance or imperil. They are decisions of a kind for which the Judiciary has neither aptitude, facilities nor responsibility and which has long been held to belong in the domain of political power not subject to judicial intrusion or inquiry.[67]

The present writer has no quixotic intention of tilting a lance in favor of full judicial review over Presidential decisions in the field of foreign affairs. That there must, in fact, be some judicial self-limitation in cases which have immediate repercussions on external affairs, few will deny. Thus, our courts may not, as the Supreme Court pointed out in 1943, so exercise their jurisdiction, by the seizure and detention of the property of a foreign sovereign, as to embarrass the executive arm of the Government in conducting foreign relations. In such a case, our national interest will be better served if the wrongs to suitors, involving our relations with a friendly foreign power, are righted through diplomatic negotiations rather than by the compulsions of judicial proceedings.[68] The basic rule where foreign relations are directly involved must be that the

President, as the personification of external sovereignty, must have the final word. The highest Court itself conceded over a century ago that:

If this were not the rule, cases might often arise in which, on most important questions of foreign jurisdiction, there would be an irreconcilable difference between the executive and judicial departments. By one of these departments, a foreign island or country might be considered as at peace with the United States; whilst the other would consider it in a state of war. No well-regulated government has ever sanctioned a principle so unwise, and so destructive of national character.[69]

To admit this much does not, all the same, necessarily bar one from wondering whether the Supreme Court, in its post-1937 jurisprudence, has not gone too far in its assertions of abstention in this field. Two 1948 decisions of the highest tribunal can be used to illustrate the kind of case which may leave the commentator with some doubt. The first is *Chicago and Southern Air Lines v. Waterman Steamship Corp.*[70] This is the case in which the Court delivered its strong statement, already quoted, in support of judicial indulgence of executive foreign affairs authority. It concerned the power of the Civil Aeronautics Board to license those seeking to engage in aerial transport. The Board is the administrative agency authorized to grant licenses to engage in both domestic and foreign air transportation, though, in the latter case, its decision is subject to the approval of the President. The relevant statute provides for review by the federal courts of any order of the Board, "except any order in respect of any *foreign* air carrier subject to the approval of the President." * This statutory exception did not expressly cover the instant case, which concerned an application by a citizen carrier to engage in overseas transportation. Despite this, the Court held that review of the Board's decision was precluded, because of the effect which it might have upon the field of foreign affairs. Although Justice Jackson, who delivered the opinion, conceded that a literal reading of the statute would subject the administrative decision to re-examination by the courts, he asserted that the letter of the statute need not govern here. Because of the impact of the Board's order on foreign relations, the courts should not intervene. Decisions such as this "are decisions of a kind for which the Judiciary has neither aptitude, facilities nor responsibility."[71]

In the *Chicago and Southern Air Lines* case, the Supreme Court held that it could not exercise jurisdiction even though the challenged governmental action clearly affected adversely the property

* Author's italics.

of the individual seeking review. Even in such a case, review is precluded because of the foreign affairs aspects of the Board's decision. As stated by the dissenting Justices, "no matter how extreme the action of the Board, the courts are powerless to correct it under today's decision." [72] The individual affected may doubtless find it difficult to comprehend why he is in a worse position than if he were applying only for a license to engage in domestic transport. The effect upon him of a refusal by the Board is essentially the same, whether he is applying for a domestic or an overseas license; yet, so far as judicial review is concerned, the Court's decision does make for a substantial difference in his rights. If his license relates to overseas traffic, the administration can act in a lawless way,[73] without fear of restraint by the courts.

The second 1948 decision referred to, *Ludecke v. Watkins*,[74] was even more drastic in its impact upon the private individual. The question at issue there was the power of the President to order the deportation of a German alien on January 18, 1946, almost a year after the cessation of actual hostilities with Germany. The President had acted under the Alien Enemy Act of 1798, which authorized him to deport enemy aliens "whenever there is a declared war between the United States and any foreign nation or government." The alien claimed that he could not be deported as a "dangerous" enemy alien without a fair hearing to determine whether he was "dangerous" and without some judicial inquiry into the truth of the executive finding that he was dangerous. The majority of the high Court rejected this claim, holding that, in this field, the executive action was not subject to any judicial review. And, though the Court's decision was rendered over three years after the physical end of the war in Germany, the Court held that it could not question the President's judgment that we were still at war with that country:

It is not for us to question a belief by the President that enemy aliens who were justifiably deemed fit subjects for internment during active hostilities do not lose their potency for mischief during the period of confusion and conflict which is characteristic of a state of war even when the guns are silent but the peace of Peace has not come. These are matters of political judgment for which judges have neither technical competence nor official responsibility.[75]

The weakness of the Court's decision in *Ludecke v. Watkins*, like that of its decision in the *Chicago and Southern Air Lines* case, arises from its drastic impact upon the personal or property right of the individual concerned, who would normally in our system have a right to judicial review. This right to review is completely denied the alien in *Ludecke* because of the supposed effect of the case upon our external security. As one of the dissenting Justices there states:

The effect of this holding is that any unnaturalized person, good or bad, loyal or disloyal to this country, if he was a citizen of Germany before coming here, can be summarily seized, interned and deported from the United States . . . , and that no court of the United States has any power whatever to review, modify, vacate, reverse, or in any manner affect the . . . deportation order.[76]

It is all very well to assert that the President should be free from judicial interference in the conduct of foreign affairs. But when the action at issue has direct impact upon the person or property of particular individuals, is it not opening the door to executive lawlessness to free such action entirely from judicial review? The executive decision in *Ludecke* may, as Justice Brandeis once eloquently put it, result "in loss of both property and life; or of all that makes life worth living." [77] Yet, under the Court's decision, it is one for the conclusive fiat of the executive, based upon the unreviewable finding of the President—purely a fiction in actual fact—that we were still at war with Germany.

Executive Agreements

In a lecture which could not be delivered because of his death in 1954, but which has since been published posthumously, Justice Jackson referred to "the gap that exists between the President's paper powers and his actual powers. The real potency of the Executive office does not show on the face of the Constitution." [78] One of the most important areas in which Presidential authority has become vastly greater in practice than in the blueprint of executive authority laid down in Article II of the Constitution is that of the execution of international agreements. The constitutional provisions in this matter clearly contemplate a division of authority between the President and the Senate. The President, states the organic document, "shall have Power, by and with the Advice and Consent of the Senate, to make Treaties, provided two thirds of the Senators present concur." Under this provision, it is the President, to be sure, who negotiates treaties with other countries; but the treaties made by him are not valid as obligations of the United States unless and until they are ratified by a two-thirds vote of the Senate.

It is not within the purview of the present work to attempt a critique of the constitutional distribution of the treaty-making power. It may well be that, as Secretary of State John Hay put it at the turn of the century, the Constitution "puts it into the power of one-third + 1 of the Senate to meet with a categorical veto any treaty negotiated by the president, even though it may have the approval of nine-tenths of the people of the nation." [79] At the same time, it cannot be denied that the deficiency thus criticized by Hay has lost at least some of its force during the present century. As is so often the case where a written constitution reveals flaws not foreseen by its draftsmen, an attempt has been made to ameliorate the situation by increasing reliance upon methods which do not come precisely within the letter of the constitutional provision in question. In the case of the treaty-making power, the deficiencies which many have seen in the system set up by our Constitution have been avoided in many cases by executive agreements entered into by the President with other countries which are not submitted to the Senate for its approval. The constitutional delegation to the President and the Senate of the treaty-making power does not exhaust the capacity of the United States to enter into international agreements. From the establishment of the Republic, it has been recognized that the President has had authority to make agreements with other nations that did not have to be submitted to the Senate for ratification. An international agreement, in other words, need not always be a treaty which requires the participation of the Senate. The President himself may, as the sole organ of the Nation in foreign relations, enter into executive agreements which are binding international obligations of the United States.

It is true that most executive agreements comprise the ordinary daily grist of the diplomatic mill.[80] Most such agreements have dealt with comparatively trivial matters, such as the settlement of minor disputes, which hardly deserve the dignity of resolution by formal treaty. It is, nevertheless, a mistake to think that all executive agreements, in contrast to treaties, concern mere international trifles. On the contrary, particularly in recent decades, executive agreements have touched upon matters which constitute the very warp and woof of the Nation's external sovereignty.

If one bears in mind the tremendous expansion in Presidential action in this field, it is not going too far to conclude, as did a study published at the end of the last war, that executive agreements concluded by the President have come to be used interchangeably with treaties in the conduct of the foreign relations of the United States.[81] Thus, such agreements have been used to accomplish the acquisition of territory; the settlement of international claims; the adherence to international organizations; international commercial agreements; control of international communications; and international financial and war debt agreements. Some of the most important moves in the evolution of our foreign policy have, indeed, been brought about by executive agreements, rather than by formal treaties: The famous "Open Door" policy, upon which American policy in the Far East has been based during most of this century, was laid down in an agreement concluded by the Secretary of State in 1900 with the principal countries of Europe and Japan. The so-called "Gentleman's Agreement" entered into between President Theodore Roosevelt and the Japanese ambassador regulated Japanese immigration to the United States for some seventeen years, until it was put an end to by an act of Congress. And, to take some more recent examples, one has only to cite the celebrated exchange of bases for destroyers between President Franklin D. Roosevelt and the British government, and the many agreements entered into by him after American participation in the war, such as those concluded at Teheran, Yalta, and (by President Truman) at Potsdam. And, since the war, as is well known, our Presidents have entered into many agreements with other governments that have approximated temporary alliances. The executive agreement has, in fact, now become in an era characterized by the instability of international relations a principal instrument of Presidential initiative in the field of foreign relations.

In two important cases decided by it in the past two decades, the Supreme Court took advantage of the opportunity to deal with the question of the legal effects of executive agreements. And it cannot be denied that the way in which the Court resolved that question has given strong impetus both to Presidential assertions of a treaty-making power without the aid or consent of the Senate and, more recently, to efforts to curb both the President's power to make international agreements and the constitutional treaty-making power itself.

The Supreme Court decisions referred to arose out of the so-called Litvinov Assignment, which involved the first important utilization of the executive agreement device by President Franklin Roosevelt. The Assignment in question was part of an exchange of diplomatic correspondence between the President and the Soviet Foreign Commissar, whereby American recognition was extended to the U.S.S.R., in consideration of certain pledges made by the latter. In addition, the two governments sought to bring about a final settlement of the claims and counterclaims between them.

The Litvinov Assignment itself was an assignment by the Soviet government to our Government of all claims due to that government by American nationals. Relying upon this Assignment, the United States brought an action against a New York private banker to recover a sum of money which had been deposited with him by a Russian corporation prior to the Russian revolution. After the revolution, the Soviet government had enacted a decree by which it dissolved the corporation in question and nationalized and expropriated all of its assets, including the deposit account with the New York banker. Our Government, in bringing its action, relied upon the fact that, under the Soviet decree, all assets of the corporation, including the deposit, became the property of the Soviet government. Hence, the deposit was an amount owing to the Soviet government by an American national, which became the property of the United States under the Litvinov Assignment. It was, however, contended by defendant that, though the Soviet decree was fully competent to affect property within the territorial jurisdiction of the Soviet government, it did not automatically have the same effect in this country, where the bank deposit in question was located. The Soviet decree involved an act of confiscation. To enforce it here, it was claimed, was contrary to the public policy of the State of New York against giving effect to confiscatory acts.

The Supreme Court wholly rejected this argument in its 1937 decision in *United States v. Belmont* [82]—a decision which gave the broadest scope to the legal status of executive agreements. In the first place, said the Court's opinion, the compact between President Roosevelt and Commissar Litvinov was a valid international agreement between the two countries, even though it had never been submitted to the Senate: "An international compact, as this was, is not always a treaty which requires the participation of the Senate. There are many such compacts, of which a protocol, a modus vivendi, a postal convention, and agreements like that now under consideration are illustrations." [83] Though this might not be a treaty requiring ratification by the Senate, it was a compact negotiated and proclaimed under the authority of the President, and as such, said the Court, had the legal effect of a treaty. But, if this was true, it was plain that the President's agreement had to prevail over the contrary public policy of the State of New York. A treaty ratified by the Senate clearly supersedes contrary state law or policy. The *Belmont* case is of such significance because it endows an executive agreement entered into by the President alone with precisely the same overriding legal effect. As the Court has clearly stated it, while the rule of supremacy over state law, "in respect of treaties is established by the express language of cl. 2, Art. VI, of the Constitution, the same rule would result in the case of all international compacts and agreements from the very fact that complete power over international affairs is in the national government and is not and cannot be subject to any curtailment or interference on the part of the several states." [84]

In *United States v. Pink*,[85] decided in 1942, the Court reiterated the *Belmont* rule—and, if anything, with added emphasis. In the *Pink* case, the United States sought, under the Litvinov Assignment, to recover the New York assets of a Russian company which had been nationalized by Soviet decree. Creditors of the Russian company contested the recovery, asserting that the Soviet decree should not be given effect contrary to New York's public policy against recognizing confiscatory decrees. Since the *Belmont* case, the highest court of New York had expressly articulated that state's public policy in this respect. As in *Belmont*, the Supreme Court held that the Litvinov Assignment took precedence over any inconsistent state law or judicially declared policy. Again the Court reiterated that an executive agreement like the Assignment had the legal effect of a treaty. "A treaty," said the Court, "is a 'Law of the Land' under the supremacy clause . . . of the Constitution. Such international compacts and agreements as the Litvinov Assignment have a similar dignity." [86] If this is true, the Assignment must override the public policy against giving effect to confiscatory decrees pronounced by the New York court; "state law must yield when it is inconsistent with, or impairs the policy or provisions of, . . . an international compact or agreement." [87]

In order fully to comprehend the import of the Court's holding in *Belmont* and *Pink* that an executive agreement has the same legal status as a treaty, a word must be said about the effect of treaties in American law. Under Article VI of the Constitution (the "supremacy clause" referred to by the Court in the *Pink* case), "This Constitution, and the Laws of the United States which shall be made in Pursuance thereof; and all Treaties made, or which shall be made, under the Authority of the United States, shall be the supreme Law of the Land." This supremacy clause has two important effects insofar as treaties are concerned. In the first place, under it, a treaty clearly overrides conflicting state laws. "A treaty cannot be the supreme law of the land . . . ," stated the Supreme Court as early as 1796, "if any act of a State Legislature can stand in its way." [88] In many ways, indeed, a validly made treaty is in our system placed in the same category as an act of the Congress. Like a federal statute, the treaty prevails over inconsistent state laws, but must itself give way to a conflicting later federal law. And this leads to the second important effect of the supremacy clause, namely, that a treaty, like an act of Congress, may, of itself, become an immediate part of the law of the land. As Chief Justice Marshall said in 1829, "Our constitution declares a treaty to be the law of the land. It is, consequently, to be regarded in courts of justice as equivalent to an act of the legislature, whenever it operates of itself, without the aid of any legislative provision." [89] In other words, unless it is clear from the terms of a treaty that it is not intended to have immediate effect in our internal law (that it is not, as the courts put it, "self-executing"), it takes effect of itself as part of our law, just as does a law enacted by the Congress. In our system, a court will resort to a treaty for a rule of decision for a case before it as it would to a statute.[90]

To most students of international relations, the effect of the supremacy clause of the Constitution is a most desirable one. The constant concern of international law has been to have treaties considered as binding instruments of legislation. To accomplish this, much effort has been directed toward ensuring that treaties create binding rights and duties, not only on the international plane between the signatory countries, but also on the national plane between individual citizens. As a practical matter, this can be accomplished only if treaties take effect as a part of domestic law and hence create rights and obligations enforceable at the suit of private individuals in national courts. To many, in truth, the practical existence of a true international order is conditioned upon the general acceptance of the primacy of international over national law.

What has just been said about treaties does not, however, necessarily apply to international agreements which are not formalized in treaties. A treaty is the end result of action by the Chief Executive and the upper house of the legislature. An executive agreement may enable the President to carry on foreign policy unhindered by the specter of Senatorial veto; but it also permits him to operate free from legislative control. And, in this, as in other fields, legislative control is essential, in our system of checks and balances, to ensure against overaudacious executive adventures.

The Supreme Court in its *Belmont* and *Pink* decisions completely blurred the legal line between treaties and executive agreements. According to the Court, an agreement concluded by the President alone had the same effect in American law as a treaty formally ratified by two-thirds of the Senate. The result was that the President alone could act to override state law and policy, even insofar as the purely internal law of the state was concerned. There is surely no more basic policy in American law than that against the confiscation of private property; it is expressly embodied in both the Federal and all our state Constitutions. Yet, under the Supreme Court's decisions, that basic policy could be set at naught—not by constitutional amendment or even by a duly enacted statute, but by the simple device of an exchange of notes between the President and Mr. Litvinov. There is, to say the least, something paradoxical about a government like ours, based essentially upon respect for person and property, profiting pecuniarily from the expropriation decree of a government conceived and dedicated to exactly the opposite principle. Under *Belmont* and *Pink,* our courts (sworn though they may be to uphold the fundamental legal premises of *our* system) must countenance such a result when it is called for in a mere exchange of diplomatic correspondence between the President and the other government.

Though the high Court certainly intended anything but that result, it cannot be denied that its decisions in this field have contributed, perhaps as much as anything, to recent attempts to limit the power to conclude international agreements, culminating in the proposed Bricker Amendment to the Constitution. Many people, both in and outside the Congress (and not limited by any means to those who are extreme supporters of the Bricker Amendment) have become troubled over the extent of the President's power to make executive agreements. The power to conclude, solely on executive authority, agreements which have the same legal effects as treaties may enable the President to avoid the Senatorial control over treaties provided for by the Constitution. He can do this by negotiating, in any particular case, an executive agreement, which he alone can make, rather than a treaty, which must be confirmed by the Senate. There is no hard and fast line between executive agreements and treaties, and they have come to be used interchangeably in the conduct of our foreign relations. That even experts in the field cannot really draw other than a purely formal line between treaties and executive agreements is shown by a request addressed to the State Department by a senator asking them how to distinguish a treaty, which must be approved by the Senate, from an executive agreement, which need not. The State Department unhelpfully defined a treaty as "something they had to send to the Senate in order to get approval by a two-thirds vote. An executive agreement was something they did not have to send to the Senate." This reply, said the senator who had sent the request, "reminded me of the time when I was a boy on the farm, and asked the hired man how to tell the difference between a male and a female pigeon. He said, 'You put corn in front of the pigeon. If he picks it up, it is a he; if she picks it up, it is a she.' " [91]

If may well be that, under contemporary conditions, a power in the executive to make agreements with other countries which have the same effect in international law as formal treaties is an essential one. What is more debatable is whether such agreements, concluded by the executive alone, should have the same internal legal effect as federal statutes. If they are treated as having such effect, does this not, in practice, vest in the President a means of exercising the legislative power which, under the Constitution, is delegated to the Congress alone?

The extent of concern with this problem is shown by the vote in the Senate in 1954, on a proposed substitute for the Bricker Amendment (introduced by Senator George, himself certainly not one to curb unduly Presidential authority over foreign affairs), which read: "An international agreement other than a treaty shall become effective as internal law in the United States only by an act of the Congress." If adopted, this provision would, of course, do away entirely with the rule of the *Belmont* and *Pink* cases. And the Senate actually did vote 60 to 31 in its favor. But, though it was thus approved by a substantial majority, it failed, by a margin of only a single vote, to receive the two-thirds vote required by the Constitution for the proposing of a constitutional amendment by the Congress. Yet, though the Senate vote thus fell short, by the narrowest of margins, of adopting the proposed limitation on the legal effort of executive agreements, it does show clearly how widespread has become the discontent with the very broad executive power allowed by the Supreme Court decisions. *Belmont* and *Pink,* without a doubt, are the direct precursors of the Bricker Amendment.

King for Four Years?

During the past two decades, the Supreme Court has heard arguments on behalf of executive power such as have not been presented to English-speaking courts since the time of Charles I. And it cannot be gainsaid that our highest tribunal has gone further in upholding such claims than any Anglo-American judges since those appointed by Stuart kings.

It will be objected that this paints too dark a picture of the Supreme Court's control of the President since 1937. Surely, it will be said, the Court, in its *Steel-Seizure* decision, asserted a degree of control over the Chief Executive that would have been unthinkable to the judges of Charles I. The present writer has no desire to

minimize the importance of the *Steel-Seizure* case (in his writings
on the subject,[92] he has, if anything, erred in the opposite direction). The steel decision will clearly, as we have emphasized,
stand as a basic precedent in repudiating the heresy that the President alone, among all governmental officials in our constitutional
system, is wholly immune from judicial review. Henceforth, those
seeking review of the legality of Presidential action will no longer
be met with dismissal at the threshold because of specious application of the separation of powers doctrine.

The Court in the *Steel-Seizure* case did not, however, go as
far in rejecting the law laid down by the Stuart judges in the
Ship-Money case as a bare reading of the "opinion of the Court"
of Justice Black might lead one to believe. As our detailed
analysis of the case has shown,* it is probable that a majority
of the Court supported the thesis of inherent power in the President to deal with emergency. As a practical matter, to one concerned with the constant trend toward expansions of executive
authority, the most important aspect of the steel case was the
recognition by the entire Court that Presidential power in the
area which the steel-seizure order sought to enter was completely
subject to the legislative authority of the Congress. Abuses of
emergency power may thus be controlled directly by the elected
representatives of the people. There is, to be sure, an obvious
weakness in such legislative control because of the President's constitutional participation in the legislative process; Congressional attempts at control which the President opposes can only become law
if enacted with the necessary two-thirds majority over his veto.

Whatever restraint the *Steel-Seizure* case imposes is limited to
the field of internal affairs. The Supreme Court has followed a consistent policy of abstaining from exercising its review authority in
the field of foreign affairs. But the cases discussed show that the
present Court has not been content with merely following the
policy of abstinence in such matters developed by its predecessors.
It has instead extended its own self-denying ordinance so that it has
come perilously close to holding that judicial review is to be denied,
not only when the conduct of foreign affairs is immediately involved
in a case, but also whenever the governmental act at issue is seen to
have some repercussions upon international relations. Its tendency
in this direction may be understandable in a tribunal firmly wedded,
as the present Court is, to the doctrine of judicial self-restraint vis-à-
vis the political branches of government. At the same time, it should

* *Supra*, p. 75.

be recognized that, if pushed too far, the Court's trend is fraught with constitutional peril.

In 1606, the king's judges decided *Bates's* case,[93] another of the great State Trials of Stuart England. It was there held that the king could, by decree, increase the tariff due on imported currants because of his absolute power over the conduct of foreign affairs. "The reason for the imposition," stated Bacon in defending the judges' decision in Parliament, "is whatsoever concerns the government of the Kingdom as it hath relation to foreign parts. The law hath reposed a special confidence in the king." [94] *Bates's* case, of course, like the other decisions upholding royal power by the Stuart judges, represents an extreme in Anglo-American law. No one suggests that our Supreme Court, in its recent jurisprudence, has gone anywhere near that extreme in upholding executive pretensions in the foreign affairs field. Yet, in the cases that have been discussed also, the Court refused to hear any challenge simply because the act at issue "concerns the government of the [country] as it hath relation to foreign parts." There is great danger in the view that, where the issues of a case touch upon foreign affairs, they are *ipso facto* not justiciable. Under present-day conditions, this view can have the effect of removing a great many executive acts from the sphere of judicial review, for a large proportion of such acts can be considered to have at least *some* effect upon foreign relations.

In one important respect, it must be admitted, the present Supreme Court may actually have gone further than the Stuart courts in upholding executive claims. Even the judges of James I refused to countenance the king's claim that he had a legislative power coextensive with that of the Parliament; in the 1611 *Case of Proclamations*,[95] they denied that the king could issue proclamations as a substitute for statutes. What the *Case of Proclamations* refused to James I has, in part, been conceded to our President by the *Belmont* and *Pink* cases.* In those cases, we saw, the highest Court recognized in the President the power to make law by mere executive agreements. Such agreements were held by the Court to take precedence, as a matter of internal law, over state law (whether legislative or judicial in origin) and, if the logic of the Court's holding that an executive agreement has the same effect as a treaty is strictly adhered to, over federal statutes as well. If, as is clearly settled in our law, a treaty may amend or repeal a prior federal statute, under *Belmont* and *Pink*, why is not the same true of executive agreements?

* *Supra*, pp. 89-90.

To a student of the Supreme Court, perhaps the most disturbing thing about that tribunal's holdings in *Belmont* and *Pink* (which do violence to what has, since the *Case of Proclamations,* been the fundamental principle of Anglo-American public law—namely, that, as is categorically expressed in the very first section of the Constitution, all legislative power is vested in the Congress) is that they were unnecessary to the decision of the two cases before the Court. This is very clear to anyone who reads the separate opinions delivered by Chief Justice Stone in those cases. In *Belmont,* as he shows, there was no need to consider whether the executive agreement should be given the effect of a treaty, for the banker, who was merely a custodian of the money deposited with him, could not set up the defense which was available only to the depositor or his creditor. It was not *his* money that the Government sought. Payment of the deposit to the United States as transferee would discharge the banker of his debt and he thus had no real interest to protect in questioning the internal effect of the Litvinov Assignment. Despite this easy way to avoid the constitutional issue (which commended itself to the three strongest members of the Court—Justices Stone, Brandeis, and Cardozo), the majority of the Court went out of its way to lay down its extreme rule equating the legal effect of executive agreements to that of treaties.

The *Pink* decision was clearly based on the authority of the *Belmont* case. Had the *Belmont* opinion not read the way it did, it is very possible that the reasoning in *Pink* would have been altogether different. This is particularly true if one bears in mind that, apart from *Belmont* itself, the Court was, as Chief Justice Stone emphasized in dissent, "referred to no authority which would sustain such an exercise of power as is said to have been exerted here by mere assignment unratified by the Senate." [96]

The Court's unnecessary haste to lay down the rule expanding Presidential power in the *Belmont* case should be compared with its meticulous observance of the rule that it would not deal with basic issues of constitutional power where the case could be decided on other grounds in a more recent case—*United States v. Guy W. Capps, Inc.*[97]—where it was the limitation, not the expansion, of executive authority that was involved. The executive agreement in the *Capps* case limited the importation of potatoes to this country from Canada. In some ways, it was similar to the executive act at issue in *Bates's* case in 1606. The Court of Appeals, in an opinion by one of our ablest judges, Chief Judge Parker, held the agreement in question void, holding that it contravened the procedure laid down by the Congress for limitations on imports in the relevant tariff act.[98] The Court of Appeals' decision imposed what seems today to be a necessary limitation on the *Belmont* and *Pink* holdings—at least if we are not to come again to the level of executive power in the foreign affairs field permitted by *Bates's* case—namely, that an executive agreement, unlike a treaty, cannot contravene the provisions of a prior federal statute. The Supreme Court, however, displaying a tenderness toward jurisdictional niceties wholly absent in its *Belmont* decision, decided the case on other grounds.

One who is familiar with the *Capps* case will, in all probability, uphold the high Court in the way that it acted in that case. It is a fundamental principle of our system that the Court should not resolve basic issues of governmental power unless it is absolutely necessary for decision of the cases before it. Yet, if this rule was sound in *Capps*, what prevented it from being such in *Belmont*? What are we to think of a tribunal which rushes in to make a decision for the President, extending his executive agreement power beyond all bounds, but which wholly withdraws into its shell of judicial timidity when a decision against Presidential authority seems called for?

It may be that the present writer is too much disposed to cavil at the Court's failure to assert effective review power over the Presidential office. Certainly, he would be the last to deny that judicial review alone can hardly prove effective in securing us against the perils of executive despotism. The Court is but one institution in our system of checks and balances and, unless its work is complemented by other checks—particularly those at the disposal of the legislative branch—it is unlikely that the Court alone can, Horatius-like, hold the constitutional bridge erected by the Founders. Subtle shifts take place in the centers of real power that do not show on the face of the Constitution and that cannot be restrained by judicial decision alone. At the same time, what is one to say of a Court that has at times shown itself even more executive-minded than the executive? The Court may be only one check, but it is a vital one, in our system. And it is the Court's constitutional role (hesitant though it may often be to exercise it) to keep even the President within the bounds of legality laid down by the Constitution and statutes of the United States. If the President alone in our system is to exercise powers unbridled by law, then, indeed, have we not progressed as far from the law of Stuart England as most of us had hoped. If the Supreme Court abdicates its responsibility to review the legality of action of the Chief Executive, then he is, in fact if not in judicial theory, not subject to law. "With all its defects, delays and inconveniences," as Justice Jackson eloquently declared, "men have discovered no technique for long preserving free government except that the Executive be under the law." [99] The alternative is to adopt the view of the Presidency attributed to William H. Seward: "We elect a king for four years, and give him absolute power." [100]

4

THE ADMINISTRATIVE AGENCY

For forms of government, let fools contest:
Whate'er is best administer'd is best . . .

So wrote Alexander Pope over two hundred years ago.[1] It cannot be denied that there are those, even at the present day, who share his view. At the same time, many people, not all of them fools by any means, would take sharp issue with Pope's couplet. For them, administration is only a means, not an end; far more important than mere efficiency in the operation of government are the ends toward which government is directed. And, to them, the form of a particular government is of supreme consequence. Rejecting the view that administration, in and of itself, is the "be all and end all" of politically organized society, they also repudiate the notion that administration should be a law unto itself. Administrative power must, like all other governmental power, be exercised in subordination to law. Even though they may concede that such power must, under contemporary conditions, be conferred to an ever-increasing degree, they insist that it must be subject to the checks and balances which restrain all exercises of governmental authority in our system.

Of course, to adherents of the opinion expressed in Pope's couplet, those who reject their simple notion that administration must be the *primus motor* in the polity, possessed of any and all powers which at any time it thinks it requires, are the victims of ignorant and insular prejudice. They consider themselves to be supporters of the most modern and up-to-date political theory, destined to be the "wave of the future." Those who support representative assemblies to fetter administrative prerogative and courts to subject it to the restraints of law are said to advocate an outmoded conception of the State, which leads to governmental inefficiency, at best, and to anarchy, at worst. To these modern advocates of a theory of absolutism much older than they like to admit, the rule of law over

99

men is to be replaced by the administration of things and the direction of the processes of production. Unrestrained administration is
to take the place of law as the instrument of social control: "The
more consistently the principle of authoritative regulation, excluding all references to an independent autonomous will, is carried
through, the less room remains for an application of the category of
law." [2] In their State, there is to be no law and but one rule of law,
namely, that there are no laws, but only administrative orders for
the individual case.[3]

This extreme view of the proper place of administration in the
political order has not by any means been confined to the totalitarian part of the world. Until recently, in fact, it was not un-
common for Anglo-Americans themselves to look upon their system
as an obsolete survival of an easier age, said to belong to the age of
etiquette, the age of overrefinement, when every practical activity
was embarrassed by cumbersome ceremonial and checks. "Not so
long ago," Justice Frankfurter informs us, "it was fashionable to find
our system of checks and balances obstructive to effective government. It was easy to ridicule that system as outmoded—too easy." [4]
More recently, we have come to see that the system of restraints
upon government laid down by our Constitution is not a mere dogmatic product of eighteenth-century political theory. Developments in other parts of the world have made us all too aware of the
dangers inherent in uncontrolled administration: "The experience
through which the world has passed in our own day has made vivid
the realization that the Framers of our Constitution were not in-
experienced doctrinaires." [5] The instructive example of those governments we disparagingly describe as totalitarian, with their
omnipotent administrations, unrestrained by any checks on their
all-pervasive regulatory activities, has certainly not led us to desire to create our administration in their image. Contemporary
foreign experience may be inconclusive on many points; but it certainly counsels us that vast administrative powers are consistent
with free government only when effective control of them is lodged
elsewhere than in the administration which exercises them.

In a constitutional republic based upon common-law concepts
and traditions, such as ours, there is a twofold control of administrative authority from outside the executive branch itself. In the
first place, there is the vital task of oversight which must be performed by the legislature. As the source of delegations of power to
administrative agencies, the Congress can and must exercise direct
supervision over the manner in which such power is employed.

Congressional control must, however, necessarily be based upon policy, not legality. It must be complemented by legal control, to ensure that administrative authority is exercised in accordance with law. Indeed, the very essence of the rule of law as it has developed in English-speaking countries has been the subordination of administration to the law of the land as administered by the ordinary courts. The historic phrase "rule of law" epitomizes the distinguishing character of our political society. When the blood, sweat, and toil of our forefathers made that phrase the base of our polity, they were not indulging in mere rhetorical flourish. The supremacy of law has meant the rejection in our system of rule by executive fiat. Every act of administration may be challenged by an appeal to law, as finally pronounced by the highest Court.

It is true that, in one sense, the rule of law involves a contradiction in terms, so far as the subordination of administration to law is concerned, for the law of the land is also made by the administration itself. But the concept of the rule of law makes the assumption that the law which is made by the administration is not on the same plane of authority as that which issues from other lawmaking organs of the State. The rule of law consequently presupposes a veritable hierarchy of lawmakers within the State.

At the apex is the constituent assembly or its equivalent, which alone has the authority to promulgate the organic instrument under which the State is governed. The provisions of the constitution enacted by it constitute the supreme law of the land. The law made by any other organ of the State is valid only so far as it does not conflict with the terms of the constitution. Next in the lawmaking hierarchy come the elected representatives of the people, given authority to enact statutes, the provisions of which are legally binding upon all, provided only that they are not inconsistent with the constitution. At the base of the lawmaking hierarchy is the administration. Strictly speaking, its only role is to execute the laws made by the legislature. But the effective performance of that role has required that it, too, be vested with substantial lawmaking authority. Thus, modern administration has the power to promulgate rules having the force of law and to render decisions in cases involving particular citizens.

The subordinate position of administration in the hierarchy of lawmakers means, nevertheless, that administrative exercises of lawmaking authority are valid only if they do not conflict with the constitution and with the statutes enacted by the legislature. Or, to put it another way, administrative action is valid only so far as it is *legal*. It is illegal if inconsistent with the prescriptions of an organ superior to administration in the hierarchy of lawmakers within the State.

Of course, there is more than the mere assertion of this "principle of legality" to the concept of the rule of law. The fact that this principle is enforced by the courts is what makes it a thing of meaning. The rule of law to which the administration is subject has two main aspects. The first is the assertion of the principle of legality—that only administrative acts in accord with law are valid. Of at least equal importance has been the enforcement of the principle of legality in particular cases by the courts. As a practical matter, the aspect of judicial enforcement is of cardinal significance. Unless the courts can intervene in cases where it is violated, the principle of legality becomes devoid of practical content.

How far has the post-1937 Supreme Court succeeded in keeping administrative authority in this country subject to the rule of law? That is the question to which this chapter is devoted; and it is certainly a crucial question to one interested in the work of the highest tribunal during the past two decades. For the years since 1937 have witnessed a drastic augmentation in the trend toward expansion of administrative power that has characterized the present century. We need not necessarily agree with Lord Acton that great men are almost always bad men; but our public law should clearly be based upon some such assumption. In fact, our whole constitutional structure has been erected upon the assumption that the king not only is capable of doing wrong but is more likely to do wrong than other men if he is given the chance. We must not today judge those in possession of governmental power more favorably than did our ancestors, with the presumption that they can do no wrong. On the contrary, if there is any presumption, it should be the other way, against the holders of power, and increasing as the power increases. In the field of administrative law, historic responsibility can never make up for the want of legal responsibility.

Delegations of Power

If the doctrine of the separation of powers were a doctrinaire concept to be made use of with pedantic rigor,[6] the rise of the modern administrative agency would have been an impossibility in our law. For the outstanding characteristic of such agency is the possession by it of powers which are both legislative and judicial in nature. The important agencies in the federal administration are vested, on the one hand, with the authority to promulgate rules and regulations having the force of law and, on the other, with the power to render decisions adversely affecting the person or property of particular individuals. The powers so vested in these agencies are comparable to those traditionally exercised by the Congress and the courts. They have, however, been vested in organs outside the legislative and judicial branches because it has been felt that, without such powers, they could not effectively perform the manifold regulatory tasks entrusted to them by the legislature. If in private life we were to organize a unit for the operation of an industry, it would hardly follow Montesquieu's lines.[7] Nor can the regulation of industry demanded by modern public opinion be adequately carried out under a rigid separation of powers. The administration has consequently been made the repository of all three types of governmental power. In the administrative process, the various stages of making and applying law, traditionally separate, have been telescoped into a single agency. As Justice Jackson well put it in 1954, administrative agencies today "combine delegated rule-making, the investigation and prosecution of complaints, and adjudication, and are supposed to unite congressional judgment as to policy, executive efficiency in enforcement, and judicial neutrality and detachment of decision."[8] Legislative and judicial powers have become the chief weapons in the twentieth-century administrative armory.

Even at this late date, there are those who deny that, in a system such as ours, dominated by the doctrine of the separation of powers, any governmental organ outside the Congress or the courts can exercise legislative or judicial authority. Such constitutional purism is wholly out of line with the facts of contemporary governmental life. In the recent words of Justice Douglas:

There is no doubt that the agency which determines that a particular individual or company should be brought within the regulatory reach of the law is a lawmaking authority. It is, in other words, clear that the administrator who by order, by rule, or by regulation extends the civil or criminal sanctions of the law to named parties indulges in legislation.[9]

The constitutional purist may claim that this sort of authority exercised by the administrator is, at most, only *quasi*-legislative in nature. Certainly, to soften a legal term by a *quasi* is a time-honored lawyer's device. Yet, in this case, it has become wholly illogical thus to grant the fact of the legislative power of the administration and still to deny the name. When the Supreme Court in 1952 upholds an indictment of a trucker for violation of a regulation promulgated by the Interstate Commerce Commission prescribing certain compulsory safety precautions for trucks transporting inflammables or explosives,[10] perhaps the ICC regulation is only a *quasi-law*.[11] But when the trucker is convicted of violating such regulation, we may be certain that they do not incarcerate him in a *quasi*-cell. To be sure, if we think of the separation of powers as carrying out the distinction between legislation and administration with mathematical precision and as dividing the branches of government into watertight compartments, we would probably have to conclude that any exercise of lawmaking authority by an administrative agency is automatically invalid. In actuality, such a rigorous application of the constitutional doctrine is neither desirable nor feasible; the only absolute separation that has ever been possible was that in the theoretical writings of a Montesquieu, who looked across at foggy England from his sunny Gascon vineyards, and completely misconstrued what he saw.

In dealing with the question of the powers that may be delegated to an administrative agency, even the pre-1937 Supreme Court recognized the truth of what has just been said. That tribunal, like the Congress itself, has had to acknowledge that the comprehensive regulation required of the contemporary State is too intricate and detailed for direct Congressional processes. Such regulation, much of which had previously been thought to be outside the scope of governmental power, could, as a practical matter, be exercised only through the medium of the administrative agency, vested, we have seen, with significant powers of lawmaking. As the Supreme Court declared in 1935:

Undoubtedly legislation must often be adapted to complex conditions involving a host of details with which the national legislature cannot deal directly. The Constitution has never been regarded as denying to the Congress the necessary resources of flexibility and practicality, which will enable it to perform its function in laying down policies and establishing standards, while leaving to selected instrumentalities the making of subordinate rules within prescribed limits and the determination of facts to which the policy as declared by the legislature is to apply. Without capacity to give authorizations of that sort we should have the anomaly of a legislative power which in many circumstances calling for its exertion would be but a futility.[12]

Under this sort of approach, the pre-1937 Court had clearly adopted the view that legislative, or rule-making, power could be vested in an administrative agency. An act of Congress was consequently not invalid merely because it, in form, delegated power legislative in nature to administrative authorities. This view was squared with the constitutional provision vesting *all* legislative powers in the Congress by distinguishing the legislative power given to the administrator with that vested in the Congress itself. The power to "legislate," it was said, when delegated by the Congress, differs basically from the Congress' own power to legislate. The Congress is vested with all of the legislative authority granted by the Constitution. But any power delegated by the Congress is necessarily a subordinate power, because it is limited by the terms of the enactment whereby it is delegated. Congress, Justice Douglas has more recently explained it,[13] may therefore be said to exercise the *primary* legislative function, the administrative agency a *secondary* one.

Implicit in this theory as it was developed by the pre-1937 Supreme Court was the proposition that, if this primary position of the Congress was to be maintained, there must be limitations upon delegations of power. Said Chief Justice Hughes in the 1935 opinion already quoted: "The constant recognition of the necessity and validity of such provisions, and the wide range of administrative authority which has been developed by means of them, cannot be allowed to obscure the limitations of the authority to delegate, if our constitutional system is to be maintained." [14] In order to preserve the position of the Congress as the primary legislator, delegations of power by it could not be inordinate. And this meant that the precise limits of the lawmaking power which the Congress intended to confer upon an administrative agency had to be defined in clear language by the statute which conferred it. Or, as the highest Court itself expressed it, the delegated power must be limited by a standard: "Congress cannot delegate any part of its legislative power except under the limitation of a prescribed standard." [15] The discretion conferred must not be so wide that it is impossible to discern its limits. There must instead be an ascertainable legislative intent to which the exercise of the delegated power must conform. If there is no precise standard in the enabling statute to limit delegations of power, the administrative agency is in actuality being given a blank check to make law in the delegated area of authority. In such a case, it is the agency, rather than the Congress, that is really the primary legislator.

The pre-1937 Supreme Court not only laid down the requirement of an ascertainable standard as a theoretical limitation upon permissible delegations of power; it did not hesitate to enforce such limitation whenever it felt it appropriate to do so. In two cases decided in 1935,[16] the Court expressly held federal laws invalid on the ground that they involved delegations not restricted by any real standard. As Chief Justice Hughes stated in the first of these cases, with regard to a law giving the administration the authority to prohibit, in its absolute discretion, the interstate transportation of so-called "hot oil" (i.e., oil produced in excess of state regulatory laws), "the Congress has declared no policy, has established no standard, has laid down no rule. There is no requirement, no definition of circumstances and conditions in which the transportation is to be allowed or prohibited." [17]

The post-1937 Supreme Court has all but abandoned the view exemplified in the two 1935 decisions just referred to—that the Court must invalidate laws delegating power which do not contain limiting standards. The change in the Court's attitude on this point is but a reflection in the field of administrative law of that tribunal's deference toward the Congress which, as has been emphasized, has tended to dominate its post-1937 jurisprudence. A Court which has consistently upheld assertions of authority by the federal legislature, even in areas previously held beyond the scope of Congressional authority, was bound to take a more lenient attitude toward delegations of power by the Congress. At the same time, it cannot be denied that the Court's new attitude has encouraged the legislature in the past two decades to make broader delegations to the administration than had formerly been its wont. A number of these delegations were made during the last war; these stand apart for their breadth and will be dealt with in our chapter on the war power.* Yet, even apart from the wartime cases, wholesale delegations have become the rule, rather than the exception.

If, as Justice Cardozo expressed it in one of the 1935 cases already referred to, delegation without a standard is "delegation running riot," [18] such delegation has, since 1937, become a normal part of the federal statute book.

The extent to which the judicial pendulum has swung in the past two decades with regard to delegations of power to administrative agencies can best be seen from an analysis of some of the cases. Under section 5(d) of the Home Owners' Loan Act, the Federal Home Loan Bank Board is empowered to prescribe by regulation the terms and conditions upon which a conservator may be appointed for a federal savings and loan association. The district court had held that this constituted an invalid delegation, in that no criterion was established to guide the Board in its exercise of the authority conferred. The Supreme Court candidly conceded that there was no express legislative standard. But that did not lead it to declare the law at issue invalid, as Justice Jackson explained.

* *Infra,* pp. 298-301.

It may be that explicit standards in the Home Owners' Loan Act would have been a desirable assurance of responsible administration. But the provisions of the statute under attack are not penal provisions. . . . The provisions are regulatory. . . . A discretion to make regulations to guide supervisory action in such matters may be constitutionally permissible while it might not be allowable to authorize creation of new crimes in uncharted fields.[19]

The Court's explicit recognition that standards are not necessary in a law of this type should be compared with its opinions dealing with grants of power under the Communications Act. Under that law, the Federal Communications Commission is given wide authority to regulate broadcasting: "The Commission was, however, not left at large in performing this duty. The touchstone provided by Congress was the 'public interest, convenience, or necessity,' a criterion which 'is as concrete as the complicated factors for judgment in such a field of delegated authority permit.' " [20] According to the Court, in a field where the subject matter of regulation is as fluid and dynamic as broadcasting, a detailed prescription of standards could have made effective administration impossible. Congress, said the Court in 1943, would have frustrated,

the purposes for which the Communications Act . . . was brought into being by attempting an itemized catalogue of the specific manifestations of the general problems for the solution of which it was establishing a regulatory agency. That would have stereotyped the powers of the Commission to specific details in regulating a field of enterprise the dominant characteristic of which was the rapid pace of its unfolding.[21]

But where does this leave the pre-1937 requirement of an ascertainable standard in legislation delegating authority to an administrative agency? The only standard provided in the Communications Act is that of the "public interest, convenience, or necessity"; the Federal Communications Commission is told by the Congress to exercise the powers vested in it as the "public interest, convenience, or necessity" may require. Plainly, such a standard is anything but mechanical or self-defining; it leaves the widest possible area of judgment and, therefore, of discretion to the administrator.[22] Indeed, one wonders whether the so-called standard of the Communications Act really furnishes an effective legislative guide. Telling the administrator to act in the "public interest" is the practical equivalent of telling him: "Here is the regulatory problem; deal with it." [23] Certainly, such a legislative direction adds little to a statute delegating powers. Would the FCC be likely to act any differently in specific cases if the Communications Act did not specifically instruct it to be guided by "public interest, convenience, or necessity"?

Prior to 1937, excessive delegations of power to administrative agencies were legal questions; under the recent jurisprudence of the Supreme Court, they have become almost exclusively political. In its post-1937 case law, the Court has relegated the requirement of a defined standard to the level of a purely formal one, devoid of most of its practical efficacy. Provided that the talismanic form of a standard (even if so vague as to be illusory) is used by the Congress, its delegations will now be upheld. Whether the Court has been right or wrong on the merits of this point, there is little doubt that its recent decisions have lowered a significant barrier against the aggrandizement of administrative authority. If there are no real standards in the relevant statute to limit the delegation of power to him, the administrator is in substance being given *carte blanche* upon which he may scribble what he pleases in the delegated area of authority. Statutes containing no effective standards may be aptly characterized as "skeleton" legislation. Under them, the flesh and the blood—not to mention the soul—of the schemes of legislative regulation are left entirely to administrative discretion. The *vires*—the limits—of the authority delegated have become so broad as to cover almost all administrative action within the particular area of regulation. The Supreme Court has now indicated that there are no longer any constitutional prohibitions against "skeleton" legislation. Now that that tribunal has all but removed itself as a controlling factor, the responsibility is solely that of the Congress to ensure that the delegations of power made by it are limited ones.

Concentration of Functions

As it has been with the question of the extent of authority which can validly be delegated, so it has been with the question of the internal structure of the administrative agency. On this matter, too, the Supreme Court has been following a basic hands-off policy, asserting that the responsibility for correcting any structural defects in the administration is vested entirely in the Congress. The extent of Congressional authority in this respect received striking reaffirmation, just before the constitutional revolution of 1937, in the celebrated *Humphrey* case.[24] There the Court upheld the power of the Congress to set up a regulatory commission, vested with significant legislative and judicial authority, and with its members immunized from the removal power which the President possesses over ordinary executive officials. The Congress could create the commission concerned as its own agent, rather than as an agency directly within the executive branch. It was the independence from Presidential control thus recognized in agencies of the type involved in the *Humphrey* case that led President Roosevelt plaintively to characterize them as a " 'fourth' branch of the Government, for which there is no sanction in the Constitution." [25]

Since 1937, the predominant authority over administrative structure which the Court in *Humphrey* acknowledged in the Congress has received its most striking vindication with regard to the so-called concentration or combination of functions. It has already been emphasized that the need for effective regulation has led the Congress to telescope the stages of making and applying law, traditionally separate, into a single regulatory agency. The result has been the merger in the one agency of what are essentially legislative, executive, and judicial functions. By concentrating these functions within the one governmental agency, the legislator has felt, there can then be performed the continuous policing function essential to effective regulation. Such concentration enables the one agency by itself to administer all the different phases of a regulatory scheme, from the promulgation of the regulatory prescriptions, to the policing of the field of regulation to ensure that they are observed, to the prosecution of those who violate them, to the adjudication of cases brought against such violators.

In these cases, the agency concerned is both policeman, prosecutor, and judge. To those who are concerned with fair play in the administrative process, the concentration of functions constitutes the great weakness, as well as great strength, of the modern regulatory agency. Concern with such concentration, Justice Brennan pointed out before his elevation to the Supreme Court,

springs from the fear that the agency official adjudicating upon private rights cannot wholly free himself from the influences toward partiality inherent in his identification with the investigative and prosecuting aspects of the case; in other words, that the atmosphere in which he must make his judgments is not conducive to the critical detachment toward the case expected of the judge. In a sense the combination of functions violates the ancient tenet of Anglo-American justice that "No man shall be a judge in his own cause." [26]

The Supreme Court has also articulated a feeling of uneasiness at the concentration of functions. Speaking through Justice Jackson in 1950, it referred to "the practice of embodying in one person or agency the duties of prosecutor and judge" as one of the administrative evils which are sought to be cured or minimized.[27] More recently, Justice Jackson has declared his own belief,

that every safeguard should be thrown about the process of administrative adjudication so that its fact-finding will be honest, unprejudiced, neutral, and competent. It should be isolated from the prosecuting function. As a prosecutor, the body serves a constituency and promotes an interest. As a judge, it should know no constituent and serve no interest except justice.[28]

This may well be the individual feeling of a Supreme Court Justice toward an administrative arrangement which appears inherently to violate the fundamentals of fair play. Such personal notions must, nevertheless, be irrelevant in a tribunal which adheres as strongly to the doctrine of deference to the legislator as does the highest Court, particularly on a matter of the internal structure of administrative agencies, where even the pre-1937 Court admitted the predominant authority of the Congress. As a judicial tribunal, the Court has acknowledged that it must recognize and accept, even though reluctantly, the Congressional power to establish agencies characterized by the combination of functions.

That such is in fact the view of the highest tribunal is shown most clearly in its 1955 decision in *Marcello v. Bonds*.[29] Petitioner there was an alien who had been ordered deported after hearing. He claimed that the deportation order was invalid because of an improper combination of functions in the administrative agency concerned, the Immigration and Naturalization Service. The officer who had presided at petitioner's hearing was subject to the supervision and control of other officials in the Service who were charged with investigative and prosecuting functions. Petitioner claimed that this procedure—which the high Court itself had described in 1950 as a perfect exemplification of the type of concentration of functions that had been so unanimously condemned [30] —was so devoid of fairness and impartiality as to be violative of due process. In the *Marcello* case, the Court rejected, almost summarily, this contention, asserting only that it was without substance when considered against the long-standing practice of the Congress in concentrating the functions of investigation, prosecution, and adjudication in the same administrative agency. In the Court's view, even though it may be felt that such concentration is unsatisfactory, it is for the Congress, not the judiciary, to remedy the evil. Deference to the legislator requires the judge to turn the other cheek before a concentration in the administrative agency which, he himself well knows, often makes the litigant feel that he has lost all opportunity to argue his case to an unbiased official and that he has been deprived of safeguards he has been taught to revere.[31]

From the point of view of the private litigant before an administrative agency, the concentration of functions is objectionable because it violates his right to have his case judged by a wholly unbiased tribunal. How, he asks, can the administrative agency decide his case with that "cold neutrality of an impartial judge" of which Burke speaks when it is the agency itself that has prosecuted the case against him? Sometimes, indeed, the prepossession in the case of such an agency seems even more invidious. An illustrative case is *Federal Trade Commission v. Cement Institute*,[32] which was presented for decision to the highest Court in 1948. It involved an order of the FTC directing the cement industry to cease and desist from using its so-called multiple basing point system of pricing. The cement companies contended that the order was invalid because of the alleged bias of the Commission. The charge of bias was based upon copies of the Commission's annual reports made by it to the Congress and the President, as it was required to do under its enabling statute. As Justice Black explains it:

These reports, as well as the testimony given by members of the Commission before congressional committees, makes it clear that long before the filing of this complaint the members of the Commission at that time, or at least some of them, were of the opinion that the operation of the multiple basing point system as they had studied it was the equivalent of a price fixing restraint of trade in violation of the Sherman Act.[33]

The FTC is set up, not only to proceed against individual businessmen guilty of unfair methods of competition, but also to investigate the state of competition in the economy and report its findings. In this case, the Commission had investigated and concluded that the pricing system of the cement industry was unfair. Could the agency at a later stage sit impartially in an adjudicatory capacity, when the cement companies were charged before it specifically with committing an unfair method of competition?

In its decision, the Court rejected the claim of bias on the part of the Commission. According to it, the fact that the Commission had entertained certain views as the result of its prior *ex parte* investigations did not necessarily mean that the minds of its members were irrevocably closed on the subject. The companies were legally authorized participants in the hearings, and were free to rebut by evidence and arguments the conclusions which the Commission had previously reached. But, once again, the real factor behind the Court's decision seems to have been deference to the federal legislator. The cement industry's contention, says the Court, "if sustained, would to a large extent defeat the congressional purposes which prompted passage of the Trade Commission Act." [34] The Congress had expressly provided that the FTC should both investigate and report to it and the President and decide cases involving specific charges of unfair methods of competition. Just as in the case where the Congress provides for a concentration of the functions of prosecutor and judge in an agency like the FTC, the Congressional will here must be respected, despite the possibility of some unfairness to the private litigant.

Morgan Cases

Nothing better illustrates the difference in approach to the administrative agency as between the pre-1937 Supreme Court and that tribunal since that time than the celebrated *Morgan* cases. Those cases, which arose out of the fixing by the Secretary of Agriculture of the maximum rates to be charged by market agencies for buying and selling livestock at the Kansas City stockyards, were before the Court in 1936, 1938, 1939, and 1941. They are perhaps the most famous among the administrative law decisions of the high bench and dealt with what many see to be, next to the concentration of functions, the key problem of the administrative agency— that of what is usually called the "institutional" decision, i.e., the decision of cases by an agency as an administrative entity rather than the personal decision by a known individual administrator.

Wordsworth begins a well-known poem with the words, "Oh, what's the matter? what's the matter?" A prosaic question like that is not always easy to answer. Nor is it easy to express in a simple sentence, for the information of the average rider of the metropolitan subways, the precise nature of the problem of the institutional administrative decision. The problem is one which arises out of the very nature of the process of administrative hearing and decision that has become common in this country. As already mentioned, powers of decision affecting private rights and obligations have been vested by the Congress in the different administrative agencies in the Federal Government. The administrative decisions must, at the same time, normally be preceded by notice and hearing, to give those affected an opportunity to present their side of the case. So much, at least, is demanded by procedural due process. For, as Justice Douglas has recently reminded us, "Notice and opportunity to be heard are fundamental to due process of law." [35]

For practical reasons, it has been impossible for the heads of the different agencies personally to hear and decide all the cases before their agencies. The great volume of administrative adjudication makes such personal hearing and decision on the part of the agency heads all but impossible. The validity of this comment is clear to anyone who is at all familiar with the facts of modern administrative life. A large federal agency like the National Labor Relations Board decides more cases each year than all the federal courts of appeals combined; obviously the Board members cannot give to each case the individual attention that is customary on the part of the federal judges. Since the workload of the agency heads has normally made it impossible for them personally to perform all the duties imposed upon the agencies by law, they have had to resort extensively to the device of delegation. The result has been that, instead of the personal hearing and decision that is familiar in the judicial process, the administrative process has been characterized by what may be termed a vicarious type of hearing and decision.

An institutional decision of an administrative agency is a decision made by an organization and not by an individual nor solely by agency heads. A trial judge's decision is personal; the judge hears evidence and argument and decides. In the administrative process, evidence may be taken before an examiner, other subordinates may sift the evidence, various specialists on the agency's staff may contribute to the writing of proposed and final reports, and the agency heads may in fact lean so heavily on the work of the staff as to know next to nothing about the problems involved in many of the cases decided in the agency's name.[36] The customary modes of internal procedure which the agencies have developed have thus been along the lines of making their decisions institutional ones— made by the agency as a whole, with the work being done almost entirely by anonymous members of the agency's staff—rather than the personal decisions of the agency heads in whose names they are rendered.

It may well be that the development of this type of institutional procedure was essential if federal administration was not to come to a virtual standstill. At the same time, the institutional decision does raise a fundamental question on the part of those subject to administrative adjudicatory authority. This is the question of whether the resolution of their cases by institutional decisions does really give them the full and fair hearing and decision to which they are entitled.

The institutional decision of an agency exercising adjudicatory authority is, from the point of view of those affected, just as unsatisfactory as that type of decision would be if rendered by a court exercising similar power. The great objection to a purely institutional decision is that nobody knows exactly how it is arrived at. One can take the procedure in the *Morgan* cases as an example. The private individuals there were, it must be conceded, granted a hearing before an examiner and oral argument before the Assistant Secretary of Agriculture. But the decision took place in the recesses of the Department of Agriculture and the private parties heard no more of the case until they were served with the agency order. The order was signed by the Secretary of Agriculture, but we know from the *Morgan* cases that the decision was his only in a formal sense. It is impossible to say who made the actual decision—what official in the Department really directed his mind to the evidence and arguments and drew therefrom the final conclusions adopted by the Secretary. The examiner probably discussed the case with his superior, and the latter discussed it with a bigger flea, and so ad infinitum. Ultimately the order got the seal of the Secretary.

As the conduct of an administrative hearing becomes divorced from responsibility for decision two undesirable consequences ensue. The hearing itself degenerates, and the decision becomes anonymous.[37] The decision of his case by a known tribunal before whom one can state his case and meet the contentions of his opponents is vital to the fostering of a belief that justice is being done. One must satisfy that requirement of the individual who comes before an administrative agency, that feeling that he wants to talk to the man who is going to decide his case. The decision by a vast departmental anonymity falls far short of satisfying that feeling. Nowhere is this thought better expressed than in the following comment of Dean Acheson, himself certainly anything but an inexorable opponent of administration:

The agency is one great obscure organization with which the citizen has to deal. It is absolutely amorphous. He pokes it in one place and it comes out another. No one seems to have specific authority. There is someone called the commission, the authority; a metaphysical omniscient brooding thing which sort of floats around the air and is not a human being. That is what is baffling. . . . There is no [sic] idea that Mr. A heard the case and then it goes into this great building and mills around and comes out with a commissioner's name on it but what happens in between is a mystery. That is what bothers people.[38]

In the first of the *Morgan* cases, decided in 1936,[39] the Supreme Court sought to strike a death blow against the type of administrative practice of which Mr. Acheson complains. The federal agencies had, we have seen, developed the practice of the institutional decision; the Court in *Morgan I* held that the responsibility of decision was vested in the agency head and this was a personal duty that could not be delegated to others. The *Morgan* cases arose out of actions to restrain the enforcement by the Secretary of Agriculture of the rates he had fixed for the Kansas City stockyards. There had, as has been noted, been a hearing before an examiner and oral argument. The plaintiffs alleged, however, that the order was not actually the personal decision of the Secretary in whose name it had been rendered. Their claim was that, although the challenged order had ostensibly been made by the Secretary of Agriculture, the actual deciding function was performed by someone else in the Department, whose decision had been rubber-stamped by the Secretary. The Supreme Court held that, if this allegation was true, the plaintiffs had been denied the "full hearing" to which they were entitled. Chief Justice Hughes declared:

The requirement of a "full hearing" has obvious reference to the tradition of judicial proceedings in which evidence is received and weighed by the trier of the facts. . . . The "hearing" is the hearing of evidence and argument. If the one who determines the facts which underlie the order has not considered evidence or argument, it is manifest that the hearing has not been given.[40]

Striking at the very heart of the institutional process of decision, the Chief Justice went on to assert that the power and duty of decision are vested in the Secretary of Agriculture himself and not in the agency as an institutional entity: "There is thus no basis for the contention that the authority conferred by § 310 of the Packers and Stockyards Act is given to the Department of Agriculture, as a department in the administrative sense, so that one official may examine evidence, and another official who has not considered the evidence may make the findings and order."[41] Since the duty of decision is that of the Secretary alone, he must have addressed himself to the evidence and himself have conscientiously reached the conclusions which he deemed it to justify: "That duty cannot be performed by one who has not considered evidence or argument. It is not an impersonal obligation. It is a duty akin to that of a judge."[42]

In its first *Morgan* decision, the highest tribunal held that a purely institutional administrative decision did not square with the demands of fair play. Somewhere along the line, asserted the Court, the agency head, in whose name the decision is rendered,

must personally address *his* mind to the evidence and argument
and make the decision which *he* deems them to justify. The final
decision itself must be the personal product of the agency head; his
own judgment must determine that it should be rendered.

Now this is precisely the kind of judicial interference with administrative procedure that the post-1937 Supreme Court has considered wholly inappropriate. Wedded as that tribunal has been
to the doctrine of deference to the Congressional will, it is hardly
surprising that it has sought to respect the autonomy of the administrative agents to whom the legislature has entrusted the detailed
execution of its regulatory policies. The Constitution, said the
Court in 1949, has left wide discretion to the Congress in creating
the procedures to be followed in administrative proceedings.[43]
The Court before 1937 looked upon the rise of the modern administrative process with essentially mistrustful eyes, being fully aware
that the movement toward administrative justice was, in many ways,
a trend toward the limitation of the adjudicatory authority of the
courts themselves. But the high tribunal has in the past two decades looked with far more sympathy upon the legislative intent to
have a host of controversies as to private rights resolved by means
other than the judicial process. In 1936, Justice Sutherland, speaking for the Court, likened an important administrative agency to
the Star Chamber of the Stuarts.[44] In 1939, when the *Morgan* controversy came up again to the Supreme Court, Justice Stone, in delivering that tribunal's opinion, completely repudiated the hostile
attitude expressed in such sanguinary simile.[45] Court and agency,
said he, are to be regarded as collaborators, not competitors; both
are the means adopted by our law to attain the ends of justice:
"Neither body should repeat in this day the mistake made by the
courts of law when equity was struggling for recognition as an
ameliorating system of justice; neither can rightly be regarded by
the other as an alien intruder, to be tolerated if must be, but never
to be encouraged or aided by the other in the attainment of the
common aim."[46]

To a Court which, in Justice Frankfurter's phrase, feels "that although the administrative process has had a different development
and pursues somewhat different ways from those of courts, they are
to be deemed collaborative instrumentalities of justice and the appropriate independence of each should be respected by the other,"[47]
it has been clear that its predecessor's striking down of the process
of institutional decision in the first *Morgan* case constituted an unwarranted interference with the autonomy of the administrative
process. It is true that the post-1937 Court has not directly over-

ruled the holding of that case. But its decision in the so-called fourth *Morgan* case [48] in 1941, which finally disposed of the *Morgan* controversy, all but eliminated the holding of *Morgan I* as an enforceable principle of our administrative law.

In its first *Morgan* decision, the 1936 Court had, we have seen, laid down the principle that the head of an administrative agency must himself exercise the responsibility of decision vested in him by the Congress; decisions rendered in his name must be his personal ones, rather than merely those of the agency as an institutional entity. How is a private litigant to prove that the agency head did not give to his case the personal consideration required by the rule of *Morgan I?* It would seem that, since personal consideration is a subjective matter, the only one who really knows whether he did give the required consideration is the agency head himself. It is thus only if the private party is permitted to probe into the mental processes of the agency head that he can learn whether the decision had actually been a personal one.

In the *Morgan* proceeding itself, after the Supreme Court had decided the first case, the trial court allowed the plaintiffs to do just that—to interrogate the Secretary of Agriculture to determine whether he had complied with the personal decision principle of *Morgan I*. He was questioned regarding the process by which he had reached the conclusions of his order, including the manner and extent of his study of the record and his consultation with subordinates. The Secretary's testimony on the part played by himself in the decision process has been well summarized by Chief Justice Hughes:

The bulky record was placed upon his desk and he dipped into it from time to time to get its drift. He decided that probably the essence of the evidence was contained in appellants' briefs. These, together with the transcript of the oral argument, he took home with him and read. He had several conferences with the Solicitor of the Department and with the officials in the Bureau of Animal Industry and discussed the proposed findings. He testified that he considered the evidence before signing the order.[49]

He went on to say that the order "represented my own independent reactions to the findings of the men in the Bureau of Animal Industry." [50]

The picture of Secretary Henry Wallace taking time off from the many cares of his office by dipping into the "light reading" of the *Morgan* record whenever he could get the chance is doubtless an intriguing one. The Supreme Court was, however, saved from the necessity of determining whether his examination of the case—characterized by a circuit judge as "casual and perfunctory in the extreme" [51]—satisfied the requirements of the first *Morgan* decision by holding, in the fourth *Morgan* case in 1941, that this type of interrogation of a deciding official was improper: "The short of the business is that the Secretary should never have been subjected to this examination. . . . Such an examination of a judge would be destructive of judicial responsibility. . . . Just as a judge cannot be subjected to such a scrutiny, . . . so the integrity of the administrative process must be equally respected." [52] What the Supreme Court giveth, it may also take away. By its decision in *Morgan IV*, the Court went far toward rendering practically sterile the principle that had been enunciated in *Morgan I*. As has already been pointed out, the only one who really knows whether *Morgan I* has been followed is the agency head upon whom the personal duty of decision has been imposed. If he cannot be questioned, it may be virtually impossible to prove that there has been a violation by the agency head of his duty of personal decision.

Critique of Morgan

The *Morgan* cases show clearly the inherent weakness of judicial power in the field of administrative law. A court endowed with "the judicial power" granted by Article III of the Constitution is at a serious disadvantage when confronted with a problem like that of the institutional agency decision. It can only approve or annul a specific agency action in a case presented to it. Yet the salient factor about the problem at issue in the *Morgan* cases is that it can be judicially resolved neither by approbation nor censure. What is needed is remedial legislation. And this is beyond the scope of judicial power.

When confronted with the *Morgan* cases, the Supreme Court was obviously aware of the limitations upon its authority just referred to. It knew that it could only affirm or reverse the Secretary of Agriculture's action. What was it to do in these circumstances?

The post-1937 Court has stated categorically that affirmance is the proper posture for a judicial tribunal. In doing so, it has been influenced both by its basic attitude of deference toward the agent of the legislature and by the fear of the undesirable consequences for administration that might ensue from an unduly strict judicial supervision of administrative procedure. In its view, the pre-1937 Court, in a case like *Morgan I,* was overly concerned with molding the administrative process into the judicial pattern. As Justice

Frankfurter put it in 1940, there are vital differentiations between courts and administrative tribunals and, unless they are observed, "courts will stray outside their province and read the laws of Congress through the distorting lenses of inapplicable legal doctrine." [53] In the post-1937 Court's view, such distortion is exactly what its predecessor had been guilty of in its first *Morgan* decision. The fact that decision in the judicial process is customarily a personal one does not necessarily mean that the same must be true of an administrative decision. To require the agency head to make each decision rendered by his agency his personal one would, the Court now feels, impose an intolerable burden upon administration. In fact, in the case of a large agency like the Department of Agriculture, literal application of the *Morgan I* requirement might make effective administration impossible. If the Secretary of Agriculture were to give to each order he signs the personal attention that *Morgan I* demanded, he would have to devote all his time to matters which, important though they may be to the private interests immediately concerned, must be considered rather petty from the viewpoint of a national administrator. The upshot of the Court's post-1937 attitude has been a throwing up of the judicial hands before the problem of the institutional administrative decision. The element of unfairness to the private litigant must be ignored because of the baneful consequences that might otherwise ensue to administration.

It is to indulge in unnecessary patronizing to assume that the members of the pre-1937 Supreme Court were not as fully aware as their successors on the bench have been of the impact upon effective administration which their first *Morgan* decision might have. There were brave men before Agamemnon; and it is ridiculous to believe that a Court composed of judges like Hughes, Brandeis, Cardozo, and Stone was not wholly cognizant of the effect which its decision would have upon the administrative process. But what were the alternatives that presented themselves to these great jurists and their colleagues on the 1936 Court?

The first *Morgan* Court was clearly repelled by an order being issued in the name of an agency head who had no real part in the decision process. To uphold the Secretary of Agriculture would be for it to give the seal of approval of the Nation's highest Court to an agency practice that had many faulty features. To set aside the Secretary's action might very well, by itself, be to impose an impractical burden upon the administrative process, which would render whatever rule the Court laid down unworkable. But it would, at the very least, sharply focus attention upon the problem of the institutional decision, which might, in turn, lead to legislative efforts to resolve the problem. Clearly, this was the preferable alternative and the one which the Court, in fact, chose.

If the 1936 Supreme Court considered the *Morgan* problem in the above light and chose the course it did as the better, though not necessarily the ideal, solution, its decision in *Morgan I* was intended to have primarily an educative effect and to serve ultimately as a stimulus to Congressional action. If that is true, then, as will be seen, the Court's intention has to a great extent been carried out. It may be that, as one writer expresses it,[54] the proposition of *Morgan I* is a statement of an ideal that probably goes beyond what is practicable. But it is precisely because the ideal stated is one which corresponds to the felt human need for personal justice that *Morgan I* has been of more than ephemeral significance. The first *Morgan* decision showed vividly the unsatisfactory situation which prevailed in the administrative process of decision, where neither the one who heard nor the agency head, in whose name the order was formally issued, made the actual decision. And it led directly to a Congressional attempt in 1946 to cure the procedural deficiencies that had developed in the administrative process.

Administrative Procedure Act

It is not too much to say that the Federal Administrative Procedure Act (APA), which was enacted by a unanimous vote of both Houses of the Congress in 1946, had its genesis directly in the first *Morgan* case. Solution of a problem like that of the institutional decision may well be beyond the scope of judicial power. But that does not justify a policy of complete abdication on the part of the Supreme Court. Chief Justice Hughes and his colleagues on the 1936 bench well knew that a decision by the highest Court of the land could focus the attention of the Congress and the legal profession upon the existing unsatisfactory state of administrative procedure. This is precisely what the *Morgan I* decision did accomplish. In many ways, indeed, that decision was the catalyst that made possible the success of the reform movement that ten years later culminated in the APA.

The 1946 act has been described by the Supreme Court as "a new, basic and comprehensive regulation of procedures in many agencies."[55] By its enactment of that statute, the Congress indicated its dissatisfaction with the law of administrative procedure which had come to be applied by the highest Court. It is all very well to assert, as the Court had done after the first *Morgan* case, that the basic need was autonomy in the administration to develop its own procedures. But how could such an attitude of laissez faire toward the administrative process be squared with the widespread conviction that agency power was not sufficiently safeguarded and sometimes was put to arbitrary and biased use? [56] By its passage of the APA, the Congress sought to allay the concern that had developed over administrative procedure and to correct the conditions out of which it arose. The Congress, in enacting the 1946 act, mirrored the mood of discontent which many felt toward the then-existing law of administrative procedure. And, as the Supreme Court aptly stated in 1951,[57] the Congress expressed its mood, not merely by oratory, but by binding legislation.

In our system, nevertheless, reform legislation does not necessarily accomplish its ameliorating purpose by its mere enactment into the statute book. The courts have, all too often, thwarted even a clearly expressed Congressional policy under the guise of constitutional and statutory interpretation. The APA, like other legislation, would lose its practical efficacy if its terms were to be read by the judges in a decimating spirit.

It was feared by some that the Supreme Court would construe the Procedure Act in so restricted a manner that it would lose much of its remedial effect. The present Court's attitude toward the administrative process—which, as has been shown, is one of marked friendliness compared with that of its predecessor—might, it was thought, lead it to view with hostility a statute which interfered with administrative procedural autonomy and to interpret it so as to limit its effect whenever possible. But the Court itself has given a clear indication in its 1950 decision in *Wong Yang Sung v. McGrath* [58] that it does not intend to construe the APA in so restricted a manner.

The specific question at issue in the *Wong Yang Sung* case was one of the applicability of the formal procedural requirements of the 1946 act to specific administrative proceedings. The *Wong Yang Sung* case involved a proceeding to deport an alien. In such cases there is no express statutory requirement of a hearing, and the Government asserted that, in the absence of such statutory requirement, the APA by its own terms did not apply, since its provisions apply only in cases "required by statute to be determined . . . after opportunity for agency hearing." The question to be decided came down to one of determining whether the term *statute* in the Procedure Act was to be applied literally, with the result of narrowing the applicability of the act, or whether it could be construed so as to include the concept of due process, so that its procedural safeguards were to be applicable to the case of an alien like Wong Yang Sung, for it had long been recognized that due process required a hearing in deportation cases. The answer to this question depends in large part upon the attitude of the judge toward the act. Is the statute an unwarranted restriction upon the flexibility of the administrative process and as such to be construed as narrowly as possible, or is a broader approach to be preferred?

Prior to the Supreme Court's decision in the *Wong Yang Sung* case, the lower federal courts had almost uniformly refused to hold the provisions of the APA applicable to deportation proceedings. In the *Wong Yang Sung* case, the high Court indicated that the narrow approach is not the way to read remedial legislation such as the Procedure Act. The requirements of the 1946 law had to be followed even though a statute did not specifically require a hearing in a deportation case. The Court thus adopted a very broad approach to the question of the applicability of the APA. Its requirements apply to all administrative hearings demanded by *law* (i.e., by Constitution or statute), and not only to those required by statute, in the literal sense.

Why did a tribunal like the Supreme Court which, we have seen, has indicated so clearly in its post-1937 jurisprudence its respect for the autonomy of the administrative process construe so liberally, and even against the letter of, a law that imposes important procedural requirements and hence drastically restricts administrative autonomy in the procedural field? The answer to this question should not be difficult for those who understand the basic reason for the changed attitude toward the administrative agency that the high Court has shown since 1937. The deference toward the administrator that has characterized the supreme bench is but an aspect of the deference toward the Congress that has been the keystone of the jurisprudential edifice constructed by that tribunal during the past two decades. Self-restraint toward the legislator has impelled the Court to hestitate as well before interfering with the agents chosen by the Congress to ensure the effective administration of its regulatory programs. The inclination toward restraint must, nevertheless, give way in the face of the Congressional will expressed in the APA that the courts were to enforce the remedial provisions of that act. Certainly, as the Court stated in its *Wong Yang Sung* opinion, the basic purpose behind the Procedure Act was to produce a uniform reform throughout the federal administration: "We pursue this no further than to note that any exception we may find to its applicability would tend to defeat this purpose." [59] In the Court's view, once the Congress had spoken, it was its duty, regardless of its personal views of the wisdom or policy of the APA, so to construe the law as to eliminate, so far as its text permits, the practices it condemns. This can be seen clearly from a highly revealing portion of the *Wong Yang Sung* opinion:

The [Administrative Procedure] Act thus represents a long period of study and strife; it settles long-continued and hard-fought contentions, and enacts a formula upon which opposing social and political forces have come to rest. It contains many compromises and generalities and, no doubt, some ambiguities. Experience may reveal defects. But it would be a disservice to our form of government and to the administrative process itself if the courts should fail, so far as the terms of the Act warrant, to give effect to its remedial purposes where the evils it was aimed at appear.[60]

The Administrative Procedure Act clearly marks a turning point in our administrative law. Before it, the Court had, we have seen, indicated that the essential desideratum was the freedom of the administration as the Congressional agent to develop its own modes of procedure. In the APA, the Congress itself rejected this laissez-faire approach to administrative procedure; the courts were now to play an active role in holding the agencies to the demands of the 1946 act. And the high Court, in line with its basic policy of deference toward the legislative will, has shown, in both *Wong Yang Sung* and later cases, that it would construe the Congressional enactment with what it has termed an "attitude of hospitality." [61] Henceforth, the extent to which the Court would give effect to its policy in favor of administrative autonomy would depend upon whether it conflicted with the contrary intent demonstrated by the Congress in its passage of the APA.

Judicial Review: Availability

Deference toward the Congressional will has also dominated the Supreme Court's approach to the question of whether judicial review of administrative action is available in a particular case. A member of the present Court, Justice Frankfurter, has, in fact, carried such deference to its logical extreme and insisted that whether access to the courts is open depends entirely on what the Congress has provided in the matter. In his view, "When judicial review is available and under what circumstances, are questions . . . that depend on the particular Congressional enactment." [62] But this means that, if the particular statute is silent with regard to review, access to the courts will be barred. To Justice Frankfurter, Congressional silence indicates a legislative intent to preclude review.

The trouble with Justice Frankfurter's view is that it makes the administrator the final judge of the validity of his own action in the large number of statutes where the Congress has neglected to make any provision for judicial review. To avoid such a result, the majority of the Court have refused to follow Justice Frankfurter in this matter. "Such a sweeping contention for administrative finality," said the Court in 1949, with reference to the Frankfurter view, "is out of harmony with the general legislative pattern of administrative and judicial relationships." [63] In a number of cases decided in the past decade or so, the Court has held, over Frankfurter dissents, that judicial review was available, even though the relevant statutes contained no provisions expressly authorizing access to the courts. As the Court expressed the rule in a 1946 decision, "the silence of Congress as to judicial review is not necessarily to be construed as a denial of the power of the federal courts to grant relief." [64]

Has not the Court, in rejecting the Frankfurter view that judicial review is available only when it is provided for expressly by the Congress, really acted contrary to its own policy of deference toward the legislative will? The Court has denied this, insisting that the Congressional will is not expressed only by its failure to provide expressly for judicial review in the particular case. The legislative silence must be construed in the light of the basic principle of our law that the administrator must act only within the bounds of the authority delegated to him and of the laws implementing Article III of the Constitution, setting up the federal courts and vesting them with jurisdiction to exercise the "judicial power."

The Supreme Court's answer to the question posed above is best articulated in its opinion in the leading case of *Stark v. Wickard*,[65] decided in 1944. The Secretary of Agriculture, acting under the Agricultural Marketing Agreement Act of 1937, had promulgated an order regulating the marketing of milk in the Greater Boston area. The order provided for fixing minimum prices to be paid to producers, and the prescribed formula authorized a deduction for certain payments to cooperatives. Producers, claiming that promulgation of the deduction provision was beyond the Secretary's statutory power, brought suit in the district court to enjoin him from carrying out the challenged portion of the order. The majority of the Court held that the suit could be maintained, even conceding that there was no direct judicial review granted by this statute for these proceedings. "Here, there is no forum," reads the opinion of Justice Reed, "other than the ordinary courts, to hear this complaint." [66] The silence of Congress is not to be construed as indicating a legislative intent to preclude review:

When Congress passes an Act empowering administrative agencies to carry on governmental activities, the power of those agencies is circumscribed by the authority granted. This permits the courts to participate in law enforcement entrusted to administrative bodies only to the extent necessary to protect justiciable individual rights against administrative action fairly beyond the granted powers. The responsibility of determining the limits of statutory grants of authority in such instances is a judicial function entrusted to the courts by Congress by the statutes establishing courts and marking their jurisdiction.[67]

Stark v. Wickard, by the way, is an instructive case to one interested in judging which is the better view on this point—that of Justice Frankfurter or that of the Court majority. If the Frankfurter view had prevailed in the *Stark* case, there would have been no review whatsoever of the Secretary of Agriculture's action; such action would, as a practical matter, be rendered final and not reviewable in any court, even though entered arbitrarily, without substantial supporting evidence, and in defiance of law. Such a result was avoided by the Court's *Stark* decision; under it, the milk producers could obtain judicial review of the legality of the Secretary's deductions for cooperatives from the amounts to be paid to them. And, according to a later decision of the Supreme Court,[68] the Secretary's deductions were actually not authorized by the relevant statute. Had the Frankfurter view prevailed on the question of the availability of review, the producers would have been remediless before an illegal administrative order which mulcted them of part of the milk prices to which they were entitled under the law.

The Supreme Court has in recent years gone even further than the *Stark v. Wickard* approach and upheld the availability of judicial review despite the existence of statutory provisions that appeared to indicate an express legislative intent to preclude all access to the courts. In *Estep v. United States,*[69] the Court dealt with a selective service case under a statute which provided that the decisions of the administrative authorities in such cases "shall be final." Despite this apparent provision for administrative conclusiveness, the Court held that the legality of draft board orders could be reviewed by the courts.

Surely, in a case like *Estep,* it will be said, the Court was doing violence to its own rule of respect for the Congressional will, when it held judicial review available in the face of an express statutory declaration that the administrative order should be "final." As

Justice Frankfurter plaintively declared, "One need not italicize 'final' to make final mean final." [70] Yet, even here, one wonders whether the bare provision for administrative finality really expressed a definitive Congressional intent to deprive draft registrants of the right, which they would otherwise clearly possess, to have the legality of administrative action affecting them challenged in the courts. Is it or is it not tolerably certain that the majority in the Congress were not even aware of the provision for finality in the selective service bill when they passed it, and that very few of those who were aware of it realized that it might have the effect of cutting off all access to the courts by those who might be illegally drafted? For the Congress to bar all review by the finality provision was for it to give the administrative agencies concerned a standing invitation to disregard the requirements of the act and to exceed the powers intended to be conferred on them. If the finality clause was intended to be taken literally, the Congress was really stultifying itself because, having inserted express provisions in the law for the protection of selectees, it then, by means of the finality clause, rendered such provisions nugatory.

One must, therefore, reject the view that the Congress really intended the provision for finality of the administrative order to have the effect of precluding all access to the courts. This is what the Court did in its *Estep* opinion. "It is only orders 'within their respective jurisdictions' that are made final," Justice Douglas asserted,[71] and the jurisdictional question is a judicial question. To hold otherwise would be to impute an intent to the legislature to depart drastically from our normal tradition of judicial control of legality, in a case where the legislative intent has not been expressed unequivocally: "We cannot readily infer that Congress departed so far from the traditional concepts of a fair trial when it made the actions of the local boards 'final.'" [72]

The correctness of the *Estep* approach has become even clearer with the enactment of the Administrative Procedure Act of 1946. For, in that statute, which, we have seen, was intended to work a general reform of the administrative process, the Congress expressly stated its intent to have all agency action subject to judicial review. "Any person suffering legal wrong because of any agency action," reads section 10 of the APA, "or adversely affected or aggrieved by such action within the meaning of any relevant statute, shall be entitled to judicial review thereof." The Congressional intent here expressed to have review available on the widest possible basis lends emphasis to the soundness of the *Estep* holding. This, at any rate, was the view expressed by the highest Court in a 1955 decision holding that judicial review under the APA was available to question the legality of a deportation order, despite a provision in the Immigration Act that such order should be "final." According to the Court's opinion, "It is more in harmony with the generous review provisions of the Administrative Procedure Act to construe the ambiguous word 'final' in the 1952 Immigration Act as referring to finality in administrative procedure rather than as cutting off the right of judicial review in whole or in part." [73] It is significant that even Justice Frankfurter, stalwart apostle though he has been of yielding to the Congress on the availability of judicial review, did not disagree with the Court's approach here.

Whether or not one agrees that the decisions on the availability of review just discussed are really consistent with the Supreme Court's own doctrine of deference to the legislator, few believers in the Anglo-American conception of the rule of law will disagree with the results reached in these cases. An administrative agency in our system is not an autocrat free to act as it pleases, but is an inferior tribunal subject to the restraining jurisdiction which our courts have exercised for centuries over such tribunals. The need for judicial control to be made available in all cases has been emphasized in strong language by a federal court: "If the judiciary has no power in such matter, the only practical restraint would be the self-restraint of the executive branch. Such a result is foreign to our concept of the division of the powers of government." [74] As the same principle was pithily phrased by Napoleon Bonaparte: "I do not see how there could be property owners in France if a man could be irrevocably deprived of his land by a mere administrative decision."

Standing

The fact that the Supreme Court has indicated that it will give effect to the Congressional will expressed in the Administrative Procedure Act and to the inarticulate major premises of our system (voiced at least in part in statutes) in favor of the availability of judicial review does not, by any means, signify that the Court has abandoned its attitude of friendliness toward administrative agencies, nor that it has repudiated its view that the judiciary should not unduly interfere with these Congressional agents, unless the Congress has clearly opted in favor of such interference.

The basic attitude of the Court, absent a clear indication of Congressional intent to the contrary, can be seen from its decisions on so-called "standing" to seek judicial review. It is a basic principle of our administrative law that a person seeking review must have a direct personal interest in the administrative act which he challenges before his review action will be entertained. "A petitioner does not have standing to sue," as Justice Frankfurter has expressed it, "unless he is 'interested in and affected adversely by the decision' of which he seeks review. His 'interest must be of a personal and not of an official nature.' " [75]

It is, of course, clear that a person who is directly affected in his economic interest by the administrative decision which he challenges has the required standing, and this has been recognized in the recent jurisprudence of the Supreme Court. Thus, in a 1956 decision,[76] the Court expressly rejected the claim that a broadcasting company did not have standing to obtain review of a Federal Communications Commission order which restricted the number of stations in which such companies could have an interest. The order, said the Court, directly affected the petitioning company in its business affairs. In previous decisions, the Court had recognized the economic interest of a competitor as sufficient to vest him with standing.[77]

These cases involving economic interest are not, however, such as to cause any real difficulty. It would be wholly fanciful to hold that one suffering direct injury in his pocketbook is not sufficiently aggrieved to be able to seek judicial review. Yet, to concede this much does not answer the question of how direct the adverse effect must be, and this is the question that has caused the Court hardship. In point here are the cases involving the standing of consumers. In *City of Atlanta v. Ickes*,[78] decided in 1939, the Court held squarely that a consumer had no standing to challenge the legality of an administrative order fixing the price of a product which he used. The economic interest of a consumer was felt to be too remote to permit him to challenge the price-fixing order. In addition, the Court has stated that, in such cases, there are only two necessary parties, the administrative agency and the companies being regulated; the agency must be relied upon to represent the consuming public.

These justifications for the Court's *Atlanta* holding do not really support it. If the interest of a competitor is sufficient to allow him to bring a review action, why is the same not true of a consumer? If the price he has to pay each time he purchases the product or service is increased by administrative order, is it not to deal in abstract legal learning rather than the realities of the case to hold that he does not have a direct personal interest in getting the order reviewed? The proposition that the administrative agency adequately represents the consuming public is often, at the best, a pious fiction.

What has actually led the Court, in *Atlanta* and other decisions, to adopt a restrictive approach to standing is, not these factitious reasons, but the Court's reluctance to countenance what it conceives as undue judicial interferences with administrative autonomy. To permit review by anyone, regardless of whether his personal interest is unique in himself or only an interest common to a large group such as the consuming public, the Court has feared, might be to open the floodgates of administrative-law litigation. Justice Frankfurter aptly expressed this risk in a case involving the radio broadcast industry: "So much by way of limitation seems necessary to prevent . . . mass appeals by the industry at large, with resulting hopeless clogging of the administrative process by judicial review." [79]

One wonders whether this fear, which seems to underlie the Supreme Court decisions, is not more theoretical than real. To assume that the courts will be flooded with countless cases if judicial review is made more freely available is to make an unwarranted assumption. Widespread availability of review will not inevitably lead to a plethora of cases. A review proceeding is expensive and time-consuming; it will rarely be resorted to for its own sake or merely to subject the administration to needless harassment by people who have no real interest in the administrative action they are seeking to have reviewed. As a late Lord Chief Justice of England well tells us:

Nobody outside Bedlam supposes that the reason why Courts of law exist in a civilized community is that the founders of the State have believed happiness to consist in the greatest possible amount of litigation. The real triumph of Courts of law is when the universal knowledge of their existence, and universal faith in their justice, reduce to a minimum the number of those who are willing so to behave as to expose themselves to their jurisdiction. . . . The knowledge that the machinery exists, and that when it is employed it is employed with skill and without favour, has the effect of rendering its employment unnecessary save only in the exceptional case.[80]

Not one of the Supreme Court cases adopting a restrictive approach to standing was decided after the enactment of the Administrative Procedure Act in 1946. It is to be hoped that that statute will induce the Court to modify its rigid attitude, in view of the APA's manifestation of a Congressional will to make access to the courts available on the widest possible basis. In a 1956 dissent, Justice Frankfurter, referring to the law of standing, stated, "To the laity such matters may seem technicalities in a derogatory sense of the term." [81] It may surprise the learned judge to discover that such feeling with regard to the Court's jurisprudence is not confined to men technically ignorant in the mysteries of the law. Competent jurists, too, hold the view that the high tribunal has been overly influenced by technical niceties in its handling of the question of standing. The Court, in holding that someone like a consumer has no standing, has lost sight of the overriding need in our system—to make sure that someone shall, in fact, be able to secure review of administrative action. It is only if this need is satisfied that the principle of administrative subordination to law can truly be enforced. It is in the interest of the community as a whole that illegal agency action should not be left untouched. It is for the judiciary to vindicate this interest by ensuring that there are no unnecessary obstacles in the path of those seeking to challenge the legality of administrative action. To construe the standing requirement as the high Court has sometimes done is to place an unnecessary obstruction on the road of justice.

Judicial Review: Scope

After the court before whom an action is brought to review the legality of an administrative act determines that review is available in the given case, it must then determine the merits of the arguments advanced against the challenged act. We must now measure the scope of the judicial inquiry that the Supreme Court has permitted into the merits.

It is hardly surprising that the Supreme Court had, prior to the Administrative Procedure Act, articulated a very narrow theory of the proper scope of review. In the first administrative-law opinion which he delivered, Justice Frankfurter declared: "Even when resort to courts can be had to review a Commission's order, the range of issues open to review is narrow. Only questions affecting constitutional power, statutory authority and the basic prerequisites of proof can be raised. If these legal tests are satisfied, the Commission's order becomes incontestable." [82]

In its general outlines, the post-1937 Court has applied the theory of review that had been developed by its predecessors, though, as befits a tribunal committed so strongly to upholding administrative autonomy, in a narrower form. That theory, first enunciated in the cases involving review of orders of the Interstate Commerce Commission (the pioneer modern federal agency), has been based almost entirely upon the distinction between questions

of *law* and questions of *fact*. As to the latter, the primary responsibility of decision is with the administrative expert. It is only the
former that are to be decided judicially. As the Court stated in
1943:

If the action rests upon an administrative determination—an exercise of
judgment in an area which Congress has entrusted to the agency—of
course it must not be set aside because the reviewing court might have
made a different determination were it empowered to do so. But if the
action is based upon a determination of law as to which the reviewing
authority of the courts does come into play, an order may not stand if
the agency has misconceived the law.[83]

From a historical point of view, the use of the law-fact distinction in the field of review of administrative action was a wholly
natural development. When the highest Court came to be confronted with cases involving challenges to the legality of agency
acts, it had at its disposition the fully developed law of appellate
review of lower courts as well as that governing the respective roles
of judge and jury—both of which were grounded entirely on the
law-fact distinction. In evolving the law of agency review, it was
not surprising that our judges proceeded, so far as possible, by
analogy with the principles that had been constructed so meticu-
lously by their predecessors in the fields above mentioned, and
particularly that of appellate court review.

The law-fact distinction, whose penetration into the law of review of administrative action can thus be explained historically,
may also be said to have a significant practical basis in the field of
administrative law. A theory of review grounded upon the distinction rests upon a division of labor between judge and administrator,
giving full play to the particular competence of each. Questions of
law are to be decided judicially; for the judge, both by training and
tradition, is best equipped to deal with them. Our desire to have
courts determine questions of law is related to a belief in their possession of expertness with regard to such questions.[84] These considerations do not apply to the judicial review of the factual issues
arising out of administrative determinations. There, the advantages
of *expertise* are with the administrator.

This division of labor is not, however, inexorably carried out, for
constitutional principles require some judicial review upon fact as
well as law. An approach to the problem of judicial review cannot
neglect the fact that its essence springs from the Anglo-American
conception of the rule of law. That concept calls for a judicial examination of the administrative determination to see that it has an

evidentiary basis. An administrative finding of fact that is not supported by evidence cannot be said to have been within the jurisdiction conferred upon the agency. Or, to put it another way, the
question whether the administrative finding of fact rests on evidence
is really a question of law, for a finding not so supported is arbitrary,
capricious, and obviously unauthorized.[85]

How far should the courts review administrative findings of
fact? The pre-1937 Supreme Court had developed the rule that
judicial review of facts is limited to the question of whether the administrative findings of fact are supported by "substantial evidence."
Where the challenged finding is one of fact, the court cannot substitute its judgment for that of the administrator. It is not for the
reviewing court to determine, upon its own independent judgment,
the correctness of the administrative factual determination. The
court has only to see if the finding is supported by substantial evidence; it is not concerned with the weight of the evidence: "In
such cases, the judicial inquiry into the facts goes no further than to
ascertain whether there is evidence to support the findings, and the
question of the weight of the evidence in determining issues of fact
lies with the legislative agency acting within its statutory authority." [86]

It is in its interpretation of the question of the amount of evidence deemed "substantial," and, hence, sufficient to support an
administrative finding of fact, that the post-1937 Court has differed
from its predecessor. In the old Court's view, substantial evidence
had to be more than a mere scintilla; evidence could not be substantial unless it persuaded a reasonable mind that it was adequate
to support the factual conclusion. To the Court after 1937, this
test (which was essentially one of the rational basis of administrative findings) permitted too broad a review. As one of the members
of the Court who was responsible for adoption of the post-1937 approach has himself recently told us, the new Court slowly relaxed
the requirement of substantial evidence "so that some evidence to
support the findings was sometimes substituted for substantial evidence." [87] Under the new theory of scope of review, the reviewing
court was, in effect, to look only to see if there was *some* evidence
supporting the agency; if such evidence was found, the administrative action had to be sustained and the evidence to the contrary to
be ignored. By 1942, it had become apparent that this approach
had been adopted by the Supreme Court. "If the findings of the
Board are supported by evidence," asserted that tribunal in a decision of that year, "the courts are not free to set them aside, even
though the Board could have drawn different inferences." [88] Where

the Court could not say that "the findings of fact of the Board are without support in the evidence," [89] its findings had to be upheld. As it was expressed by Justice Frankfurter in 1951, with regard to review of the National Labor Relations Board, "It is fair to say that by imperceptible steps regard for the fact-finding function of the Board led to the assumption that the requirements of the Wagner Act were met when the reviewing court could find in the record evidence which, when viewed in isolation, substantiated the Board's findings." [90]

There was understandably much criticism of so contracted a theory of review. A scope of review as narrow as that developed by the high Court, in effect, vested the administrator with the final word as to the facts; and, since, in most cases, it is the facts and not the law that are contested, finality as to facts becomes in reality finality in law. "The power of administrative bodies to make findings of fact that may be treated as conclusive . . ." reads a celebrated statement of Charles Evans Hughes, "is a power of enormous consequence. An unscrupulous administrator might be tempted to say, 'Let me find the facts for the people of my country, and I care little who lays down the general principles.' " [91]

Dissatisfaction with the restricted scope of review developed by the Supreme Court was, without a doubt, one of the factors that led to the reform movement that culminated in the Administrative Procedure Act. By inserting an express direction in section 10(e) of that act to reviewing courts to consider the "whole record" in determining whether administrative findings are supported by substantial evidence, the draftsmen of the 1946 law sought to do away with the pre-APA judicial tendency just discussed. As has been true with the other provisions of the Procedure Act, the Supreme Court has molded its jurisprudence to accord with the Congressional intent expressed in the statute; the Court's desire to leave the field to the administrative expert has yielded in the face of the legislative desire that the judge exercise positive responsibility here. In its 1951 decision in *Universal Camera Corp. v. National Labor Relations Board*,[92] the Court held that the sponsors of the APA meant just what they said in the "whole record" requirement in section 10(e). The Court's opinion on this point reads:

Whether or not it was ever permissible for courts to determine the substantiality of evidence supporting a Labor Board decision merely on the basis of evidence which in and of itself justified it, without taking into account contradictory evidence or evidence from which conflicting inferences could be drawn, the new legislation definitively precludes such a theory of review and bars its practice. The substantiality of evidence must take into account whatever in the record fairly detracts from its weight. This is clearly the significance of the requirement . . . that courts consider the whole record.[93]

What, then, does the substantial-evidence rule mean today under the Administrative Procedure Act? According to one commentator, underlying the word "substantial" is the notion of fairness. The judge must reverse if, as he conscientiously sees it, the administrative finding is not fairly supported by the record; or, to phrase it more sharply, the judge must reverse if he cannot conscientiously escape the conclusion that the finding is unfair.[94]

When, under this view, is an agency finding unfair? It would seem, to the present writer, that unfairness occurs when the finding is not a reasonable one in the light of the evidence in the whole record. Substantial evidence is, hence, such evidence as might lead a reasonable man to make the finding at issue. The evidence in support of a fact finding is substantial when from it an inference of the existence of the fact may be drawn reasonably. As a state court has expressed it, "Choice lies with the Board and its finding is supported by the evidence and is conclusive where others might reasonably make the same choice." [95]

The substantial-evidence rule under the Administrative Procedure Act tests the rationality of administrative findings of fact, taking into account all the evidence on both sides. The APA thus brings us back to the meaning of substantial evidence declared by the old Supreme Court. The substantial-evidence test is once again a test of the *reasonableness*, though not of the *rightness*, of agency findings of fact.

It should be emphasized that the Court in the *Universal Camera* case broadened the scope of review of administrative findings of fact (though not as broadly as some would like) only because it deferred to the Congressional will clearly expressed in the Administrative Procedure Act. Where not compelled to do so by the 1946 law, the Court has consistently adhered to a more narrow theory of review than had been applied by the pre-1937 Court. Thus the present Court has rejected the so-called "jurisdictional-fact" doctrine established by its predecessor in the famous 1932 case of *Crowell v. Benson.*[96] Under that doctrine, as it was enunciated by Chief Justice Hughes, there must be full judicial review of findings upon which administrative judisdiction depends. For example, where, as in *Crowell v. Benson,* the agency concerned was authorized to act only in cases involving employees, the agency finding that an employment relationship did in fact exist was a jurisdictional one and hence subject to full review upon the independent judgment of the reviewing court. The Supreme Court in the past two decades has indicated that it is now wholly out of sympathy with attempts to secure broad review based upon this "jurisdictional-fact" doctrine. In a number of cases, it has stated that such facts must be reviewed no more broadly than ordinary facts. As Justice Frankfurter put it in 1946, the doctrine that jurisdictional facts must be fully reviewed has now "earned a deserved repose." [97]

Even more significant is a change in the post-1937 Court's attitude toward review of administrative interpretations of statutes. To its predecessors on the bench, the question of the proper construction of statutes was of the very essence of a question of law to be finally resolved, in our system, by the judge, not the administrator. In the past two decades, the question of review of statutory interpretation has arisen most frequently in connection with the application of statutory language to particular states of fact. In an important 1941 decision, *Gray v. Powell*,[98] the highest Court held that the application of statutory terms or concepts to particular states of fact was to be treated more like a question of fact than one of law, for the purpose of determining the proper scope of review.

During the decade and a half since 1941, the Court has applied the doctrine of *Gray v. Powell* in a large number of cases and it now appears to be firmly ingrained in that tribunal's jurisprudence. As good a case as any to illustrate this is *National Labor Relations Board v. Hearst Publications*,[99] a 1944 case, where the Board's determination that certain newsboys were its "employees" was challenged by the employer. According to Justice Roberts, who dissented, "The question who is an employee, so as to make the statute applicable to him, is a question of the meaning of the Act and, therefore, is a judicial and not an administrative question." [100] Hence, it was one to be determined by the reviewing court upon its own independent judgment. To the majority of the Court, the proper scope of review was a more restricted one. Declared Justice Rutledge, who delivered the opinion:

Where the question is one of specific application of a broad statutory term in a proceeding in which the agency administering the statute must determine it initially, the reviewing court's function is limited. . . . the Board's determination that specified persons are "employees" under this Act is to be accepted if it has "warrant in the record" and a reasonable basis in law.[101]

Reasonableness rather than rightness has thus become the test upon review of this type of question.

Gray v. Powell and the *Hearst* case assimilate review of ques-

tions of statutory interpretation to review of questions of fact.
That is a plain statement of their effect, no matter how courts or
commentators may try to obscure their meaning. And it is because
of their effect that these cases are of such great consequence. They
blur the distinction between law and fact upon which the scope of
review in our administrative law had been grounded. They limit
review, not only of agency findings of "fact" in the narrow, literal
sense, but also of agency constructions of statute law. The latter
are matters which, under the traditional theory of Anglo-American
judicial review, are matters more legal than factual in nature and,
consequently, are for the courts to review. By conveniently labeling them matters of application, rather than interpretation, the high
Court has continued to pay lip service to the form of the traditional
theory. But the doctrine of *Gray v. Powell* and *Hearst* tends to
make the practical effectiveness of that theory a thing of the past
in our administrative law.

Deference and Administrative Law

Cases like *Gray v. Powell* and *Hearst* show that, where it is not
compelled to act otherwise by a statute like the Administrative Procedure Act, the present Court still tends to defer to agency *expertise.*
Its basic approach to the technical questions involved in most fields
of administrative regulation remains that of humility stated by Justice Frankfurter in 1942: "We certainly have neither technical competence nor legal authority to pronounce upon the wisdom of the
course taken by the Commission." [102]

The history of American administrative law has been one of the
constant expansion of administrative authority accompanied by a
correlative restriction of judicial power. It cannot be denied that
the past twenty years have seen an accentuation of this development, insofar as the Supreme Court alone has been concerned. The
doctrine against uncanalized delegations of authority to the administration has been all but done away with in the Court's post-1937
decisions. The attempt of its predecessor strictly to control the
process of administrative decision in the first *Morgan* case has been
abandoned as an unwarranted judicial interference with agency
autonomy. The scope of judicial review deemed permissible by
the highest tribunal has been narrowed. Before the Administrative
Procedure Act, review of fact findings had come to be so restricted
as to be almost illusory. And, even since the enactment of the 1946
Act, the area of "law" subject to full review has continued to narrow. Findings involving the application of statutes to particular

states of fact are assimilated to findings of fact, for purposes of review, under cases like *Gray v. Powell* and the *Hearst* case. The doctrine of full review of "jurisdictional facts" has been all but relegated to oblivion.

The balance sheet of the past decade has not, however, been all in favor of the administration. The Administrative Procedure Act gives clear evidence of a Congressional desire to call a halt to the process of administrative expansion. And, significantly enough, the high Court has given every indication that that law will be interpreted in such a way as to give full effect to its remedial intent. The Supreme Court decisions under the APA have been of the greatest consequence. While the present Court is undoubtedly far more friendly toward administrative authority than were its predecessors, it has shown by its APA decisions that it will defer to the legislative desire that it play a more active part in controlling the agencies.

The decisions under the Procedure Act may, indeed, well prove to be the most important rendered by our highest Court in the field of administrative law during the past twenty years. For they indicate at least some judicial concurrence in the widely expressed desire to put an end to the aggrandizement of administrative authority and to re-establish judicial review as a true balance of our governmental system. "Judicial review," Justice Douglas has recently written, "gives time for the sober second thought. . . . The confidence of the citizen in modern government is increased by more, rather than less, judicial review of the administrative process." [103]

Significantly, it is Justices like Douglas and Frankfurter, formerly the most ardent partisans of administrative autonomy, who have been expressing recent doubts about the wisdom of leaving the agencies a law unto themselves. Twenty years ago, it would have been almost unthinkable for one of Justice Douglas' political convictions to call for more, rather than less, judicial review. The administrative process, then, was seen by its proponents as the great hope in our governmental system. Through it they hoped to work a progressive modification of the economy and the society, comparable, at the very least, to the great English Reform Movement of the nineteenth century. Many of them, in fact, went even further and saw in the administration the ultimate supplanter of private industry, which would take over the role of economic leadership in the "public interest." This was the ultimate view that enthralled the extreme New Dealer. This was the horrid specter that terrified the world of private industry.[104]

More recently we have come to see that neither the thrill nor the chill adequately reflected the reality of the administrative process. The irrational hopes and fears of the 1930's have given way to more reasoned attempts to restrain administrative excesses, while, at the same time, recognizing and desiring to retain the essentially good features of administration. Such attempts have sought to confine the exercise of agency authority within proper procedural bounds, to subject such authority to closer judicial control, and have culminated in the Administrative Procedure Act.

The past quarter century has brought about a greater expansion of administrative authority than most people are yet aware of. The need to deal with economic depression, the exigencies of total war, and the insecurities of the postwar period have led to ever-increasing delegations of power to the administration. More and more, the Congress has been delegating to the agencies significant powers of lawmaking. Nor should it be thought that the lawmaking powers thus vested in the administration are powers of slight import. On the contrary, the exercise of rule-making and adjudicatory authority by federal agencies well-nigh dwarfs the direct exercise of legislative and judicial powers by the Congress and the courts. The *Federal Register* (in which administrative rules and regulations are published) vastly exceeds in size the *Statutes at Large* (containing the laws enacted by the Congress); and the values affected by administrative decisions exceed every year many times the dollar value of all money judgments rendered by the federal courts. Well could a distinguished judge characterize administrative law in 1954 as "the outstanding legal development of the twentieth century, reflecting in the law the hegemony of the executive arm of the government." [105]

"In the opinion of this House," reads a famous House of Commons resolution of the time of Charles I, "the power of the Executive has increased, is increasing, and ought to be diminished." There are doubtless many who would like to see a similar resolution moved in contemporary American legislatures. Yet it is not the growth of administrative authority, as such, that constitutes a great danger to our polity. Administrative power, properly controlled, is an essential tool to enable the modern State to perform its multifold tasks. The great danger is the delegation to the administration of uncontrolled discretion—of power which, in Justice Cardozo's famous phrase, [106] is not canalized within banks that keep it from overflowing. "Unless we make the requirements for administrative action strict and demanding," a member of the highest Court who has been anything but noted for his hostility toward the administrative process has asserted, "*expertise,* the strength of modern government, can become a monster which rules with no practical limits on its discretion. Absolute discretion, like corruption, marks the beginning of the end of liberty." [107]

Judicial self-restraint and deference toward the elected representatives of the people do not require the courts to leave everything to the administrative expert. "There is an obvious difference," the Supreme Court pointed out in 1933—a difference that the more recent Court has too often ignored—"between legislative determination and the finding of an administrative official . . . . the legislature acts upon adequate knowledge after full consideration and through members who represent the entire public." [108] The administrator is, it is true, presumed to be an expert in his own particular field of regulation. But this is not always an unmixed blessing. The expert tends all too often to become sterile in his outlook and to make his decisions within the narrow limits of his own restricted experience. To make the expert all-powerful would create an intolerable situation.[109] The limitations of the expert—inability to see beyond the narrow confines of his own experience, intolerance of the layman, and excessive zeal in carrying out his own policy regardless of the cost to other, more vital, interests of society—these must be subjected to the trained scrutiny of the judge who, unhindered by the professional bias of the specialist, is able to take a broader view than that of merely promoting administrative policy in the case at hand without counting the ultimate cost.

Respect for administrative *expertise* must not lead the judge to abdicate his vital function of ensuring that agency authority does not transgress legal limits. Agencies must not, in the recent words of the present Chief Justice,[110] be free to ignore limitations on their authority. Deference toward the administrator cannot, as two dissenting members of the Court urged in 1947, "be invoked to support action outside of the law. And what action is, and what is not, within the law must be determined by courts, when authorized to review, no matter how much deference is due to the agency's fact finding." [111] If the trend toward bureaucratic predominance that has occurred elsewhere in the world is successfully to be resisted in this country, the Supreme Court must not surrender control as the Congress has delegated power. Over-deference to the administrator not only reduces judicial review to a mere feint; it may even do positive harm by giving the illusion of a safeguard that does not really exist. And, in a democracy, nothing is so dangerous as a safeguard that appears to be adequate, but is really a façade.[112]

5

THE COURTS

Before his elevation to the supreme bench, Benjamin N. Cardozo was for many years a distinguished member and chief of New York's highest tribunal. With the perspective gained from judicial service in both Albany and Washington, he could note acutely a basic difference between the highest courts of state and Nation. The New York Court of Appeals, he said, "is a great common law court; its problems are lawyers' problems. But the Supreme Court is occupied chiefly with statutory construction—which no man can make interesting—and with politics." [1] Of course, as Justice Jackson has pointed out, in this statement, the word "politics" is used in no sense of partisanship but in the sense of policy making. [2]

The transition from a state court, eminent though it may be, to the supreme tribunal in Washington is more than mere promotion to a higher judicial body. When Cardozo came to Washington, he left what was, without a doubt, the greatest common-law court in the land; it dealt essentially with the questions of private law that are the preoccupation and delectation of most lawyers. The Court to which he came was not, and has not been, since the time of John Marshall, the usual type of law court. Public, not private, law is the stuff of Supreme Court litigation. Elevation to that tribunal requires the judge to make the adjustment from preoccupation with the restricted, however novel, problems of private litigation to the most exacting demands of judicial statesmanship. It was characteristic of Cardozo's devotion to lawyer's law that, when he left the New York court to ascend the bench in Washington, he wrote, "whether the new field of usefulness is greater, I don't know. Perhaps the larger opportunity was where I have been." [3] One whose mastery of the common law matched his love for it could feel a wrench at being taken from a court where he might fully indulge his talents as a legal craftsman to a Court that was, in many ways, more a political than a purely legal tribunal and one in which the judge must be even more the statesman than the lawyer.

Most observers of the American system would not share the great jurist's dubiety at whether the greater field of usefulness lay in Albany or Washington. Few today refuse to recognize, with Cardozo, that the Supreme Court is more than a law court, in the ordinary sense of that term. Even those to whom the law is the most esoteric of mysteries now know that the highest tribunal makes decisions that are political as much as legal. But this fact would not, to most people, cause the doubt which Justice Cardozo articulated. On the contrary, it is the fact that the Supreme Court is more than the usual law court that makes its work of vital significance to more than a relatively small number of jurists. The Court is primarily a political institution, in whose keeping lies the destiny of a mighty nation. Its decrees mark the boundaries between the great departments of Government; upon its action depend the proper functioning of federalism and the scope to be given to the rights of the individual. A judge on such a tribunal has an opportunity to leave his imprint upon the life of the Nation as no mere master of the common law possibly could. Only a handful of men in all our history have made so manifest a mark on their own age and on ages still to come as did Justice Holmes.[4] The same cannot be said of even the greatest of modern English judges. To be a judge, endowed with all the omnipotence of justice, is certainly among life's noblest callings; but the mere common-law judge, even in a preeminently legal polity like that in Britain, cannot begin to compare in power and prestige with a Justice of our Supreme Court. A judge who is regent over what is done in the legislative and executive branches—the *deus ex machina* who has the final word in the constitutional system—has attained one of the ultimates of human authority.

What makes the work of the Supreme Court of such moment to the people of this country is, not its common-law decisions, but those of a politico-legal nature in the field of constitutional law. It is the judge *qua* statesman who attracts public attention; the judge as lawyer is relegated to the relative obscurity of professional journals. It is, therefore, wholly natural for the present volume to be devoted almost entirely to the highest tribunal as a center of judicial statesmanship, particularly since it is focused on the constitutional revolution of the past twenty years which is the direct product of such statesmanship. At the same time, to understand the workings of the Supreme Court one must never forget, as all too many people do, that it follows the forms of a law court. This affects the work of that tribunal in two important ways. In the first place, it drastically limits the manner in which the Court's role as guardian of the ark of the Constitution may be performed. The high bench does not exercise power that is directly political in form; even its most important policy-making decisions must grow out of the traditional form of the lawsuit. In the second place, it makes it possible for some of the Court's most important functions, even in the constitutional field, to be exercised through its position as an appellate law court, charged in that capacity with ensuring the propriety of what is done in lower courts. In this respect, it should be noted that the Supreme Court is the ultimate appellate authority over two sets of courts, the lower federal courts and the courts of the different states. As we shall see,* the Court's supervisory power is not the same over these two court systems; it is the direct hierarchical superior of the federal courts, but it examines the work of the state courts only to secure against misconstructions of federal law and violations of provisions of the Federal Constitution.

What the Court Does Not Do

Justice Brandeis used to say that what the Supreme Court did not do was often more important than what it did do. The fact that the highest tribunal acts as a law court has been more important than any other factor in determining the things that it does not do in our constitutional system. The Founding Fathers deliberately withheld from the Supreme Court power that was purely political in form, such as a forthright power to veto or revise legislation. Instead, they delegated to the Court "the judicial power" alone, a power which, by the express language of Article III, extends only to the resolution of "Cases" and "Controversies." This, Justice Jackson rightly notes,[5] is the most significant and the least comprehended limitation upon the way in which the high Court can act. Judicial power, the Court pointed out in 1911, "is the right to determine actual controversies arising between adverse litigants, duly instituted in courts of proper jurisdiction." [6] The result of the constitutional restriction is that the Court's only power is to decide lawsuits between opposing litigants with real interests at stake, and its only method of proceeding is by the conventional judicial process. Justice Frankfurter, more than any other member of the Court, has insisted that the need for the limitations upon the Court's power in this respect be observed fastidiously (the "keeper of the Court's jurisdictional conscience," he has been termed[7]), and, as he has explained it, the "Case or Controversy" requirement means,

that a court will not decide a question unless the nature of the action challenged, the kind of injury inflicted, and the relationship between the

* *Infra,* pp. 160-61.

parties are such that judicial determination is consonant with what was, generally speaking, the business of the Colonial courts and the courts of Westminster when the Constitution was framed. The jurisdiction of the federal courts can be invoked only under circumstances which to the expert feel of lawyers constitute a "case or controversy." [8]

Of course, in a system such as ours, where the highest Court plays so prominent a political role, there might be great advantages in knowing at once the legal powers of the Government. It would certainly be convenient for the parties and the public to know promptly whether a particular statute is valid. The desire to secure these advantages led to strong efforts at the Constitutional Convention to associate the Supreme Court as a Council of Revision in the legislative process; but these attempts failed and, ever since, it has been deemed, both by the Court itself and most students of its work, that the disadvantages of such a political role by the judiciary were far greater than its advantages. Similarly, from the beginning of the Republic, the high Court has rejected the notion that it could avoid the difficulties inherent in long-delayed judicial invalidation of legislation by an advisory opinion procedure. The very first Court felt constrained to withhold even from the Father of his Country an advisory opinion on questions regarding which Washington was most anxious to have illumination from the highest tribunal.[9] Ever since that time, it has, in Chief Justice Stone's phrase, been the Court's "considered practice not to decide abstract, hypothetical or contingent questions." [10] A party cannot, in other words, bring an action for what Justice Holmes once called "a mere declaration in the air"; [11] on the contrary, "A case or controversy in the sense of a litigation ripe and right for constitutional adjudication by this Court implies a real contest—an active clash of views, based upon an adequate formulation of issues, so as to bring a challenge to that which Congress has enacted inescapably before the Court." [12]

With the highest tribunal's refusal to render advisory opinions, it is believed, few informed observers will disagree. The great weakness of decision without a true case is that, being rendered *in vacuo*, it is divorced from the real life of actual facts. Advisory opinions are thus bound to move in an unreal atmosphere and to be based upon sterilized and mutilated issues.[13] A body which functions in the form of a law court cannot, by an omnibus answer to an omnibus question, adjudge in advance the rights of all. That is not the way in which a system of case law properly develops. A court deals with the particular instance; and it waits till it arises.[14]

The judicial approach described above is not the product of the post-1937 Supreme Court's handiwork; the "Case" and "Controversy" limitation has, on the contrary, as has been mentioned, had a history from the very first Court and had been extensively developed by the predecessors of those who have sat on the Court during the past two decades. Yet, though the restriction against adjudication in the abstract thus antedated by many years the recent Court, it is that Court that has been more inexorable in applying it than any other. And the reason is not far to find. Abstention in advance of concrete controversy is an indispensable component of the deference to the political departments that has dominated the Court in the last twenty years. For the Court to refuse to adjudicate in the abstract is for it to give the impression that it does not exercise its authority except when it is absolutely imperative for the decision of a case between hostile parties presented to it for decision. Indeed, the rule of self-limitation in this respect has done the post-1937 Court an even greater service. By construing the requirement of an actual case more strictly than had any of its predecessors, the Court has, in recent years, been able to avoid a significant number of the important constitutional issues pressed upon it for decision. This has, to be sure, enabled the Court to carry its doctrine of deference to the other branches to the extreme of a complete hands-off policy toward challenged governmental action. But it has also produced the anomaly in our system of vital constitutional questions left wholly unanswered by the one tribunal competent to resolve them and the spectacle of legislative and executive action (federal and state), tainted though they may be by claims of unconstitutionality, left undisturbed by any possibility of constitutional attack.

The extent to which the high Court in recent years has applied the "Case" or "Controversy" limitation to foreclose access to its bar may be seen from its cases dealing with "standing" to secure review of the constitutionality of governmental acts. We saw, in Chapter 4,* that, before an individual can bring a suit for judicial review of the legality of an administrative act, he must show that he has standing to maintain the review action. The same is true of anyone who seeks to test the constitutionality of a statute or other governmental act. In the settled view of the Supreme Court, there can be no actual "Case" or "Controversy" if the individual bringing the particular action does not have a real personal interest in having the act which he challenges declared unconstitutional. Unless he is adversely affected personally, as an individual, he is seeking only a judgment in the abstract upon the constitutionality of such an

* *Supra,* p. 128.

act. Such a proceeding, we have seen, is not enough to call for the exercise by the Court of its judicial power.

As was true of the administrative-law cases discussed in Chapter 4, the Supreme Court since 1937 has also applied the requirement of standing in cases involving constitutional issues so strictly as, in effect, to overlook the need for ensuring that someone *will* be able actually to challenge the validity of governmental acts. In *Tennessee Power Co. v. Tennessee Valley Authority*,[15] decided by it in 1939, the Court held that private power companies had no standing to challenge the constitutionality of the distribution of electricity by the government-owned TVA, even though such electricity was sold in competition with the companies concerned in areas served by them. According to the Court's opinion, an interest in freedom from competition is not such a legally protected right as will justify a suit. As its doctrine was stated by Justice Frankfurter in a later case,[16] a determination whether the Government is within its powers in distributing electric power may have great financial impact upon a private company, but it has no standing to raise the issue.

Now it is certainly true, as the learned judge states,[17] that the common law does not recognize an interest in freedom from honest competition. Yet this does not, despite his apparent view to the contrary, conclude the issue of standing raised in the *Tennessee Power* case. It is unreal to say plaintiffs in that case had no direct personal interest when, as Justice Frankfurter plainly concedes, the governmental action they were challenging was of such enormous financial consequence to them. Perhaps no one has a right to be free from competition; but does that apply to government competition that is illegal? Justice Frankfurter assumes that the competition against which the power companies complained was "honest," when that was the very question presented to the Court and the question which it was precluded from resolving by its decision on the standing issue. In a system such as ours, based upon judicial enforcement of a written Constitution, it is of the utmost importance that governmental acts should not be placed in a position of practical immunity from constitutional attack. Yet that is what the Court's decision in *Tennessee Power* really did, since the plaintiff companies there were the only parties with sufficient interest to bring suit. It is highly doubtful on the merits, to say the least, that, under the recent cases discussed in Chapter 2,* the Court would hold that a statute authorizing the governmental generation and sale of electric energy is beyond the power of the Congress. All

* *Supra*, pp. 34-46.

the same, under the Court's *Tennessee Power* decision, the constitutional question is one which must remain unanswered, since, without anyone's possessing the requisite standing, the Congressional exercise of authority is placed beyond constitutional inquiry.

Another case which well illustrates the Court's restrictive approach to standing to challenge constitutionality is *United Public Workers v. Mitchell*,[18] a 1947 decision. Plaintiffs there were government employees who sought to challenge the validity of the Hatch Act, which made unlawful certain political activities on the part of federal employees. Except for one of these employees, none had actually violated the act, but they did assert that the law interfered with their desire to engage in the forbidden political activities. The majority of the Court held that, except for the employee who had actually violated the statute being challenged, there was no standing to sue. In the Court's view, for standing to exist in a case like this, the plaintiffs would have had to violate the law's prohibition and run the risk of its penalties. This is, however, to impose too great a burden upon those who are directly affected by the statute. No one would deny that all the plaintiffs here were members of the class subject to the Hatch Act's restrictions or that the act did limit the political activities in which civil servants like the plaintiffs could engage. Why should these men have to violate the statute and lose their jobs in order to test their rights? As a commentator has aptly put it, in this case, the Court's restrictive interpretation is like requiring that somebody actually walk the plank and fall into the water before he can find out whether it was necessary to make the trip at all.[19] There is here no real danger of adjudication in the abstract; all the plaintiffs were concededly subject to the act's restrictions upon their otherwise legitimate activities. It is a blot upon a system of law and procedure if there is no way by which a decision on the legality of a law can be obtained by one subject to its prohibitions, without putting himself in the invidious position of suffering the law's penalty.

The approach of the Supreme Court to the standing question has become so rigid that it has been rejected by most state courts. Thus, the high Court had held as early as 1923 that a federal taxpayer had no standing *qua* taxpayer to challenge the constitutionality of a Congressional enactment.[20] Most states have, on the contrary, permitted such suits by taxpayers. And, until recently, the Supreme Court had upheld the right of the states so to liberalize their standing requirements. In its 1952 decision in *Doremus v. Board of Education*,[21] the Court repudiated this earlier leniency toward state policies on this point. *Doremus* involved an attack upon a New Jersey statute which provided for the reading of certain Old Testament verses at the beginning of each public-school day. Plaintiffs claimed that this law violated the Federal Constitution, alleging the interests of citizens and taxpayers. The Supreme Court held that such interest was not enough to raise the federal question, even though the action had originally been brought in a New Jersey court, and the highest court of that state had allowed such a taxpayer suit. Thus, the Court rejected the view which its predecessors had adhered to and refused to follow the more liberalized approach toward standing adopted by the state for constitutional actions in its courts. Yet, in a case like this, it would seem that the law was in better balance before *Doremus*. If the case is one to enjoin a federal law, the high Court can well follow its own standing rule (rigid though it may doubtless be). At the same time, why should not New Jersey be able to fashion her own rules governing the institution of suits in her courts? If she wants to give taxpayers standing to sue, there is nothing in the Constitution to prevent it. In a case where the clash of interests is as real and as strong as it is over laws such as that involved in the *Doremus* case, it is pure fiction to hold that there is no real case or controversy.

The "Case" or "Controversy" restriction—barring consideration of constitutional issues by the Supreme Court unless they arise in the course of actual litigation between interested adverse parties—is only one of the limitations on the Court's activity in this area. Even in true cases presented to it for decision, not all constitutional issues will be determined by the highest Court. For certain questions have, by their very nature, been considered inappropriate for decision by a tribunal vested only with "the judicial power." These are questions which have been felt to be suitable for final determination by the political branches of government. The Court has kept its hands off them because it has feared the consequences of interfering in matters that are deemed primarily political. As Justice Frankfurter has put it, "Courts ought not to enter this political thicket." [22]

The doctrine of political questions is one which had been developed by the Supreme Court many years before its recent period upon which the present book is focused. In fact, as early as *Marbury v. Madison* in 1803, the Court declared that "Questions in their nature political . . . can never be made in this court." [23] Yet it has been in the highest Court of the past twenty years that the political question doctrine has been pushed to its extreme as a means of enabling the Court to refuse to deal with matters that its predecessors might well have deemed justiciable. In the post-1937 Court, the term "political questions" has all too often been a magical formula to enable that tribunal to be relieved of the necessity of thinking further about a particular problem. As such, it has, of course, fitted in neatly with the Court's basic policy of deference to the elected departments of government, since it has, in practice, had the effect of transferring ultimate responsibility for decision to those departments.

The doctrine of political questions has (ever since its first application there in 1796 [24]) been used most widely in the field of foreign affairs. We have already had occasion to discuss the Court's recent extensions of the rule of nonreviewability in such cases in our analysis of judicial control of Presidential action in Chapter 3.* We saw there that the Court has refused to intervene in cases that had any repercussions on our external relations, even though there was a direct effect on the person or property of individuals in this country. But the Court in recent years has not confined its refusal to take jurisdiction, on the ground that political questions were involved, to cases in the foreign affairs field. On the contrary, its most controversial applications of the political question doctrine have been made in two cases involving what is, perhaps, the most important domestic right of citizenship, namely, the right to vote.

Colegrove v. Green,[25] which came before the high bench in 1946, involved an action by Illinois voters seeking to invalidate that state's law governing the apportionment of its seats in the Federal House of Representatives. The law at issue gave voters in some districts a vote disproportionate to that given voters in other districts; indeed, the population of the election districts in the state (each of which elected one representative) ranged, at the time of the case, from 112,000 to over 900,000. Petitioners—voters in three of the districts which had the largest populations—claimed that the apportionment law denied them the equal protection of the laws guaranteed by the Federal Constitution. Despite the fact that their claim in this respect touched upon such an essential attribute of citizenship as the right to vote, the majority of the Supreme Court dismissed the action on the ground that it involved a political question beyond judicial competence. The remedy for unfairness in districting, said Justice Frankfurter, is in the legislature, not the courts. Nor does it matter that, under petitioners' allegations, the constitutional command of equality was violated: "The Constitution has many commands that are not enforceable by courts because they clearly fall outside the conditions and purposes that circumscribe judicial action." [26]

* *Supra,* pp. 84-86.

The holding in *Colegrove v. Green* was applied in even more extreme circumstances in the 1950 case of *South v. Peters*.[27] It involved an effort by voters to restrain adherence to the so-called county unit system prescribed by Georgia law. Under that system, each county was allowed a number of unit votes, ranging from six, for the most populous, to two, for those which had the smallest populations. The votes of citizens of the most populous county had only a fraction of the weight of those in the other counties. The disproportion here was, in fact, so great that petitioners, voters in Georgia's most populous county, were able to show that in one county a vote would be worth over 120 times each of their votes. To the Court, however, even if more extreme, this was essentially the same case as *Colegrove v. Green*, calling again for dismissal of the action as one involving a nonjusticiable political question.

It would have been one thing for the Court to hold that the Illinois and Georgia distributions of electoral strength among their political subdivisions were not contrary to federal law. Thus, the Court in *Colegrove* could have upheld the Illinois apportionment law on the ground that the Congressional act governing the districting for the election of representatives had no requirement of equality, or near equality, in the population of districts. By so holding, the Court would have been consistent with its policy of deferring to Congressional judgment, where such judgment did not pass the bounds of reason (though it might well be argued here that the inequality in voting was so great as to be an arbitrary violation of constitutional equality). But the Court went much further, removing the question of the legality of the two state election schemes entirely from judicial cognizance. It may be that the Court itself would hesitate before carrying its doctrine to its logical extreme, drawing the line, for example, at a state law which reduced the votes of Catholics or Jews, so that each got only one-tenth of a vote. Yet that, it should be noted, is precisely the effect, according to the record, which the Georgia system has upon the heavy Negro population in the large cities of that state (and, it may be pertinent to note, the record showed that only in such cities were Negroes in Georgia able to vote in important numbers).

The Court was clearly swayed by the fear of becoming unseemly embroiled in politics. "It is hostile to a democratic system," declares Justice Frankfurter's *Colegrove* opinion, "to involve the judiciary in the politics of the people. And it is not less pernicious if such judicial intervention in an essentially political contest be dressed up in the abstract phrases of the law."[28] Strange language from a tribunal that has, from the very nature of its constitutional function, been making political decisions from the very beginning of its history! Strange timidity from a Court that has since become embroiled, *via* its school segregation decisions,* in one of the most significant political issues of our times! In truth, all the Court's decisions protecting the right to vote (which will be discussed in Chapter 7 †) are, in one sense, "political"; voting is, of course, a part of elections and elections are preeminently political in nature. It is, nevertheless, as Justice Holmes once said, "little more than a play upon words" to call a suit by individual voters to enforce their right to vote a political suit and therefore a nonjusticiable one. [29] Such individual voters are seeking to enforce personal rights guaranteed them by the Constitution. It is difficult to see how a policy of deference toward either the Congress or the state legislatures requires the Court to refuse even to hear the claim that so important a constitutional right has been violated. Under the Court's decisions, as a leading critic aptly notes, "out of judicial deference to the action of the two state legislatures, the equal protection clause faded out of the Constitution and with it fundamental rights of citizens of Georgia and Illinois." [30] This is the true effect of these decisions and it can hardly be obscured by the Court's Pilate-like washing of its hands in its jurisdictional doctrine.

Even more important for an understanding of what the Supreme Court does not do than the restrictions upon jurisdiction, imposed by the "Case" or "Controversy" requirement or the doctrine of political questions, is the fact that the Court's jurisdiction is almost entirely discretionary. This means that it is almost exclusively up to the Court itself to determine what cases it will hear and decide. Under the Judiciary Act of 1925, the right to appeal to the Supreme Court as a matter of course was taken away. Instead, the Court itself was made the judge, in the vast majority of cases, of whether or not it would receive an appeal to it. If it feels that the question involved is not one of sufficient importance, or has any other reason for wishing to do so, it may refuse to hear the case.

The reason behind the 1925 Act is not difficult to determine. "The Judiciary Act of 1925," says Justice Frankfurter, "was aimed to extend the Court's control over its business by curtailing its appellate jurisdiction drastically. Relief was given by Congress to enable this Court to discharge its indispensable functions." [31] In a country as large as ours, the right of appeal to the highest tribunal must be restricted, lest the Court be swamped with more cases than it can properly dispose of. If litigants were allowed to appeal to

* *Infra,* pp. 271-73.
† *Infra,* pp. 266-67.

the Supreme Court whenever they desired, the cases would be too numerous for that tribunal to handle expeditiously. The result of such a needless clog on the Court's proper business would be that cases of wide general importance would be unduly delayed in coming to decision, while the Court frittered away its time on cases of slight importance. It is erroneous to think of the supreme bench, even purely as a Court, as merely an ultimate appellate tribunal. Its discretionary power to determine the cases to be heard by it has made it more than the ordinary judicial body, which can be given jurisdiction by the action of the litigants before it. The discretionary authority of the highest Court is based primarily upon public, rather than private, interest. The Court is a tribunal of special resort for the settlement only of such questions as it deems to involve a substantial public concern, rather than the concerns only of private litigants as such.

No one familiar with the workings of the high bench and the evils of the overburdened docket that afflicted it prior to the Judiciary Act of 1925 will dispute the wisdom of the 1925 law. At the same time, it does not take the acumen of one trained in the intricacies of Supreme Court practice to perceive that the discretionary jurisdiction vested in the high Court can be a two-edged sword. True, it enables the Court to dismiss inconsequential matters and concentrate upon cases of consequence; but it also gives that tribunal an easy way out when, for one reason or another, it wishes to be relieved of the necessity of deciding a particular case. Important though the issues in a case may be, and anxious though the country may be to have them resolved, the Court can always dispose of them by the easy, perhaps too easy, expedient of denying certiorari.

The Court since 1937, and more particularly in the last ten years, has made ever increasing use of its power to deny review. The wholesale use of denials of certiorari in the past decade has, in fact, cut down the work-load of the recent Court to a twentieth-century low. Where the Court in Charles Evans Hughes's day used to decide from a hundred and fifty to almost two hundred cases a year with formal opinions, that in the first year of Earl Warren's tenure handed down only sixty-five full-fledged decisions, less than any Supreme Court had done in over a century. The niggardly use by the recent Court of its power to grant review by certiorari has enabled it to avoid decision on many of the most important constitutional problems presented to it. Recent studies [32] have shown how many issues of moment the Court has been able to eschew by simply refusing to hear the cases in which they were presented. These range from important cases in the field of racial discrimination to other, less publicized, though no less legally consequential, matters. Truly, the sparse use by the Court, in the past ten years, of its certiorari power well illustrates the soundness of the previously mentioned statement of Justice Brandeis *—that what the Court does not do may be even more important than what it does do.

A Century of Error?

One of the first victims of the constitutional revolution of 1937 was one Harry Tompkins. In the mid-thirties, he took a walk along the Erie Railroad Company's right of way in Pennsylvania. He was injured by the swinging door of a car on a passing freight train. He then took a trip to law, and there he got hit by a swinging Supreme Court,[33] and his experience well illustrates the way in which changes in jurisprudence by the highest tribunal have direct impact upon parties to litigation.

Tompkins did not bring suit in the courts of Pennsylvania. The railroad had been incorporated in the State of New York; Tompkins, who was a citizen of Pennsylvania, could therefore bring his action in a federal court, since such courts have jurisdiction over cases arising between citizens of different states (and the railroad was, for jurisdictional purposes, treated as a citizen of New York). From Tompkins' point of view, this was most fortunate, for the court decisions in Pennsylvania were highly unfavorable to a trespasser on a railroad right of way. The federal district court in New York in which Tompkins sued, on the other hand, applied a rule much more advantageous to trespassers, and Tompkins was awarded a jury verdict of thirty thousand dollars. When the Circuit Court of Appeals affirmed, Tompkins must have felt reasonably sure of his judgment, particularly since it was based upon an oft-followed 1842 decision of the Supreme Court. He reckoned, however, without that Court itself, for it overruled its century-old precedent and reversed the judgment in Tompkins' favor.

To make possible an understanding of the Court's 1938 decision in *Erie Railroad Co. v. Tompkins*,[34] a word must first be said about the doctrine discarded by that case. That doctrine arose out of a Congressional attempt to answer the question of what law the federal courts should apply in cases before them arising from controversies between citizens of different states. Section 34 of the Judiciary act of 1789 directed that "The *laws* of the several states

* *Supra*, p. 142.

. . . shall be regarded as rules of decision in trials at common law in the courts of the United States in cases where they apply." *
This was a simple rule to apply if there chanced to be an applicable state statute.[35] But what happened if there was no such statute relevant to the case? Did the Congressional command require the federal courts to apply the decisional law of the state courts as well as the statutory laws of the several states?

In its 1842 decision in *Swift v. Tyson*,[36] the Supreme Court answered this query in the negative, holding that the federal courts were not bound by state court decisions, at least insofar as those in the field of commercial law were concerned. Commercial transactions, its opinion asserted, should not be governed by the decisions of purely local tribunals; instead, there was a general commercial law, applied throughout the common law world, which should control in the federal courts. In matters of "general law," such as those governing commercial transactions, the decisions of the state courts were not binding on the federal courts sitting in the state; the federal courts were free to follow the rules of the common law in accordance with their judgment of what those rules were. Quoting Cicero's famous statement that the law is not one thing in Rome and another in Athens, the Court concluded that the same must be true of New York and Boston.[37] The word "laws" in section 34 of the Judiciary Act applied only to statutes and matters of purely local concern (such as the rights and title to real property), not to court decisions on matters of "general law," such as the law governing ordinary commercial transactions. As to such matters, the federal courts were free to apply rules of their own, different though they might be from those which would be applied if the case were tried in a state court.

The opinion in *Swift v. Tyson* was entirely the handiwork of Joseph Story, perhaps the greatest scholar who ever sat on the highest Court and certainly one of the most respected Justices in its history. After the Court had adhered to Story's doctrine for the better part of a century, the legal profession might have been pardoned for assuming that it was fully settled in federal jurisprudence. (Even counsel for the Erie Railroad, we shall see, did not have the temerity to question the doctrine of *Swift v. Tyson*.) Nor was the seeming finality of that doctrine affected by the fact that it was attended by serious inconveniences. Under *Swift v. Tyson*, the federal courts fashioned their own "federal common law" which they would apply in matters of "general law." This concept of a "federal common law," which Justice Story had held should govern in

* Author's italics.

commercial transactions, was extended by later Courts so as to cover most nonstatutory aspects of the law, including the field of torts which was to be involved in Harry Tompkins' case. But, since the state courts continued to follow their own rules of decision, even when they were contrary to the "federal common law," the result in many instances was the existence of two conflicting rules of law in the same state, with the outcome of suits dependent upon whether they were brought in the state or federal courts. *Swift v. Tyson* made the rights enjoyed under the general common law vary according to whether enforcement was sought in the state or federal courts. "This dual system," to quote from a recent discussion by Justice Jackson, "for application of state laws was bound to produce conflicts, for if a litigant could get his case into a federal court, it might be decided by a more favorable rule than that of the state court. There was much shopping for favorable forums, and no doubt there were serious abuses." [38]

If these abuses were all that *Swift v. Tyson* had produced, its doctrine would hardly have lasted ninety-six years. There is actually no easy answer to the problem at issue in *Swift v. Tyson;* the mere overruling of that case by *Erie Railroad Co. v. Tompkins* has, we shall see, by no means settled that problem. Section 34 of the Judiciary Act of 1789 placed before the Supreme Court a dilemma and it has since, as the learned judge just quoted neatly characterized it before his appointment to the Court,[39] shifted from horn to horn, finding either position very uncomfortable. For the federal courts to apply their own rules would lead to the difficulties, already mentioned, arising from conflicting rules in the state and federal courts. On the other hand, for the Supreme Court to be bound by the decisions of the state courts would be for it to declare one rule of law one day and another the next, depending on the state whose laws were applicable. This would wholly defeat the dream of a uniform system of common law, a dream which has moved men ever since the days of the Roman republic. No matter which view the highest tribunal might adopt, it could not escape from the quandary inherent in section 34 of the Judiciary Act: if the federal courts were to be uniform among themselves, they must be at variance with some of the states; if they were to try to be uniform with the state in which they sat, they would then be at variance among themselves.

With no sure way out of the dilemma, one would have thought the balance was in favor of adhering to the hundred-year-old precedent, despite the difficulties arising from it. And, in fact, the Court in *Erie Railroad Co. v. Tompkins* did state expressly: "If only a question of statutory construction were involved, we should not be prepared to abandon a doctrine so widely applied throughout nearly a century." [40] According to the Court, however, more than mere interpretation of the Judiciary Act was involved. In its view, the Constitution itself had been misconstrued in *Swift v. Tyson*. For the 1842 Court to interpret the Judiciary Act as it had was for it to invade rights reserved to the states. According to the *Erie Railroad* opinion:

Except in matters governed by the Federal Constitution or by Acts of Congress, the law to be applied in any case is the law of the State. . . . There is no federal general common law. Congress has no power to declare substantive rules of common law applicable in a State whether they be local in their nature or "general," be they commercial law or a part of the law of torts. And no clause in the Constitution purports to confer such a power upon the federal courts.[41]

The Court's decision in *Erie Railroad Co. v. Tompkins* overruling *Swift v. Tyson* is remarkable in a number of ways.[42] It reversed a century-old precedent, which counsel before it had not even questioned. The Erie Railroad declared expressly: "We do not question the finality of the holding of this Court in *Swift v. Tyson*." [43] Despite this, the Court's opinion opens with the statement that "The question for decision is whether the oft-challenged doctrine of *Swift v. Tyson* shall now be disapproved." [44] The *Erie* decision is truly, as Justice Jackson termed it,[45] a volunteered confession by the high bench of a century of error. Even more striking, perhaps, is the fact that the *Erie Railroad* opinion, for the first and only time in our constitutional history, held action of the Supreme Court itself to have been unconstitutional. In doing so, the Court in effect declared one of the greatest of American jurists, Justice Story, and his successors in all the federal courts for ninety-six years to be guilty of a usurpation of power wholly unwarranted by the Constitution. This is a most startling conclusion, especially when one recalls that the *Swift v. Tyson* Court was only interpreting a Congressional law which prescribed rules of decision for the federal courts, as the federal legislature appears to have the perfect right to do. Well might a contemporary comment on the *Erie Railroad* case assert that "Harry Tompkins probably thinks courts as unpredictable as car doors." [46]

What was it that led the 1938 Court to a decision that seems such an aberration, even for a tribunal that has not been noted in recent years for conformity to pre-existing canons of judicial action? Two main reasons are given in the Court's opinion. In the first

place, an article published by Charles Warren had convinced the
Court that *Swift v. Tyson* had misinterpreted section 34 of the 1789
Judiciary Act, at least insofar as the intent of its draftsmen was concerned.[47] That may well be true; but the Judiciary Act in 1938 is
not necessarily only what its words meant to its Framers in 1789.
The gloss of a century of interpretation is not to be blithely disregarded only because of a scholarly suggestion that it was probably
erroneous. By 1938, *Swift v. Tyson* was at least as much a part of
the Judiciary Act as the words of which that act was originally
composed. Even more important was the belief of the 1938 Court
that the doctrine of *Swift v. Tyson* had revealed "defects, political
and social"[48] so great as to call for its repudiation. These defects
have already been mentioned. To the *Erie Railroad* Court, it was,
in Chief Justice Hughes's language in 1940, "inadmissible that
there should be one rule of law for litigants in the state courts and
another rule for litigants who bring the same question before the
federal courts owing to the circumstance of diversity of citizenship."[49]

If it was the defects which experience had revealed in *Swift v.
Tyson* that led to its overruling, one may logically ask whether the
situation in this respect has actually been improved under *Erie
Railroad Co. v. Tompkins.* Just before his death in 1954, Justice
Jackson asserted that *Erie Railroad* "did not end the confusion, the
conflict or the shopping for forums."[50] If anything, the confusion
and conflict are even more inevitable today when the Supreme
Court has pushed the *Erie Railroad* decision to its logical extreme.
The Court's 1938 decision repudiated the *Swift v. Tyson* view that
the federal courts could apply their own rules of law; instead, the
Court held, they must henceforth follow the rules laid down by the
courts of the state in which they sit, unless only a question of
federal law is involved in the particular case. This does not, it is
true, present too much difficulty in a case like *Erie Railroad* itself,
where the applicable rule on the question of tort law had been laid
down authoritatively in a line of decisions by the highest court of
the state. All too often, however, the application of the *Erie Railroad* doctrine is not so obvious. As the high Court has interpreted
that doctrine, the federal courts must frequently decide cases on the
basis of a theoretical "state law" which really does not exist because there is no state decision in point.[51] The Supreme Court has
held that, if there is no decision of the highest court of the particular state, the federal courts in that state must follow the relevant
decisions of the lower courts of the state. As the Court put it in

1940, "a federal court is not free to reject the state rule merely because it has not received the sanction of the highest state court, even though it thinks the rule is unsound in principle or that another is preferable." [52] In another case, the Court went even further and held that a federal court had to follow the decisions of a state court of original jurisdiction.[53] It is true that, in 1948, the Court drew the line and refused to rule that a federal court in South Carolina was bound by an isolated decision by a trial court of that state, whose decisions were not reported and not considered as precedents under state law.[54] But this refusal to reduce *Erie Railroad* to absurdity does not really answer for the federal courts the question of what is the binding state rule where the point has never been passed on by the highest state court.

The difficulties for lower courts under the *Erie Railroad* case have been well stated by a member of the highest Court. Where the federal judge,

has to divine what the state law is, he often has to proceed on fragmentary data. The court of last resort in the State may not have spoken. There are rulings of intermediate tribunals that squint one way and rulings of lower courts that squint another. What is the main current of the state law? What would the highest court of the State decide if the question were put to it? [55]

Under the Supreme Court's doctrine, lower state court decisions often control the final result of litigation in the federal courts, even though such decisions might be reversed if they reached the highest state court. This, in substance, is to subordinate the federal to the state courts and to make their judgments subject to changes in policy or personnel of the latter. And what happens if there are no decisions by courts of the particular state or they are hopelessly in conflict? According to the Supreme Court, the difficulty of determining state law does not excuse a federal court from following the *Erie Railroad* case.[56] It must, as best it can, determine what the state law would be if there were an authoritative decision on the point. Even if the state law is not clear, the federal judge may not exercise his own judgment of what the proper rule should be and do justice according to his best lights; he must instead try to place himself in the shoes of a member of the state's highest court and make his own determination of what that court would probably rule in a similar case. This is, in effect, to make federal law merely a prophecy of what the state courts are likely to do in fact.[57] This is all very well as a definition of law from the point of view of

Justice Holmes's celebrated "bad man"; [58] it is, to say the least, disconcerting when it is the concept of law upon which courts must decide questions on which important interests both of property and person may turn.

One who has read this far will find it hard to disagree with the judgment on the effect of *Erie Railroad* rendered off the bench by Justice Jackson:

The problem of which court has jurisdiction and which state law is applicable and whether it has been applied exactly as a state court would have done, is perplexing to the point of frustration to any person who tries to solve the question in a particular case without the consolation of a retainer. A vast and utterly unjustifiable part of federal litigation concerns only the question of jurisdiction, on which great time and labor and expense are expended before the merits of a question are ever reached.[59]

It may be, as Justice Frankfurter stated only last year, that the *Erie Railroad* doctrine's essence is that the difficulties of ascertaining state law are fraught with less mischief than the doctrine it repudiated.[60] But is such mischief so much less that it justified the Court in overturning a doctrine that proved workable for so long a period?

Perhaps the most important effect of the *Erie Railroad* case is one that has yet to occur, and that is the elimination of the diversity jurisdiction of the federal courts (i.e., their competence to decide cases between citizens of different states, even though no question of federal law is involved). *Erie Railroad v. Tompkins* may not have ended the difficulties of the federal courts with regard to what law they should apply in diversity cases, but it does end the last vestige of justification for continuing our system of dual jurisdictions based on diversity of citizenship. This was the conclusion of Robert H. Jackson in his last published work [61] and, in the opinion of the present writer, it is wholly justified. The diversity jurisdiction of the federal courts is certainly not founded in reason. On the contrary, ours is the only federation that has set up a dual system of state and federal courts, with the latter authorized not only to protect federal rights but also to enforce state law in cases between citizens of different states. The diversity jurisdiction given to the federal courts in the Constitution was based solely on the desire of the Framers to assure out-of-state litigants courts free from local bias. The experience after the Revolution led to the fear that parochial prejudice by the citizens of one state toward those of another would lead to unjust treatment of citizens of other states in the state courts: "Such was the reason for enabling a citizen of one State to press a claim or stand on a defense, wholly state-created, against a citizen of another in a federal court of the latter's State." [62]

The fear of the Founders may have been a valid reason for diversity jurisdiction in the fledgling Republic, still dominated by the excessive sectionalism that had rendered the Articles of Confederation unworkable. Over a century and a half later, these reasons are much less compelling. The permeation of national feeling and the mobility of modern life have destroyed most of the prejudice that formerly existed against the out-of-stater. And, even if some sectionalism still persists, it hardly affects the ability of the now-mature state court systems to do justice to all who come before them. Justice Frankfurter recently pointed out how Madison believed that Congress would return to the state courts judicial power vested in the federal courts "when they find the tribunals of the states established on a good footing." [63] Can anyone fairly deny that the state courts are now established on a sufficiently "good footing" so as to be trusted to mete out justice to citizens and non-citizens alike?

It is plain that, under the present system, a flood of state litigation is being diverted into the federal courts. And it is this flood that is, more than anything, responsible for the swamping of the federal courts by litigants in recent years. Over half of the civil cases in the federal courts are diversity of citizenship cases; most of them involve no questions of federal law. An act for the elimination of diversity jurisdiction could, in Justice Frankfurter's apt characterization, [64] fairly be called an act for the relief of the federal courts.

But such an act would have an even more important beneficial effect. It is essential to a vital federal system that the state governments should not be deprived of powers rightly theirs. An effective state court system to dispense state law is a fundamental element in state government. But how can the state courts be truly effective when they are deprived of so large a proportion of the cases that are rightfully theirs? Under *Erie Railroad v. Tompkins,* according to a recent Supreme Court statement, the federal court enforcing state law in a diversity case is in substance "only another court of the State." [65] Yet, if that is true, what justification is there any longer for diversity jurisdiction? "The whole purpose of diversity jurisdiction is to give one of the parties a better break in federal court than he would expect in state court. Take that away, use the same jurors, make the federal judge rule as a state judge would rule, and the purpose sought in diversity jurisdiction is gone." [66]

It may be objected that the caliber of most state courts is still below that of the federal courts. That alone is not, all the same, a justification for diversity jurisdiction. On the contrary, the best way to improve state tribunals is to make litigants realize that they have only those tribunals to resort to on state issues: "Is it sound public policy to withdraw from the incentives and energies for reforming state tribunals, where such reform is needed, the interests of influential groups who through diversity litigation are now enabled to avoid state courts?" [67]   In addition, the elimination of the present emasculation of their jurisdiction may be expected to have a correcting influence within the state courts themselves. We should not forget the wisdom contained in Justice Brandeis' dictum [68] that responsibility is the great developer of men.

Criminal Law and the Bill of Rights

The Supreme Court is, of course, the apex of the federal judicial system. This means that it is the ultimate appellate tribunal above all of the federal courts. It is the hierarchical superior over all those courts and is directly responsible for the adequacy of the justice dispensed by them. As far as the federal courts are concerned, the Supreme Court's supervisory power is not limited to the enforcement of constitutional guarantees. The Court must also ensure the fairness of the procedures followed and the soundness of the decisions reached themselves (at least within the permissible scope of appellate review in our law). This is particularly true in that aspect of the high bench's appellate work that has received the most public attention in recent years, namely, in the field of criminal law. The extent of the Supreme Court's supervisory power in federal criminal cases was well stated in 1943 by the Court itself: "The scope of our reviewing power over convictions brought here from the federal courts is not confined to ascertainment of Constitutional validity. Judicial supervision of the administration of criminal justice in the federal courts implies the duty of establishing and maintaining civilized standards of procedure and evidence." [69]

The appellate authority of the Supreme Court in criminal cases is not, at the same time, limited to convictions secured in the federal courts. The very first Congress, in 1789, gave the Court power to review decisions of the state courts on constitutional grounds. Though this jurisdiction has often been challenged, it has never been taken away or even basically altered. Indeed, it is difficult to see how it could be changed consistently with the fundamental principle of the supremacy of the Constitution as interpreted by the nation's highest Court. Where the decision of a state court involves a federal constitutional question, it must be subject to review by the Supreme Court, if that principle is to be maintained. All the same, one must note an essential distinction between the review power which the high Court exercises over the decisions of state courts and the appellate authority which it possesses over the lower federal courts. The Supreme Court, as already noted, is the direct hierarchical head of the federal judicial system; its relation to the other federal courts is that of chief to subordinate. The same is not true of its relation to the state courts. The latter are coordinate judicial tribunals, wholly independent in their own sphere. Despite some recent arguments to the contrary, it was never intended by those who drew up the Constitution to compound the state and federal judicial systems into one common mass, subject to the overriding supervisory authority of one Court in Washington. The appellate jurisdiction of the Supreme Court was not intended to reduce all state courts to a subordinate position.

As far as the criminal law is concerned, this makes for a substantial difference between Supreme Court review of convictions secured in the states and those appealed from the lower federal courts. Administration of criminal law in the states is not subject to the direct supervision which the Court may exercise over the federal courts. Review by the high bench of such administration must, on the contrary, be based upon respect for coordinate tribunals in a federation and upon the desire to avoid needless conflicts with such tribunals. In its 1943 decision, already quoted, the Court stated: "Considerations of large policy in making the necessary accommodations in our federal system are wholly irrelevant to the formulation and application of proper standards for the enforcement of the federal criminal law in the federal courts." [70] But such considerations should dominate the Court's review of state criminal cases. At best, as Justice Frankfurter has aptly expressed it, "intervention by this Court in the criminal process of States is delicate business. It should not be indulged in unless no reasonable doubt is left that a State denies, or has refused to exercise, means of correcting a claimed infraction of the United States Constitution." [71] The power of the highest Court to undo convictions in state courts is limited to the enforcement of those rights secured by the Constitution.

This distinction between the Supreme Court's review power over state and federal convictions has been clear for the better part of our constitutional history. More difficult for the post-1937 Court has been the question of what constitutional rights may not be violated in state criminal cases. As far as federal trials are concerned, it is clear that they are governed by the requirements of the Bill of Rights; in fact, one of the primary purposes of its draftsmen was to safeguard us from the abuses of the English criminal law of the late eighteenth century. It was, however, held in an opinion by Chief Justice Marshall in 1833,[72] that the Bill of Rights placed restraints on the Federal Government only, not on the state governments. Under this holding, the Constitution left the states free to carry out their own notions of criminal justice. This situation was basically changed with the ratification in 1868 of the Fourteenth Amendment. That Amendment placed no specific restraints upon the states in the formulation or the administration of their criminal law, similar to those which the Bill of Rights had imposed on the Federal Government. It did, nonetheless, provide that no state could thereafter "deprive any person of life, liberty, or property, without due process of law." It also prohibited the states from abridging the "privileges and immunities" of citizens of the United States and from denying to any person the equal protection of the laws.[73]

These provisions of the Fourteenth Amendment revived the constitutional question that had been laid to rest by Marshall's 1833 decision. It was clear that the Amendment, and particularly its due process clause, imposed upon the Supreme Court some responsibility over the caliber of criminal justice dispensed in the states; the difficult question was how much responsibility the Court was supposed to assume. To put it more specifically, did the due process clause of the Fourteenth Amendment impose upon the criminal law of the states all the restrictions contained in the Bill of Rights, or did it require something less?

As early as 1884,[74] the Supreme Court rejected the view that the Fourteenth Amendment absorbed all the provisions of the Bill of Rights and hence placed upon the states the limitations which the specific articles of the first eight Amendments had theretofore placed upon the Federal Government. The leading case until recently was *Twining v. New Jersey*,[75] a 1908 decision. That case held unequivocally that the Fourteenth Amendment was not simply a shorthand summary of the Bill of Rights; the due process clause did not incorporate verbatim the first eight Amendments as restrictions upon state power. On the contrary, the Court's view was that the due process clause of the Fourteenth Amendment expresses a demand for standards of fair procedure which are not defined by the specifically enumerated guarantees of the Bill of Rights. In accordance with this view, the Court before 1937 had held that indictment by a grand jury,[76] trial by jury,[77] and protection against self-incrimination [78] (all of which are clearly required in criminal proceedings in the federal courts by the Bill of Rights) were not fundamental attributes of the fair trial demanded of the states by due process. And, during 1937 itself, the Court held that the same was true of the prohibition against double jeopardy in federal prosecutions contained in the Fifth Amendment.[79] Thus, it seemed settled that the Fourteenth Amendment did not withdraw from the states the freedom to enforce their own conceptions of fairness in criminal proceedings; the Supreme Court would not reverse a state conviction merely because a similar federal conviction would be reversed as contrary to the Bill of Rights.

Those who supposed the law so to be settled reckoned without some of the more militant members of the post-1937 Supreme Court, who, despite the more than half-century of precedents against them, chose to give renewed life to the claim that the Fourteenth Amendment included, through its due process clause, all the provisions of the Bill of Rights, which were thus made as applicable to the states as they had previously been to the Federal Government. The strongest exponent (and, indeed, the originator) of this claim on the post-1937 Court has been Justice Black. His position was best stated in the 1947 case of *Adamson v. California.*[80] Defendant there had been convicted under a California procedure permitting the failure of the accused to testify to be commented upon by the court and counsel and to be considered by the court and jury. The Court assumed that such a procedure would violate the privilege against self-incrimination under the Fifth Amendment if this were a federal trial. However, repeating the holding that the due process clause of the Fourteenth Amendment did not draw all the rights of the Bill of Rights under its protection, the Court decided that the California procedure did not violate the Constitution. It was this decision, and the holding upon which it was based, that called forth a vigorous dissent by Justice Black explaining his contrary view. Rather than accept the view of the majority, he declared, "I would follow what I believe was the original purpose of the Fourteenth Amendment—to extend to all the people of the nation the complete protection of the Bill of Rights." [81]

Adamson v. California was the high-water mark of the Black position, for four Justices were there recorded in support of it. Yet, though subsequent changes in personnel have reduced the supporters of that view to only two, the reasoning in Justice Black's

Adamson opinion is still of more than mere academic interest, for it illustrates neatly a basic difference in approach to their functions among the members of the post-1937 Court. As has already been emphasized, from 1884, the Supreme Court had, by a constant jurisprudence, adhered to the view followed by the majority in *Adamson*. That view had received the support of every great liberal judge on the Court, including Miller, Holmes, Brandeis, Hughes, Stone, and Cardozo. In truth, the only Justice who had recorded his dissent in the last important case raising the issue had been Justice Butler [82]—hardly a jurist whom Justice Black has normally looked to as a precursor of his views. What was it then that made Justice Black reject all the weighty precedents against him and take issue with what seemed so settled in Supreme Court doctrine?

Justice Black's answer is given near the beginning of his *Adamson* dissent. His statement is so suggestive that it deserves detailed consideration:

My study of the historical events that culminated in the Fourteenth Amendment, and the expressions of those who sponsored and favored, as well as those who opposed its submission and passage, persuades me that one of the chief objects that the provisions of the Amendment's first section, separately, and as a whole, were intended to accomplish was to make the Bill of Rights, applicable to the states.

This historical background, he goes on, "has never received full consideration or exposition in any opinion of this Court interpreting the Amendment." [83]

Hugo L. Black, legal historian, has, in other words, convinced Mr. Justice Black that all his distinguished predecessors had completely misread the historical purpose of the Fourteenth Amendment, and this was enough to persuade the learned judge blithely to reject both the wisdom of prior Courts and the weight of the precedents which they had made. This is true despite the fact that some of the earlier judges thus disregarded were themselves witnesses of the adoption of the Fourteenth Amendment (an advantage even historian Black did not claim to possess). Perhaps we are being too censorious here. After all, one has only to compare *Adamson v. California* with the previously discussed case of *Erie Railroad Co. v. Tompkins* to note the progress made in the use of legal history by the highest Court. Mr. Charles Warren wrote an article attacking the historical basis of *Swift v. Tyson* and the 1938 Court jumped to reject the wisdom of a century.* Historian Black had no such luck;

* *Supra,* p. 156.

equally bold in his historical analysis, he could convince only a
minority of the Court to leave the rock of settled jurisprudence for a
jump off the deep end.

Historian Black's analysis, like that of Charles Warren before
him, was made *ex parte*. Without the benefit of discussion and
argument at the Court's bar, or an opportunity for refutation by
other scholars, it should hardly be enough to overthrow a settled
precedent. In this connection, it is pertinent to note that a pains-
taking post-*Adamson* analysis by two impartial professors has indicated that Justice Black's history on the subject is as dubious as his
law; Black's research, according to them, was both "inadequate and
misleading." [84] But, even if the judge turned historian *had* ma-
terialized into another Maitland, that alone would not have justified
the course of decision which he advocated.

The life of the law may not, as a famous statement of Justice
Holmes has it, be logic, but experience. Logic must, all the same,
remain a prime desideratum of any system of legal interpretation.
To read a portion of a legal document—be it a constitution, a statute, a contract, or a will—in a manner that is not logically consistent
with other portions of the document is, to say the least, to violate
sound canons of construction. Yet that is precisely what the Black
interpretation of the due process clause in the Fourteenth Amendment does. Even Justice Douglas, the strongest supporter on the
Court, next to Justice Black himself, of the view that the Fourteenth
Amendment made the entire Bill of Rights applicable to the states,
has recently conceded the strong logic of the contrary position. As
he well states, "The Fifth Amendment, like the Fourteenth Amendment, banned the deprivation of a person's 'life, liberty, or property
without due process of law.' That clause must, therefore, mean less
in the Fifth Amendment than it does in the Fourteenth, if in the
latter it is given a scope so broad as to include all of the Bill of
Rights." [85] The logical refutation of the Black view has been stated
far more strongly by Justice Frankfurter (as befits the judge who
has, more than anyone else, persuaded the majority of the Court to
reject Justice Black's position). To follow the Black view, he says,
is to charge the Framers of the Bill of Rights with writing into it a
meaningless clause:

The Fifth Amendment specifically prohibits prosecution of an "infamous
crime" except by indictment; it forbids double jeopardy and self-incrimination, as well as deprivation of "life, liberty, or property, without due
process of law." Not to attribute to due process of law an independent
function but to consider it a shorthand statement of other specific clauses
in the same Amendment is to charge those who secured the adoption of

this Amendment with meretricious redundancy by indifference to a phrase—"due process of law"—which was one of the great instruments in the very arsenal of constitutional freedom which the Bill of Rights was to protect and strengthen. Of course the Due Process Clause of the Fourteenth Amendment has the same meaning. To suppose that "due process of law" meant one thing in the Fifth Amendment and another in the Fourteenth is too frivolous to require elaborate rejection.[86]

Certainly, the short answer to the Black view—that the due process clause of the Fourteenth Amendment was a way of saying that every state is now bound by the entire Bill of Rights—is that it is a singularly strange way of saying it.[87]

Against this seemingly irrefutable logical argument, historian Black has marshalled some statements by Congressional supporters of the Fourteenth Amendment which appear to him to bear out his thesis. Yet, even if these statements had the effect he thinks they do (and this, it must be said, is by no means certain to outside observers), that would hardly justify distortion of the clear language of the Fourteenth Amendment, when taken together with the similar phraseology in the Fifth Amendment. It need hardly be emphasized today that legal interpretation must focus primarily on the words used, rather than on the presumed intent of the draftsman. Constitutional construction must be based upon analysis of the language instead of upon psychoanalysis of the Framers. As pithily put by Justice Frankfurter in the *Adamson* case, "Remarks of a particular proponent of the Amendment, no matter how influential, are not to be deemed part of the Amendment. What was submitted for ratification was his proposal, not his speech." [88] Statements of legislators may be relevant to explain ambiguous wording, but they can hardly be used to change the meaning of otherwise clear language. It is one thing to rely on legislative history in a proper case; it is quite another to extrapolate entirely new meaning from surmises and speculation and free-wheeling utterances in the Congress, especially when that is done in utter disregard of the terms in which the legislator has finally chosen to express his purpose.[89]

The kind of approach used by Justice Black (even if it gave the results he thought it did) is illegitimate in the case of a provision like the Fourteenth Amendment, which is clear in itself, or clear when read in the light of a mass of subsequent case law. Justice Black forgets that the primary question is not what Congressmen said they meant, but what the language they enacted into law means. The framer of a legal document all too often confuses what he actually said with what he might have said, had he been bolder; the judge must give meaning only to the language in fact used, unless it is equivocal. This would be true even if the question of meaning had never before been judicially considered. How much more true was it at the time of the *Adamson* case, when a whole volume of precedents had been handed down contrary to the Black position! Even if the provision at issue had originally meant what Justice Black contended, a prudent judge should still have hesitated to change the meaning acquired by the gloss of a century. In certain fields of endeavor, the palm may well go to the boldest innovator; yet the bench is hardly one of them. To read the Fourteenth Amendment as Justice Black has urged is a process that is not interpretation, but creation, of a constitutional provision.

Jus Naturale Redivivum?

We have just seen that the Supreme Court has refused to follow the view that the due process clause of the Fourteenth Amendment requires the states in their administration of the criminal law to comply with all the demands of the Bill of Rights. Upon what basis, then, does the highest tribunal act in reviewing the constitutionality of state convictions? More specifically, what rights of the accused are included in the concept of due process contained in the Fourteenth Amendment?

The answer which the Supreme Court gives to this question still depends, in the given case, upon its answer to the basic query posed half a century ago in *Twining v. New Jersey:* Is the right which the accused claims that the state has violated "a fundamental principle of liberty and justice which inheres in the very idea of free government and is the inalienable right of a citizen of such a government"? [90] If the answer is in the affirmative, then the right in question is one which is included in the concept of due process; otherwise, it is not, and the state violation of it does not call for Supreme Court correction, even if the similar violation in a federal trial would be held to contravene a specific provision of the Bill of Rights, such as the privilege against self-incrimination involved in the *Adamson* case. More recently, the *Twining* test has been somewhat more precisely stated. According to Justice Cardozo in 1937, the line of division depends upon whether the particular right is one that has "been found to be implicit in the concept of ordered liberty"; is it one that is "of the very essence of a scheme of ordered liberty"? If it is, the Fourteenth Amendment has absorbed it, in the belief that neither liberty nor justice would exist if such a right were sacrificed. [91]

Under the Court's view, not all the rights guaranteed in the Bill of Rights are included within the concept of due process. Some provisions of the Bill of Rights seem to protect petty preferences, not basic principles, as for example the right to jury trial in cases where the amount in controversy exceeds twenty dollars. That right may have value and importance; few today are so narrow or provincial as to maintain that a fair and enlightened system of justice is impossible without it—at least in civil cases and those involving only minor offenses. The same is true of the Fifth Amendment's provision requiring prosecutions to be initiated via the grand jury route. This too might be lost, and justice still be done.[92] Rights of this type, which reflected temporary preferences of the Framers, are not the kind of rights protected by due process. They grew out of transient experience which time might well improve. Other safeguards, however, do have perdurable validity.[93] They are principles so rooted in the traditions of justice and the conscience of civilized people as to be ranked as fundamental. These are the kinds of safeguard that are included in the concept of due process. These are the rights which are of the very essence of a scheme of ordered liberty. The question of whether a state conviction is consistent with the requirements of the due process clause of the Fourteenth Amendment imposes upon the Supreme Court, in the language of a 1952 decision of that tribunal itself, "an exercise of judgment upon the whole course of the proceedings [resulting in a conviction] in order to ascertain whether they offend those canons of decency and fairness which express the notions of justice of English-speaking peoples even toward those charged with the most heinous offenses."[94] Or, to paraphrase a characteristic more earthy criterion of Justices Holmes, state administration of the criminal law offends due process "if it makes you vomit."[95]

It should be obvious that a test, such as that adopted by the Supreme Court in these cases, is anything but a precise mathematical one. It is neither mechanical nor self-executing, but, instead, leaves wide areas of judgment and discretion to the judge. In effect, the Court is applying the rule that a state, in enforcing its criminal law, cannot resort to methods that offend what may fairly be deemed the civilized standards of the Anglo-American world.[96] When will the Court hold that such standards have been violated? It is not enough that there has been a mere violation of a specific provision of the Bill of Rights; the state method must be one which the highest Court finds repulsive.[97]

Of course, such a test is one which no two judges will apply in exactly the same way; what is loathsome to one judge may well seem venial to another. It was this element of subjective application that has led Justice Black to deride the Court's conception of the due process clause of the Fourteenth Amendment as resort to a revival of "natural law." In the learned judge's view, the majority of the Court is substituting natural law concepts for the Bill of Rights. "This decision," he asserted in his *Adamson* dissent, "reasserts a constitutional theory . . . that this Court is endowed by the Constitution with boundless power under 'natural law' periodically to expand and contract constitutional standards to conform to the Court's conception of what at a particular time constitutes 'civilized decency' and 'fundamental liberty and justice.' " [98]

It cannot be denied that Justice Black's characterization of the Supreme Court's conception of due process as a natural-law notion is an acute one. And it must be admitted that, in accusing the Court of arrogating to itself a power to judge the validity of state criminal proceedings in the light of the subjective opinions of its individual members' notions of civilized decencies, he has put his finger on one of the great weaknesses in such a natural-law concept. The judge himself must determine, on his individual judgment, whether a particular conviction violates a right that is of the very essence of a scheme of ordered liberty, or only some lesser right. Is there not in such subjective approach an element of serious uncertainty, and a temptation to judicial arbitrariness? Declaring himself the servant of the natural-law principle, the judge is, in fact, its creator. Such a philosophy must inevitably have what Justice Black terms "accordion-like qualities," [99] expanding and contracting according to the personal notions of the individual judge.

Must we then echo in our day, against the Supreme Court's application of due process, the complaint of the seventeenth-century common lawyers against the Court of Chancery, that the justice dispensed by it is so uncontrolled by fixed principles that it might just as well depend on the size of the particular Justice's foot? To assume, however, that a conception of due process, such as that applied by the high Court in reviewing state convictions, must rest wholly on the unfettered discretion of the judge is to go too far. Justice Black's criticism proves too much, for it might with equal validity be directed against a large part of the law. What the Court is applying in these cases is a broad standard, rather than a closely defined precept. But the same thing is done in most of the important areas of modern law. Indeed, it is in its application of such standards, instead of only mechanical rules, that a developed legal system differs most from a primitive one.

The primitive mind, unable to differentiate between varying degrees of the same type of conduct, brands all equally and metes out similar consequences to those concerned. As the law grows more mature, differentiations are made and the judge is allowed to make differences of degree instead of visiting with society's vengeance the visible source of any evil result. Thus, to take an obvious example, the mechanical rule of absolute liability for torts, characteristic of the formative period of a legal system, gives way to liability only for culpability, with culpability in each case being judged by the standard of the reasonable man. Certainly the standard of the reasonable man applied in our modern law of torts leaves much to the inclinations and idiosyncrasies of the individual judge or jury; yet few suggest replacing it (except in certain special fields) with the unmoral rule (mechanical though it may be) of liability regardless of the culpability of the actor. As Justice Holmes has aptly expressed it, the whole law depends upon differences of degree as soon as it is civilized. Between the differences of degree, in a standard like that of the reasonable man or that of due process, "and the simple universality of the rules in the Twelve Tables or the Leges Barbarorum, there lies the culture of two thousand years." [100]

It is erroneous to assert that the natural-law aspects of due process, as it is interpreted by the Supreme Court in the cases under discussion, leave judges at large. The Court itself stated in 1952, with regard to this criticism: "We may not draw on our merely personal and private notions and disregard the limits that bind judges in their judicial function. Even though the concept of due process of law is not final and fixed, these limits are derived from considerations that are fused in the whole nature of our judicial process." [101] Due process thus interpreted is not a mere matter of judicial caprice. Judges are men and partake fully of what has been well termed man's sense of injustice.[102] They share with others the natural rebellion that is awakened in the human conscience in the face of injustice: "The Foole hath sayd in his heart, there is no such thing as Justice; and sometimes also with his tongue." [103] Others deny neither the concept of justice, nor man's natural revulsion in the face of its violation. Justice, like the reason of which Cicero spoke two thousand years ago, has existed, derived from the nature of the universe, urging men to right conduct and diverting them from wrongdoing, and this justice did not become law when it was written down, but when it first came into existence. In reaction to repulsive acts, whether in the field of criminal law or elsewhere, there wells up in us an irrepressible sense of injustice. Justices of the highest tribunal are no more exempt from this feeling than lesser mortals. If anything, they are better placed, both by training and position, to give fuller effect to this basic human feeling. The judge can be expected both to be keenly perceptive to violations of basic canons of justice and to be sufficiently detached to avoid imposing his purely personal notions, not shared by other men, upon society. Thus, a judge's individual sense of injustice may be violated by the death penalty; he must, nevertheless, suppress such purely personal feeling if he is to remain true to his judicial office.[104] Justice Frankfurter, speaking for the Court in 1952, well expressed this point when he said:

To practice the requisite detachment and to achieve sufficient objectivity no doubt demands of judges the habit of self-discipline and self-criticism, incertitude that one's own views are incontestable and alert tolerance toward views not shared. But these are precisely the presuppositions of our judicial process. They are precisely the qualities society has a right to expect from those entrusted with ultimate judicial power.[105]

It is not realistic to fear that the judge, relying in these cases upon his sense of injustice, and using it to strike down abhorrent acts, will apply merely erratic, capricious, or idiosyncratic standards. "Our judges are products of our society, and . . . they will generally think along with the beliefs of some substantial segment of the citizenry. A man who uses a moral standard that no one shares in a population of 150 million probably does not belong at large, much less on the bench." [106] To be sure, there will be individual variations and accordionlike expansions and contractions of the due process concept. But that is the very essence of a system of case law, which enables it to adjust itself to the ebbs and flows of the civilization it is supposed to regulate.

Trial by Jury

The best way to determine whether Justice Black's criticism of the way in which the majority of the high Court has applied the Fourteenth Amendment in the field of criminal law is justified is to analyze the post-1937 cases involving violations of rights of defendants. This will be done with regard to four basic rights which have given rise to an abundance of Supreme Court decisions. These are the right of trial by jury, the right to counsel, the right against coerced confessions, and the right against unlawful searches and seizures. While, strictly speaking, only the cases involving review of state convictions are directly relevant to the present inquiry, those cases can be placed into clearer focus if they are compared with the decisions involving appeals from convictions in the lower federal courts. Consequently, cases involving both federal and state convictions will be discussed.

There is little doubt that, to the Founding Fathers, trial by jury was, in Hamilton's phrase, "the very palladium of free government." [107] It was this which led them to insert in the Bill of Rights an absolute guarantee of trial by jury in all civil and criminal cases. This means, of course, that defendants in federal criminal cases have a clear right to be tried by a jury—a right which includes all the essential elements of jury trial which were recognized in this country and in England when the Constitution was adopted. It should be noted, however, that though the Sixth Amendment expressly states that the right to trial by jury exists in *all* federal criminal prosecutions, the Court has not given literal effect to this seemingly absolute language. It has been settled for many years that the Sixth Amendment right does not extend to so-called "petty" offenses. In 1937, the Court held that the offense of engaging, without a license, in the business of a dealer in secondhand personal property, punishable by a fine of not more than three hundred dollars or imprisonment of not more than ninety days, was to be classed as a petty offense, which might be tried without a jury.[108] The result here is somewhat paradoxical, since, under the Seventh Amendment, a jury trial is assured in all civil suits involving over twenty dollars. While a jury is guaranteed in trifling civil cases, it is denied where imprisonment for a considerable time or liability for fifteen times twenty dollars confronts the accused.

In view of the Court's decision in such a case, it is not surprising that it has held that the right to trial by a common-law jury of twelve men in all criminal cases is not one of the basic rights safeguarded by the due process clause of the Fourteenth Amendment. Consequently, a state procedure providing for a jury of less than twelve men or dispensing with the rule of unanimity (at least in noncapital cases) has been upheld.[109] The right to trial by jury in its unmodified common-law form is, in Justice Cardozo's language, not a *sine qua non* of a fair and enlightened system of justice.[110]

The fact that the states are not bound by the jury-trial requirements of the Sixth Amendment had been decided many years before the present Court. What has concerned the Court since 1937 has been, not so much the right to a jury trial, as such, but the question of the impartiality of the jury. The right to an impartial jury is one specifically guaranteed by the Sixth Amendment. In the federal courts, this necessarily contemplates an impartial jury drawn from a cross section of the community. For the jury system to function properly, the high Court has said, the jury must be a body truly representative of the community, and not the organ of any special group or class.[111] If one class or group in the community is systematically excluded from a jury, it is evident that this standard has not been met. Thus, the wholesale exclusion from the federal jury lists of all persons who work for a daily wage was held improper in 1946,[112] and a similar decision was reached the same year with regard to a jury panel from which women were systematically excluded.[113] "Jury competence," declared the Court in the first of these cases, "is an individual rather than a group or class matter. That fact lies at the very heart of the jury system. To disregard it is to open the door to class distinctions and discriminations which are abhorrent to the democratic ideals of trial by jury." [114]

Perhaps the most difficult federal cases, involving the question of jury impartiality, have been those dealing with the qualification of government employees to serve on juries in the District of Columbia. In 1948, the Court held that government employees, as a class, were not disqualified by bias from serving on a jury in a prosecution for violation of the federal narcotics law.[115] Two years later, the same holding was made in the prosecution of a high officer of the Communist Party charged with willful failure to appear before a Congressional committee in compliance with a subpoena.[116] The Court in both cases declared that government employees were subject to challenge only for "actual bias"; there was no implied bias against persons charged with violations of federal law merely by reason of government employment. The Court's decisions here may well have been necessitated by the practical necessity of securing properly qualified jurors in an area where government employees constitute the largest part of the population. All the same, one cannot help but feel somewhat uneasy about a jury that, in the phrase of a dissenting Justice,[117] is composed of members in the hire of one of the litigants. This appears to be particularly true in the case of the Communist defendant. In the words of Justice Black, in such a case, "the prevailing pattern of loyalty investigations . . . makes it wholly unrealistic to expect government employees to enter the jury box with that quality of disinterestedness essential to complete impartiality." [118]

In the federal cases just discussed, the Supreme Court, in enforcing the standard of jury impartiality, is exercising its supervisory power over the administration of justice in the federal courts. As we have seen, the high bench has no such supervisory authority over administration of criminal law in the states. However, since, as the Court stated, in a passage already quoted, lack of jury impartiality is "abhorrent to the democratic ideals of trial by jury," [119]

the right to an impartial jury is treated by it as one of the fundamental rights guaranteed by the Fourteenth Amendment. Most of
the state cases involving the question of jury impartiality that have
reached the highest Court in the past two decades have raised
claims of discrimination against Negroes in the selection of juries.
As a starting point, it seems clear that a jury from which Negroes
have been excluded because of their race violates the right of the
defendant to an impartial jury truly representative of the community. "For racial discrimination to result in the exclusion from
jury service of otherwise qualified groups," eloquently declared Justice Black for the Court in 1940, "not only violates our Constitution
and the laws enacted under it but is at war with our basic concepts
of a democratic society and a representative government." [120] Certainly, a Court which feels this way about the right to an impartial
jury will find its violation repulsive and, hence, forbidden to the
states by the due process clause of the Fourteenth Amendment. In
addition, where the accused is a Negro, to try him by a jury from
which members of his race have been systematically excluded is to
deny him the equal protection of the laws guaranteed by the same
Amendment.

Where the defendant does make out a case of state discrimination in the selection of juries, the Supreme Court will reverse the
conviction just as speedily as it would if a similar violation of the
right to an impartial jury had occurred in a federal court. In a
number of cases since 1937, the high tribunal has applied this principle to void convictions of Negroes in southern states. And, it
should be noted, the principle applies both to the grand jury, which
indicts, and the petit jury, which convicts.[121] Nor is the prohibition
against discrimination in jury selection limited to discrimination
against Negroes. In 1954, the Court reversed a Texas conviction
where it was shown that that state systematically excluded persons
of Mexican descent from jury service. "The Fourteenth Amendment," said Chief Justice Warren, "is not directed solely against discrimination due to a 'two-class' theory—that is, based upon differences between 'white' and Negro." [122] On the contrary, it requires
juries to be chosen indiscriminately from among all qualified persons, regardless of national origin or descent.

The federal cases involving juries composed of government employees, which, we have seen, have caused the highest Court some
embarrassment, have their counterparts in state cases dealing with
the so-called "blue ribbon" jury. Such jury is drawn from a special
panel composed of citizens deemed to be of a higher caliber than
the general run of jurors: "That group was chosen because they pos-

sessed some trait or characteristic which distinguished them from the general panel of jurors, some qualification which made them more desirable." [123] Thus, under the New York system, which was the one ultimately put to the constitutional test, the selection of the "blue ribbon" panel rested upon the "degree of intelligence" as revealed by the questionnaire sent to prospective jurors, augmented by personal interviews. The aim behind the selection of such a panel is, of course, to improve the quality of jury personnel, particularly in important cases. No one will deny that this is a laudable intention; but is it consistent with the concept of the jury as a representative cross-section of the community?

The high Court answered this question in the affirmative, though only by a bare majority, in the 1947 case of *Fay v. New York.*[124] The Court held that, in the absence of a showing that there was discrimination against specific groups or occupations, the state procedure was not subject to Fourteenth-Amendment attack; the state could apply legitimate standards to improve jury personnel. It must be admitted that there is much truth in the claim of the dissenters that the "blue ribbon" panel is inconsistent with the normal notion of a jury chosen from a fair cross section of the community. Traditionally, the accused has been entitled to be tried by a just sampling of his neighbors, not only those with superior intelligence and learning.[125] Does it, all the same, necessarily follow from this that the states are to be barred from nondiscriminatory attempts to improve the caliber of their juries? In the pure Athenian democracy, all citizens were entitled to public office on the basis of lot, regardless of their individual qualifications. Such an ideal is no longer practical, if it ever was. Today we recognize the right of the state to prescribe nondiscriminatory qualifications for public employment. Why should not the same right extend to public service? To apply the rule of the dissenters to its logical extreme, one would have to invalidate all tests of jurors' qualifications, including tests of ability to read and write the English language. If the state is permitted to test the literacy of prospective jurors (or, indeed, even to impose property qualifications for jury service), it should be able to impose other tests, provided they are not discriminatory in purpose, designed also to select only qualified jurors. "Society also has a right to a fair trial." [126]

Right to Counsel

On the question just discussed, of an impartial jury, the Supreme Court has reached basically similar results in the federal and state cases, despite the different theories underlying the Court's review-ing power in the two types of case. When we consider the de-fendant's right to counsel, on the other hand, we find that there is a basic difference in result as between federal and state cases. The Sixth Amendment unequivocally provides that, in all criminal prose-cutions, the accused shall enjoy the right "to have the Assistance of counsel for his defence." In its 1938 decision in *Johnson v. Zerbst*,[127] the Court held that this provision imposed the duty on the federal courts to furnish counsel to all defendants in criminal cases. "The Sixth Amendment," categorically declared the Court, "withholds from federal courts, in all criminal proceedings, the power and authority to deprive an accused of his life or liberty un-less he has or waives the assistance of counsel." [128]

The Sixth Amendment is not, anymore than the other provisions of the Bill of Rights, directly binding upon the states through the coercion of the Fourteenth Amendment. Whether the right to coun-sel will be enforced by the Supreme Court against the states conse-quently depends upon whether such right is considered to be one that inheres in the very essence of our ordered liberty and, as such, included in the concept of due process. In the 1932 case of *Powell v. Alabama* [129]—the famous *Scottsboro* case—the Court had held that, in a capital case, the right to counsel was one that could not be violated by the states. In such a case, it was the absolute duty of the court to assign counsel as a necessary requisite of due process of law. Yet the Court expressly left open the question of whether the denial of counsel in criminal cases involving less than capital offenses was equally violative of the due process clause of the Four-teenth Amendment. It has fallen to the Court in the past fifteen years to answer that question.

The case in which the Court's answer was given is *Betts v. Brady*,[130] decided in 1942. Speaking through Justice Roberts, the Court refused to hold that, in a noncapital case, violation of the right to counsel was always a violation of due process. Instead, the opinion stated that,

the Fourteenth Amendment prohibits the conviction and incarceration of one whose trial is offensive to the common and fundamental ideas of fairness and right, and while want of counsel in a particular case may result in a conviction lacking in such fundamental fairness, we cannot say that the Amendment embodies an inexorable command that no trial for any offense, or in any court, can be fairly conducted and justice accorded a defendant who is not represented by counsel.[131]

The Court here was laying down what has since been termed the "fair trial" test: The denial of counsel by a state in a noncapital case does not automatically violate due process; whether it does depends upon whether, under all the circumstances of the case, it is possible for the accused to obtain a fair trial even without counsel. As the Court explained its rule in 1951, "the Due Process Clause of the Fourteenth Amendment requires states to afford defendants assistance of counsel in noncapital criminal cases when there are special circumstances showing that without a lawyer a defendant could not have an adequate and a fair defense." [132] In *Betts v. Brady* itself, defendant, indicted in a Maryland court for robbery, was held not to have been denied due process merely because he was not furnished counsel. The Court found that this alone did not deny a fair trial to one of forty-three years of age, of ordinary intelligence, and of ability to take care of his interests.

Justices Black and Douglas (and, when they were alive, Murphy and Rutledge as well) have strenuously opposed the doctrine of *Betts v. Brady*—that "ill-starred" decision, Justice Douglas has termed it.[133] And for a time, in fact, it seemed as though their view, first expressed by Black in dissent in *Betts v. Brady* itself, might prevail on the Court. Since 1947, however, the "fair trial" test of *Betts v. Brady* has been consistently applied by the highest tribunal. *Bute v. Illinois*,[134] a 1948 case, well illustrates the approach of the majority of the Court. The decision there held that due process did not require the state to furnish counsel before accepting a plea of guilty to a charge of indecent liberties with female children, the maximum penalty for which was twenty years, from a fifty-seven-year-old defendant, who received from the state court a full explanation of the consequences and penalties resulting from his plea. After a lengthy analysis, the Court reaffirmed the *Betts v. Brady* holding and found that, under it, due process was not violated here; in the circumstances of this case, the lack of counsel did not make a fair trial impossible. On the other hand, where the accused is not in a position to take care of his interests (even though advised by the trial judge) because of his immaturity,[135] his ignorance of the English language,[136] his lack of mental capacity,[137] or because of the unfairness of the trial itself,[138] then circumstances are present which indicate that a fair trial was lacking because of the absence of counsel. In such cases, the state convictions will be reversed. Perhaps the best summary of the high Court's view was stated in 1948 by Justice Reed in delivering the opinion in *Uveges v. Pennsylvania*.[139] The majority of the Court, he said, rejects the claim that the services of counsel to protect the accused are guaranteed by the Constitution in every instance.

[They] think that when a crime subject to capital punishment is not involved, each case depends on its own facts. . . . Where the gravity of the crime and other factors—such as the age and education of the defendant, the conduct of the court or the prosecuting officials, and the complicated nature of the offense charged and the possible defenses thereto—render criminal proceedings without counsel so apt to result in injustice as to be fundamentally unfair, . . . the accused must have legal assistance under the Amendment whether he pleads guilty or elects to stand trial, whether he requests counsel or not.[140]

The present writer must confess his sympathy with the dissenting Justices in these cases on the right to counsel. His disagreement with the Black view, that the due process clause of the Fourteenth Amendment incorporates the Sixth Amendment (as it does all of the Bill of Rights) as a safeguard against the states, has already been made manifest.* But adherence to the Court's general due process approach does not necessarily lead to approval of *Betts v. Brady* and the manner in which its doctrine has been applied. True, the Fourteenth Amendment does not make the Sixth Amendment, as such, applicable to the states. Yet it does bar the states from practices that make fair trials impossible; such practices constitute what the *Betts v. Brady* Court termed "a denial of fundamental fairness."[141] It is most difficult to see why the refusal of counsel in a serious criminal case does not constitute just such a denial. In considering this matter, we should, with Justice Douglas, ask ourselves this question: Of what value is the right to a fair trial if an accused does not have counsel to advise and defend him?[142] Even the educated and intelligent layman is at a serious disadvantage without counsel to aid him. Not only is he usually not fully informed of the law applicable to his case but, even more important, he is wholly ignorant of the manner in which to develop his defense in the courtroom and to counter the case which the trained advocate for the prosecution is preparing against him. Nor does it make any difference that the accused has, in fact, pleaded guilty. A layman might rush to confession where counsel would see advantages in a trial.[143] Without the guiding hand of counsel at every stage of the proceeding, he is at a serious disadvantage.

It is recognized that the high Court was led to its *Betts v. Brady* doctrine by the fact that in the past the question of the right to counsel had normally been deemed one of legislative policy. Certainly, the right to counsel was not generally recognized in English or American law, either at the adoption of the Bill of Rights or the ratification of the Fourteenth Amendment. And it is also true that

* *Supra,* pp. 164-67.

the growth of the right to be assigned counsel on request has been a slow one under state laws (though by the time of *Betts v. Brady* it had been safeguarded in thirty-five states). But the virtue of the Court's due process approach is that it does not imprison criminal procedure in an eighteenth-century strait jacket. Instead, it enables the Court to expand the rights that may be guaranteed in accordance with altered conceptions of fairness. That counsel may once have not been deemed a fundamental right is irrelevant if the absence of counsel shocks our present-day sense of justice. It is hard to believe that most people today (the majority of the Supreme Court notwithstanding) would not recoil from the suggestion that a defendant in a serious criminal case, who was unable to secure counsel, could obtain a wholly fair trial. In our system, no man should be condemned to run the gauntlet of the criminal law without counsel at his side. Any other practice seems so repugnant to the fundamentals of fair play that it is difficult to see how it can be squared with the Court's own notion of due process.

Coerced Confessions

Fundamental in any system of ordered liberty is antipathy toward the use of confessions coerced from an accused. As Justice Black eloquently stated for a unanimous Supreme Court in 1940:

The testimony of centuries, in governments of varying kinds over populations of different races and beliefs, stood as proof that physical and mental torture and coercion had brought about the tragically unjust sacrifices of some who were the noblest and most useful of their generations. The rack, the thumbscrew, the wheel, solitary confinement, protracted questioning and cross questioning, and other ingenious forms of entrapment of the helpless or unpopular had left their wake of mutilated bodies and shattered minds along the way to the cross, the guillotine, the stake and the hangman's noose. And they who have suffered most from secret and dictatorial proceedings have almost always been the poor, the ignorant, the numerically weak, the friendless, and the powerless.[144]

A tribunal which feels this way will not hesitate to void either federal or state convictions based upon coerced confessions. Conviction based upon compulsion is so repugnant to civilized concepts of justice that it cannot be condoned by a Court that seeks to hold the states to the standard of due process: "The Due Process Clause bars police procedure which violates the basic notions of our accusatorial mode of prosecuting crime and vitiates a conviction based on the fruits of such procedure."[145] The basic difference in the high Court's authority when reviewing federal convictions and those from the states has, nevertheless, led that tribunal to follow a different approach in the two types of case in answering the question of whether a confession has in fact been secured by coercion.

The leading case involving federal convictions is *McNabb v. United States*,[146] decided in 1943. In that case, the defendants were arrested and placed in a detention room by federal officers; they were questioned intermittently for two days before being taken before a magistrate. During that period, incriminating statements were obtained which were used to secure their conviction. The detention and questioning of defendants was in violation of a federal statute commanding officers arresting persons to arraign them promptly before a United States Commissioner or judicial officer. The Court in *McNabb* held that confessions secured while defendants were thus illegally detained could not be used against them. The fruits of unlawful action on the part of federal officers could not be employed in the federal courts.

The *McNabb* rule has been criticized as an undue restriction upon police officials. Of course, it does impose limitations upon police efficiency. But is it for that reason alone undesirable? Since the Petition of Right in the time of Charles I, Anglo-American law has abhorred unlawful detentions. Prompt production before a magistrate or other proper official is essential to the prevention of such illegal acts. And it is particularly important that the period between arrest and arraignment not be prolonged so as, in effect, to turn the detention of the accused into a process of wrenching evidence from him. As a member of the highest Court has recently put it, "When the police use the arrest to detain the prisoner and to exact a confession from him the processes of the law are perverted. The period of detention before the accused is brought before the police is the awful lull. Then the accused is completely at the mercy of the police." [147] Though the highest Court has, since 1943, retreated somewhat from the logical extremes some have seen to inhere in *McNabb*,[148] it has remained true to the substance of its holding there. Today, as in 1943, illegal detention is sufficient to bar from evidence in the federal courts a confession to police officers during unlawful detention.[149]

In its *McNabb* opinion, the high Court stated expressly that its decision was based, not on constitutional grounds, but on its supervisory authority over the administration of justice in the federal courts. As far as state convictions are concerned, on the other hand, the Court can intervene only to secure the observance of the due process clause of the Fourteenth Amendment. Does the use in a state trial of a confession secured in violation of the *McNabb* rule violate due process? This question was answered in the negative in the 1952 decision of *Gallegos v. Nebraska.*[150] The rule of the *McNabb* case, categorically stated the Court there, is not a limitation imposed by the due process clause. The fact that it was made during illegal detention is only one of the factors to be used in determining whether a state confession was coerced; it does not, as in the federal courts, automatically invalidate such confession.

How then does the Supreme Court determine whether a confession used to secure a state conviction was the result of compulsion? In *Ashcraft v. Tennessee,*[151] decided in 1944, the Court held that, where the accused had been held incommunicado for thirty-six hours, during which time, without sleep or rest, he had been interrogated by relays of officers, the situation was "so inherently coercive that its very existence is irreconcilable with the possession of mental freedom"[152] by the accused. Any confession secured under such circumstances must be treated as the result of compulsion. In other words, though the fact that it was made during unlawful detention will not of itself invalidate a state, as it would a federal, confession, where the circumstances under which it was made were such as to be "inherently coercive," the state confession must fall. When is the situation in which a confession is secured such as to be "inherently coercive"? Continuous questioning without rest or sleep was held to be such in *Ashcraft.* Other cases reaching a similar result involved (1) the confession of a fifteen-year-old Negro arrested at midnight and questioned for five hours with no friend or counsel present ("The age of petitioner, the hours when he was grilled, the duration of his quizzing, the fact that he had no friend or counsel to advise him, the callous attitude of the police towards his rights combine to convince us that this was a confession wrung from a child by means which the law should not sanction."[153]); (2) the confession of a man held without arraignment, without the aid of counsel or friends, and without advice as to his constitutional rights for a week, during which period he was held much of the time in solitary confinement and was interrogated by relays of police officers, usually until long past midnight;[154] (3) the confession under similar circumstances of a man held five days, where the prosecutor "admitted that a hearing was withheld until interrogation had produced a confession";[155] and (4) the confession in a southern state of an illiterate Negro arrested and confined in a small hot room for almost a week, without being informed of the charge, denied access to counsel or friends, and interrogated day and night by relays of police officers.[156] It makes no difference in cases like these that defendant cannot show that his confession was caused by physical constraint; there is torture of mind as well as of body. "When a suspect speaks because he is overborne, it is immaterial whether he has been subjected to a physical or a mental ordeal." [157]

The Court's application of the "inherently coercive" doctrine of the *Ashcraft* case led in 1949 to an expression of strong dissent by Justice Jackson, who felt that the judicial pendulum had swung too far for the good of society in the direction of protecting suspected criminals. In his view, in cases like these involving unwitnessed crimes, "no one suggests that any course held promise of solution . . . other than to take the suspect into custody for questioning. The alternative was to close the books on the crime and forget it, with the suspect at large. This is a grave choice for a society in which two-thirds of the murders already are closed out as insoluble." [158]

What Justice Jackson was asking for here was essentially a more restricted application of the Court's confession test. And his view in this respect has been receiving the concurrence of the Court since 1949. Though the high bench has, since that time, continued to adhere to *Ashcraft*, it has applied its rule in a much more cautious manner. Thus, in 1952, it was held that the mere length of unlawful detention by a state did not, without more, invalidate confessions made during that period.[159] And, in the 1953 case of *Stein v. New York*,[160] confessions secured during an illegal detention of thirty-two hours, during twelve hours of which defendants were questioned by police officers, were held not barred by due process. The Court emphasized that defendants were mature men, experienced with police practices, asserting that "What would be overpowering to the weak of will or mind might be utterly ineffective against an experienced criminal." [161] That may well be true; but it cannot be denied that the Court's decision in *Stein* does constitute a watering down of the *Ashcraft* approach.

There is another aspect of the *Stein* decision worthy of comment. The Court there held (though only by way of obiter) that, even if the state jury had rejected the confessions as coerced, it could still have returned a conviction if there was other evidence before them sufficient to convict. As Justice Frankfurter, dissenting, expresses it,

the Court now holds that a criminal conviction sustained by the highest court of a State, and more especially one involving a sentence of death, is not to be reversed for a new trial, even though there entered into the conviction a coerced confession which in and of itself disregards the prohibition of the Due Process Clause of the Fourteenth Amendment.

The Court now holds that it is not enough for a defendant to establish in this Court that he was deprived of a protection which the Constitution of the United States affords him; he must also prove that if the evidence unconstitutionally admitted were excised there would not be enough left to authorize the jury to find guilt.[162]

This ruling is both needlessly broad and contrary to settled principles. A constitutional right is not a rule of evidence, to be governed, like the latter, by the harmless error rule. The denial of a right guaranteed by the Constitution should not be treated as a matter of mere error, which may be disregarded if deemed harmless. To hold to the contrary is not, as the *Stein* Court claims, to avoid making constitutional doctrines "mere technical loopholes for the escape of the guilty"; [163] it is, in Justice Frankfurter's phrase,[164] to take a retrogressive step in the enforcement of fundamental rights.

Unlawful Search and Seizure

The double standard employed by the Supreme Court in judging the legality of federal, as compared to state, convictions is clearly evident in cases involving claimed violations of the right to be secure against unlawful searches and seizures. The Fourth Amendment contains an unqualified prohibition against violation of "the right of the people to be secure in their persons, houses, papers, and effects, against unreasonable searches and seizures." This provision of the Bill of Rights has been aptly characterized as central to enjoyment of the other guarantees of the Bill of Rights.[165] Search and seizure at the discretion of government officials more than anything else characterizes the police state. The Fourth Amendment's prohibition is clearly binding upon federal officers, and the high Court has intervened in many cases in the past two decades where it has been transgressed by them. While the Court has had a great deal of difficulty in determining whether, in individual cases, federal officers have engaged in illegal search or seizure, there is no doubt that it is quick to intervene when it feels that the Fourth Amendment has been contravened. More than that, the Court has been consistent in applying the doctrine of a 1914 decision [166] making evidence secured as the result of illegal search and seizure wholly inadmissible in the federal courts. This is, of course, the real sanction behind the effectiveness of the Fourth Amendment; to deny the fruits of unlawful violation of the constitutional provision to police officers is the best way to ensure against such violation in the first place.

In its 1949 decision in *Wolf v. Colorado*,[167] the Court found that

the right against unlawful search and seizure was an essential element of due process. "The security of one's privacy against arbitrary intrusion by the police . . . ," declares its opinion, "is basic
to a free society. It is therefore implicit in 'the concept of ordered
liberty' and as such enforceable against the States through the Due
Process Clause." [168] But the Court refused to go further and enforce
a rule that evidence secured through an unlawful search and seizure
could not be used in the state courts. The Fourteenth Amendment,
said the Court, did not impose upon the states the federal rule making evidence obtained in violation of the Fourth Amendment inadmissible in federal courts. The Court was strongly influenced by
the fact that the great majority of Anglo-American jurisdictions have
not barred evidence secured by unreasonable search and seizure:
"When we find that in fact most of the English-speaking world does
not regard as vital to such protection the exclusion of evidence thus
obtained, we must hesitate to treat this remedy as an essential ingredient of the right." [169] In the face of the mass of contrary evidence from the existing practice in the English-speaking world, the
Court felt that it could not hold the federal rule excluding illegally
obtained evidence to be a basic notion of justice. Here we can see
clearly the way in which the due process test is applied by the high
bench. To the conscience of the individual judge, the use of illegal
evidence may well be obnoxious; but how can he hold it contrary to
civilized standards of decency and fairness when it is so prevalent
throughout the Anglo-American world?

At the same time, it must be admitted that the Court's decision
in *Wolf v. Colorado,* which it has consistently adhered to,[170] despite
vigorous dissents, tends to make all but impossible the enforcement
against the states on a federal level of the prohibition against unreasonable searches and seizures, which *Wolf* itself admitted was
contained in the Fourteenth Amendment. The *Wolf* decision refused to invalidate a state conviction based upon illegally secured
evidence and, in 1951, the Court declined to allow a federal injunction to be issued against the use, in pending state criminal proceedings, of evidence obtained by an unlawful search by state police.[171]
It is true that, in a 1956 decision, the highest tribunal did hold that
a federal agent could be enjoined from testifying in a state court
prosecution with respect to evidence obtained by him in the course
of an unlawful search, which had been suppressed in a prior federal
prosecution under the federal rule barring illegal evidence.[172] But
this hardly changes the practical effect of the *Wolf* holding in the
vast majority of state cases. As a result of *Wolf,* it cannot be denied
that the prohibition against illegal searches and seizures by the

states (which, under *Wolf* itself, is included in the due process clause of the Fourteenth Amendment) may become only a form, and its enforcement an illusion. Nonetheless, the Court has refused to reach a different result because it has not been convinced that imposition of direct judicial enforcement, by a rule barring use of illegal evidence in the states, is a proper function of the highest federal tribunal, in view of the extent to which the states and other countries have declined to resort to such enforcement by their own courts.

The Judge's "Notion"

A Lincoln anecdote about an Illinois jury has it that the jury foreman asked the judge if he could help him out with a question that he had, and the judge said that he would be glad to give any help he could. "Well judge," said the foreman, "the jury wanted to know: Was that there you told them the law or just your notion?" [173]

Justice Black's criticism of the Supreme Court's application of the due process clause of the Fourteenth Amendment is based precisely upon the claim that the majority Justices are applying only their own notions of the law. Of course, that is so, at least in part; but cannot the same criticism be directed against the most important portion of Supreme Court jurisprudence? All too often, the highest tribunal decides on the basis of its notions of proper policy, rather than on the basis of law in the traditional common-law sense. Yet that, as has already been emphasized, is the primary purpose of the supreme bench in our polity. We have endowed a judicial tribunal with the authority to decide disputes that, in other systems, are fought out at the political level. By elevating those disputes to the judicial plane, we have ensured their decision in an atmosphere of detachment, removed from the immediate strife of partisan politics. But we have inevitably had to sacrifice in the deciding tribunal itself something of the nature of the common-law court. Without a doubt, the highest Court translates its own notions into the supreme law of the land. And being composed of fallible men, the Court may make the wrong policy decisions. Yet that is part of the price we pay for a system in which every governmental act must be confined within constitutional limits.

The cases we have discussed show clearly that the high Court's application of the due process concept in the field of criminal law makes for different results in the federal, as compared with the state, cases which it reviews. They do not, all the same, substantially support the fear expressed by Justice Black that the Court's approach inevitably means a reliance upon the arbitrary caprice of the individual judge's application of a revived natural law. On the contrary, in most of the cases discussed, the Court has applied standards not unfamiliar to those conversant with Anglo-American law, even though the personal feelings of particular members of the Court may have been completely opposed to such standards. It is true that such standards can be applied only when there is relevant experience in the English-speaking world from which the supreme tribunal may draw. If there is no such experience because the problem at issue is a new one, then the Court is inevitably left at large. In such a case, how is the judge to decide? What answer is he, for example, to give to the following cases, all of which have been before the highest Court in recent years?

1. May a state, consistently with due process, order the electrocution for the second time of a convicted murderer after a first attempt at electrocution had failed because of a mechanical defect? [174]

2. May a state, without offending due process, put to death a condemned murderer who became insane while awaiting execution? [175]

3. May a state, without violating the Constitution, require an accused in a murder case to assume the burden of proving his defense of insanity beyond a reasonable doubt? [176]

4. Even under the rule of *Wolf v. Colorado,* may a state allow the use in its courts, in a prosecution for violating a law forbidding the possession of morphine, of two morphine tablets forcibly extracted from the accused through stomach pumping? [177]

In answering such questions, it is not to be wondered at if no two judges adopt exactly the same approach. Here, it is the judge's "notion," more than anything else, that will determine the law. But, once again, that is exactly the reason why there has been established an ultimate tribunal to resolve even the most difficult legal problems; the fact that he may be furnished with no relevant authoritative guide is no reason for the judge to refuse to decide a wholly novel question. In these cases, he must decide as best he can in the light of his conceptions of the fundamental principles of our legal order. These are precisely the type of questions to which we have a right to expect the answer from the depositories of the law whom we have endowed with the judicial power.

Not only is the application of the due process clause in close cases, like the examples given above, one which may vary from judge to judge; it is also one which may be different at different times. This is, however, one of the great advantages of a plastic concept like due process—it can expand or contract to meet changing conceptions of the essentials of justice. Due process is, thus, a concept that both has its roots in Magna Carta and, at the same time, contemplates advances in the conceptions of justice and freedom by a progressive society. Due process does not express only the restricted views of eighteenth-century Englishmen; it is an enduring reflection of experience with human nature.

Griffin v. Illinois,[178] a 1956 decision of the highest Court, well illustrates the dynamic aspect of due process in the field of criminal law. The majority there held that it violates the Fourteenth Amendment for a state to deny to defendants alleging poverty free transcripts of the trial proceedings, which would enable them adequately to prosecute appeals from convictions for armed robbery. It is certainly true, as a dissent points out, that the right to a free transcript in most jurisdictions is a relatively recent one. Nevertheless, Illinois' failure to furnish transcripts to indigent defendants is, today, one which shocks the conscience. A rule which effectively denies the poor an adequate appellate review, accorded to all who have money to pay the costs in advance, appears at present an utter misfit in a country dedicated to affording equal justice to all. If a state has a general policy of allowing criminal appeals, it cannot, consistently with present-day notions of the Fourteenth Amendment, make lack of means an effective bar to the exercise of this opportunity.

It cannot be overemphasized that the Supreme Court's power to include new rights in the due process concept is one which should be exercised with the greatest caution. Previously accepted practice should be declared invalid only when it has become so completely out of line with more modern standards of justice that it is repugnant to the present-day judge. Otherwise, the high bench must constantly remember that it is not a Court of Criminal Appeal from the state courts. Nor is the Court to use due process as a device to import all its personal ideas of decency into the states. Due process, as we have stressed, is something more than a mere mirror for the idiosyncrasies of the individual judge. The Fourteenth Amendment must not, above all, be used by the Supreme Court as a ready instrument to expand federal, and incidentally its own, authority over the state courts. The high Court should give the freest possible scope to the states in the choice of their methods of criminal procedure, intervening only when state procedures do actually violate fundamental principles of justice. The state courts, too, have a vital role to play in a flourishing federalism. Conflict with state courts should be eschewed unless utterly unavoidable. Of course, it is the duty of the Supreme Court to review denials by states of claimed federal rights. But this hardly requires that tribunal to undermine the state courts by closely supervising the merits of state criminal proceedings. The high bench should not, in these cases, forget the truth stated by Justice Jackson in 1953, that the mere fact of its reversal of a state court is not proof that justice was thereby better done: "There is no doubt that if there were a super-Supreme Court, a substantial proportion of our reversals of state courts would also be reversed. We are not final because we are infallible, but we are infallible only because we are final." [179]

6

THE STATES

"The question of the relation of the States to the federal government is the cardinal question of our time," wrote Woodrow Wilson in 1908.[1] In the resolution of that question, the Supreme Court has an essential part to play. Indeed, it is not too much to say that, in our system, the high tribunal is the arbiter of the federal system. "Scarcely any political question arises in the United States," acutely observed de Tocqueville over a century ago, "that is not resolved, sooner or later, into a judicial question."[2] And so it was to be expected that the division of authority between states and Nation, too, would ultimately give rise to controversies for adjudication by the Court in Washington. In deciding such controversies, the function of the Court is to maintain the constitutional equilibrium between the states and the Federal Government. "The Constitution," Justice Douglas has declared, "is a compact between sovereigns."[3] It is for the high Court, standing outside and above both the states and the central government, to hold the balance between sovereignties in our system. As Chief Justice Taney aptly stated in 1859: "So long . . . as this Constitution shall endure, this tribunal must exist with it, deciding in the peaceful forms of judicial proceeding the angry and irritating controversies between sovereignties, which in other countries have been determined by the arbitrament of force."[4]

The Court's role as arbiter of federalism is one which it has exercised from the foundation of the Republic. At the same time, it can hardly be gainsaid that the manner in which that role has been performed has been drastically altered in recent years. "It is," in Justice Jackson's words, "undeniable that . . . we have been in a cycle of rapid centralization, and Court opinions have sanctioned a considerable concentration of power in the Federal Government with a corresponding diminution in the authority and prestige of state governments."[5] In the first part of our history, the Supreme Court could strive to hold an equal poise between federal and state authority; more recently, it has tended to place ever-increasing weight on the federal side of the balance. In Chapter 2 we discussed in some detail the extent to which the Court has, since 1937, upheld exertions of federal regulatory power.* We saw there that it has all but abandoned its former position as controller of Congress. This means, of course, that federal authority can be exerted today, even in areas that were formerly deemed purely within the competence of the states. Few, if any, economic activities are now deemed so local as to be beyond the expanded reach which the Court has given to the Congressional commerce power: "If it is interstate commerce that feels the pinch," colloquially declared the Court in 1949, "it does not matter how local the operation which applies the squeeze." [6]

In Chapter 2, we dealt with the augmented scope which the post-1937 high Court has given to federal power. In the present chapter, we shall be looking at the other side of the coin—the authority recognized by the Court in the states themselves. Even in an age of ever-expanding federal power, this is a crucial subject to one who believes in federalism as a flourishing system. It may well be true that, as a matter of constitutional law, under the decisions on Congressional authority discussed in Chapter 2, we have reached the stage, prophesied by Chief Justice Hughes in 1935, where state authority even over its domestic concerns exists only by sufferance of the Federal Government.[7] But that does not mean that, in a country such as ours, there is not still a vital role for the states to play. There is a vast difference between the possession of power and the propriety of its exercise. The fact that, under the recent jurisprudence of the Supreme Court, the Congress can assert regulatory power at will, so as to supersede almost all state authority, does not, by itself, answer the question of how far the federal legislature has actually acted to override state power.

In a country like ours, where local patriotism and attachment to the individual state still retain much of their vigor, it is unlikely that the legislators whom we send to Washington will knowingly seek to reduce the states to governmental sterility. Yet, as is true of all laws, statutes involving federal regulatory authority receive their final form and content through interpretation by the courts. It is, thus, ultimately the Supreme Court which must determine whether the Congress has, in particular exertions of its authority, intended to make federal power all-pervasive in the given field, or whether it has been willing to leave untouched the local authority of the states, to be exerted as a complement to federal regulation. Few types of case have given the high Court more difficulty in recent years than

* *Supra,* pp. 34-46.

those concerned with the interplay of federal and state authority. And few have been of greater importance to the working of our federal system. For, at a time when few, if any, powers are denied by the Court to the National Government, the extent to which national authority is deemed compatible with the possession of similar state power will be cardinal in determining what powers the states may legitimately exercise.

It is true that, even if the highest Court should construe federal laws with a strong presumption in favor of the exercise of concurrent state authority wherever possible, our present system will still be a far cry from the classical concept of federalism. To the theoretical purist, in truth, even a state with a federal income tax is no longer a genuinely federal state. But pure federalism is utterly inconsistent with the stresses of twentieth-century political evolution. To seek to recreate it in its eighteenth-century classical image is to indulge in a hunt for the chimera. Certainly, no tribunal entrusted with the highest judicial power can reasonably be expected to engage in so quixotic an undertaking. Yet the Court can be looked to for the realization of more attainable goals, and, specifically, to vindicate a primary function of constitutional law in a present-day federation—to ensure to the states whatever powers they may still be legitimately permitted to exercise. State authority should be scrutinized with anything but a jealous eye by a tribunal cognizant of the values which even a watered-down federalism may still possess.

Substantive Due Process

One respect in which the post-1937 Court has differed drastically from its predecessors has been in its application of the doctrine of substantive due process to the states. In Chapter 5, we discussed the procedural aspects of the due process clause of the Fourteenth Amendment.* Fair or proper procedure is, of course, the literal meaning of due process. From about 1890, however, due process acquired a substantive aspect as well, which came, in many ways, to be even more important. Henceforth, the substantive as well as the procedural aspect of state legislation would be subject to the scrutiny of the highest Court. How did the Court determine whether the substantive parts of a state law were consistent with due process of law? In the view of the 1890–1936 Court, such a determination required an inquiry by the judge into the reasonableness of a challenged law. If the Court was of the opinion that

* *Supra,* pp. 162 ff.

a statute was arbitrary, it could not hold it to be consistent with due process of law; as the Court put it in an 1884 case, anticipating the expansion of the due process clause that was shortly to occur, "arbitrary power, enforcing its edicts to the injury of the persons and property of its subjects, is not law, whether manifested as the decree of a personal monarch or of an impersonal multitude." [8]

It is the 1905 decision of the highest tribunal in *Lochner v. New York*,[9] already referred to in a previous chapter,* that is the classic case illustrating the pre-1937 approach to the issue of substantive due process. According to the Court there, the question to be determined in cases involving challenges to state legislation on due process grounds was: "Is this a fair, reasonable and appropriate exercise of the police power of the State, or is it an unreasonable, unnecessary and arbitrary interference with the right of the individual to his personal liberty or to enter into those conducts . . . which may seem to him appropriate or necessary." [10] Under the *Lochner* test —is the statute unreasonable, unnecessary, and arbitrary?—the Court was able to set itself up as the Supreme Censor of the wisdom of state legislation. The due process clause was thus expanded from its origins, designed to provide a fair trial, to a device for judicial control of the whole range of both the national and local economic systems.

Judicial utilization of substantive due process was not, it should be noted, mere control in the abstract of the wisdom of state legislation. Court control was directed to a particular purpose, namely, the invalidation of state legislation that conflicted with the doctrine of laissez faire which dominated thinking in this country at the turn of the century. What Justice Frankfurter has termed "the shibboleths of a pre-machine age . . . were reflected in juridical assumptions that survived the facts on which they were based. . . . Basic human rights expressed by the constitutional conception of 'liberty' were equated with theories of *laissez-faire*." [11] The result was that the Fourteenth Amendment became the rallying point for judicial resistance to the efforts of the states to control the excesses and relieve the oppressions of a rising industrial economy.[12] "The paternal theory of government," declared Justice Brewer, one of the principal architects of the post-1890 doctrine of due process, "is to me odious. The utmost possible liberty to the individual, and the fullest possible protection to him and his property, is both the limitation and duty of government." [13] To a Court which adopted the Brewer philosophy, the "liberty" protected by the Fourteenth Amendment became synonymous with governmental hands-off in the

* *Supra*, pp. 13-14.

field of private economic relations. Any legislative encroachment upon the existing economic order became suspect as infected with unconstitutionality.[14]

Of particular importance to the pre-1937 Court was liberty of the individual to contract. "The general right to make a contract in relation to his business," asserted the opinion in the *Lochner* case, "is part of the liberty of the individual protected by the Fourteenth Amendment." [15] Freedom of contract became the formula for striking down scores of state statutes. This was especially true in the case of laws regulating labor conditions and, by such regulation, seeking to eliminate many of the worst abuses of a free competitive economy. Nor did it make any difference to the high tribunal that, particularly in the labor field, the notion of equality between contracting parties, upon which freedom of contract must be based, is wholly out of line with the facts of a modern industrial society— that, in the words of Justice Stone, "There is grim irony in speaking of the freedom of contract of those who, because of their economic necessities, give their services for less than is needful to keep body and soul together." [16]

Despite the fact that freedom of contract is really a misnomer as applied to a contract between an employer and an ordinary employee, it was in the name of freedom of contract that the Court prior to 1937 outlawed state statutes regulating the hours of labor,[17] minimum wages,[18] barring so-called "yellow dog" contracts [19] (making it a condition of employment that the worker should not join a union), or restraining the granting of injunctions in labor disputes.[20] Indeed, as late as 1936, the Court held that a minimum-wage law was beyond the power of the state of New York.[21] And the due process clause was similarly used to invalidate a host of other state legislation seeking to regulate other abuses of the economic system, from laws to protect purchasers from excessive ticket brokerage charges to those fixing maximum fees which employment agencies might charge.[22] As Justice Jackson has stated, after 1890, it was a fortunate and relatively innocuous piece of state reform legislation that was able to run the gauntlet of due process.[23] The impact of the judicial veto on state power is perhaps best seen from statistics: in the period between 1890 and 1937, the Supreme Court held invalid 228 state statutes.[24] Well could Justice Holmes protest, in one of his most celebrated dissents, "As the decisions now stand, I see hardly any limit but the sky to the invalidating of [state laws] if they happen to strike a majority of this Court as for any reason undesirable." [25]

Few, today, doubt that the high tribunal went too far before

1937 in its application of the doctrine of substantive due process, or that the Court since that time has been correct in deliberately discarding its predecessor's extreme due process philosophy. There is, to paraphrase a 1945 opinion of Justice Black,[26] a strong emotional appeal in words like "fair and reasonable" or "freedom of contract." But they were not chosen by those who wrote either the Constitution or the Fourteenth Amendment as a measuring rod for the Supreme Court to use in invalidating state laws. Not even those who have most feared democratic government have ever formally proposed that the Court should be given power to annul legislation under such elastic standards. It is not for a judicial tribunal to set itself up as judge of the wisdom or desirability of measures taken by the states to deal with supposed economic evils. The Fourteenth Amendment was not intended to prevent the state legislatures from choosing whether to regulate their economies or leave them to the blind operation of uncontrolled economic forces, futile or even noxious though the particular choice might seem to the individual judge. Economic views of confined validity are not to be treated as though the Framers had enshrined them in the Constitution.[27] "The Fourteenth Amendment," Justice Stone well protested in 1936, "has no more embedded in the Constitution our preference for some particular set of economic beliefs than it has adopted, in the name of liberty, the system of theology which we may happen to approve." [28]

In his dissent in the *Lochner* case, Justice Holmes asserted, "This case is decided upon an economic theory which a large part of the country does not entertain." [29] In the period since 1937, both the economic and legal theories upon which *Lochner* rested have been repudiated by the Supreme Court. Early in 1937, the high tribunal overruled its earlier holdings that a minimum-wage law violated due process by impairing freedom of contract between employers and employees. "What is this freedom?" asked the Court's opinion. "The Constitution does not speak of freedom of contract. It speaks of liberty and prohibits the deprivation of liberty without due process of law. In prohibiting that deprivation the Constitution does not recognize an absolute and uncontrollable liberty." [30] The liberty safeguarded by the Constitution is liberty in a society which requires the protection of the law against evils which menace the health, safety, morals, or welfare of the people. Regulation adopted in the interests of the community, the Court concluded, is due process.

The extent to which the post-1937 Court has followed the view that regulation adopted in the interest of the community is consistent with due process is shown by a 1952 decision. At issue, there, was a Missouri statute which provided that any employee entitled to vote might absent himself from his employment for four hours on election days, and that it was unlawful for his employer to deduct wages for that absence. It was argued that such a law constituted an invalid deprivation of the employer's property without due process. Such an argument, said the Court, is reminiscent of the philosophy of *Lochner v. New York* and other like due process decisions of the pre-1937 period. To be sure, the Missouri law requires the employer to pay wages for a period in which the employee performs no services. But that does not mean that it makes for a taking of property without due process. The statute at issue was seen to be basically similar to a minimum-wage law, like that upheld in 1937. Though not, like the earlier legislation, designed to protect the health and morals of the citizen, this statute is equally enacted in the interest of the community. It is designed to eliminate any penalty for exercising the right of suffrage and to remove a practical obstacle to getting out the vote: "The public welfare is a broad and inclusive concept. The moral, social, economic, and physical well-being of the community is one part of it; the political well-being, another. The police power which is adequate to fix the financial burden for one is adequate for the other." [31] It is true, the Court conceded, that the judgment of the legislature— that time out for voting should cost the employee nothing—may be a debatable one. But that is the whole point about the Court's changed approach to review under the due process clause. Under it, the Court leaves debatable issues, as respects business, economic, and social affairs, to legislative decision. "Our recent decisions," declares the Court, "make plain that we do not sit as a super-legislature to weigh the wisdom of legislation nor to decide whether the policy which it expresses offends the public welfare." [32] A law like that at issue, asserted the opinion, could be invalidated only if the Supreme Court were to return to the philosophy of pre-1937 cases like *Lochner v. New York*.

A case, like that just discussed, shows how far the highest tribunal has retreated from that earlier philosophy. It is one thing to uphold a minimum-wage law; yet, because a state may require payment of a minimum wage for hours that are worked, it does not follow that it may compel payment for time that is not worked. All the same, such a law must be upheld under the theory that regulation adopted in the interests of the community is due process. In the Court's present view, the state legislatures have constitutional authority to experiment with new techniques; they are entitled to maintain their own standard of the public welfare; they may, within extremely broad limits, control practices in the business-labor field.

Since 1937 the high bench has had occasion directly to overrule only one other due process decision of its predecessors. It occurred in 1941, when a 1928 decision,[33] voiding as inconsistent with due process a state statute regulating the fees charged by employment agencies, had been relied on by a lower court to invalidate a similar Nebraska law; the Supreme Court speedily reversed, holding that the earlier case could no longer be deemed a controlling authority.[34]

Though, as just stated, the Court has had no occasion directly to repudiate other specific due process decisions of the pre-1937 period, there is no doubt that it would do so if the need arose. For decisions like that upholding the Missouri election-pay law show how clearly the Court has rejected the earlier due process philosophy. From 1890 to 1937, the high bench used the due process clause as a device to enable it to review the desirability of state regulatory legislation. In 1955, that tribunal could declare: "The day is gone when this Court uses the Due Process Clause of the Fourteenth Amendment to strike down state laws, regulatory of business and industrial conditions, because they may be unwise, improvident, or out of harmony with a particular school of thought." [35] Before 1937, the Court tested state laws by its own judgment of whether they were reasonable, in the light of the overriding bias of the law against unnecessary governmental interferences with the free working of the economic system. Since that time, the Court has tended more and more to defer to the judgment of the state legislature on the desirability of the particular law. In many ways, in fact, the Court's deference to the state legislature, when a question of substantive due process is at issue, has moved close to the deference which, we have seen,* that tribunal now shows to the Federal Congress. Here, too, the tendency is to adopt the test of whether a rational legislator could have regarded the statute as a reasonable method of protecting the public welfare. It is enough, said the Court in its 1955 opinion just quoted, that there is an evil at hand for correction, and that it might be thought that the particular legislative measure was a rational way to correct it.

Interestingly enough, one of the strongest recent attempts to induce the high Court to return to the pre-1937 notion of due process was made in 1949 by a labor union, which had, of course,

* _Supra_, Chapter 2.

been the very economic group most severely affected by the earlier decisions invalidating laws on due process grounds. By 1949, however, the shoe was on the other foot, for at issue then was a so-called "right-to-work" law which forbade employers to enter into closed shop agreements, obligating themselves to exclude from employment persons not members of unions. This type of law, unlike those that had been at issue in the pre-1937 period, was intended to protect the nonunion worker. It was thus wholly natural for organized labor to challenge its constitutionality; what was more surprising was that it used the sword—of which it had so often been the victim in earlier days—against such social legislation. The union claimed that the state law at issue deprived both employers and union members of their freedom of contract. This, the Court itself aptly noted, was to ask for a return to the due process philosophy that had been deliberately discarded since 1937. Such a return was one which could not be taken by a Court which adhered to the doctrine that the due process clause is no longer to be so broadly construed that state legislatures are put in a strait jacket when they attempt to suppress business and industrial conditions which they regard as offensive to the public welfare: "Just as we have held that the due process clause erects no obstacle to block legislative protection of union members, we now hold that legislative protection can be afforded non-union workers." [36]

It should be obvious to one who has read thus far that the high Court's due process decisions since 1937 have made for a drastic change in the law of judicial review of the constitutionality of state legislation. Such departure from the jurisprudence of its predecessors by a judicial tribunal should, to be sure, be suspect as undermining the stability of the law. In the field under discussion, nevertheless, the rejected precedents had themselves been based upon an unwarranted departure from the more limited meaning originally given the due process clause. There is little doubt that, to paraphrase Justice Jackson,[37] the 1890–1936 Court had, by its undue expansion of the concept of due process, torn that concept loose from its ancient connotations and, by so doing, had magnified the doctrine of judicial supremacy beyond all legitimate bounds. In rejecting the pre-1937 due process philosophy, the Court has, in Justice Black's words in 1949, "consciously returned closer and closer to the earlier constitutional principle that states have power to legislate against what are found to be injurious practices in their internal commercial and business affairs, so long as their laws do not run afoul of some specific federal constitutional prohibition, or of some valid federal law." [38] In so doing, the Court has returned to a more reasonable view of the proper scope of judicial power.

It can hardly be denied that there may be dangers in too restricted a judicial role. Undue deference to the state may allow it to enforce laws whose real purpose is to perpetuate family monopolies [39] or to drive competitors of an established industry out of business.[40] Even in such cases, deference to the legislator may result in judicial findings that challenged laws may be rational regulatory devices. To the possibility of abuse, if the states are all but unrestrained by the judiciary, the Court only two years ago repeated an earlier statement of a nineteenth-century Chief Justice: "For protection against abuses by legislatures the people must resort to the polls, not to the courts." [41] Once again, deference to the legislator has led the Court all but to abandon the field to him. The zone for legislative action has so broadened as almost to eliminate substantive due process as a restraint against everything except the most arbitrary state action. But, the Court would say, that is precisely the situation that is consistent with a democratic system. In such a system, the forum for the correction of ill-considered legislation must be, not the courts, but a responsive legislature.

Intergovernmental Tax Immunities

The post-1937 reversal in jurisprudence, just discussed, has, without any doubt, been most favorable toward exertions of state authority, for it has almost entirely eliminated substantive due process as an effective limitation upon the states' police power. Another important change in case law by the highest Court in the past twenty years has taken place in a field that is of vital importance to the proper functioning of a federal system, namely, that of intergovernmental tax immunities. Here, however, the practical results of the change have not been entirely favorable to the states.

The doctrine of intergovernmental tax immunity is one that is inherent in the nature of federalism. It grows out of the possession by both the Federal Government and the states of powers of taxation. But the fact that we are a federation raises a basic problem with regard to such powers, which was well stated by Justice Frankfurter: "Since two governments have authority within the same territory, neither through its power to tax can be allowed to cripple the operations of the other. Therefore state and federal governments must avoid exactions which discriminate against each other or obviously interfere with one another's operations." [42]

The legal starting point for intergovernmental tax immunities was the 1819 case of *McCulloch v. Maryland*,[43] in which John Marshall delivered one of his most celebrated opinions. In holding that a state could not levy a tax upon an agency of the Federal Government operating within the state, the great Chief Justice made his famous statement that the power to tax involves the power to destroy. To permit the states to tax federal agencies would be to place in the states the power to nullify federal operations.

Implicit in the Marshall holding is a broad doctrine of intergovernmental immunity, which protects the states as well as the Federal Government. If state power to tax federal agencies involves the power to destroy them, the same is also true of federal authority to tax state agencies. As Justice Frankfurter has explained it,

the fear that one government may cripple or obstruct the operations of the other early led to the assumption that there was a reciprocal immunity of the instrumentalities of each from taxation by the other. It was assumed that there was an equivalence in the implications of taxation by a State of the governmental activities of the National Government and the taxation by the National Government of State instrumentalities.[44]

At the same time that the Supreme Court extended the immunity doctrine to protect state, as well as federal, instrumentalities, it gave an expansive scope to what were deemed to be "instrumentalities of government" for purposes of tax immunity. The Court assumed that the economic burden of a tax on any interest derived from a government imposes a burden on that government so as to involve an interference by the taxing government with the functioning of the other government.[45] Acting on this assumption, it held in the leading 1870 decision of *Collector v. Day* [46] that the Federal Government could not tax the salary paid to a state officer. In other words, the immunity from taxation by the other vested in the state and National Governments was also accorded to the officials through whom those governments operated.

It did not take the post-1937 Court long to reject this extension of intergovernmental immunity to government officials. In 1938, the high tribunal decided that the salary of a state employee was not immune from federal income tax; [47] the next year, the Court reached the same result with regard to the immunity of a federal employee from state income taxation, at the same time sweeping out the protection from taxation which the doctrine of intergovernmental immunity had been construed to give public officers.[48] A nondiscriminatory tax laid on the income of all members of the community, said the Court in both decisions, casts no unconstitutional burden on the government whose employees are taxed: "The theory, which once won a qualified approval, that a tax on income is legally or economically a tax on its source, is no longer tenable." [49]

Once again, the post-1937 Court had overruled established doctrine of its predecessors. But here, too, it can hardly be said that the reversal was unwarranted. *Collector v. Day* and its progeny were themselves an unprecedented extension of the intergovernmental immunity principle—an extension by no means logically inherent in that principle. In Justice Jackson's expression, "However persuasive the argument for governmental immunity, there was little reason in law and none at all in sound government for holding that officeholders shared the government's immunity from tax." [50] To suggest that it makes inroads upon a state government's immunity by making its employees pay their aliquot share of the cost of maintaining the National Government is to trivialize the whole notion of intergovernmental immunity. To subject public employees to a general income tax is merely to recognize that they are also citizens, and that their particular function in government does not generate an immunity from sharing with their fellow citizens the material burdens of both state and Federal Governments. [51]

The pre-1937 Court had not only held that a tax on government employees imposed a burden on the government concerned, but also applied the same theory to a tax on any interest derived from government. Thus, it had been held in 1928 that a state could not impose any tax upon a contractor with the Federal Government, where the result of the tax would be to increase the amount which the Government would have to pay under the contract. [52] In such a case, the theory ran, the burden of the tax was really not on the contractor, but on the Government, which was, of course, wholly immune from state taxation. This theory was basically similar to that which had supported the pre-1937 immunity of government employees from taxation; so it is hardly surprising that it, too, was abandoned by the post-1937 Court as early as possible. At the end of 1937, the high tribunal held that a state may impose an occupation tax upon an independent contractor, measured by his gross receipts under contracts with the Federal Government. [53] And, in 1941, in *Alabama v. King & Boozer*, [54] a state sales tax imposed on a contractor, in respect of materials which he purchased for the performance of a "cost-plus-fixed-fee" contract with the United States, was sustained. In this case, it was clear that, since the Federal Government, pursuant to the "cost-plus" contract, had to reimburse the contractor for the amount of the tax, the state tax did increase the amount the United States had to pay under the contract. According to the Court, nonetheless, that did not mean that there was an infringement of the Federal Government's immunity. So far as a nondiscriminatory state tax upon the contractor enters into the cost of the materials to the Government, that is but a normal incident of the organization within the same territory of two independent taxing sovereignties. The asserted right of the one to be free of taxation by the other does not spell immunity from paying the added costs, attributable to the taxation of those who furnish supplies to the Government. And the Court went on expressly to overrule the earlier cases, like its 1928 decision already referred to, which had upheld government contractors' immunity.

Alabama v. King & Boozer is of basic importance to the states in an age when government, to operate properly, must seek to tap all possible legitimate sources of revenue. It is one thing to say that instrumentalities and activities of the Federal Government must not be subject to state taxation. But the pre-1937 Court had created what were, in effect, a vast area of private immunities for those who dealt with the National Government. To wipe out these private immunities and limit the immunity that remains to the activities of the Government itself is not to infringe upon the tax immunity of the United States. Today, as Justice Frankfurter has expressed it,

it is not enough that the Government may ultimately have to bear the cost of a part or even the whole of a tax which a State imposes on a third person who has business relations with the Government, when a State could impose such a tax upon such a third person but for the fact that the transaction which gave rise to it was not with a private person but with the Government.[55]

To state it another way, under post-1937 decisions like *Alabama v. King & Boozer,* the Court has moved forward from the time when a state's power to tax was nullified whenever the federal treasury was even remotely affected.

It may, at the same time, be necessary to impose a caveat here, lest the reader overestimate the freedom to tax given the states by the *King & Boozer* decision. It is important, in the first place, to bear in mind that *King & Boozer* dealt with the state's taxing power where there has been no Congressional provision on the matter. And, under the prevalent attitude of the high Court toward Congressional exertions of authority, there is no doubt that that tribunal will respect a federal statute immunizing those who deal with the National Government from sales and other taxes which the states, under cases like *King & Boozer,* are otherwise free to impose. This view is confirmed by *Carson v. Roane-Anderson Co.,*[56] decided in 1952, which denied to Tennessee the power to apply its use tax to private contractors for the Atomic Energy Commission on articles used in the performance of contracts with the Commission. This holding was based on a prohibition, contained in the Atomic Energy Act, of any state taxes upon AEC "activities," and on the finding that the contracts involved in the case and their performance were Commission "activities" within the meaning of the prohibition. It is thus clear that what the Supreme Court giveth to the states, the Congress can take away.

Just as important is the fact that what the Court gave to the states in *King & Boozer,* it can itself also take away. In an age of ever-mounting Government expenditures and consequent attempts to cut down burdens on the federal treasury by decreasing the cost to the Government on "cost-plus" type contracts, there has been constant pressure by Government counsel on the Court to repent its *King & Boozer* generosity. These pressures are difficult for the Court to withstand in the face of the plain fact that state taxes on contractors under "cost-plus" contracts do ultimately result in increased costs to the United States. In its 1954 decision in *Kern Limerick, Inc. v. Scurlock,*[57] indeed, the majority of the Court took a substantial step toward giving in to such pressures. It there held that a state sales tax could not validly be applied to a sale by which certain contractors acquired two tractors for use in constructing a naval ammunition depot for the United States under a "cost-plus" contract. The Court justified this holding because of the fact that here, unlike *King & Boozer,* the contract purported to make the contractors purchasing agents for the Federal Government, and the purchase order involved in the sale in question provided: "This purchase is made by the Government." This, said the Court, distinguished this case from *King & Boozer,* for here the United States was the real purchaser and would have had to pay the tax. The only trouble with this reasoning is that the Government was the real party in interest in both cases; but the Court, in *King & Boozer,* held that that did not prevent the state from taxing the sale to the contractor. In actual fact, the form of the particular contract and purchase order in the *Kern Limerick* case had been drafted by the Navy Department to avoid the effect of the *King & Boozer* decision and, thus, to conserve federal funds. That is, of course, a laudable purpose; but is it enough to defeat the right of the states to impose nondiscriminatory taxes on private sales within their borders? If the *King & Boozer* rationale was sound, it should have been applied in this case as well. Instead, the Court allowed the Government contracting officers to draw the line of permissible state taxation by changing a few words in a contract.[58]

Under the pre-1937 cases in this field, the emphasis was clearly on immunity from taxation. The more recent cases, already dealt with, reveal a shift in emphasis to limitation upon immunity. They have, however, concerned themselves with eliminating the immunity formerly given to private individuals because of their participation in governmental functions. None of them involved direct taxation of government itself. In the 1946 case of *New York v. United States*,[59] on the other hand, the federal tax at issue was one imposed directly upon the state. It arose out of an action by the Federal Government to recover taxes assessed against the State of New York on the sale of mineral waters taken from springs on state-owned land at Saratoga Springs and bottled and sold by a state agency. The federal tax in question is one imposed on all mineral waters sold in this country. New York claimed that it was immune from this tax, but its claim was rejected by the Supreme Court. In a case like this, the Nation may tax the state activity upon the same basis as it does private individuals engaged in that activity. When a state enters the market place seeking customers it divests itself of its sovereignty pro tanto, and takes on the character of a private trader, at least so far as the federal taxing power is concerned. "If Congress . . . ," states Justice Frankfurter, who announced the judgment of the Court, "taxes all vendors of mineral water alike, whether State vendors or private vendors, it simply says, in effect, to a State: 'You may carry out your own notions of social policy in engaging in what is called business, but you must pay your share in having a nation which enables you to pursue your policy.' " [60]

New York v. United States permits the Federal Government to include the states in levying a tax also exacted from private persons engaged in the same business. But the case is far from holding that state immunity from federal taxation is now entirely done away with. There are certain activities which are so essential to the existence of state governments that to allow the Federal Government to tax them would be to allow it to interfere unduly with the states' performance of their sovereign functions of government.

There are, of course, State activities and State-owned property that partake of uniqueness from the point of view of intergovernmental relations. These inherently constitute a class by themselves. Only a State can own a Statehouse; only a State can get income by taxing. These could not be included for purposes of federal taxation in any abstract category of taxpayers without taxing the State as a State.[61]

State immunity is now limited to those activities which are considered essential to government as we have traditionally known it. When the state takes over an activity men have been accustomed to carry on as a private and, therefore, taxable enterprise, then the activity can be taxed by the Nation: "so long as Congress generally taps a source of revenue by whomsoever earned and not uniquely capable of being earned only by a State, the Constitution of the United States does not forbid it merely because its incidence falls also on a State." [62]

A decision like *New York v. United States* tends drastically to change the nature of the doctrine of intergovernmental tax immunity. Heretofore, the predominant theme had been that of equality between states and Nation, insofar as tax immunity was concerned. Under the *New York* case, there is no longer equivalent intergovernmental immunity. The states are now immune from federal taxation only with regard to activities deemed essential to their continuance as independent governments. But the Congress can tax all functions deemed nongovernmental—such as the sale of mineral waters—even though they may be carried on by a state: "Not the extent to which a particular State engages in the activity, but the nature and extent of the activity by whomsoever performed is the relevant consideration." [63] The Federal Government, on the other hand, remains wholly immune from state taxation. The immunity of federal agencies does not turn on their nature or the nature of their activities; as the Court has put it in two post-1937 decisons, all the activities of a federal agency must be considered as governmental and, as such, entitled to whatever immunity attaches to functions performed by the Federal Government.[64]

It must be recognized that underlying, at least in part, the *New York v. United States* decision were the ever-present pressures, already referred to, to increase federal sources of revenue. As Justice Rutledge candidly declared, in a concurring opinion, "Competitive considerations unite with the necessity for securing the federal revenue, in a time when the federal burden grows heavier proportionately than that of the states." [65] At the same time, it can hardly be denied that the implications for our federalism of the *New York* decision are of great consequence. If federal power to tax the states is conceded, they no longer have the independence which they have always been assumed to have: "They are relegated to a more servile status. They become subject to interference and control both in the functions which they exercise and the methods which they employ. They must pay the federal government for the privilege of exercising the powers of sovereignty guaranteed them by the Constitution." [66]

It is true, as has been pointed out, that the states still retain a certain amount of tax immunity—so far as their essential governmental activities are concerned. But the area of state activity from which immunity has been removed is precisely that of especial significance to modern government, which is more and more undertaking social functions that half a century ago were thought to be beyond the sphere of government:

A State's project is as much a legitimate governmental activity whether it is traditional, or akin to private enterprise, or conducted for profit. . . . A State may deem it as essential to its economy that it own and operate a railroad, a mill, or an irrigation system as it does to own and operate bridges, street lights, or a sewage disposal plant. What might have been viewed in an earlier day as an improvident or even dangerous extension of state activities may today be deemed indispensable.[67]

Recognition of federal taxing power over state so-called nongovernmental activities gives to Washington a ready means of controlling the social service functions of the states. And that is why the removal of state tax immunity, with regard to such functions, may be an important step in that magnification of federal authority which is now the dominant theme of our federal system. As a dissenting member of the Supreme Court has asserted:

A tax is a powerful, regulatory instrument. . . . If the federal government can place the local governments on its tax collector's list, their capacity to serve the needs of their citizens is at once hampered or curtailed. The field of federal excise taxation alone is practically without limits. Many state activities are in marginal enterprises where private capital refuses to venture. Add to the cost of these projects a federal tax and the social program may be destroyed before it can be launched.[68]

Regulation of Commerce

In Chapter 2, we dealt with the regulatory authority vested in the Congress under the commerce clause of the Constitution.* It is, however, important to realize that, as Justice Douglas has recently

* *Supra,* pp. 28-46.

pointed out, "The Commerce Clause has a negative as well as a positive aspect. The Clause not only serves to augment federal authority. By its own force it also cuts down the power of the constituent State in its exercise of what would normally be a part of its residual police power." [69]

The grant of the commerce power to the Congress does not of itself divest the states of all authority to regulate commerce. It has, on the contrary, always been recognized that there is still a residuum of power in the states to make laws governing their local commerce; this is true even though such laws in some measure affect interstate commerce or even, to some extent, regulate it. "Every State . . . ," said Chief Justice Taney over a century ago, "may regulate its own internal traffic, according to its own judgment and upon its own views of the interest and well-being of its citizens." [70] From the time of John Marshall, nevertheless, it has been recognized that the power of the states over commerce within their boundaries must be exercised consistently with the overriding purpose of the commerce clause. That clause sought to put an end to the economic autarchy of the states. If there were no commerce clause, each state could shut out the products of other states or admit them only on conditions. But this is precisely the sort of Balkanization of our economy that the commerce clause sought to end. It is not for the states, in pursuit of their local interests, to decide what products from without may cross their boundaries or to admit products on condition that they satisfy local economic policy. [71] The states may shelter their people from menaces to their health or safety and from fraud, even when those menaces emanate from interstate commerce, but they lack power to retard, burden, or constrict the flow of such commerce for their economic advantage. The Constitution, in the apt words of Justice Cardozo, "was framed upon the theory that the peoples of the several states must sink or swim together, and that in the long run prosperity and salvation are in union and not division." [72]

It is thus clear that the commerce clause, in and of itself, affords protection from state legislation inimical to national commerce. The basic principle is that our economic unit is the Nation; and its corollary is that the states are not separable economic units, which may place themselves in positions of economic isolation. The commerce clause was intended to promote a system of free trade among the states, and to do so by denying to the states the power to impede the free flow of commerce from state to state. And there are few lessons more clearly taught by history than the beneficial consequences of such promotion of free trade between the states. Certainly, the material success that has come to the inhabitants of the states that make up our federal free-trade unit has been the most impressive in the history of commerce.[73]

From the splintered confederation of the 1780's, cut asunder by commercial warfare between the states, has grown the United States of today. No constitutional provision has played a larger part in that growth than the commerce clause. The Supreme Court itself recognized this when it eloquently declared in 1949:

Our system, fostered by the Commerce Clause, is that every farmer and every craftsman shall be encouraged to produce by the certainty that he will have free access to every market in the Nation, that no home embargoes will withhold his exports, and no foreign state will by customs duties or regulations exclude them. Likewise, every consumer may look to the free competition from every producing area in the Nation to protect him from exploitation by any. Such was the vision of the Founders.[74]

We must now inquire whether it has been given reality by the recent decisions of the highest Court.

Our first inquiry will be into the question of the effect of Congressional silence, with regard to the particular subject of regulation, upon state power over commerce. Even when Congress has not acted, the commerce clause creates a large area of free trade, of which the Supreme Court is often the main guardian.[75] Furthermore, the Court is not aided by the Constitution itself in determining the boundaries of that area. On the contrary, on the subject of what powers the states may exercise when Congress has not spoken, the Framers left the high Court almost wholly at large. As that tribunal has expressed it:

While the Constitution vests in Congress the power to regulate commerce among the states, it does not say what the states may or may not do in the absence of congressional action. . . . Perhaps even more than by interpretation of its written word, this Court has advanced the solidarity and prosperity of this Nation by the meaning it has given to these great silences of our Constitution.[76]

Perhaps the most important step in the process of advancement referred to was taken roughly a hundred years ago in the basic case of *Cooley v. Board of Port Wardens*.[77] At issue in that case was the validity of a Pennsylvania law requiring vessels coming into or leaving Philadelphia to use local pilots. Since there was no federal law on the subject, the question for the Court was that of the extent of state regulatory power over commerce where the Congress was silent on the matter. According to the now classic opinion of Justice Curtis, whether state regulatory power exists in such a case depends upon the subjects of the power, and particularly upon whether they are of such a nature as to require exclusive legislation by Congress:

Now, the power to regulate commerce, embraces a vast field, containing not only many, but exceedingly various subjects, quite unlike in their nature; some imperatively demanding a single uniform rule, operating equally on the commerce of the United States in every port; and some, like the subject now in question, as imperatively demanding that diversity, which alone can meet the local necessities of navigation.[78]

Whether the states can regulate in a case of this type, the opinion goes on, depends upon whether it is imperative that the subjects of the regulation be regulated by a uniform national system:

Whatever subjects of this power are in their nature national, or admit only of one uniform system, or plan of regulation, may justly be said to be of such a nature as to require exclusive legislation by Congress. That this cannot be affirmed of laws for the regulation of pilots and pilotage is plain . . . . the nature of this subject is such, that until Congress should find it necessary to exert its power, it should be left to the legislation of the States; that it is local and not national; that it is likely to be the best provided for, not by one system, or plan of regulations, but by as many as the legislative discretion of the several States should deem applicable to the local peculiarities of the ports within their limits.[79]

The *Cooley* case has remained the polestar for judicial decisions on state power under the commerce clause, where Congress has made no provision in the matter. The high Court's law in this field still rests upon the distinction between subjects of regulation which require nationally uniform exertions of regulatory authority and those where uniformity is not demanded. In 1937, the Court had before it a state law which regulated motor-driven tugs not regulated by federal law, this regulation providing for inspection of the hull and machinery of such vessels in order to insure safety and seaworthiness. In determining whether such a state regulatory law was valid, Chief Justice Hughes, speaking for the Court, relied entirely upon the *Cooley* test. Is the inspection of these tugs to insure safety and seaworthiness, he asks, "a subject which necessarily and in all aspects requires uniformity of regulation and as to which the State cannot act at all, although Congress has not acted? We hold that it is not." [80] Consequently, the Court concluded, the state could enact a regulatory law like that at issue.

A more recent case where the application of the *Cooley* doctrine caused a split within the Court is *Southern Pacific Co. v. Arizona*,[81] decided in 1945. At issue in it was an Arizona train-limit law which made it unlawful for any person or corporation to operate within the state a railroad train of more than fourteen passenger or seventy freight cars in length. This statute, said the Court, "imposes a serious burden on the interstate commerce conducted by appellant. It materially impedes the movement of appellant's interstate trains through that state and interposes a substantial obstruction to the national policy proclaimed by Congress, to promote adequate, economical and efficient railway transportation service." [82] The regulation of interstate train lengths, if any be necessary, must be prescribed by a single body having nation-wide authority. The state cannot prescribe uniform control, such as is essential to a national transportation system, which Congress alone can prescribe. If one state may regulate train lengths, so may all the others, and they need not prescribe the same maximum limitation. The result would be that interstate railroads would have to conform to "a crazy-quilt of State laws" [83] which imposed different regulations in each state. This result was well described in the Court's opinion:

Compliance with a state statute limiting train lengths requires interstate trains of a length lawful in other states to be broken up and reconstituted as they enter each state according as it may impose varying limitations upon train lengths. The alternative is for the carrier to conform to the lowest train limit restriction of any of the states through which its trains pass, whose laws thus control the carriers' operations both within and without the regulating state.[84]

Though two dissenting Justices took sharp issue with the propriety of the *Cooley* test as the standard by which to judge the challenged Arizona law, that test seems peculiarly appropriate, even a century after its articulation, to aid the decision of cases like *Southern Pacific Co. v. Arizona*. If the national interest demands a single system of regulation, then state regulatory power must give way, even though no federal law on the subject has been enacted. Where national uniformity is necessary, no regulation at all is preferable to the confusion and difficulty with which interstate commerce would be burdened under a patchwork of state legislation. In a case like *Southern Pacific*, to permit Arizona to enforce her law, while train lengths remain unregulated or are regulated by varying standards in other states, must inevitably result in an impairment of uniformity of efficient railroad operation, because the railroads are subjected to regulation which is not uniform in its application. Of course, the state has an interest in securing the safety of train operation within her borders. But the state interest cannot be maintained at the expense of the national interest in uniformity of regulation by an enactment which regulates interstate train lengths without securing such uniformity. To such a matter of national concern, the state interest must be subordinate. Where national uniformity is deemed necessary, to allow the states to regulate would be to countenance the very sort of thing that the commerce clause was intended to put an end to.[85]

Chief Justice Stone, who delivered the *Southern Pacific* opinion, felt compelled to distinguish *South Carolina Highway Department v. Barnwell Bros.*,[86] a 1938 case in which he also announced the opinion of the Court. In that case, the state law in question was a South Carolina statute which prohibited the use on the highways of the state of motor trucks and "semi-trailer" motor trucks whose width exceeded ninety inches, and whose weight, including load, exceeded twenty thousand pounds. This South Carolina law was upheld by the Court in the *Barnwell Bros.* case, despite the fact that it appears to be the counterpart, in the field of motor vehicle regulation, of the Arizona law in the field of train regulation, later declared invalid in the *Southern Pacific* case. How did Chief Justice Stone explain this seeming inconsistency in his *Southern Pacific* opinion? According to him, the difference between the two cases stems from the difference in the type of transportation involved: "There are few subjects of state regulation affecting interstate commerce which are so peculiarly of local concern as is the use of the state's highways. Unlike the railroads local highways are built, owned and maintained by the state or its municipal subdivisions. The state is responsible for their safe and economical administration."[87] In the field of motor vehicle regulation, in other words, an added element is present which tips the scale in favor of state regulatory power, namely, that motor vehicles use highways furnished and maintained by the state. It is this that gives the state a far more extensive control over motorcars passing interstate over its highways than over interstate railroads. The law at issue in the *Barnwell Bros.* case, which regulated the width and weight of vehicles in the state, had a direct relation to the safety and cost of maintenance of the highways provided by the state and was, therefore, upheld.

Basing its action directly upon the reasoning which led it to sustain the South Carolina law just discussed, the highest Court has, in more recent cases, upheld other state laws regulating motor vehicles, even though their prescriptions applied to interstate as well as purely local traffic. Thus, a Pennsylvania statute, which prohibited the operation on its highways of any motor vehicle carrying any other vehicle over the head of the operator of such carrier vehicle, was declared valid in 1940; [88] and the year before, a New Hampshire law fixing maximum hours for drivers of vehicles on its highways was held binding on interstate as well as local vehicles.[89] In 1949, the *Barnwell Bros.* reasoning was applied to sustain a New York traffic regulation forbidding the operation of any advertising vehicle in the streets, even though it was enforced against trucks delivering goods from New Jersey. As the Court's opinion expressed it, "Where traffic control and the use of highways are involved and where there is no conflicting federal regulation, great leeway is allowed local authorities, even though the local regulation materially interferes with interstate commerce." [90]

The Court in recent years has not, however, stopped at upholding state regulations of the type just dealt with, which are clearly adopted to promote safety upon state highways and to insure their conservation and convenient use by the public. It has gone further and held that, if the state can regulate by such laws, it can also regulate by means of licensing schemes. Under its decisions, it is clear that a state can require all motor carriers using its highways to obtain licenses from the relevant state agency, and this requirement may validly be applied to interstate as well as intrastate carriers. In a 1952 decision, the Court held that Arkansas could require a person engaged exclusively in the interstate transportation of goods by motor vehicle to obtain a certificate of necessity and convenience from Arkansas.[91] This case clearly settles (although its holding is implicit in earlier decisions) that a state can impose the condition of obtaining a state license as a prerequisite for using its highways, even on one engaged exclusively in interstate commerce. Nor is this power to license confined to carriers using the highways. In 1941, the high Court upheld a state law requiring every transportation agent (i.e., one who negotiates for the transportation of passengers in motor vehicles over the highways of the state) to obtain a license.[92] A 1927 decision had declared such a law invalid,[93] but the Court stated that the cases which uphold the power of the states closely to regulate their highways justified this regulation of transportation agents, and the 1927 decision was accordingly overruled.

In other cases, the Court has gone even further, holding that the power to license includes the power to tax. Consequently, a state may impose a reasonable fee upon interstate motor carriers for the use of its highways. As the Court put it in 1939, "a State may impose upon vehicles used exclusively for interstate transportation a fair and reasonable tax as compensation for the privilege of using its highways for that purpose." [94] Such state fees must be upheld if they bear some reasonable relation to the cost of maintaining and policing the highways. [95] This is true even though they do impose substantial burdens upon the interstate carriers concerned. In a 1952 case, an Illinois tax, imposed for the use of the public highways and measured by the gross weight of the vehicles involved, was sustained, although the amount of the tax was as high as $1,580 per truck. [96]

Despite the Court's attempt to distinguish these motor vehicle regulation decisions from the Arizona train limit case, one is left with an uneasy feeling that those decisions permit the states to carry on the very restrictive practices that the commerce clause was intended to preclude. In the Court's view, highway regulation is not a subject requiring national uniformity; road conditions vary from state to state and, in addition, there is the factor, already mentioned, that the highways are furnished and maintained by the state itself. These may, to be sure, differentiate road regulation from train regulation of the type at issue in *Southern Pacific Co. v. Arizona*. At the same time, one cannot help but feel that separate regulation in each state results in the same impediment to interstate commerce by a "crazy-quilt" of state laws as that which the Court pointed to with alarm as the inevitable result of the Arizona train limit law. It is paradoxical that, in a country dominated by the free-trade concept of the commerce clause, interstate commerce must obtain separate permits and pay toll every time it crosses a new state line. Interstate commerce is faced with a rampart of economic barriers, which constitute a constant clog upon that mobility of commerce that the Constitution was designed to foster.

If separate state regulation of interstate commerce, such as that sustained in the recent decisions discussed, is to be tolerable at all, it must be scrutinized with a jealous judicial eye. For the power to regulate also involves, to paraphrase the famous Marshall dictum, the power to destroy. State regulation can all too easily be employed as a device to eliminate competition from out of state or to discriminate against such competition. Of course, outright embargo [97] on interstate commerce by a state or patent discrimination [98] by it against such commerce will be stricken down without any difficulty. But the states are hardly ever so artless as to avow such obviously unseemly uses of authority. When a state employs its regulatory power for an improper purpose (such as discrimination against interstate commerce), it is not so naive as to admit it.

It disguises the true motives of its action and seeks to give some legal pretext (e.g., that its action is based upon the need for highway safety). The Supreme Court must then unmask the ruse—not always a simple matter.

The authority to license may easily be used as a device to protect those already in the field from interstate competition. However, this clearly contravenes the policy of the commerce clause. In an important 1925 case, the Court had held that a state could not use its power to license interstate carriers to deny access to its market by out-of-state carriers on the ground that the community was already adequately served; such regulation was, in effect, being used to effect a ban on interstate competition.[99] In its 1952 decision, already referred to, upholding the power of Arkansas to require an interstate carrier to obtain a state certificate of necessity and convenience,[100] the Court stated that its decision was based upon the denial by the relevant state licensing agency of any discretion to deny a certificate to anyone engaged in interstate carriage. Here the state was plainly not going to use its licensing authority to exclude out-of-staters from its roads.

More recently the high Court has gone even further in holding that interstate commerce cannot be barred from a state's highways. In *Castle v. Hayes Freight Lines*,[101] a 1954 case, the Court held that, where an interstate carrier held a certificate of convenience and necessity from the Federal Interstate Commerce Commission, a state could not suspend the carrier's state permit to use the state's highways, even though such suspension was imposed as a punishment for repeated violations of the state law regulating the weight of loads of freight that might be carried on the state's highways. This decision supplies a needed corrective (though only in part) to the cases, already dealt with, which allow interstate commerce traveling on roads to be regulated directly by the states. Under the *Castle* decision, even violators of state regulatory laws cannot be excluded from state highways, if they are engaged in interstate commerce. State regulatory authority may thus not be employed to keep interstate commerce off its roads. It should, all the same, be emphasized that the *Castle* case does not in any way affect the states' powers to enact regulatory laws of the type under discussion. Nor does it affect the liability of carriers who violate such laws under the conventional sanctions of the criminal law. Though the interstate carrier may not be driven from the state's highways, the threat of fine or imprisonment will normally be enough to compel him to comply with the state regulations.

Taxation of Commerce

In the cases just discussed, involving the regulation of commerce, the normal predilection of the present writer in favor of state authority gives way to the overriding need to promote the policy which called forth the commerce clause, if not the Constitution itself. If some of its recent decisions have been criticized, it is because the high Court has at times tended to lose sight of this basic need in a country like ours. It is more vital today even than in 1787 that we remain an undivided economic aggregation and not, what Justice Jackson aptly termed, a collection of parasitic states preying upon each other's commerce. With that judge, "I make no concealment of and offer no apology for my philosophy that the federal interstate commerce power should be strongly supported and that the impingement of the states upon that commerce which moves among them should be restricted to narrow limits." [102]

This philosophy must also be the guiding principle in cases involving the power of the states to tax commerce. Here, too, the post-1937 Court has gone further than its predecessors in upholding state authority. Of course, interstate commerce benefits as much as local commerce from local government and should share with local commerce the burdens and costs of it. Interstate commerce should pay its way and should not secure competitive advantage from tax immunity denied to local commerce. At the same time, if we hold an interstate industry subject to the unlimited taxing power of each state in which it does business, we open the door to the destruction of interstate commerce by local efforts to secure revenue. It may be, as the high Court stated in 1940, that the question is "whether the state has given anything for which it can ask return." [103] But that test, too, can be pushed too far—even, indeed, to its *reductio ad absurdum,* as a member of the Court aptly showed in 1942. In a very real sense, he said,

every State and Territory in the Union has conferred very real benefits upon every inhabitant of the Union. Some States have seen to it that our food is properly produced and inspected; others have fostered and protected the industry upon which we are utterly dependent for the ordinary conveniences of life and for life itself. All of them have yielded up men to provide government at home and to repel the enemy abroad. I am the very real debtor, but am frank enough to say I hope not a potential taxpayer, of all.[104]

If the commerce clause means anything, it means that interstate commerce cannot be taxed to the full limit by every state through which it passes. Physical power alone cann.ot be the criterion in a country governed by a Constitution such as ours; might cannot always make right in the field of taxation.[105] Even if interstate commerce should be required to pay its own way, that does not mean that it should be required to do more. If interstate commerce were subject to the full taxing power of each state through which it moved, the interstate trader would be at a tremendous disadvantage compared with local industries. For this to be avoided, the tax situation must be equalized as between interstate and local commerce. The goal, in the words of one commentator,[106] seems to be that the interstate transaction should not be saddled with an aggregate tax burden higher than it would bear if it had taken place in the same volume and over the same distance within a single one of the pertinent states.

How is this goal, which seeks basically to place interstate and local commerce upon a plane of tax equality, to be attained, when the taxing power of a state is sought to be exerted against a multistate enterprise? The answer must be in terms of an apportionment between the taxing state and the other states in which the taxpayer carries on his commerce. Without such allocation to the taxing state of only its fair share of the interstate business enterprise, the latter could be seriously hampered by excessive taxation in each state in which it operates. Thus, in *Adams Mfg. Co. v. Storen,*[107] a 1938 case, the Court had before it an Indiana tax on all the gross receipts of a company which sold 80 per cent of its products outside the state. Such a tax, said the Court, was invalid insofar as it affected the company's interstate business. If Indiana could impose such tax, so could the states where the goods were sold, and the company's interstate commerce would thus be subjected to the risk of double taxation. As Justice Stone put it the next year, in an opinion invalidating a similar Washington tax:

If Washington is free to exact such a tax, other states to which the commerce extends may, with equal right, lay a tax similarly measured for the privilege of conducting within their respective territorial limits the activities there which contribute to the service. The present tax, though nominally local, thus in its practical operation discriminates against interstate commerce, since it imposes upon it, merely because interstate commerce is being done, the risk of a multiple burden to which local commerce is not exposed.[108]

For such a tax to be valid, it must be apportioned to the company's activities within the taxing state. Consequently, when the Indiana gross receipts tax was applied only to the sales within the state of an interstate company, it was upheld.[109]

There have been many cases in the past twenty years in which state taxes based upon apportionments have been sustained. A few examples will suffice to illustrate what the states may do in this field. A Texas franchise tax on the Ford Motor Co., measured by a charge upon such proportion of the outstanding stock, surplus, and undivided profits of the company as the gross receipts from its Texas business bore to its total gross receipts, was upheld in 1939.[110] And the same result was reached in 1942 with regard to a California franchise tax on corporations, measured by a formula calculated to allocate to the state that portion of the net income reasonably attributable to the business done in California. The apportionment formula averaged the percentages which (1) value of real and tangible personal property, (2) wages, salaries, commissions, and other compensation of employees, and (3) gross sales, attributable to the California branch of the company taxed, bore to the corresponding items of all its branches.[111] A number of these cases involve companies engaged in interstate transportation, whose travel routes run through several states; here again, the states can tax upon an apportioned basis. Thus, an interstate railroad could be assessed within a state by taking such part of the value of the railroad's entire system, less the value of its "localized" property (terminal buildings, shops, and nonoperating real estate), as was represented by the ratio which the railroad's mileage within the state bore to its total mileage.[112] And an interstate bus company's gross receipts could be taxed, but only if apportioned as to the mileage within the taxing state.[113] Similarly, a state tax on barges doing business on an interstate river was valid where the assessments were based on the ratio between the number of miles of line within the taxing state and the total number of miles of the entire barge line.[114]

It must be admitted that the apportionment theory, upon which state taxes in this field must be based, is far from a perfect one. Certainly, it cannot be denied that any method of allocating to one state its fair share of a nation-wide unitary business must be, at best, a rough approximation. And, in the Court's decisions, there is a definite tendency to accept almost any bona fide state attempt to work out some allocation, mathematically inexact though the formula used may be. As the Court stated in 1947, rough approximation, rather than precision, is all that is required: "Unless a palpably disproportionate result comes from an apportionment, a result which makes it patent that the tax is levied upon interstate commerce rather than upon an intrastate privilege, this Court has not been willing to nullify honest state efforts to make apportionments." [115]

Yet, even with its imperfections conceded, the apportionment theory remains the best practical (even if not wholly logical) device to prevent duplication of tax burdens. It has been found workable, even though particular formulae of apportionment may have to be more or less arbitrary.

The merits of the apportionment theory are best seen when the high Court does not adhere to it, as has happened at times in recent years. Perhaps the most striking case of this kind was *Northwest Airlines v. Minnesota*,[116] decided in 1944. That case considered for the first time constitutional limitations upon state power to tax airplanes. The Court's decision upheld a tax by Minnesota upon all the property of an airline incorporated within the state and having there its principal place of business, which was listed as the home port registered with the Civil Aeronautics Authority. The tax was upheld, even though it was not apportioned as between the flying or the business done in the state and that done in other states. Tax apportionment was deemed unnecessary because Minnesota was the state of domicile and such state was not limited in its taxing power. The only trouble with this is that it ignores the possible claims of the other states in which the airline operates. There is nothing in the *Northwest Airlines* decision to bar states, other than the domiciliary state, from taxing planes in interstate commerce upon an apportionment basis in accordance with their use in the taxing state, and a 1954 decision actually upholds such taxing power.[117] But, if other states can tax on an apportionment basis, the *Northwest Airlines* case, holding that the state of domicile is not limited by that basis, means that the result will be multiple taxation of the interstate enterprise. That result can be avoided only if the Court returns to the apportionment basis and permits the domiciliary state to tax upon that basis alone.[118]

Another important class of cases where the post-1937 Court has appeared to overlook the dangers of multiple taxation are those involving sales and use taxes. In its 1940 decision in *McGoldrick v. Berwind-White Coal Mining Co.*,[119] the high tribunal sustained a New York City sales tax on a contract of sale made in New York for shipment of coal from Pennsylvania to a New York purchaser. Thus, for the first time, the Court sustained a direct tax upon an interstate sale; yet this was the kind of state barrier to free intercourse that the commerce clause was intended to remove. The Court in *Berwind-White* speaks of the need not to give interstate commerce an exemption which local commerce does not have. But a state may not lay a direct tax upon interstate commerce even if it is nondiscriminatory; such a tax amounts to a customs duty of the type which destroys the concept of free trade upon which the commerce clause is based. In addition, a tax like that sustained by the Court opens the door to multiple taxation—if New York can tax the sale of coal delivered in New York, why cannot Pennsylvania tax its shipment from that state, or New Jersey the transshipment through its borders?

The so-called *use* tax is a direct result of efforts by the states to avoid competitive advantages otherwise enjoyed by sister states without sales taxes. As the Court explained it in a 1954 opinion, the

use tax, not in itself a relatively significant revenue producer, usually appears as a support to the sales tax in two respects. One is protection of the state's revenues by taking away from inhabitants the advantages of resort to untaxed out-of-state purchases. The other is protection of local merchants against out-of-state competition from those who may be enabled by lower tax burdens to offer lower prices.[120]

Such a tax is imposed on the privilege of using in the state products brought in from other states. In 1937 the high Court upheld such a use tax in *Henneford v. Silas Mason Co.*,[121] a decision announced by Justice Cardozo. According to him, the states can tax the privilege of use of property within their borders, even though such property was acquired through interstate commerce. But such a use tax is subject to at least the same objections as a sales tax upon commerce; the theory that the commerce has come to an end cannot change the fact that the tax is a direct charge upon interstate commerce. It is true that, in the Washington tax law upheld in the 1937 case, there was a provision exempting from the tax any property which had already been subjected to an equal or greater sales tax in another state. This offset provision eliminates the possibility of double taxation; the stranger from afar is, in Justice Cardozo's phrase, subject to no greater burdens than the dweller within the gates. But the Court overlooks the basic fact that, if the purpose of the tax is to create equality as between interstate and local commerce, its effect is exactly like that of a protective tariff. It may be advantageous for the state to be able to say to interstate commerce: You may come into my borders as you please, but your products must be subject to the same tax burdens as local products. There is no doubt that a sovereign country could make such a statement and levy protective tariffs to carry it into effect. The whole point about our system, nevertheless, is that the states are barred from laying such tariffs upon commerce from sister states. In place of the immunity of interstate commerce contemplated by the Constitution, the *Berwind-*

White and *Henneford* decisions have fostered the erection between states of what amounts to tariff walls designed to offset the competitive advantages of lower taxes in other states.

The Supreme Court itself has been coming to see this, for, though it has never overruled the two cases discussed, it has more recently been imposing some limits in the sales-use tax field. In *McLeod v. Dilworth Co.*,[122] decided in 1944, Arkansas was not permitted to levy a sales tax on purchases of goods in Tennessee for consumption in Arkansas. The *Berwind-White* case was distinguished on the ground that there the seller had an office in New York and the sale was consummated there; here the sales were made in Tennessee. Though this decision does mark what the dissenting Justices called a retreat from *Berwind-White* (now, a sales tax cannot be imposed unless the sale is made in the taxing state by a seller who maintains an office there), it does not affect the taxing state's power to substitute a use tax for the sales tax, even under a fact pattern like that presented in the *McLeod* case.[123]

The effectiveness of a use tax depends upon the scheme by which it is collected. Such taxes are all but impossible to collect from the thousands of individuals who make purchases across state lines. To overcome these difficulties, the states have attempted to make the sellers collect use taxes for them. In its 1954 decision in *Miller Bros. Co. v. Maryland*,[124] however, the high Court denied such power to the state of the purchaser to make the out-of-state seller its tax collector, refusing to permit the state to enforce the duty to collect the tax imposed by it by seizure of a truck used by the seller to do business within the state. This is an important restriction upon the effectiveness of the use tax. But it does not alter the power of the states to impose such taxes and to attempt to collect them as best they can, though it is as clear today as it was two decades ago, when such taxes were first upheld, that they are wholly contrary to the purpose of the commerce clause. The Court in the past decade has been quick to strike down state taxes imposed directly on the privilege of doing interstate commerce. The use tax imposes just as effective a barrier to free commerce. To be sure, as a dissenting opinion urges in the *Miller Bros.* case: "Unless the States can collect a sales or use tax upon goods being purchased out-of-state, there is a fertile opportunity for the citizen who wants state benefits without paying taxes to buy out-of-state." [125] Yet it is exactly this opportunity to deal freely beyond his state's borders that is given to the citizen by the commerce clause. The Court itself in *Miller Bros.* recognized that the use tax has the same effect as a protective tariff.

Under the Court's decisions upholding the use tax, it is precisely with this type of "protective tariff" that our former free-trade economy is now honeycombed.

Propriety of Judicial Review

Our discussion till now has assumed the propriety of the Supreme Court acting to nullify state legislation on the ground that it is contrary to the commerce clause. That assumption has not, it should be noted, gone unchallenged on the post-1937 Court. It is true that, from the very beginning of our constitutional history, the high tribunal has exercised the authority to enforce the policy behind the commerce clause. Though the power of the Court to nullify state action in these cases was disputed in the 1840's by Chief Justice Taney,[126] ever since his day the exercise of judicial power in this field has gone unquestioned; in fact, for much the better part of a century, not a single member of the Supreme Court had cast any doubt upon the settled principle that the drawing of a line between permissible and illegal state regulation and taxation of commerce was a judicial function.

This century of unanimity did not daunt Justice Black; shortly after his appointment to the high bench, he seized the opportunity to assert, in dissent,[127] his view that his predecessors had again been wrong, and that the many cases in which the Court had acted in this field had merely been unconstitutional assumptions of power which "cannot be justified or validated by claiming prestige from advanced age." [128] In Justice Black's view, the commerce clause means that Congress can regulate commerce and that the courts cannot. The Court is, therefore, acting beyond its province in nullifying state legislation deemed in conflict with the commerce clause: "Whether state legislation imposes an 'undue burden' on interstate commerce raises pure questions of policy, which the Constitution intended should be resolved by the Congress." [129] In 1945, indeed, the learned judge went so far as to accuse the majority of the Court, which had refused to follow his view, of assuming the role of a "super-legislature" in these cases [130]—thus reviving one of the chief charges that had been directed against the pre-1937 high Court.

In Chapter 5,* we dealt at some length with another instance where Justice Black rejected the jurisprudence of a century in favor of his own notion of what the law should be. What was said there, about the seemliness of judicial casting off of established case law, need not be repeated here; some fields of thought may be advanced

* *Supra,* pp. 163-67.

by heresy based upon sudden revelation, but the law is not one of them. Since the cases just discussed in this chapter are, all the same, of such consequence to the proper working of our federalism, it is important here to demonstrate the unsoundness of the Black view on the merits.

According to Justice Black, only the Congress, not the courts, should be permitted to deal with state transgressions of the commerce clause. Only the legislature, says he, can not only consider whether particular state legislation is consistent with the best interests of our national economy, but can also, on the basis of full exploration of the many aspects of a complicated problem, devise a national policy fair alike to states and Nation.[131] Such a view betrays such ignorance of the practical working of the legislative process that it is hard to believe that it is advanced by one who spent over a decade in the Senate. As a practical matter, how is the Congress able to deal with the myriad problems of state impediments to national trade? Even if we assume that an assembly so reflective of sectional interests could acquire the broad view and impartiality necessary to resolve these matters, it is hard to see where it would find the time, when it is now swamped by the pressures of its normal legislative tasks. And where is the legislative body to acquire the machinery and the personnel to operate it, which are required to deal speedily and effectively with cases of improper state action as they arise? It is only the judicial process that is able actively to deal with these cases so as to give immediate practical effect to the policy behind the commerce clause. Justice Douglas (until recently the strongest supporter on the Court of the Black view) aptly pointed this out in a 1955 lecture. Speaking of state barriers to commerce, he says, "Congress, of course, could have removed those barriers and probably would have done so. But the judiciary has moved with speed. As a result of the case by case approach, there has been no great lag between the creation of the forbidden barrier or burden and its removal by the judiciary." [132]

No one (and least of all the present writer) would claim that the Supreme Court has been a perfect instrument for the implementation of the commerce clause, or even that it has been as effective in all cases as it might have been. On the whole, nonetheless, the performance of the judiciary in the field has produced a record far more commendable than might be expected from a legislative assembly. Free trade has, in fact, flourished under the fostering impact of the high Court's commerce-clause decisions. That tribunal has been at its best when it has pierced the veil of ostensible regulation in the interest of public health or safety and brought to light a scheme of state discrimination against interstate commerce.[133] Certainly, it has been the American experience that the fulfillment of a policy like that of the commerce clause must depend primarily upon the courts: "Constitutions can say that commerce must be free; but over the years the courts will be largely the ones who will implement these provisions." [134] Perhaps the best answer to the Black view on the impropriety of judicial power was given some years ago by Justice Holmes, when he said:

I do not think the United States would come to an end if we lost our power to declare an Act of Congress void. I do think the Union would be imperilled if we could not make that declaration as to the laws of the several states. For one in my place sees how often a local policy prevails with those who are not trained to national views and how often action is taken that embodies what the Commerce Clause was meant to end.[135]

Federal-State Conflicts

Thus far in this chapter we have been dealing with cases involving the validity of state legislation where there has been no Congressional law on the subject. At the same time, in an era of ever-expanding federal authority, federal legislation under the commerce clause has penetrated more and more deeply into areas once occupied exclusively by state regulatory power. The result has been that state laws have come under increasingly frequent attack as being incompatible with acts of Congress operating in the same field. How has the Supreme Court dealt with such attacks? That is the question to which we must now turn.

If the Congress acts, its action is, of course, the supreme law of the land (subject, to be sure, to the rule that such action must itself be within the constitutional boundaries of Congressional power). Any state law incompatible with such Congressional act must, therefore, fall. Yet, it should be emphasized that the mere fact that Congress has chosen to speak does not automatically silence the states. That Congress has legislated in a particular field does not of itself divest the states of whatever powers they otherwise possess in that field. As Justice Frankfurter stated in 1945, "when Congress has spoken, although not as fully as the Constitution authorizes, that is, when a federal enactment falls short of the Congressional power to legislate touching commerce, the States may still speak where Congress is still silent." [136] In such a case, a state statute must give way only if it is in clear conflict with the federal enactment or if the Congress has, in such enactment, expressed an intent to take over the field of regulation. In the latter case, Congress has spoken so as to silence the states—has acted so as to bar any state action at all in the particular field.

As is true of most legislation, the Congressional intent on the question of compatibility between its laws and state legislation in the field covered is one which must be determined by the courts, and ultimately by the supreme bench in Washington. The high Court's determination in particular cases whether state laws are consistent with exertions of federal power is, as was emphasized at the beginning of this chapter,* of crucial importance to the present-day functioning of our federalism. At a time when the Court denies few, if any, powers to the Congress, the extent to which it deems Congressional authority compatible with similar power in the states will be vital in determining what authority the states may still exercise.

Our discussion of state action touching interstate commerce was dominated by an overriding policy against local interferences with the national economy. That policy led us to scrutinize state regulations of commerce with a jealous eye. But that is not the way to regard state laws in cases involving the interplay of federal and state regulatory authority. Here we are dealing with state action confined to its own boundaries, where the state could clearly regulate, except for the Congressional act that is claimed to sweep away state power in the particular field. The starting point in such a case should be, not judicial suspicion, but respect for an allowable area of state law, with a strong presumption in particular cases in favor of state authority. The Court should not lightly infer that the Congress, by the mere passage of a federal act, has impaired the traditional sovereignty of the states.[137] It is one thing for a state law to be stricken down as incompatible with an act of Congress where the repugnance is direct and positive, so that the two laws cannot be reconciled or consistently stand together. It is, Chief Justice Stone well stated in 1942,

quite another to infer a purpose, which Congress has not expressed, to deprive the states of authority which otherwise constitutionally belongs to them, over a subject which Congress has not undertaken to control. Due regard for the maintenance of our dual system of government demands that the courts do not diminish state power by extravagant inferences regarding what Congress might have intended if it had considered the matter, or by reference to their own conceptions of a policy which Congress has not expressed and is not plainly to be inferred from the legislation which it has enacted.[138]

* *Supra,* pp. 190-91.

If the high Court's decisions in recent years, nullifying state laws as incompatible with Congressional enactments, have been subjected to very strong criticism, it is, in part at least, because that tribunal has all too often lost sight of the basic wisdom expressed in the Chief Justice's statement. In the very case where that statement was made, Chief Justice Stone was speaking for a minority who protested against the striking down by the Court of an Alabama statute regulating packing stock butter used in the manufacture of renovated butter because of the existence of a federal law regulating the manufacture and transportation of renovated butter. Yet it is clear, even from the majority opinion, that the federal law did not give to the relevant federal agency the power to condemn or destroy unwholesome packing stock butter before it was used in the manufacture of renovated butter. Nevertheless, the majority held, the Alabama law must fall because Congress intended to take over the field—and this despite any clear indication in the federal law of legislative intent to exclude state regulation like that at issue and despite the fact that the federal and state regulatory schemes had been administered in harmonious cooperation for many years. The result of the Court's gratuitous assumption of Congressional intent to destroy all state butter regulation was to deny the state the power to protect the health of its citizens without replacing such protection by that of the Federal Government.[139]

This case illustrates an important practical factor which the Court seems to have lost sight of in some of its recent decisions. All too often, its decision invalidating state power is purely destructive; the Court takes power away from the states but is unable to ensure its exercise by the Federal Government.[140] Thus, in a 1947 decision, the Court held that the system of warehouse regulation established by Illinois was completely superseded by the Federal Warehouse Act, even though the Court conceded that the federal scheme was a more modest, less pervasive regulatory scheme than that of the state. A dual system of regulation which had operated successfully for thirty years was ended by this decision, not because the operation of the state law conflicted with that of the federal law (concededly it did not), but because of the Court's theory that Congress, just by regulating, intended to nullify the extensive network of state regulatory laws in the field. It is not too far fetched to say, as did Justice Frankfurter, in a dissent, that what the Court had really done was to introduce laissez faire outside the relatively narrow scope of the federal act. In his apt words,

surely one does not draw on idle fears in suggesting that as a result of today's decision the gates of escape from deeply rooted State requirements will be open, although Congress itself has not authorized federal authority to take over the regulation of such activities and though their State enforcement does not at all conflict with, but rather promotes, the limited oversight of warehouses thus far assumed by the Federal Government. The Court displaces settled and fruitful State authority though it cannot replace it with federal authority.[141]

Due regard for our federalism, in its practical operation, favors survival of the reserved authority of the states, unless Congress has clearly swept the boards of state power. Instead, the Supreme Court has even held state regulation invalid because incompatible with federal laws, in the face of express indications of a Congressional intent not to displace existing state regulation. This has occurred several times in the field of natural gas regulation where the Court has extended federal, to the exclusion of state, authority, despite provisions in the relevant federal law indicating that it was intended only to supplement—not to supplant—state legislation. The most controversial, perhaps, of the Court's decisions in this field has been that which it rendered in 1954 in *Phillips Petroleum Co. v. Wisconsin*.[142] There, notwithstanding an express provision in the federal statute that it "shall not apply . . . to the production or gathering of natural gas," the Court held that federal, rather than state, regulation was called for over an independent producer engaged solely in the production and gathering of natural gas, and this despite the fact that the federal regulatory agency had decided that the statutory provision left jurisdiction in the matter to the states. "Language could not express a clearer command," caustically declares Justice Clark in his dissent, "but the majority renders this language almost entirely nugatory by holding that the rates charged by a wholly independent producer and gatherer may be regulated by the Federal Power Commission."[143]

Another case worthy of note where the high Court has needlessly overridden state authority is *Bethlehem Steel Co. v. State Labor Relations Board*,[144] a 1947 decision. That case involved the regulation of labor relations, where both the Congress and New York had enacted similar regulatory laws, with the state statute confined to intrastate commerce. The relevant federal agency, the National Labor Relations Board, had entered into an agreement under which it ceded jurisdiction to the New York Labor Relations Board in cases arising in certain specified trades and industries, which, it was felt, were best handled on a local level. The Supreme Court held, however, that the Congress had intended to occupy the field, so far as the decision of appropriate units of labor representation (the issue in the case) was concerned, so that the NLRB's declining of jurisdiction did not leave the state free to intervene. Regardless of the consent of the National Board, said the Court, New York was excluded from enforcing rights of collective bargaining in all industries within its borders as to which Congress had granted opportunity to invoke the authority of the National Board. Completely frustrated was the practical federal-state working arrangement, arrived at by the agencies carrying the responsibility for breathing life into the bare bones of the legislation.[145] The cooperative agreement between federal and state agencies was nullified by a metaphor —"occupied the field"—which did service for close analysis.[146] Surely it should not be beyond the power of the National Board to agree with state agencies enforcing similar laws to divide, with due regard to local interests, the domain over which Congress had given the National Board abstract authority, but which the latter feels cannot practically be covered by it alone.

Many of the Court's controversial decisions invalidating state laws on the ground of irreconcilability with federal statutes have been in the same field as that involved in the *Bethlehem Steel* case —that of labor relations. In 1945, the high tribunal invalidated a Florida statute which required business agents of a union operating in the state to file annual reports and pay a fee of one dollar.[147] This was true although the matter regulated by Florida was not at all regulated by the relevant federal labor law. In 1950, the strike vote provisions of the Michigan mediation law, which prohibited a strike unless a majority of the employees voted in its favor, were held void [148] and, the following year, a like decision was reached with regard to the Wisconsin Public Utility Anti-Strike Law, which sought to outlaw strikes which would interrupt essential public utility services.[149] In both these cases, too, the states were dealing with aspects of their labor relations which were not regulated by the federal law.

This is not to say, of course, that the federal labor statute has left state laws in that field wholly unimpaired. Thus, where a union was engaging in an unfair labor practice for which the Congress had provided a federal remedy before the National Labor Relations Board, a state court could no longer issue an injunction against such practice, even though such injunction was authorized under state law.[150] Nor can a state "right-to-work" law (outlawing closed shops) prevail in the railroad field in the face of a provision in the Federal Railway Labor Act expressly permitting closed shop agreements, notwithstanding the law of any state.[151] But these are cases of patent conflict between state and federal statutes. It is when the inconsistency of the two regulatory schemes is not so obvious that the high Court often appears to be too ready to override state authority. Judicial disregard of the need for maintaining state regulation is particularly undesirable in the labor field. For that is one field where few will contend that our law has achieved anything like an adequate accommodation of conflicting interests. Yet, in our federal system, we have at hand a magnificent means of experimentation with new solutions, without the necessity for imposing them on the entire country. As Justice Brandeis once said, "It is one of the happy incidents of the federal system that a single courageous State may, if its citizens choose, serve as a laboratory; and try novel social and economic experiments without risk to the rest of the country." [152] Thus, long before there was any federal regulation of utilities, courageous states took the initiative and almost the whole body of our modern utility law has resulted from their experience. The same might happen in the field of labor regulation, if state experimentation in that field is not judicially choked off at the outset. A system of compulsory arbitration may or may not be the answer which will enable us to avoid the drastic effects of strikes that curtail essential services; but we are deprived of the experience of states experimenting with such novel regulatory devices by the 1951 decision, already referred to, annulling a Wisconsin law which provided for such a way of dealing with public utility strikes.

Diversity of experimentation in the field of regulation has values which centralization and uniformity destroy. Regulatory measures (even though they attain to the dignity of being embodied in an act of Congress) are, in Justice Jackson's phrase,[153] temporary expedients—not eternal verities. The highest Court should not utilize its centralizing authority to destroy the diversity between states which is possible in our federalism. Yet this is what the Court has been doing in all too many of its recent decisions. Such judicial action is inconsistent with the basic premises of a flourishing federal system, particularly, as in most of these cases, where the Congress has not manifested any clear intention to sweep aside all state authority. This was acutely noted by Justice Frankfurter who declared in 1947:

Since Congress can, if it chooses, entirely displace the States to the full extent of the far-reaching Commerce Clause, Congress needs no help from generous judicial implications to achieve the supersession of State authority. To construe federal legislation so as not needlessly to forbid preexisting State authority is to respect our federal system. Any indulgence in construction should be in favor of the States, because Congress can speak with drastic clarity whenever it chooses to assure full federal authority, completely displacing the States.[154]

There are, to be sure, those, both on and off the high Court, who will dismiss strictures like those of the present writer as based upon an outmoded appeal to "states' rights," in an age when effective regulation must be carried out upon a national level. These people, however, ignore the strength which still remains in the American tradition of federalism. It retains and will continue to retain its vitality because it has values which, difficult though they may be to articulate, have not been destroyed by rapid transportation and the growth of national markets. Maintenance of strong state governments imparts a democratic strength to our system, not found in centralized, monolithic administration. If, now and then, some state does not regulate according to the federal standard, that may be a small price to pay for preserving the vigor of our federal system. Of course, the destruction of state authority and the setting up of a wholly centralized administrative system, with all regulatory authority flowing from Washington, may be the realization of many a federal bureaucrat's fondest dreams. To many of us, all the same, it could well signalize the commencement of the Orwellian nightmare of 1984, dominated by its omnipotent administration, unrestrained by any checks on its all-pervasive regulatory activities.

It was with most keen insight that, more than a century ago, Alexis de Tocqueville expressed the basic dangers inherent in over-centralized administration. In a celebrated passage, he wrote:

I cannot conceive that a nation can live and prosper without a powerful centralization of government. But I am of the opinion that a centralized administration is fit only to enervate the nations in which it exists, by incessantly diminishing their local spirit. Although such an administration can bring together at a given moment, on a given point, all the disposable resources of a people, it injures the renewal of those resources. It may ensure a victory in the hour of strife, but it gradually relaxes the sinews of strength. It may help admirably the transient greatness of a man, but not the durable prosperity of a nation.[155]

Would that our highest Court were equally alive to the values inherent in the diffusion of authority under our federal system!

7

THE INDIVIDUAL

Summing up his political faith in defense against a charge of high treason, Thomas Wentworth, Earl of Strafford, declared in 1641: "God, his majesty, and my own conscience, yea, and all those who have been most accessary to my inward thoughts and opinions, can bear me witness that I ever did inculcate this, That the happiness of a kingdom consists in a just poize of the king's Prerogative and the Subject's Liberty: and that things would never go well, till they went hand in hand together." [1]

The happiness of a State consists in a "just poize" between Authority and Liberty. To describe the interplay between Authority and Liberty in these terms requires acute perception. It recognizes that both are essential elements in the functioning of any polity and that their coexistence must somehow be reconciled. But there are all too few who frankly acknowledge that Authority and Liberty are complementary, not competing, elements in a political society. Most often, the problem is stated, not in terms of necessary reconciliation between the two, but in terms of one or the other taking over the entire field. Even so discerning an observer as John Stuart Mill begins his essay *On Liberty* by referring to the "struggle between Liberty and Authority" as the most conspicuous feature in history. This implies a constant battle between two contending principles, with one or the other ultimately destined to dominate in the political arena. Such a view may have validity in a society in which there is a sharp distinction between those who govern and those who are governed. In such an order, the rulers are in a necessarily antagonistic position to the people whom they rule. Liberty, then, means protection against the political rulers, and history is, indeed, a continuing effort to set limits to their powers. There comes a time, at last, when such effort has succeeded, not merely in curbing the tyranny of the rulers, but in effecting a complete transformation in the political system. The ruling power comes to emanate from the periodical choice of the ruled and the dichotomy between governors and governed becomes blurred. The rulers are identified with the people; their interest and will become the interest and will of the nation.

It is not, to be sure, true that the problem of Authority versus Liberty is wholly resolved merely because demos comes to be king. The notion that the people have no need to limit their power over themselves is one which we have rejected in our very concept of constitutionalism. What is true is that, in a representative system dominated by a constitution, the just claims of both Authority and Liberty must be recognized. For the proper functioning of the polity, each must be given its proper place; we must seek to partition the field between them, not to exclude the one or the other. Which brings us back, of course, to Strafford's need for a "just poize" between Authority and Liberty. Both are essential: "They are fellows and companions, that are and ever must be inseparable in a well-governed kingdom." [2] But how is this proper balance to be secured?

In the American system, it is the Supreme Court that is entrusted with the task of securing a "just poize" between Authority and Liberty. Our Constitution vests in the Government all the powers needed to enable it to function effectively. At the same time, the Framers recognized that it was not enough thus to grant the authority needed for government to be carried on. For the first time in an organic instrument, they provided for the safeguarding of the liberties of the individual. The Bill of Rights drew up the inventory, since become classic, of modern Liberty. Thus, both Authority and Liberty are adequately provided for in the Constitution. A constitution is not, however, self-executing, and power continues, even in a democracy, to be (in Madison's phrase) of an encroaching nature. What happens, then, if Authority seeks to circumscribe Liberty? The answer, without a doubt, is that the validity of restrictions upon Liberty is, like other matters in our constitutional system, ultimately a judicial question. It is for the Supreme Court to determine whether such restrictions are consistent with the balance between Authority and Liberty provided for in the Constitution.

As Justice Jackson wrote just before his death in 1954, "Perhaps the most delicate, difficult and shifting of all balances which the Court is expected to maintain is that between liberty and authority." [3] It is not as easy as doctrinaire advocates of civil liberties suppose to determine what serves Liberty best by way of restriction of Authority. It should not be forgotten that, in a democracy such as ours, the protection of individual freedom usually means a limitation of the power of the majority. To quote Justice Jackson again, "the power of the Court to protect individual or minority rights has on the other side of the coin the power to restrain the majority." [4] Most Bill of Rights cases involve asserted infringements by the Authority of the majority upon the Liberty of the minority or the individual. In a democratic society, how is the high Court to assess the competing interests of majority power and individual rights? In our system, the Court cannot be given free choice in determining which interest is to prevail. Here, too, primary responsibility must be left with those to whom the people have directly delegated political power and accountability. At the same time, the function of the judiciary must not be so limited that it must sanction the use of its power as mere rubber stamp to the will of the majority of the day. The high bench has no reason for existence if it is only to reflect the pressures of the day. On the contrary, the function of the Court is to give proper scope to the legitimate demands of both Authority and Liberty. Above all, it is that tribunal's job to see that there is maintained that balance between Authority and Liberty that is indispensable to a well-ordered polity. Attainment of "just poize" between the two must still be the guiding aim; for, as Strafford so felicitously expressed it over three centuries ago: "As on the lute, if any one string be too high or too lowly wound up, you have lost the harmony; so here the excess of [Authority] is oppression; of pretended Liberty in the subject, disorder and anarchy." [5]

Firstness of First Amendment?

It has been strongly urged that this theory of harmony between Authority and Liberty is contrary to both the language and purpose of the Constitution. Far from striking a balance between Authority and Liberty, it is said, the Founders of the Republic placed all their weight on the side of the latter. The Constitution, unequivocally declares a leading exponent of this view, "does not give equal status to the duty of self-preservation and the duty of maintaining Political Freedom. On the contrary, our 'experiment' in self-government makes that freedom an absolute." [6] This absolutist position is based upon the unqualified language of the First Amendment, which provides that "Congress shall make no law" abridging the freedoms of religion, speech, press, and assembly therein guaranteed. As one of the members of the high Court most closely associated with the absolutist interpretation of the First Amendment has recently said, with regard to its language, "The mandate is in terms of the absolute. . . . The prohibition is all-inclusive and complete. The word 'no' has a finality in all languages that few other words enjoy." [7] In this view, when the First Amendment says that no laws of a given type shall be made, it means flatly that *no* laws of that type shall, under any circumstances, be made.

One undisciplined in the law may be forgiven if he reads the First Amendment in a literal vacuum. It is, therefore, not surprising that the leading exponent off the high bench [8] of the absolutist view of Liberty has had no legal training or experience. What is unexpected is that his opinion should have found an echo among some of the Justices of the highest tribunal themselves. For it should be self-evident to one of any discernment in the law that the absolutist interpretation of the First Amendment carries within it its own *reductio ad absurdum*. There is to be unqualified freedom of speech under the language of the Amendment, say the absolutists. Yet it has been clear, from the beginning of our history, that the Constitution does not provide for a wholly unfettered right of expression. Justice Holmes's famous example [9] of the man falsely shouting "fire!" in a theatre, whom not even the most stringent protection of free speech would protect, is simply the most obvious example of speech which can be controlled. There shall be *no* restriction on the free exercise of religion, categorically declares the First Amendment. But all recognize today that religious belief cannot be pleaded as a justification for action outlawed by the criminal law. A sect whose religion looks with favor on polygamy cannot practice its religious belief, despite the constitutional guarantee. "Crime is not the less odious," in the words of an 1890 decision, "because sanctioned by what any particular sect may designate as religion." [10]

The words of the First Amendment thus cannot be given the absolute effect in law which they have in language. Without the freedoms guaranteed by that Amendment, there would, to be sure, be no free society at all. But the rejection of the one extreme—giving no effect to the Amendment—does not mean that we must embrace the opposite extreme—giving them unlimited effect. The First Amendment freedoms are not ends in themselves, but only means to the end of a free society. As such, they are qualified by the requirements of the Constitution as an entirety for the maintenance of a free society. The First Amendment freedoms are vital, but their exercise must be compatible with the preservation of other rights essential in a democracy and guaranteed by our Constitution.[11] The application in practice of the First Amendment can no more be governed by absolute rules than can that of other constitutional provisions. The demands of First Amendment freedoms, as well as the competing claims of governmental authority to secure other recognized interests, are "better served by candid and informed weighing of the competing interests, within the confines of the judicial process, than by announcing dogmas too inflexible for the non-Euclidian problems to be solved." [12] "Just poize," rather than absolutism, should be the guiding principle behind interpretation of the First Amendment.

In the Supreme Court, during the past two decades, those Justices who have veered toward the absolutist interpretation of the First Amendment have rejected the doctrine of deference toward the legislator in cases involving rights secured under that Amendment. These judges, who were among the strongest advocates of judicial self-restraint and who deplored most strongly the lack of such restraint on the part of the pre-1937 Court, have felt that a subdued judicial role is inappropriate in First Amendment cases. In such cases, on the contrary, they have urged that the Court must play a more active part, refusing to defer at all to the legislative judgment when alleged infringements of the First Amendment are at issue. For the rule that a challenged law must be presumed valid unless its unconstitutionality is proved beyond all reasonable doubt, these members of the Court have asserted the new doctrine that, when a statute appears to encroach on a First Amendment right (i.e., freedom of speech, press, religion, or assembly), the presumption is that the law is invalid. The command of the First Amendment, declared Justice Douglas in 1953,

is that there shall be *no* law which abridges those civil rights. The matter is beyond the power of the legislature to regulate, control, or condition. The case is therefore quite different from a legislative program in the field of business, labor, housing, and the like where regulation is permissible and the claim of unconstitutionality usually can be determined only by the manner or degree of application of the statute to an aggrieved person.[13]

That there is a sharp difference between cases involving the First Amendment and other cases, in the view of these Justices, may be seen even from the position taken by the least extreme of them, Justice Stone. In the 1936 case of *United States v. Butler*,[14] where the Court nullified the Agricultural Adjustment Act (one of the most important of the New Deal laws), Justice Stone delivered a now classic dissent pleading for judicial self-restraint in the face of Congressional assertions of regulatory power. "Courts are not the only agency of government," said he, "that must be assumed to have capacity to govern"; [15] nor is the responsibility for the preservation of our institutions the exclusive concern of the judicial branch.

Two years later, however, Justice Stone implied that the rule of restraint might not be applicable to cases arising under the Bill of Rights. Delivering the opinion in *United States v. Carolene Products Co.,*[16] a case involving economic regulation, where the usual rules of deference and presumption of constitutionality unless there is no rational basis to support the law have been the judicial lodestars since 1937, he stated, with what has been termed the casualness of a footnote,[17] that "there may be narrower scope for operation of the presumption of constitutionality" when a law appears on its face to be within a specific prohibition of the Bill of Rights; such legislation may be subjected to more exacting judicial scrutiny.[18] Though a footnote hardly seems to be an appropriate way of announcing a new constitutional doctrine, the Stone footnote has in fact been the foundation upon which some members of the high Court have attempted to construct the doctrine that the judicial function in reviewing statutes restricting a First Amendment freedom differs sharply from the Court's normal duty in sitting in judgment on legislation.

How can the Justices who have urged the view that any law touching a First Amendment right is infected with presumptive invalidity, while adhering wholeheartedly to the opposite view when any other law is at issue, square their position with the logical consistency required of the judicial process? They would answer by denying that there is any inconsistency in their position; for, they assert, there is a basic difference between the rights guaranteed by the First Amendment and all other constitutional rights. The First Amendment freedoms, they declare, are the very matrix, the indispensable condition, of nearly every other form of freedom. Their view with respect to the place of the First Amendment in a system such as ours was most eloquently stated by Justice Black in 1941. In deciding a case of alleged infringement of constitutional rights, he maintained, we cannot and should not lose sight of the nature and importance of the particular liberties at stake. He went on,

I view the guaranties of the First Amendment as the foundation upon which our governmental structure rests and without which it could not continue to endure as conceived and planned. Freedom to speak and write about public questions is as important to the life of our government as is the heart to the human body. In fact, this privilege is the heart of our government. If that heart be weakened, the result is debilitation; if it be stilled, the result is death.[19]

Believing as he has "that the First Amendment is the keystone of our Government," [20] it has been natural for Justice Black and those in accord with his view on the high Court to have embraced the philosophy that the First Amendment gives a preferred status to the liberties it protects. As Justice Rutledge, a partisan of the Black position, stated in 1945, "the usual presumption supporting legislation is balanced by the preferred place given in our scheme to the great, the indispensable democratic freedoms secured by the First Amendment. . . . That priority gives these liberties a sanctity and a sanction not permitting dubious intrusions." [21]

In 1945, when Justice Rutledge made this statement of the "preferred-position" philosophy, he spoke for a majority of the Supreme Court. At that time, the view that the First Amendment freedoms were on a higher plane was accepted by Justices Black, Douglas, Rutledge, Murphy, and Chief Justice Stone. The result was that the Court at that time applied more or less a double standard in exercising its review power. In the normal case, the basic theme was deference to the legislator; the narrow limits of judicial authority set by the constitutional revolution of 1937 were to be scrupulously observed. If a First Amendment right was involved, on the other hand, judicial self-restraint went by the board. In such a case, the 1945 Court majority seemed to act on premises of legislative limitation and *judicial* supremacy.[22] Statutes restricting First Amendment freedoms, stated Justice Rutledge for the Court in the 1945 opinion already cited, "must be justified by clear public interest, threatened not doubtfully or remotely, but by clear and present danger. The rational connection between the remedy provided and the evil to be curbed, which in other contexts might support legislation against attack on due process grounds, will not suffice." [23]

The preferred-position philosophy, emphasizing the firstness of the First Amendment, was accepted by a majority of the Court from about 1943 to 1948. What this meant in practice can be seen from the Court's two decisions in the celebrated compulsory flag-salute cases. They dealt with the validity of state regulations requiring pupils in the public schools to participate in daily flag-salute ceremonies, as applied to children whose religious beliefs were opposed to such flag-salutes. In the first case, *Minersville District v. Gobitis*,[24] decided in 1940, the Court upheld the challenged regulation. Deference to the legislative judgment * required the Court to sustain the state action if it bore a reasonable relation to a legitimate end. Here, the end of inculcating a common feeling for the common country was said surely to be legitimate; and the wisdom

---

* For purposes of review, it should be noted, the Court treated the challenged regulation as though it had been directly enacted by the state legislature itself.

of the means chosen to attain that end was not a question for the Court. By 1943, as already pointed out, the majority of the high tribunal had adopted the preferred-position philosophy with regard to the First Amendment. Under it, restrictions upon freedom of belief, like that involved in the compulsory flag-salute, must be much more closely scrutinized than ordinary laws; respect for the legislature alone is not enough to sustain a First Amendment limitation. In such a case, the judicial starting point must be, not the normal presumption of constitutionality, but the taint of presumptive invalidity. A Court which proceeds from this starting point will, of course, be more likely to find unconstitutionality than a Court dominated by the doctrine of deference. So it is not surprising that the 1943 case of *West Virginia Board of Education v. Barnette* [25] reached a result diametrically opposed to that of the *Gobitis* decision. This time, the Court majority rejected the notion, upon which the earlier case had been based, that the legislative judgment should be respected. The *Barnette* opinion emphasized the difference in approach which must be followed as between First Amendment cases and other cases: "The right of a State to regulate, for example, a public utility may well include, so far as the due process test is concerned, power to impose all of the restrictions which a legislature may have a 'rational basis' for adopting. But freedoms of speech and of press, of assembly, and of worship may not be infringed on such slender grounds." [26] The adoption by the 1943 Court of the preferred-position philosophy led it directly to overrule its earlier decision and hold that the compulsory flag-salute was contrary to the First Amendment.

It can hardly be gainsaid that the view that treats the First Amendment freedoms as in a preferred position presents much attraction in a country in which those freedoms constitute so vital an article of faith. Certainly, as Justice Frankfurter well stated in 1949, "those liberties of the individual which history has attested as the indispensable conditions of an open as against a closed society come to this Court with a momentum for respect lacking when appeal is made to liberties which derive merely from shifting economic arrangements." [27]

One who is cognizant of the values for our society involved in the rights guaranteed by the First Amendment cannot help but feel sympathetic toward the results sought in individual cases by adherents of the preferred-position philosophy. Predisposition toward the libertarian result does not, all the same, necessarily mean that the doctrine used to reach the result in given instances must be approved. In a judicial tribunal, the result alone is not the test of a

decision. A judge must do more than import his individual preferences into the Constitution. If the function of the reviewing Court
is to be no different from that of the legislature, with each member
casting his vote for or against a law on the basis of his personal
predilections on the results achieved by the law, then, indeed, is
the Court turned only into a third house of the legislature. Consistency in a Court committed to the overriding values of a democratic society is not only consistency in seeking the libertarian result
in all cases. Even restrictions on First Amendment freedoms must
be upheld when they are required for the preservation of other
rights essential in a democracy.

The basic weakness of the preferred-position philosophy is that
pointed out by Justice Jackson in 1949. "We cannot," he said, "give
some constitutional rights a preferred position without relegating
others to a deferred position; we can establish no firsts without
thereby establishing seconds." [28] Under the preferred-position approach, the First Amendment freedoms may be elevated to an exalted status; but the clear implication is that other constitutional
rights are marked as only secondary, to be relegated to a deferred
position.

What is it that makes for such a distinction between first-class
and second-class constitutional rights? The answer is to be found
neither in the text nor the structure of the Constitution, but in the
personal hierarchy of values of the particular judge. In 1922, a
federal judge could state, "It should be remembered that of the
three fundamental principles which underlie government, and for
which government exists, the protection of life, liberty, and property, the chief of these is property." [29] Today we see that such a
view made for a distorted interpretation of the Constitution. It led
the pre-1937 high Court to an exaggerated concern for property
rights, which induced it to invalidate what are now seen to have
been reasonable legislative attempts to accommodate property rights
to the superior interests of the community. Today we acknowledge
that the pre-1937 Court, under the guise of merely interpreting the
Constitution, was really giving effect to its personal prepossessions
on the predominance of property in the constitutional order of
things. Yet is not this sort of creation of a personal scheme of constitutional values exactly what the preferred-position philosophy requires of its partisans?

To be sure, the stress has shifted from what it was in the pre-
1937 period—now it is personal, rather than property, rights that are
asserted to be in the preferred position. But the judicial posture is
(save for the shift in emphasis with regard to the rights that are

deemed to have the primacy) strangely akin to the now discredited attitude toward the Constitution of the old apostles of property. In both cases, the judge seeks to nullify laws which conflict with his conception of the hierarchy of values upon which the Constitution is based. In neither case is the use of such undefined destructive power, based upon the personal scheme of values of the judge, justified. It cannot be admitted today, any more than it should have been before 1937, that judges can strike down legislation because to them as individuals it seems opposed to the basic "plan and purpose" of the Constitution. That, in Justice Frankfurter's phrase, "is too tempting a basis for finding in one's personal views the purposes of the Founders." [30]

It is hard to see why, when they are concerned with interests other than property, the members of the highest Court should have a wider latitude for enforcing their own predilections, than when they are concerned with property itself. To draw a distinction between first-class and second-class constitutional rights is to distort the Constitution. That document is based not upon a hierarchy but upon an equality of values. The Founders were, of course, firm believers in the personal rights secured by the First Amendment. Yet that did not lead them in any way to subordinate the right of property. On the contrary, if anything is clear from the words and actions of the men of 1787, it is that to them property was as important as liberty. Without property rights, they well knew, personal rights were devoid of practical content: "Property must be secured," declared John Adams, "or liberty cannot exist." [31] The result was that the Constitution which they drafted places both person and property upon a plane of protection—each is equally essential to the kind of society contemplated by the Framers. "Life and liberty," as Daniel Webster stated, "are, no doubt, to be protected by law; but property is also to be protected by law." [32]

In refusing to differentiate qualitatively between the rights safeguarded by the instrument they were drafting, the Founders acted with acute perception. A hierarchy of values reflects, all too often, the temporary judgment of the day, rather than the perduring wisdom that is essential in a document intended to abide through the ages. We should be able to perceive, today, more than we could have some years ago, that person and property are equally essential props of a free society. From contemporary experience, we can see all too clearly what the result is for personal liberty when rights of property are abrogated. In truth, personal rights and property rights are the two faces of a single coin—which is the specie of a free society. A philosophy that gives a preferred position to either (with its necessary corollary of a subdued position for the other) ignores the basic equality of values that must underlie a society in which both person and property are to be given their fullest expression.

As already stated, it was during the period 1943–48 that a majority of the Supreme Court adopted the view that the First Amendment freedoms are in a preferred position as compared with other constitutional rights. Since 1948, however, the Court majority has receded from the preferred-position philosophy. It is usual to date the change in the Court's view from the deaths in 1949 of Justices Murphy and Rutledge (both staunch supporters of the primacy of the First Amendment). It should, nevertheless, be pointed out that, even while those two judges were still on the bench, the Court had begun to retreat from its adherence to the preferred-position doctrine. What the deaths of Murphy and Rutledge made clear was that the doctrine, which for roughly a five-year period had won the acceptance of the controlling wing of the Court, was henceforth doomed to be adhered to by only a small minority of that tribunal.

From 1949 on, the decisions of the Court definitely reject the notion that there is any difference between the reviewing function in cases involving the First Amendment and that in other cases. "It is a *non sequitur*," stated Justice Reed for seven members of the high Court in 1953, "to say that First Amendment rights may not be regulated because they hold a preferred position in the hierarchy of the constitutional guarantees of the incidents of freedom. This Court has never so held and indeed has definitely indicated the contrary." [33] Of course, despite Justice Reed's disclaimer, the Court had so held in the 1943–48 period; what is true, nonetheless, is that, by 1953, his rejection of the preferred-position philosophy was clearly consistent with the prevailing view of the high bench. It is fair to say, in fact, that, at the present time, only Justices Black and Douglas are still partisans of a preferred status for First Amendment rights. The remainder of the Court has come around to the view, supported most vigorously in the 1943–48 period, in dissent, by Justice Frankfurter, that the Court's approach in reviewing statutes must be basically the same in all cases. If self-restraint before the legislator is the proper posture for a judicial tribunal in cases involving property rights, there is no reason why, in the Court's present view, the same should not be true in cases involving personal rights. The Court has thus come back to the view that the Constitution does not create first-class and second-class rights. Equality, not hierarchy, of guarantees is the dominant constitutional theme. Absolutist interpretation of personal rights is recognized as no more justifiable today than was absolutist interpretation of property rights prior to 1937.

Freedom of Speech

The First Amendment to the Constitution guarantees both freedom of speech and freedom of religion. That they are thus linked together in the same constitutional provision is no mere accident. For the Founders knew that the great constitutional struggles of the seventeenth century were struggles for both political and religious freedoms. It was religious disagreements that aggravated the political controversies of the time and made their resolution impossible except by the sword. Their understanding of the experience that led to the establishment of the rights of Englishmen led the Framers to perceive that the right to speak and the right to believe were inextricably linked. Out of refusals to compromise religious creeds had arisen some of the most important principles of freedom of expression; and it was not until political freedom was established that religious toleration, which left each man free to pursue his own faith without hindrance from the State, became possible. It was, thus, only if both freedom of speech and of religion were identically provided for, the Founders knew, that the system of ordered liberty they were establishing could endure.

It will be said that the link between expression and belief is nowhere near as close today as it was in the seventeenth and eighteenth centuries. In a country of diverse faiths, dominated by the doctrine of toleration, there is surely no place for religious conflict of the kind that preponderated two and three centuries ago. The fact that toleration is engraved in a Constitution does not, nevertheless, necessarily mean that it is always practiced. It was with keen discernment that John Stuart Mill wrote that "so natural to mankind is intolerance in whatever they really care about that religious freedom has hardly anywhere been practically realized, except where religious indifference . . . has added its weight to the scale." [34] When something occurs to do away with indifference to doctrinal quarrels, then, regardless of how categorically toleration may be enjoined in the basic law, there is a reversion to intolerance. Then, too, is the time for the law to vindicate the fundamental right to freedom of religion, even on behalf of a vilified and despised sect, whose views may be odious to most people. In doing so, the law will find once again that, in protecting the religious beliefs of some, it is vindicating the freedom of expression of all.

In our own day, it is the sect known as Jehovah's Witnesses that has demonstrated once again the close link between the different freedoms of the First Amendment. Certainly, there are few people, apart from adherents of that sect, who do not find much that is offensive in both its teaching and its actions. Especially obnoxious to many has been the Witnesses' persistent attacks upon other religious groups, particularly the Catholic Church, against which they have directed the most intemperate language. Couple this with their extremely unorthodox methods of evangelism, their tenacious door-to-door campaigns to secure proselytes (which their own leader aptly likened to an invasion of locusts), accompanied by the blare of phonograph records censuring religion as a "snare and racket," and one can well understand why the Witnesses have been in constant conflict with law-enforcement officers and local and state regulations. But the principles involved in particular cases are not dependent upon the desirability of those in whose favor such principles are asserted. In many ways, indeed, the converse is true. The law, to paraphrase Justice Murphy,[35] knows no finer hour than when it cuts through transitory emotions and protects even those who may be deemed least deserving personally of such protection.

The Jehovah's Witnesses who became involved in troubles with the law were only seeking to propagate their unpopular creed. But they furnished to the Supreme Court its most fruitful opportunities in the past two decades to strike down arbitrary restraints upon the freedoms guaranteed by the First Amendment. It should be emphasized, furthermore, that the impact of the Jehovah's Witness decisions of the high tribunal is not confined to those using speech as a means of evangelism. For this is one of the areas where there is a close interrelation between freedom of speech and of religion. Regulation used to block religious evangelism today may be employed to stifle political expression or other speech tomorrow. This can be seen clearly from the first case involving the Jehovah's Witnesses to come before the Supreme Court, Lovell v. Griffin.[36] It was decided in 1938 and involved a municipal ordinance which prohibited the distribution of literature of any kind without the prior permission of the city manager. Such an ordinance, said a unanimous Court, is invalid on its face. Though used in this case against the distribution of religious literature, it could equally be applied to all other printed matter, including newspapers. It amounted to a previous restraint upon publication and distribution of a type wholly inconsistent with the notion of freedom of speech and of the press.*

* Parenthetically, it should be stated that, ever since Gitlow v. New York, 268 U.S. 652 (1925), it has been held that the First Amendment rights are among the fundamental liberties protected by the Fourteenth Amendment. Hence, they can no more be violated by the states than they can be by the Federal Government.

As the Court put it, "Legislation of the type of the ordinance in question would restore the system of license and censorship in its baldest form." [37]

In the 1940 decision of *Cantwell v. Connecticut*,[38] the same approach was applied in a case involving the offensive type of vilification of religion by phonograph records generally associated with the Witnesses. Cantwell had been convicted under a state law which forbade any person to solicit for any religious cause without first securing a permit from a designated official, who was required to determine whether such cause was a bona fide religious one and who might withhold the permit if he determined that it was not. Here, said the Court, the challenged law gave the relevant official what amounted to a power to censor religions; unless he approved a religious cause, its partisans could not solicit for it: "Such a censorship of religion as the means of determining its right to survive is a denial of liberty protected by the First Amendment." [39] In *Cantwell*, it may be said, only the freedom to solicit for religious purposes was involved. But the type of licensing attempted there can be used to restrain distribution of other literature as well. Thus, a 1943 case dealt with an ordinance which made it unlawful for any person to solicit orders or sell books or literature without a permit from the mayor, who was to issue such permit only if he "deems it proper or advisable." This was basically the type of restraint stricken down in *Cantwell*, though here, of course, not confined to restraint of religion. In the words of the Court, "This is administrative censorship in an extreme form. It abridges the freedom of religion, of the press and of speech." [40]

The principle of these cases has been applied more recently in two 1951 decisions. In *Niemotko v. Maryland*,[41] Jehovah's Witnesses had been denied a permit to use a city park for Bible talks, for no apparent reason except the city authorities' dislike of the Witnesses and disagreement with their views. This case, said the Court, pointed up clearly the type of abuse inherent in the licensing schemes condemned in the prior cases. The licensing authorities here had the same type of unlimited discretion and they used it to discriminate against this religious sect. The right to exercise freedom of speech and religion, declared the Court's opinion, has a firmer foundation than the whims or personal opinions of a local governing body. The second 1951 decision, *Kunz v. New York*,[42] involved basically the same situation. New York City had a licensing system to control the use of its streets and parks for religious meetings. The Police Commissioner was authorized to grant or withhold permits, but there was no standard to guide his action. Kunz, a Baptist minister, was refused a permit because the Commissioner found that he had ridiculed and denounced other religions. Again, the Court invalidated the restriction upon expression, holding that New York cannot vest restraining control over the right to speak in an official where there are no appropriate standards to guide his action.

The cases just discussed restrain government from imposing arbitrary previous restraints upon expression, whether of religious beliefs or of other types of speech. The state or municipality may not condition the right to speak on the prior approval of an official vested with absolute discretion in the premises. That gives the official concerned what amounts to an unlimited power of prior censorship; he can easily use his authority as a means of preferring one religious or political group over another. As the high Court put it in a 1953 case where the officials concerned did actually employ their authority in this way against the Jehovah's Witnesses, "Baptist, Methodist, Presbyterian, or Episcopal ministers, Catholic priests, Moslem mullahs, Buddhist monks could all preach to their congregations in Pawtucket's parks with impunity. But the hand of the law would be laid on the shoulder of a minister of this unpopular group for performing the same function." [43]

It should be emphasized that these cases turn upon the lack of controls contained in the laws or ordinances setting up the restrictions upon expression. "The vice to be guarded against," in Justice Frankfurter's phrase, "is arbitrary action by officials." [44] But these cases do not bar the authorities concerned from imposing reasonable and proper restraints even upon the right of speech, whether for religious or other purposes. Freedom of speech, like other constitutional rights, must not be considered in the abstract. Even the right of speech may be exercised so as to impinge upon the rights of others; that is why, despite the absolutist view of the First Amendment asserted by some, there can be no absolute right of free speech, save possibly for a Robinson Crusoe. [45] Few cognizant with the Constitution will deny the right of a sect like the Jehovah's Witnesses to express their doctrines, offensive though they may be to most of us. Their rights in this respect are, and should be held to be, as extensive as those of the most accepted religious or political groups. But the real question is not that of their rights to speech and belief; the real question is where their rights end and the rights of others begin. [46] Speech in the streets may conflict with the right of the community to keep order and to provide for orderly movement of pedestrian and vehicular traffic. Speech in a public park may conflict with the right of the community to peaceful relaxation in its

parks. Unrestrained solicitation to help religious or political programs may conflict with the right to protect the public from fraud
and from criminals who use solicitation as a device to enter homes.
Unrestricted right of zealots to descend like locusts upon the front
doors of others may conflict with the rights of householders to be
free from undesired intrusions. "Freedom of speech or press does
not," as the Supreme Court stated in 1951, "mean that one can
talk or distribute where, when and how one chooses. Rights other
than those of the advocates are involved."[47] Freedom of the
streets, of public parks, and of the home may be as important as
freedom of speech. The real task of the high Court in these cases
is that of balancing the different rights that are in contention, and
it cannot be met by mere general pronouncements about freedom
of speech.

The cases already discussed do not bar local authorities from imposing reasonable restraints in the interest of order in the streets.
In the words of a 1941 opinion of the highest Court, "The authority
of a municipality to impose regulations in order to assure the safety
and convenience of the people in the use of public highways has
never been regarded as inconsistent with civil liberties but rather
as one of the means of safeguarding the good order upon which
they ultimately depend."[48] In accordance with this view, the Court
upheld the power of New Hampshire to prohibit processions upon
public streets in its cities without a license and sustained the convictions of Jehovah's Witnesses who had engaged in a religious
procession without a permit. Similarly, a municipality can restrain
the use of abusive epithets tending to cause a breach of the peace
on its streets. What was wrong in the cases we discussed before
was not that restraints were imposed, but that such restraints were
arbitrary, in that they permitted the relevant officials to bar speech
entirely or to discriminate against those, like Jehovah's Witnesses,
with whose views they strongly disagreed. Where local authorities regulate, to preserve order on the streets or to ensure reasonable
peace and quiet to those seeking some escape in the parks, and the
regulation neither bars all speech nor is it applied in a discriminatory
manner, then such use of the police power will be upheld. Free
speech is not an absolute right; it is entitled only to reasonable
protection; it may not be used as an iron standard to crush the
living rights of others to public order and individual repose.[49] Illustrative of the police power here is the 1953 decision of *Poulos v.
New Hampshire*,[50] where a city ordinance providing for licensing
of meetings in public streets and parks was sustained, in view of
the fact that the highest state court had construed the ordinance

as leaving no discretion as to the granting of licenses to the officials concerned, and hence vesting no power in them to discriminate. Said the Court, "The principles of the First Amendment are not to be treated as a promise that everyone with opinions or beliefs to express may gather around him at any public place and at any time a group for discussion or instruction." [51] On the contrary, reasonable nondiscriminatory regulation by governmental authority that preserves peace, order, and tranquility is not prohibited by the Constitution.

What has just been said with regard to the power of public authorities to impose reasonable regulations even upon speech has particular relevance in connection with our large metropolitan areas, with their polyglot millions who must be enabled to live in peace and tolerance. Street preaching in the large city is done in a milieu quite different from preaching on a New England village green.[52] *Kunz v. New York*, already discussed,* involved the largest of our metropolitan areas. As we have seen, the Court there invalidated New York's regulation of speech because unfettered discretion was vested in the Commissioner of Police with regard to the granting or withholding of permits. In the words of a concurring opinion, "if a municipality conditions holding street meetings on the granting of a permit by the police, the basis which guides licensing officials in granting or denying a permit must not give them a free hand, or a hand effectively free when the actualities of police administration are taken into account." [53] The *Kunz* decision is, nevertheless, far from holding that a city like New York is restrained by the Constitution from protecting completely the community's interest in relation to its streets. On the contrary, if anything is clear it is that New York need not give unlimited license to those who seek to use its thoroughfares to peddle their doctrines and beliefs. Unrestricted freedom of speech is quixotic in a human beehive like New York City—that "frightening aggregation" of people, as Justice Jackson termed it—in whose streets and public places, "all races and nationalities, and all sorts and conditions of men walk, linger and mingle." [54] May not the city protect these persons from fanatics who play with the twin explosives of race and religion in its public streets?

Not only can a city use regulatory power administered with an equal hand to impose reasonable restraints upon speech; it can also act against those who abuse their right of expression to commit breaches of the peace. This is shown by the 1951 case of *Feiner v. New York*.[55] Feiner had made a street corner speech in Syracuse.

* *Supra,* pp. 242-43.

He spoke from a box and made use of sound amplifiers attached to an automobile. A crowd of seventy-five to eighty persons gathered around him, and several pedestrians had to go into the street in order to pass by. Two policemen observed the meeting. In the course of his speech, Feiner referred to the Mayor of Syracuse as a "champagne-sipping bum," to the President as a "bum," and to the American Legion as "Nazi Gestapo agents." He also indicated in an excited manner that Negroes did not have equal rights and should rise up in arms. His audience included a number of Negroes. One man indicated that if the police did not get the speaker off the stand, he would do it himself. The crowd, which consisted of both those who opposed and those who supported the speaker, was restless. There was not yet a disturbance but, in the words of the arresting officer whose story was accepted by the trial judge, he "stepped in to prevent it from resulting in a fight. After all there was angry muttering and pushing." Having ignored two requests to stop speaking, Feiner was arrested on a charge of disorderly conduct. His conviction was upheld by the Supreme Court. While the police could not be used as an instrument for the suppression of unpopular views, when the speaker passed the bounds of argument and undertook incitement to riot, the police were not powerless to prevent a breach of the peace. Feiner could be arrested and convicted, not for the making or the content of his speech, but for the reaction which it actually engendered.

The weakness of the *Feiner* decision, even if one agrees that the police can act against those who use speech to commit breaches of the peace, lies in the implication that, not the words or the intent of the speaker, but the effect on his audience can make him guilty of a breach of the peace. But this gives an audience, or any part of it, an easy means to suppress a speaker with whom it disagrees. Any group which wishes to silence a speaker can create a disturbance in the audience, and that will justify the police in stopping the speaker.[56] Thus, a hostile reception destroys the right to speak, despite the fact that, as an abstract proposition at least, all would agree with Justice Jackson that "Tolerance of unwelcome, unorthodox ideas or information is a constitutionally protected policy not to be defeated by persons who would break up meetings they do not relish." [57] In a case like this, while we may agree with the principle applied by the Court permitting the police to intervene where speech has caused a breach of the peace, we may still insist that the Court review carefully to determine that there was, in fact, a real, immediate, and serious threat to the peace when the police acted.[58]

The problem of balancing the interest of the individual in freedom of speech with that of the community in regulating its streets and public places is complicated by the fact that those who exercise their right of expression normally do not do so only with the naked voice. Like Feiner in the case just discussed, they make use of mechanical amplification devices, which alone enable them to attract and hold an audience of any size. It may well be that, under contemporary conditions, sound amplifiers are a necessary medium in the expression of ideas. "Loud-speakers," said the Supreme Court in 1948, "are today indispensable instruments of effective public speech." [59] At the same time, it must be recognized that, from the point of view of the public, there is a vast difference between the human voice alone and the voice magnified by mechanical devices. This difference was acutely noted by Justice Frankfurter:

The native power of human speech can interfere little with the self-protection of those who do not wish to listen. They may easily move beyond earshot. . . . But modern devices for amplifying the range and volume of the voice, or its recording, afford easy, too easy, opportunities for aural aggression. If uncontrolled, the result is intrusion into cherished privacy. The refreshment of mere silence, or meditation, or quiet conversation, may be disturbed or precluded by noise beyond one's personal control.[60]

Loud-speakers blaring forth in a small park in a small city may destroy the one outdoor retreat available for quietness, contemplation, and repose.

Since the sound amplifier is an essential implement of present-day speech, it can no more either be prohibited absolutely or be made dependent upon the unfettered discretion of a designated official than can speech with the naked voice alone. On the other hand, the abuses to which speech by loud-speaker is subject makes such speech peculiarly appropriate for reasonable, nondiscriminatory regulation. Thus, it is clear, as the high Court stated in 1948, that "Noise can be regulated by regulating decibels. The hours and place of [loud-speaker use] can be controlled." [61] In 1949, the Court upheld a municipal ordinance which forbade the use on the public streets of sound trucks or other amplifying devices which emitted "loud and raucous" noises. "We think," said the Court, "it is a permissible exercise of legislative discretion to bar sound trucks with broadcasts of public interest, amplified to a loud and raucous volume, from the public ways of municipalities." [62] As the Court appeared to interpret the regulation at issue, it applied only to bar abuses by sound trucks which were "loud and raucous."

There are two difficulties in squaring this interpretation with the decision. In the first place, since there is no standard in the ordinance defining when a sound truck is "loud and raucous," is it not really leaving the restraint of this particular speech to the uncontrolled discretion of the relevant authorities? Secondly, it is hard to see how a sound truck can be other than "loud and raucous"— that is the nature of the animal. If that is true, does not the ordinance at issue really prohibit amplification devices? Such absolute prohibition is, however, unwarranted under all the decisions we have been discussing. In actuality, speech by loud-speaker should be a question of degree. If it is too "loud and raucous" (i.e., exceeds a specified decibel volume), it can be prohibited; but the regulation should clearly define when the permitted bounds are passed.

Speech on the streets and in public places may, we have seen, conflict with the rights of the community to maintain order and to unrestricted use of parks and other areas for relaxation. Just as great a clash may occur between the right of expression and the right of a householder to be free from undesired intrusions. Thus, the door-to-door canvassing of a sect like the Jehovah's Witnesses may confront the community with a real problem. On the one hand, there is the constitutional right of the sect to express its religious beliefs; on the other, there is the certainty of annoyance to those to whom homes are the principal sanctuaries from invasions upon privacy. May the State in such a case give preference to the maxim "a man's house is his castle" when it conflicts with freedom of expression?

The city of Struthers, Ohio, attempted to give such preference to the householder's rights by enacting an ordinance forbidding any person to knock on doors, ring doorbells, or otherwise summon to the door the occupants of any residence for the purpose of distributing to them any handbills or circulars. In its 1943 decision in *Martin v. Struthers*,[63] the Supreme Court held that such an attempted resolution of the competing interests of speech and privacy was invalid. Whether visiting in the home shall be permitted, said the Court, should depend upon the will of the individual master of each household, and not upon the determination of the community. To be valid, any community regulation must give "due respect for the constitutional rights of those desiring to distribute literature and those desiring to receive it, as well as those who choose to exclude such distributers from the home."[64]

The Court's emphasis of the rights of those desiring to receive literature seems, to put it mildly, somewhat unrealistic. The rights of peddlers in ideas should not be sanctified in disregard of the rights of those within doors. The *Struthers* decision is at odds with the realities of life in a small industrial community, some residents of which work at night, so that for portions of the city's inhabitants opportunities for rest and refreshment require, during the day as well as the night, whatever peace and quiet are obtainable in a modern industrial town.[65] Upon such a community, a door-to-door campaign of the Jehovah's Witness type may have devastating effect. This is recognized by so faithful a fighter for free speech as Zechariah Chafee, who writes of house-to-house canvassing:

Of all the methods of spreading unpopular ideas, this seems the least entitled to extensive protection. The possibilities of persuasion are slight compared with the certainties of annoyance. Great as is the value of exposing citizens to novel views, home is one place where a man ought to be able to shut himself up in his own ideas if he desires. There he should be free not only from unreasonable searches and seizures but also from hearing uninvited strangers expound distasteful doctrines.[66]

To emphasize only the rights of the house-to-house canvasser, while ignoring those of the community to protect its inhabitants from such canvasser, is to rely upon a doctrinaire approach to the First Amendment, which conceives of the rights guaranteed by it as absolutes, to be enforced to their extremes with pedantic rigor.

Fortunately, the high Court itself has come to see that its *Martin v. Struthers* decision ignores the realities of organized front door intrusions. In its 1951 decision in *Breard v. Alexandria*,[67] it has recognized that these cases involve more than the right of those seeking to distribute from house to house; they turn, instead, upon a balancing of the conveniences between the householder's desire for privacy and the desire to disseminate speech in the precise way that may be felt to bring the best results. The issue brings into collision the rights of the householder and those of the house-to-house solicitor. But, this time, unlike the result in *Martin v. Struthers*, it is the right of the householder that prevails. Consequently, a municipal ordinance that prohibits door-to-door solicitation without the prior invitation of the householder was upheld. The First Amendment, said the Court, is not to be treated as an absolute. A community which finds door-to-door campaigns "obnoxious may control them by ordinance. It would be, it seems to us, a misuse of the great guarantees of free speech and free press to use those guarantees to force a community to admit the solicitors of publications to the home premises of its residents." [68]

Picketing and Free Speech

In a striking passage written in 1943, Justice Jackson drew attention to a tendency to which the post-1937 Supreme Court has been all too prone. "This Court," said he, "is forever adding new stories to the temples of constitutional law, and the temples have a way of collapsing when one story too many is added." [69] In recent years, the Court almost added one story too many in its cases treating picketing purely as speech to be protected by the First Amendment.

The starting point here was a celebrated 1937 dictum of Justice Brandeis. Delivering the opinion in a case involving a state law authorizing peaceful picketing, he stated, "Members of a union might, without special statutory authorization by a State, make known the facts of a labor dispute, for freedom of speech is guaranteed by the Federal Constitution." [70] This is, of course, a truism; but it was soon distorted to the dogma of a juristic absolute. In the 1940 case of *Thornhill v. Alabama*,[71] the Court, in outlawing a state law prohibiting all picketing, extended the Brandeis dictum to equate picketing with speech and held, hence, that, like speech, it was an activity protected by the First Amendment. The safeguarding of picketing, said the Court, "is essential to the securing of an informed and educated public opinion with respect to a matter which is of public concern." [72] The states may set the limits of permissible contest open to industrial combatants. Yet, according to the *Thornhill* Court: "It does not follow that the State in dealing with the evils arising from industrial disputes may impair the effective exercise of the right to discuss freely industrial relations which are matters of public concern. A contrary conclusion could be used to support abridgment of freedom of speech and of the press concerning almost every matter of importance to society." [73]

Several subsequent cases adopt the view that picketing is speech which can no more be restrained by the states than can the dissemination of political ideas or religious beliefs.[74] Such a starting point for a system of labor law, however, wholly ignores what actually occurs in a present-day industrial dispute. The objection to summarizing by the phrase "picketing is speech" is that it reduces a complicated problem to a deceptive formula. And it was Justice Holmes who admonished us that "To rest upon a formula is a slumber that, prolonged, means death." [75] Such a formula, at the least, makes for mechanical jurisprudence. It also furnishes the judge with a deceptively simple way of dealing with cases, but one which is unfortunately all too often far removed from the actualities that underlie such cases. Unless we are to reach judgments as did Plato's men, who were chained in a cave and saw nothing but shadows, we must not allow reliance upon syllogistic formula to substitute for analysis of the realities for which the formula is a façade.

Picketing is more than mere speech. It is a form of economic persuasion which, in the realities of industrial strife, may easily amount to economic coercion. The picket line today is more an instrument of compulsion than information. A powerful union can impose an economic quarantine by posting a single picket. It is to deal in pernicious abstraction to compare this kind of picketing to the kind of speech contemplated by the constitutional guarantee. Picketing is a process of proscription—it contemplates a "psychological embargo" (which often becomes a *de facto* physical embargo) around the picketed premises.[76] Most people hesitate to cross picket lines, not because they are persuaded intellectually by the worth of the picketing union's cause, but because they wish to avoid trouble and the scorn that would be directed against them for being anti-union. Without a doubt, the members of a union have a right to disseminate their point of view; and, under present-day conditions, labor also has a legally protected right to peaceful picketing. But the two are not the same right and should not be confused by the law. The first is protected by the First Amendment; the second is subject to the State's power to set permissible limits to industrial, as to other forms of, combat. Our system presupposes the deliberative process as a condition of thought and of responsible choice by the people. To the Founders, it would hardly seem a proof of progress that a hybrid like picketing—comprising, as it does, elements of persuasion, information, economic pressure, and signals for action—must be treated as a necessary medium of the deliberative process.[77] In the actualities of acute industrial strife, uncontrolled picketing may make calm deliberation impossible: "The very presence of a picket line may induce action of one kind or another, quite irrespective of the nature of the ideas which are being disseminated."[78]

Unlike pure speech, picketing must be subject to regulation by the community as a whole to keep it within what the community regards as lawful bounds. Speech alone, even when directed toward illegitimate ends, should not be prohibited unless it be combined with incitement to unlawful action or is itself accompanied by some overt act which can be outlawed. Yet, even if picketing does involve an element of speech, by its very nature, it is always combined with action. And it is this that should render it far more subject to state regulation in the general interest than is ordinary speech alone. The State must have the same power to keep industrial weapons within reasonable bounds that it has over other instruments of contention with harmful potential to society.

If picketing, though peaceful, is carried on for a purpose in conflict with a state law on restraint of trade, is it the state law that must give way? The Supreme Court itself conceded that an affirmative answer could not be required of the state in its 1949 decision in *Giboney v. Empire Storage Co.*[79] A union of retail ice peddlers tried to obtain agreements from all wholesale distributors of ice in the area that they would not sell ice to nonunion peddlers. Under a state statute, such agreements were outlawed restraints on trade. Empire Co. refused to sign such agreement, and its place of business was picketed by the union. The state court enjoined such picketing as carried on for a purpose made unlawful by the anti-trade-restraint statute, and the Supreme Court affirmed, despite the claim that the picketing was protected by the First and Fourteenth Amendments. The state could clearly prohibit competing dealers and their aiders and abettors from combining to restrain freedom of trade. And, said the Court, there is nothing in the Constitution to prevent a state from prohibiting picketing engaged in to induce a violation of a valid state law. The basic issue, according to the Court's opinion, was whether the state or the union had paramount power to regulate trade practices. And, of course, the state's power was held paramount. To construe picketing only as speech immune from this type of state regulation would make it practically impossible ever to enforce laws against agreements in restraint of trade as well as many other agreements and conspiracies deemed injurious to society.

A Court which decided the *Giboney* case as it did had, we may be sure, receded from the extreme *Thornhill v. Alabama* view of the protected nature of picketing. In a series of significant recent cases, the high tribunal seems definitely to have given up its untenable equation of picketing with mere speech. Picketing, declared the Court in 1950, "is more than speech and establishes a *locus in quo* that has far more potential for inducing action or nonaction than the message the pickets convey."[80] Or, as it put it in another 1950 opinion, "picketing, not being the equivalent of speech as a matter of fact, is not its inevitable legal equivalent."[81] And this means that picketing is stripped of the broad constitutional protection given it by the *Thornhill* case. It is true that a state could still not outlaw all picketing. But it can prohibit picketing carried on for an unlawful purpose; and, just as important, the state is free to define the public purposes which override picketing rights. Thus, the Supreme Court has upheld state restraints on picketing carried on to induce the firing of nonunion employees, in violation of a "right to work" statute, or to bring about violation of a law forbidding employers to coerce their employees' choice of a bargaining representative.[82] Similarly, the Court has affirmed the power of the state courts to enjoin picketing deemed by them to be for an unlawful object; [83] the state courts, no less than the legislature, could determine what picketing was contrary to the public policy of the state.[84] Though one may not wholly agree with the decisions in all of these recent cases, he cannot help but feel that the high Court has taken a substantial step forward in abandoning its untenable earlier view. As the Court itself stated in one of the cases just referred to, "we must start with the fact that while picketing has an ingredient of communication it cannot dogmatically be equated with the constitutionally protected freedom of speech." [85] There is nothing in the Constitution to bar the states from choosing not to put picketing on a par with advertisements in the press.

Press and Censorship

Few, today, would deny the relationship between a free press and a free society. "Democratic government," writes Bryce, "rests upon and requires the exercise of a well-informed and sensible opinion by the great bulk of the citizens." [86] Without a free and fearless press, the informed public opinion upon which democracy rests is impossible. The censored press has always been the hallmark of the despot. Ideas are dangerous; and traffic in them has always been the concern of dictators.[87]

There is no doubt that the Founders were well aware of the importance of a free press in the system they were establishing. Perhaps Jefferson went too far when he asserted, in an oft-quoted passage, "were it left for me to decide whether we should have a government without newspapers, or newspapers without a government, I should not hesitate a moment to prefer the latter." But he and his compatriots knew, both from personal experience and their reading of history, that laws restricting freedom of the press were incompatible with free government. With Blackstone, they firmly believed in the right of every freeman to lay what sentiments he pleases before the public. And, in the Bill of Rights, they clearly intended, at the very least, to follow the English law, which, by Blackstone's time, had done away with that system of previous restraint upon publication by a licensing system which had formerly

characterized it.   As Justice Holmes, speaking for the Court in 1907,
stated, the "main purpose" of the First Amendment is "to prevent
all such *previous restraints* upon publications as had been practiced
by other governments." [88]

There has been no occasion for the post-1937 Court to deal with
attempts directly to censor the publication of newspapers, periodicals, or books.   Except during wartime, we have not had overt
prior censorship of published materials in this country.   The Court
has, all the same, had occasion to concern itself with a possible
threat of censorship inherent in the power of the Postmaster General to exclude publications from second-class mailing privileges.
The second-class mail privilege is a form of subsidy, since second-
class mail is carried at much less than cost.   But, since the privilege
is vital to commercial publications today, it can be turned into a
censorship device.   This is, in fact, what the Postmaster General
tried to do in withdrawing second-class mailing privileges from
Esquire magazine.   His withdrawal was based on his opinion that
Esquire contained writings and pictures which, though not obscene,
were "indecent, vulgar, and risque."   According to him, the special
rate afforded to magazines possessing the privilege was only for
those which contributed to "the public good and the public welfare."   In actuality, this was asserting in himself a power to determine whether a particular publication conformed to his norm
as to what was "good" or "bad."   To uphold the withdrawal
order would, therefore, said the Court, be to grant the Postmaster
General a power of censorship: "Such a power is so abhorrent
to our traditions that a purpose to grant it should not be easily
inferred." [89]   A requirement that literature or art conform to some
norm prescribed by an official smacks of an ideology foreign to our
system.

The press intended to be protected by the Framers of the First
Amendment was the conventional press of newspapers, periodicals,
and books.   In our time, as Justice Douglas points out,[90] science has
produced other methods and media of communication which are
just as basic and probably as enduring.   The mass media of radio
and television are such, by their physical characteristics, as to make
impossible the literal application of the Blackstonian theory of freedom of the press.   Every freeman may be able to distribute handbills or even (if he has the financial means) to publish a newspaper
or magazine without any previous license from the State.   But the
same cannot be true of operating a radio or television channel.
There the State cannot sit by and allow all who choose to use the

new media. In the words of a 1943 opinion of the Supreme Court: "Unlike other modes of expression, radio inherently is not available to all. That is its unique characteristic, and that is why, unlike other modes of expression, it is subject to governmental regulation." [91] Owing to their physical characteristics, radio and television must be both regulated and rationed by the Government. Otherwise, there would be chaos. These practical considerations have led the Congress to authorize, and the high Court to approve, a scheme of selective licensing by the Federal Communications Commission. The right of free speech does not, in the Court's phrase, include the right to use the facilities of radio or television without a license.[92] The relevant statute does, to be sure, expressly bar the Commission from using its authority for censorship purposes. Yet there are censorship pressures that may inhere in the very nature of the type of licensing regulation administered by the FCC, though they are pressures of the type that are unlikely ever to see the light of day in the Supreme Court Chamber.

The motion picture does not share the physical limitations of radio and television, which demand that they be closely regulated by licensing, lest their usefulness be destroyed. On the other hand, the movies, like broadcasting, are more media of entertainment than information and are part of a large-scale business operation conducted for private profit. In 1948, however, the Court gave a clear indication that, for purposes of the First Amendment, there was no real line between the entertaining and the informing medium: "What is one man's amusement, teaches another's doctrine." [93] And, in its 1952 decision in *Joseph Burstyn, Inc. v. Wilson*,[94] the case involving the movie *The Miracle,* the high Court expressly held motion pictures to be within the ambit of protection which the First Amendment secures to freedom of the press. In doing so, the Court squarely overruled a 1915 case, decided in the infancy of the motion picture industry, which refused to hold movies within the constitutional guarantee, on the ground that moving pictures were "a business, pure and simple, originated and conducted for profit." [95] The 1952 Court rightly pointed out that this was irrelevant to the First Amendment issue, since books, newspapers, and magazines are also published and sold for profit. The Court's opinion declared:

It cannot be doubted that motion pictures are a significant medium for the communication of ideas. They may affect public attitudes and behavior in a variety of ways, ranging from direct espousal of a political or social doctrine to the subtle shaping of thought which characterizes all artistic expression. The importance of motion pictures as an organ of public opinion is not lessened by the fact that they are designed to entertain as well as to inform.[96]

As organs of public opinion, they fall within the First Amendment's aegis.

It may be thought from this that motion pictures are now no more subject to censorship restraints than are printed materials. This is, it is true, the view of at least two members of the high Court, Justices Douglas and Black. As they see it, "If a board of censors can tell the American people what it is in their best interests to see or to read or to hear . . . , then thought is regimented, authority substituted for liberty, and the great purpose of the First Amendment to keep uncontrolled the freedom of expression defeated."[97] To Justices Douglas and Black, all censorship of motion pictures is unconstitutional.[98] The rest of the Court has not gone so far. The movie *The Miracle* had been banned under a New York law permitting the relevant officials to deny a license to exhibit films on the ground that they were sacrilegious. The majority of the Court expressly stated that it was not deciding whether a state might censor motion pictures under a clearly drawn statute. It held only that the New York statute, in giving its censor the power to ban films deemed "sacrilegious," was really vesting the authority to grant or refuse a license in the unbridled discretion of the censor. The term *sacrilegious* is so broad and ill defined that it furnishes no standard to control the censor's discretion: "In seeking to apply the broad and all-inclusive definition of 'sacrilegious,' . . . the censor is set adrift upon a boundless sea amid a myriad of conflicting currents of religious views, with no charts but those provided by the most vocal and powerful orthodoxies. New York cannot vest such unlimited restraining control over motion pictures in a censor."[99] The case is thus treated like some of the Jehovah's Witness and other free speech cases, already discussed,* which hold that the state cannot vest the approval of speech in the absolute discretion of an official. One wonders, all the same, whether the censoring of motion pictures should be treated on the same basis as speech in a street or public place which, we have seen, is subject to regulation under properly drawn statutes. If the movie is treated like the newspaper under the First Amendment, should it not also be wholly free from previous restraints? In Blackstone's words, "To subject the press to the restrictive power of a licenser, as was formerly done, . . . is to subject all freedom of sentiment to the

* *Supra,* pp. 241-44.

prejudices of one man, and make him the arbitrary and infallible judge of all controverted points in learning, religion and government." [100] Today, few will controvert this, as far as the conventional press is concerned. But, if the motion picture now has First Amendment protection similar to that enjoyed by the newspaper or the magazine, it should also be the beneficiary of full freedom from previous restraints. In this Nation, everyone protected by freedom of the press, no matter what medium of expression he may use, should be freed from the censor.

Church and State

Few cases have given the Supreme Court more difficulty and have given rise to more searching public scrutiny than those which have been before the high tribunal in the past decade on the question of the separation of church and State, provided for under the First Amendment. "Probably few opinions from this Court in recent years," Justice Black has stated with regard to the decision in one of these cases, "have attracted more attention or stirred wider debate." [101] In a country such as ours, composed, in the Supreme Court's phrase, of "a religious people whose institutions presuppose a Supreme Being," [102] where so many religious faiths coexist and form so important a part of the life of the community, few things that the Court does affect so intimately the daily lives of the people as its decisions on the permissible relationships between church and State.

We have already dealt with the right to express and propagate religious beliefs in our section dealing with freedom of speech.* Yet the right to evangelize in the Jehovah's Witness sense is but a small part of the freedom of religion guaranteed by the First Amendment. To most of us, it is not the right to preach, but the right to believe and pray in our own way (or not to believe and pray, if it so behooves us) that is the essence of the constitutional guarantee. While we may recognize that we are amenable to society for our conduct which concerns others, we deny that society has any rights over that which only concerns ourselves. Over his own mind, the individual is sovereign. We feel that this is particularly true insofar as our religious beliefs are concerned. "The Religion then of every man," reads Madison's famous *Remonstrance*, "must be left to the conviction and conscience of every man; and it is the right of every man to exercise it as these may dictate." [103]

* *Supra,* pp. 240-45.

Under the First Amendment, we are accountable to no man for what we may believe or fail to believe. Religion with us is a wholly private matter beyond the scope of governmental power.[104]

The First Amendment, it should be emphasized, gives us more than the right to have our own beliefs reign in the private kingdom of the individual mind. It ensures us that we will not be penalized by the State for the particular faiths that we follow or refuse to follow. Our forebears had too much experience, both in the Old World and the New, of what it means to be discriminated against for not being a member of the established church, not to have intended wholly to outlaw all power in government to continue such discriminations. Eliminated by the First Amendment is the possibility of religious tests upon which the right to vote or to hold public office may turn.[105] The Protestant and the Catholic, the Calvinist and the Greek Orthodox, the Jew and the Mohammedan, the agnostic and the atheist, all may sit down at the common table of our councils without any inquisition into their faiths or modes of worship, or their lack of same.[106]

In 1945, the Supreme Court rendered a decision which seems inconsistent with the right of individuals not to be penalized or discriminated against for their religious beliefs. In *In re Summers*,[107] it upheld the refusal of a state to admit an otherwise qualified applicant to the practice of law solely because his religious scruples forbade him from swearing to use force to support the Constitution. It is hard to deny that the individual concerned was refused the right to practice his profession because of his religious conviction. And, under our Constitution, men may be punished for what they do or fail to do, not for what they believe. The *Summers* case, it should be noted, was decided by a 5–4 vote. And, only a year after it had been decided, the Court itself indicated that it no longer held the same view, for in *Girouard v. United States*,[108] it was held that the fact that an alien's religious convictions made him refuse to bear arms in defense of this country did not make him ineligible for admission to citizenship. This decision is inconsistent with the *Summers* approach; under it, one may adhere to what he deems to be his obligation to God without forfeiting any rights that he might otherwise have.

The religious freedom accorded by the First Amendment is, however, not exhausted by the right to practice one's religion, free from penalty or discrimination. The First Amendment provides, not only that Congress shall make no law prohibiting the free exercise of religion, but that it shall also make no law "respecting an establishment of religion." The constitutional guarantee is thus divided into two parts. In substance, it means that the State shall neither prefer nor penalize religion: as Justice Frankfurter puts it, "The essence of the religious freedom guaranteed by our Constitution is therefore this: no religion shall either receive the state's support or incur its hostility." [109]

It is the first part of the constitutional guarantee—that forbidding governmental preference for religion—that has given the Supreme Court the difficulty in recent years. "Congress shall make no law respecting an establishment of religion." * What exactly does this mean? Of course, it is clear that the Congress cannot, without violating this provision, provide for an established church of the type that existed in many of the American colonies and is still set up in England. But this prohibition of an established church by no means exhausts the scope of the "establishment of religion" provision of the First Amendment. "We are all agreed," stated Justice Frankfurter in 1948, "that the First and the Fourteenth Amendments have a secular reach far more penetrating in the conduct of Government than merely to forbid an 'established church.'" [110] The difficulty is in determining exactly how much farther the Amendments do reach.

In its 1947 decision in *Everson v. Board of Education*,[111] the Supreme Court indicated that the constitutional division between church and State was sharper than many people had realized. Said Justice Black, speaking for the high tribunal there:

The "establishment of religion" clause of the First Amendment means at least this: Neither a state nor the Federal Government can set up a church. Neither can pass laws which aid one religion, aid all religions, or prefer one religion over another. Neither can force nor influence a person to go to or to remain away from church against his will or force him to profess a belief or disbelief in any religion. No person can be punished for entertaining or professing religious beliefs or disbeliefs, for church attendance or non-attendance. No tax in any amount, large or small, can be levied to support any religious activities or institutions, whatever they may be called, or whatever form they may adopt to teach or practice religion. Neither a state nor the Federal Government can, openly or secretly, participate in the affairs of any religious organizations or groups and *vice versa*. In the words of Jefferson, the clause against establishment of religion by law was intended to erect "a wall of separation between church and State." [112]

The "wall of separation" metaphor may be a striking formula, but, as with all jurisprudential formulas, we must take care lest it

---

* Under the *Gitlow* case, *supra* p. 241, this First Amendment prohibition is just as binding upon the states, through the due process clause of the Fourteenth Amendment, as it is upon the Federal Congress.

serve as a substitute for reflection and reasoning. Certainly, to paraphrase one member of the high Court,[113] even if we agree, in the abstract that the First Amendment was intended to erect a "wall of separation between church and State," that hardly tells us what it is that the wall separates. In its *Everson* decision, the Supreme Court held that the wall did not bar the state of New Jersey from providing free transportation to children attending Catholic parochial schools, upon the same basis as that provided to public school children. According to the opinion of the Court, "we cannot say that the First Amendment prohibits New Jersey from spending tax-raised funds to pay the bus fares of parochial school pupils as a part of a general program under which it pays the fares of pupils attending public and other schools." [114]

How can the Court's decision in *Everson* be reconciled with its insistence there that the First Amendment has erected a wall between church and State? It insists that that wall must be kept high and impregnable; but has it not actually permitted New Jersey to breach such wall? The answer depends upon what is really meant by the "wall of separation" metaphor. Despite the contrary implication contained in it, it does not require that there be an absolutely watertight division between church and State. The First Amendment, said the high Court in 1952, "does not say that in every and all respects there shall be a separation of Church and State." [115] What is it then that the wall between church and State prohibits? It is believed that a clue to the answer is given by consideration of that part of the First Amendment which bars government from penalizing or discriminating against religion. As has already been stated, it places the religious beliefs or nonbeliefs of the individual outside the sphere of governmental power. But this does not mean that all matters on which religious beliefs may pronounce are wholly outside the sphere of government. Much that is the concern of temporal authority may affect the spiritual interests of men. Thus, it is clear that religious belief cannot be pleaded as justification for a criminal act. The State may not penalize a man for his religion, but if he commits a crime he cannot defend on the ground that his act is sanctioned by his religion. Practices opposed to the health, safety, morals, or welfare of the community may be regulated, although such regulation may impinge upon the professed doctrines of religious belief. Consequently, the individual cannot claim freedom from compulsory vaccination on religious grounds.[116] Nor can the right of a parent to have his child practice his religion freely prevail against the child labor law of a state.[117] Were it otherwise, instead of the separation of church and State, there would be the subordination of the State on any matter deemed within the sovereignty of the religious conscience.[118]

These cases show that the prohibition against penalizing religious beliefs does not prevent the State from compelling conduct in the enforcement of legislation of general applicability, even though the religious consciences of particular individuals may rebel at the exaction.[119] The State may proceed without discrimination against conduct deemed undesirable, even though such conduct may, in the particular case, be sanctioned by religious belief. What the State may not do is to single out and penalize religion *as religion.*

But is not the converse of this also true? The State may not single out and aid religion (one or all faiths) *as religion.* Yet if the State, in applying legislation of general applicability, in a nondiscriminatory manner, happens to aid a religious, as well as a nonreligious group, then the State is giving no prohibited aid to religion. We can take the *Everson* case as a good illustration. New Jersey, there, was administering a general state program of aid to education, involving free transportation for school children. As the Court put it, "Its legislation, as applied, does no more than provide a general program to help parents get their children, regardless of their religion, safely and expeditiously to and from accredited schools." [120] Those attending parochial schools were given aid, not because they were Catholics, but because they were school children whom it was the policy of the state to aid. In other words, religion here, if aided, was not aided because it was religion but as part of a general nondiscriminatory state program designed to make education expeditious to all. In such circumstances, to bar the parochial school children from the state program would be to discriminate against them for their faiths. Such discrimination is, of course, not demanded by the First Amendment. It "requires the state to be a neutral in its relations with groups of religious believers and non-believers; it does not require the state to be their adversary." [121] A philosophy of such hostility to religion cannot be read into the Bill of Rights.

In *Everson,* religion was not singled out and aided *as religion;* hence the fact that a religious group was helped, along with other groups, by the New Jersey law did not render that law invalid. In the 1948 case of *McCollum v. Board of Education,*[122] on the other hand, it was religion as such that was aided by the State and this, the high Court held, was contrary to the First Amendment. At issue was a "released-time" program of religious education in the public schools of Champaign, Illinois. Under it, religious instruction was given once a week in the school buildings during the regular school hours by representatives of the Catholic, Protestant, and Jewish faiths. Pupils whose parents so requested were excused from their secular classes during the periods of religious instruction and were required to attend the religious classes. Pupils compelled by the state's compulsory education law to go to school for secular purposes were thus released in part from their legal duty upon the condition that they attended the religious classes. According to the Court, "This is beyond all question a utilization of the tax-established and tax-supported public school system to aid religious groups to spread their faith. And it falls squarely under the ban of the First Amendment." [123] Under the Champaign program, it was religion as such that was singled out and aided. Pupils not participating in the program of religious instruction were not released from their compulsory school duties. Here, secular power was placed at the disposal of sectarian groups and of them alone: "This is not separation of Church and State." [124]

In the more recent case of *Zorach v. Clauson*,[125] decided in 1952, a New York City "released time" program similar in many ways to that involved in *McCollum* was before the high Court. The New York scheme permitted its schools to release pupils during school hours, on written requests of their parents, so that they might leave the school buildings and go to religious centers for religious instruction or devotional exercises. Those not released stayed in the classrooms; and the churches reported to the schools the names of children released from the public schools who failed to report for religious instruction. This program, said the Court, differed sufficiently from that in *McCollum* to be upheld. The New York program, the Court emphasized, involved neither religious instruction in public school classrooms nor the expenditure of public funds. That being the case, there was no prohibited aid to religion: "Here . . . the public schools do no more than accommodate their schedules to a program of outside religious instruction." [126]

It is, to be sure, true that the difference emphasized by the Court did exist as between the "released time" programs at issue in *McCollum* and *Zorach*. Without any doubt, there is less of a commingling of secularism and sectarianism in the New York City type of program. One wonders, all the same, whether even it is free from the type of interrelationship between church and State that the First Amendment attempted to prevent. Under it, the state gives to religion aid which it does not extend to others: this is help to religion *as religion* and not as part of nondiscriminatory administration of a state scheme intended to aid all education. Even the *Zorach* Court concedes that, under the Constitution, the state "may not coerce anyone . . . to take religious instruction." [127] Yet New York was permitted to use its compulsory education law to induce students to take religious instruction: "The state thus makes religious sects beneficiaries of its power to compel children to attend secular schools." [128] The pith of the New York program is that formalized religious instruction is substituted for other school activity which those who do not participate in the released-time program are compelled to attend. As one of the dissenting Justices neatly characterized it, the classroom "serves as a temporary jail for a pupil who will not go to Church." [129] It is hard to see how this type of state aid to religion as such is consistent with the view of the First Amendment taken in the *Everson* case. Surprisingly enough, nonetheless, the *Zorach* opinion asserts that it is consistent with both *Everson* and *McCollum*. To be sure, as already shown, the programs at issue in *McCollum* and *Zorach* were not exactly alike. But the distinction does not appear to alter the basic defect which the Court found in the *McCollum* program. Indeed, to assume that *Everson, McCollum,* and *Zorach* are compatible with each other is, in Justice Jackson's pungent phrase, "to make the legal 'wall of separation between church and state' as winding as the famous serpentine wall designed by Mr. Jefferson for the University he founded." [130]

Equal Protection and the Negro

In few respects has the post-1937 Supreme Court differed more from its predecessors than in its readiness to give full effect to the Constitution's guarantee of equal protection of the laws for the Negro. And, as is well known, it is the Court's decisions in this field that have given rise to the greatest constitutional controversy since the "Court-packing" fight of twenty years ago. It is the strife that has grown up around these decisions, even more than the intrinsic importance of the decisions themselves, that makes analysis of them of moment. Has the high bench, as has been charged, distorted the Constitution, in accordance with the personal prepossessions of its members, to deprive the states of their sovereign powers over their educational systems? Are the Court's decisions abolishing segregation in public schools based upon a cavalier disregard of settled law and a judicial attitude that regard for precedents and authorities is obsolete, that words no longer mean what they have always meant to the Court, and that the Court itself knows no fixed principles? Few questions are of greater import to those concerned with the working of our constitutional system; if they must be answered in the affirmative, few can deny that the diminishing respect shown for the Supreme Court in certain quarters is a proper manifestation, even toward a tribunal endowed with such power and prestige.

As a starting point in any discussion of the decisions on the Negro and the law, we can do no better than to do what almost all of the critics of the Court fail to do, namely, refer to the relevant constitutional provisions. These are the Thirteenth, Fourteenth, and Fifteenth Amendments to the Constitution. The Thirteenth Amendment prohibits slavery and involuntary servitude, except as a punishment for crime. The Fourteenth Amendment provides that "No State shall make or enforce any law which shall abridge the privileges or immunities of citizens of the United States; nor shall any State deprive any person of life, liberty or property without due process of law, nor deny to any person within its jurisdiction the equal protection of the laws." And, under the Fifteenth Amendment, "The right of citizens of the United States to vote shall not be denied or abridged by the United States or by any State on account of race, color, or previous condition of servitude."

At the outset, it seems that three points are evident with regard to these Amendments. In the first place, it is hardly surprising if their provisions are contrary to the viewpoint of the southern states. These Amendments were adopted after the Civil War to attain some of the most important objectives for which the North had fought that conflict. Though they were ratified by most of the southern states, it is certainly untrue that such ratification was approved by the free will of their citizens. As far as the South was concerned, the postbellum Amendments were part of the terms imposed by the victors upon the vanquished. But this does not at all alter the legal effect of the Amendments in question; coerced or not from the South's point of view, they are parts of the Constitution and must be treated by the Supreme Court as such.

In the second place, it is hard to see how, legally speaking, it can be denied that these Amendments override the powers reserved to the states under the Tenth Amendment. This is true both because they were adopted after the Tenth Amendment and because of the settled rule of legal construction that a specific provision of an instrument takes precedence over a general provision. "The powers not delegated to the United States by the Constitution," reads the Tenth Amendment, "nor prohibited by it to the States, are reserved to the States." But the Thirteenth, Fourteenth, and Fifteenth Amendments are specific provisions which prohibit certain powers to the states, and, as far as their prohibitions are concerned, there can be no state reserved power.

The third point to be noted about the post-Civil War Amendments is that, like all provisions in legal documents that are not ambiguous, they were intended to mean exactly what they say. This may seem self-evident; yet it needs must be reaffirmed at the outset if the high Court's actions in this field are to be evaluated fairly. What is it that the Amendments in question say? If their language means anything, it means that slavery is abolished, that the right to vote cannot be made dependent upon the race or color of the would-be voter, and that the states cannot deny the protection of equal laws to those within their jurisdictions. Laws cannot, of course, be equal if they discriminate against the members of a given race or color. But the guarantee of equal protection goes even further. It does not require the states to treat all persons identically; the states may base their laws upon reasonable legislative classifications, which differentiate between people or groups in different circumstances. Legislative classification based upon race or color is, however, lacking in the rational basis that is necessary for such classification to be sustained. Even if we concede that there may be differences between the races, can we say that we know enough, scientifically speaking, about racial differences to conclude that classification based on race is other than irrational? If we are frank, we must admit that racial classification reflects not objective science, but racial animosity. If the equal protection clause means what it says, such irrational classification cannot mount the hurdle of the Fourteenth Amendment.

It is, without a doubt, the Supreme Court's decisions in the field of school segregation that have attracted the most public attention. But school segregation has been only a part of the general pattern established in the South to govern relations between the races. Before we deal with segregation in education itself, it will be necessary to turn briefly to other parts of that pattern which have been before the high Court in recent years.

From the point of view of the Negro's position in the community, the Supreme Court decisions that have been of the greatest moment (aside perhaps from the school segregation cases themselves) have been those enforcing his right to vote under the Fifteenth Amendment. "The very essence of political equality," in the recent language of a member of the highest tribunal, "is the right to vote. Once it is conceded that every man is equal in the voting booth, there is the beginning of real democracy."[131] To the

Negro, in truth, the right to vote is more than a symbol of his role in a democracy. In a system such as ours, political action is a principal instrument for the protection of individual and group rights. As a disenfranchised minority, the Negro would have little hope of exerting political pressure to bring about an end to discriminatory practices.

The Fifteenth Amendment secures the right to vote to all citizens irrespective of race or color. As far as general elections are concerned, the Amendment automatically put an end to state attempts to limit the franchise at such elections to members of one race. This was clearly established in the decisions of the highest Court even before 1937, and it is not with the question of discrimination at general elections that the Court has been concerned in recent years, but with that of discrimination in primary elections. As is well known, in most of the South the primary is the only election of real significance; if the Negro can be excluded from the Democratic primary, he can be effectively barred from the political process in southern states. Does disenfranchisement of the Negro at the primary stage violate the Fifteenth Amendment? It clearly does when exclusion of the right to vote in primaries is required by state law; such direct state action barring the Negro from an important stage of the voting process was held to fall within the constitutional ban in 1927.[132] But what happens if it is the Democratic Party of the state alone that resolves to limit participation in its primaries to whites only? It is only *state action* that is affected by the Fifteenth Amendment; if the action of a political party is not state action, it is not touched by the Amendment. In 1935, the Supreme Court held that the action of the Democratic Party was not action of the state, and its resolution barring Negroes from its primaries did not consequently violate the Fifteenth Amendment.[133]

Such a result might well be satisfying to those who believe that the law must be imprisoned in formal fictions. But it cannot be denied that it is pure fiction to assimilate the Democratic Party in a southern state to any purely private club and to assert that the qualifications for membership established by it are as far aloof from the impact of constitutional restraints as are those for membership in a golf club or a Masonic lodge.[134] Regardless of the technical form, the result of such approach was to bar the Negro from participation in the only stage of the election procedure which was of practical significance in the South. It was, therefore, not surprising that the Supreme Court itself in 1944 refused to countenance what was really a transparent violation of the Fifteenth Amendment. In *Smith v. Allwright*,[135] the Court held that primaries, though operated by political parties, are conducted under state authority. And the parties, in this respect, are agencies of the state, insofar as they determine the participants in primaries. The Fifteenth Amendment, said the Court, "is not to be nullified by a State through casting its electoral process in a form which permits a private organization to practice racial discrimination in the election. Constitutional rights would be of little value if they could be thus indirectly denied." [136] *Smith v. Allwright*, it must be conceded, dealt only with the matter of the constitutional right to vote. It did not and could not affect the extra-legal pressures that may still be brought to deter the Negro in the South from exercising his right to the ballot. That the extra-legal imponderables are still of importance in practice can hardly be controverted. Yet, even with them, the effect of *Smith v. Allwright* has been profound. Attempts at disfranchisement can no longer be legally condoned, and this is bound to mean a gradual improvement in the political status of the Negro.

The right to vote is the most important attribute of citizenship in a democracy. Access to the ballot enables any group of consequence ultimately to make its voice heard in the community. To the average citizen, all the same, particularly in a country like ours where representative government is securely established, vindication of the right to vote tends to be a relatively abstract matter. Of greater immediate moment to him are violations of his civil rights that affect him in his day-to-day living. To the Negro in the South, without a doubt, nothing is of more immediate impact than the all-pervasive institution of segregation:

Legally enforced segregation has been followed throughout the South since the close of the Reconstruction era. In these States it is generally illegal for Negroes to attend the same schools as whites; attend theaters patronized by whites; visit parks where whites relax; eat, sleep or meet in hotels, restaurants, or public halls frequented by whites. This is only a partial enumeration—legally imposed separation of races has become highly refined. In the eyes of the law, it is also an offense for whites to attend "Negro" schools, theaters and similar places. The result has been the familiar system of racial segregation in both public and private institutions which cuts across the daily lives of southern citizens from the cradle to the grave.[137]

Various aspects of segregation have been before the highest Court in the past twenty years. In the first place, there is the question of residential segregation. It has been settled since 1917 that such segregation cannot be required by state or local law; such governmentally enforced segregation of the races constitutes a patent violation of the equal protection clause of the Fourteenth Amendment.[138] Since 1917, residential segregation (and not only in the South) has been accomplished by private restrictive covenants entered into by property owners forbidding the transfer of property to persons of a certain race or color. In 1926, the Court had upheld the validity of such private covenants.[139] The Fourteenth Amendment inhibits only state action; it erects no shield against merely private conduct, however discriminatory or wrongful.[140] But the holding that the Constitution does not prohibit "private individuals from entering into contracts respecting the control and disposition of their own property" [141] did not really get to the core of the restrictive covenant problem. None will deny the freedom of individuals to contract even in a discriminatory way, but can such contracts be enforced except through state action? The sanction behind restrictive covenants is the possibility of legal relief if they are violated, and such relief is provided by the state through its courts.

In the 1948 case of *Shelley v. Kraemer*,[142] the Supreme Court held that such enforcement by a state of a covenant restricting the use or occupancy of property to persons of the Caucasian race denied the equal protection of the laws to a Negro against whom the covenant was enforced. Said Chief Justice Vinson for a unanimous Court: "We hold that in granting judicial enforcement of the restrictive agreements in these cases, the States have denied petitioners the equal protection of the laws and that, therefore, the action of the state courts cannot stand." [143] In a more recent case, the Court denied the power of a state court to award damages for breach of a restrictive covenant, stating that such judicial action is also state action forbidden by the Fourteenth Amendment.[144] *Shelley v. Kraemer* and this more recent decision clearly remove the legal sanction behind residential segregation. They have not, to be sure, by themselves completely altered the residential pattern of the South (nor even, for that matter, of other sections of the country where *de facto* residential segregation is practiced). At the same time, the high Court, in denying the possibility of judicial enforcement, has removed the legal "teeth" from restrictive covenants and this will surely help in ultimately making equal protection of the laws, in the field of property ownership, more than a mere slogan for the Negro and other minority groups.

Perhaps the best known laws providing for the segregation of the races are the so-called "Jim Crow" laws, which have made it unlawful for any common carrier to transport whites and Negroes in the same vehicle or the same portion thereof. Such enforced segregation might seem to be a patent transgression of the Fourteenth Amendment, since it is compelled by state law. In the celebrated case of *Plessy v. Ferguson*,[145] decided in 1896, the Supreme Court held, nonetheless, that mere segregation in transportation did not violate the equal protection clause. The Court rejected "the assumption that the enforced separation of the two races stamps the colored race with a badge of inferiority."[146] Under the Court's doctrine, so long as laws requiring segregation did not establish unequal facilities for the Negro, he was not denied the equal protection of the laws. As the Court has more recently explained it, "Under that doctrine, equality of treatment is accorded when the races are provided substantially equal facilities, even though these facilities be separate."[147]

The "separate but equal" doctrine, thus enunciated in *Plessy v. Ferguson*, has been the legal cornerstone of segregation in the South. It should, however, be noted that the *Plessy* case itself involved only transportation. Despite a widespread assumption to the contrary, the Supreme Court has never approved its employment in other fields and particularly, we shall see, has never sanctioned it in that of education. It is pertinent also to state that the approach of the *Plessy* Court was diametrically opposed to the clear language of the equal protection clause. The Court's holding was based on the assertion that segregation as such does not mean discrimination; if the Negro felt discriminated against, said the Court, it was "not by reason of anything found in the act, but solely because the colored race chooses to put that construction upon it."[148] To anyone familiar with the techniques of racial discrimination, this view is completely out of line with reality. The device of holding people deemed inferior separate—whether by confinement of Jews to the ghetto, by exclusion of untouchables from the temple, or by segregation of the Negro—is a basic tool of discrimination.

Yet, even if the *Plessy* Court were correct in its assumption that segregation is not discrimination, that would not make its doctrine consistent with the equal protection clause. For that clause bars the states from making legal distinctions that are not supported by reasonable legislative classifications, and, as already emphasized, classification on the basis of race must be deemed irrational. Our Constitution, to use the apt description of the dissenting Justice in the *Plessy* case, is color-blind; it neither knows nor tolerates classification on racial grounds.[149] "What is this," as the high Court asked in 1880, "but declaring that the law in the States shall be the same for the black as for the white?"[150] Nor is it an answer to the Negro who claims that segregation denies him equal protection to assert that his race may be given equal facilities from which the white race is barred. The rights created by the Fourteenth Amendment are guaranteed to the individual; they are personal rights. It is no answer to the individual Negro to say that the law also segregates whites: "Equal protection of the laws is not achieved through indiscriminate imposition of inequalities." [151] The Negro as an individual has the right to the same treatment by the law as others in the community; provision of separate facilities for his group (though they be equal) does not affect his personal right not to be barred by law from access to the same (not only to similar) facilities as those open to others in the community.

It is in the field of transportation that the "separate but equal" doctrine of *Plessy v. Ferguson* was announced. But, as is well known, it has been in the field of education that that doctrine has had its most widespread application. Before the high Court's recent decisions in that field are dealt with, it is important to emphasize that, as already stated, the Court had never, prior to 1954, considered directly the validity of the *Plessy* doctrine in education cases. In the 1899 case of *Cumming v. County Board of Education*,[152] the Court held only that an injunction which would force the discontinuance of white schools till operation of a Negro school was resumed was not the proper remedy to aid the Negro children denied adequate educational facilities. This holding, which was essentially one that two legal wrongs did not make a right, did not at all touch upon the validity of school segregation. The 1927 case of *Gong Lum v. Rice* [153] concerned a child of Chinese descent who contended that the state education authorities had erred in classifying him with Negro children and requiring him to attend a Negro school. Here, too, the validity of the *Plessy v. Ferguson* doctrine in the field of education was not at all challenged. It may be true that, by 1937, such validity had come to be widely assumed; but such assumption can hardly take the place of a direct Supreme Court decision.

From 1937 to 1954, the education cases before the Court all concerned education on the graduate level and the Court's decisions tended toward the doctrine that, where higher education is concerned, separate facilities for the Negro are inherently unequal. In these cases, the Court has ordered states to admit qualified Negro students to their regular law schools and to nonsegregated instruction at a state university for a postgraduate degree.[154] The Court's holding in these cases that segregation in higher education was inherently unequal and hence violative of the equal protection clause made it unnecessary for the Court to consider the validity of *Plessy v. Ferguson* in the field of education. Since, even under the *Plessy* case, segregation at the postgraduate level is contrary to the Constitution, the Court in these cases did not have to determine the question of the applicability of *Plessy* to education in order to determine whether to grant relief to the Negro plaintiffs.

In 1954 that question was presented directly in *Brown v. Board of Education.*[155] It is important to bear in mind that, despite charges subsequently made that the Court's decision there was contrary to all the settled precedents, the *Brown* case was really the first in which the validity of the "separate but equal" doctrine in the field of public education was squarely before the highest tribunal. The plaintiffs in *Brown* were Negroes of school age who sought the aid of the courts in obtaining admission to the public schools of their community on a nonsegregated basis. They had been denied admission to schools attended by white children under laws requiring or permitting segregation according to race. The lower courts had found expressly that the Negro and white schools involved were equalized or being equalized, with respect to buildings, curricula, qualifications and salaries of teachers, and other "tangible" factors. But the plaintiffs contended that this made no difference, asserting that segregated public schools are not "equal" and cannot be made equal. The Supreme Court was thus presented with the question: Does segregation of children in public schools solely on the basis of race, even though the physical facilities and other "tangible" factors may be equal, deprive the children of the minority group of equal educational opportunities? This question could not be answered without considering the applicability of the *Plessy v. Ferguson* doctrine to the field of public education.

In its *Brown* decision, the Court seized the constitutional issue squarely by the bit and held unanimously that segregation in public schools as such violated the equal protection clause. According to Chief Justice Warren's opinion, "in the field of public education the doctrine of 'separate but equal' has no place. Separate educational facilities are inherently unequal." [156] This is true because the mere fact of segregation discriminates against Negro pupils: "To separate them from others of similar age and qualifications solely because of their race generates a feeling of inferiority as to their status in the community that may affect their hearts and minds in a way unlikely ever to be undone." [157] Of course, this is contrary to the basic justification given for its decision by the *Plessy v. Ferguson* Court, namely, that segregation is not of itself discriminatory. The *Brown* opinion acknowledges this and states expressly that the *Plessy* rationale is contrary to what we now know about the psychological effects of segregation.

The Supreme Court itself has been the first to admit that the implementation of its *Brown* decision outlawing school segregation would be no simple matter. Immediately after declaring the fundamental principle that racial discrimination in public education was unconstitutional, the Court requested further argument (from the parties, the United States Attorney General, and the attorneys general of all states permitting or requiring segregation in schools) on the question of what specific relief the Court should give to implement its *Brown* decision. In 1955, the Court delivered a further opinion on this question of relief.[158] It conceded at the outset that there were complexities connected with the transition to a system of public education freed of racial discrimination. This led it to recognize both that desegregation was not a matter to be achieved in a day and that the tribunals best equipped to determine the specific relief to be granted in each case where the *Brown* principle was invoked were the trial courts themselves, which were most cognizant with local conditions in each case. If time is needed in the public interest before the *Brown* principle can be implemented in practice in a locality, the lower courts are authorized to grant such time. At any rate, the lower courts are instructed to take such action in each case as is necessary and proper to ensure that Negroes are admitted to public schools on a racially nondiscriminatory basis "with all deliberate speed." [159]

"With all deliberate speed"—this is surely far from the irresponsible decree of a body of radical extremists that desires by judicial fiat to subvert the reserved powers of the states. Even though segregation in public education is found to violate the equal protection clause, the Court does not command immediate wholesale compliance with its ruling. Instead, it recognizes that desegregation cannot be attained overnight throughout the country. Different local conditions may require different desegregation timetables, and the Court is willing to leave the fixing of specific schedules to the lower courts in the localities concerned. All that the high Court asks is that the state authorities involved "make a prompt and reasonable start toward full compliance" with the desegregation ruling and that there be such compliance "at the earliest practicable date." [160]

To be sure, one can be persuaded of the reasonableness of the course taken by the Supreme Court only if he does not feel that the *Brown* decision constitutes a usurpation of judicial power, as all too many critics of that decision claim to feel. It is hardly likely that any such extreme critics can be persuaded by any legal arguments that the present writer can make. Though such critics of the Court profess to base their strictures on legal grounds, such professions are primarily a cover for an antipathy toward desegregation grounded on sociological and psychological considerations. It is true that the emotional response which the Court's desegregation ruling has met in the South is neither unnatural nor wholly unwarranted. The *Brown* case strikes at the core of the South's way of life—a way of life that has roots far deeper than the actions of legislatures and courts. The reaction of those whose established modes of existence are thus disrupted is not to be expected to be either fair or rational. In singling out the Supreme Court as the cause of the destruction of the interracial pattern developed by it, the South is letting its natural desire for a scapegoat obscure the real origin of its present difficulties. The fault (if it be a fault) is not in the Court but in the Constitution. Nor is it surprising that this is so, in view of the fact, already alluded to, that the relevant constitutional provision (the Fourteenth Amendment) was imposed upon the South as part of the price of defeat on the battlefield. Without a doubt, the post-Civil War Amendments were intended to work hardship on the South and to do so without regard to southern inclinations and desires; that is the normal purpose of terms imposed upon a defeated power, and particularly after a civil war.

Imposed by coercion or not, the Fourteenth Amendment is now clearly a part of the Constitution, accepted as such even by the southern states. When it is confronted with a claimed violation of the Constitution, what is the Supreme Court to do? It must lay the constitutional provision that is invoked beside the act that is challenged and decide whether the latter squares with the former. In making that decision, the Court cannot be at all influenced by what it deems the desirability of the constitutional provision or the opposition its implementation may meet among those affected by it. As Chief Justice Warren aptly stated in the 1955 *Brown* opinion, "it should go without saying that the vitality of these constitutional principles cannot be allowed to yield simply because of disagreement with them." [161] If the Fourteenth Amendment outlaws legislative classifications based on race, is a Court to be blamed if it holds that the Amendment means what it says, even in the field of educational segregation?

One point needs to be emphasized in any consideration of the constitutional storm stirred up by the desegregation ruling of the highest tribunal, and it has nothing to do with the merits of that ruling as a matter of constitutional law. Successful defiance by the South of the decision of the Supreme Court will result in a far more radical change in our constitutional system than even the most extreme critic of the Court asserts was brought about by the *Brown* decision. A constitutional system such as ours, governed by a written organic instrument, must of necessity be a Law State par excellence. That such a system can flourish only in a society imbued with a legal spirit and trained to reverence the law is as certain as any conclusion of political speculation can be. For such a system properly to operate, there must be some machinery set up to ensure that the provisions of the Constitution are adhered to. A Constitution whose provisions are enforced only by the voluntary adherence of those subject thereto is a mere paper instrument. "To what purpose," as John Marshall so eloquently stated, "are powers limited, and to what purpose is that limitation committed to writing, if these limits may, at any time, be passed by those intended to be restrained?" [162] For a Constitution to be effective in practice, it must, the Founding Fathers themselves knew, incorporate a "coercive principle"; the only question is whether it should be "a coercion of law, or a coercion of arms." [163]

In our early history, the answer to this question may not have been entirely certain. But if the civil conflict of a century ago settled anything, it was the need to have issues of constitutional power settled by legal rather than physical coercion. We now see that there can be no Constitution without law administered through the highest Court. But this necessarily presupposes respect for and compliance with the law declared by the Court. When, in a real controversy, an appeal is made to law, the issue must be left entirely to the judgment of the high Court and not the personal judgments of those interested. This principle is a basic postulate of our constitutional system. Indeed, respect for the Court's decisions is the *sine qua non* of our structure; draw out this particular bolt, and the machinery falls to pieces. To make even one exception to the principle that the Supreme Court alone is the trustee of the law is to take the fatal first step toward abrogation of the rule of law: "If one man can be allowed to determine for himself what is law, every man can. That means first chaos, then tyranny." [164] Covenants without the sword, says Hobbes, are but empty words. The same is true of a Constitution that cannot be enforced by the courts. How vain are such words if they may be heeded or not at will! Of what importance is it to say, the states are prohibited from doing certain acts, if the states recognize no legitimate authority to decide whether an act done *is* a prohibited act? If the states alone have the right to decide on their own powers, does any Constitution remain? Does not the power of the states become absolute and uncontrolled? Can anyone talk to them of transgressing their constitutional powers, when they deny that anyone has a right to judge of those powers but themselves?

8

THE WAR POWER

"Laws are commanded to hold their tongues amongst arms; and tribunals fall to the ground with the peace they are no longer able to uphold." Thus reads a striking passage from Burke's *Reflections on the Revolution in France*. One familiar with the practical working of a constitutional system realizes that Burke's dictum all too often accords with the realities of wartime. War begets necessities not required by the lesser exigencies of more normal periods. War calls into play the full power of government in extreme emergency. It compels invention of legal, as of martial, tools adequate to deal with supreme necessity.[1] Inevitably some of the instruments for waging total war will be inconsistent with the rights of individuals that could ordinarily not be impaired. Basic provisions of the Constitution, normally and perfectly adapted to conditions of peace, may not have the same complete and universal application in time of war. Even constitutional doctrine, it is felt, must give way if it conflicts with the national necessity. "By general law," declared Abraham Lincoln at the height of our greatest national emergency, "life and limb must be protected, yet often a limb must be amputated to save a life; but a life is never wisely given to save a limb." [2]

Few will disagree with the Lincoln view that a nation fighting for its existence cannot be fettered by all the legal technicalities that obtain in time of peace. Total war cannot be waged in complete subordination to law. On the contrary, total war means the total subjection of the individual to the State. Manpower, labor, property, material, profit, rent, and even food—both property and life, and all that makes life worth living—all are subject to the overriding authority of the modern war power. The war power, said the Supreme Court at the height of the last conflict, "is 'the power to wage war successfully.' . . . It extends to every matter and activity so related to war as substantially to affect its conduct and progress. The power is not restricted to the winning of victories in the field and the repulse of enemy forces. It embraces every phase of the national defense." [3]

At the same time, to quote a concurring opinion, which was delivered in a 1948 case,

No one will question that this power is the most dangerous one to free government in the whole catalogue of powers. It usually is invoked in haste and excitement when calm legislative consideration of constitutional limitation is difficult. It is executed in a time of patriotic fervor that makes moderation unpopular. And, worst of all, it is interpreted by judges under the influence of the same passions and pressures.[4]

What Justice Jackson has termed "the planned economy and galloping socialism of modern war"[5] may be accepted as a patriotic necessity in times of conflict. But their impact may extend far beyond the immediate needs of the war emergency. The war power may set a pattern that is not easily changed when peace is restored. If laws are required entirely to hold their tongues amongst arms, who is to say when they will again become fully articulate?

Certainly we must reject the view that the war power must be exercised in strict conformity to all legal forms and limitations. Yet this is far from saying that the war power must be permitted to carry before it our basic constitutional structure. The demands of war must somehow be reconciled with those of law; if either takes over the field completely in a period of emergency, it may carry down with it all else that we value.

It was during the extreme emergency of our Civil War that there were presented the extreme claims of both war and law. The former was personified by President Lincoln, the latter by Chief Justice Taney. To deal with the unprecedented situation in which the Government found itself after the fall of Fort Sumter, Lincoln purported to exercise thitherto unparalleled powers. On his own authority, he suspended the writ of habeas corpus and ordered wholesale arrests without warrants, detentions without trials, and imprisonments without judicial convictions. Private mail was opened and persons ordered arrested and held incommunicado by military officers acting under Presidential authority. As Taney well put it, the President had "thrust aside the judicial authorities and officers to whom the constitution has confided the power and duty of interpreting and administering the laws, and substituted a military government in its place, to be administered and executed by military officers."[6]

The passage just quoted was part of an opinion delivered in May, 1861, by Taney, in which he sharply condemned as illegal the suspension of habeas corpus by the President and the arrest, without warrant and hearing, of a civilian by military order. Taney's vindication of the letter of the law against executive claims of emergency was drowned out by cannons and marching feet. In truth, however, neither the Lincoln nor the Taney philosophy alone is adequate for the times' necessity in a war period. What is needed is some reconciliation of the extreme demands of war and law, not the complete exclusion of the one or the other. It was with most keen perception that Justice Jackson wrote shortly before his death in 1954, "Had Mr. Lincoln scrupulously observed the Taney policy, I do not know whether we would have had any liberty, and had the Chief Justice adopted Mr. Lincoln's philosophy as the philosophy of the law, I again do not know whether we would have had any liberty." [7]

Military Tribunals

The conflict between war and law personified in 1861 by the great President and Chief Justice is one which has occurred many times in our history. But it has rarely, if ever, taken place in a more dramatic setting than that presented in the Supreme Court building on July 29–31, 1942. For it was on those days that the high tribunal heard and decided the case of the eight German saboteurs who had been landed on our shores from submarines in June, 1942. The eight had been arrested by FBI agents soon after their landings and tried by a Military Commission specially appointed by President Roosevelt for offenses against the law of war and the Articles of War. The Commission had found them guilty of violating the law of war by attempting sabotage of our war facilities and had ordered death sentences for six of them and prison terms for the other two. The officers who had been appointed to defend the Germans before the military tribunal then sought habeas corpus, first from a district court, then from the federal court of appeals in Washington, and then from the Supreme Court. To deal with the case "without any avoidable delay," the Court convened in July in Special Term pursuant to a call to the vacationing Justices from Chief Justice Stone. It was during this special three-day session that the legality of the saboteurs' convictions was argued and determined, though the formal opinion of the Court explaining its brief July 31 announcement that the military trial had been valid was not filed until three months later, weeks after the death sentences ordered by the Military Commission had been carried out.

The case of the German saboteurs differs strikingly from that of almost a century earlier in which Chief Justice Taney eloquently though unavailingly asserted the illegality of military detentions. In 1861, an aide-de-camp in full military uniform and appropriately wearing a sword appeared before the Chief Justice and declined obedience to a writ of habeas corpus upon the ground that the writ had been "suspended." Said Taney plaintively then: "I have exercised all the power which the constitution and laws confer upon me, but that power has been resisted by a force too strong for me to overcome." [8] In 1942, too, the President's proclamation appointing the Military Commission and directing it to try the saboteurs provided expressly that the Germans were not to be permitted "to seek any remedy or maintain any proceeding directly or indirectly, or to have any such remedy or proceeding sought on their behalf, in the courts." But this part of the proclamation was quietly ignored, the Court stating only, "neither the Proclamation nor the fact that they are enemy aliens forecloses consideration by the courts of petitioners' contentions that the Constitution and laws of the United States constitutionally enacted forbid their trial by military commission." [9] The saboteurs were thus given a full judicial hearing on the legality of their convictions, despite the President's attempt completely to bar the courts from the case.

Yet, though the Court in 1942 refused to give effect to the Presidential effort to prevent the saboteurs from testing their military trial and sentences before the courts, its decision on the merits was anything but favorable to the Germans. They had contended that they could not validly be tried by a military tribunal, asserting that they were entitled to be tried in the civil courts with the safeguards, including trial by jury, which the Fifth and Sixth Amendments guarantee to all persons tried in such courts for criminal offenses. The Court rejected their contention, holding that the constitutional safeguards did not apply to offenses against the law of war. The law of war draws a universal distinction between lawful and unlawful combatants. Lawful combatants are subject to capture and detention as prisoners of war. Unlawful combatants are likewise subject to capture and detention, but in addition they are subject to trial and punishment by military tribunals for acts which render their belligerency unlawful. The spy who secretly passes the military lines of a belligerent in time of war, seeking to gather military information and communicate it to the enemy, or an enemy combatant who without uniform comes secretly through the lines for the purpose of waging war by destruction of life or property, are examples of belligerents who are deemed not to be entitled to the status of prisoners of war, but to be offenders against the law of war and subject to trial and punishment by military tribunals. According to the Court, the German saboteurs were clearly such offenders against the law of war. Said Chief Justice Stone for a unanimous tribunal: "those who during time of war pass surreptitiously from enemy territory into our own, discarding their uniforms upon entry, for the commission of hostile acts involving destruction of life or property, have the status of unlawful combatants punishable as such by military commission." [10]

Not many people, it is felt, will take issue with the Court's decision in the case of the German saboteurs. The saboteurs were actual invaders. Their penetration of our boundary, effected from hostile submarines, was basically a military operation; their capture was a continuation of that operation. The punishment by military tribunal of such enemies who, with the purpose of destroying war materials and utilities, entered our territory without uniforms was not forbidden by the Constitution. Unlawful enemy belligerents, both in the field and on our own soil, could be proceeded against without adherence to the safeguards of indictment and trial by jury in the civil courts.

The principle upon which the high Court based its decision in the case of the German saboteurs was applied by that tribunal in 1946 to uphold the convictions by military commission of the captured Japanese generals Yamashita and Homma.[11] Both generals had been tried by military tribunals, appointed by the commanding general of the American forces in the Philippine Islands, on charges of violating the law of war. The gist of the charges was that the defeated generals had failed in their duty as army commanders to control their troops and had permitted them to commit specified atrocities against the civilian population and prisoners of war. Both Yamashita and Homma attacked the legality of their trials and convictions, but the Supreme Court, as already stated, relied upon its decision in the case of the German saboteurs in rejecting their legal attacks. The Japanese generals, like the saboteurs four years earlier, were charged with violations of the law of war. Moreover their violations had been committed in the actual theater of military operations. Military tribunals, competent to try the German saboteurs for unlawful belligerency in 1942, were no less competent to try Yamashita and Homma for offenses against the law of war after they were captured.

Even Justice Murphy, who (along with Justice Rutledge) delivered a vigorous dissent, agreed with the Court's conclusion that the military commissions which had tried the Japanese generals were lawfully created and had jurisdiction to try them for recognized war crimes. To the majority of the Court, this conclusion meant the end of the defeated generals' cases. One wonders, nevertheless, whether such a result follows as imperatively as the Court thought it did.

Though one may agree with the holding in the case of the German saboteurs and recognize that it justifies the Court in upholding the jurisdiction of the tribunals that tried Yamashita and Homma, that alone does not justify the sustaining of their convictions. For the difficult issue in the cases of the Japanese generals was not the existence of military jurisdiction but the manner in which such jurisdiction was exercised in the particular cases.

To be sure, as already stated, the military tribunals had jurisdiction to try Yamashita and Homma for recognized war crimes, such as the commission of atrocities against civilians or prisoners of war. What gives one pause is the question of whether the Japanese generals were really charged with having personally committed any recognized war crimes. Thus, Yamashita was accused of having failed to control the operations of troops under his command, permitting them to commit brutal atrocities. Nowhere was it alleged that he personally committed any of the atrocities, or that he ordered their commission, or that he had any knowledge of the commission thereof by members of his command. Actually, during the period covered by the charges against him, Yamashita had all but lost effective control over the forces under him—and that because of the fact that our invading troops in the Philippines had crushed the Japanese defense, leaving Yamashita's troops scattered and his command wholly disorganized. In these circumstances, it is hard to disagree with Yamashita's counsel when he asserted, "The petitioner is charged not with having done something or failed to do something. He is charged with having *been* something—the commanding officer of a Japanese force." [12]

Just as disturbing as the failure to charge Yamashita with any personal act, order, or even knowledge were the conditions under which he was tried and convicted. Yamashita was rushed to trial under a hastily drawn charge, given insufficient time to prepare an adequate defense, deprived of the benefits of some of the most elementary rules of evidence, and summarily sentenced to be hanged. The charge against Yamashita was served only three weeks after his surrender. When he was arraigned, he was served with a bill of particulars alleging sixty-four specific crimes by troops under his command. When his trial began, twenty-one days later, he was served with a supplemental bill alleging fifty-nine more crimes. His counsel thus had only three weeks to investigate and prepare to meet all the charges in the original bill. They asked for additional time to prepare to meet the charges in the supplemental bill (which had, as already stated, only been served at the beginning of the actual trial), but their request was denied. It may well be that, to the military mind that supervised his trial, Yamashita, in protesting on this point, was acting the ingrate; for had he not been given a full three weeks after his arraignment to prepare his defense, while his compatriot Homma had been given only fifteen days? To an impartial outsider, on the other hand, the shortness of the time allowed for the preparation of the defense was wholly inconsistent with any semblance of a fair trial. And the trial itself was conducted in a manner most lawyers would consider shocking where a capital offense is concerned. The customary safeguards relating to the reception of evidence were abrogated; so far as the admissibility and probative value of evidence was concerned, the directive setting it up made the tribunal that tried Yamashita a law unto itself. Thus left completely at large, the military commission, over the constant objections of the defense, admitted into evidence everything the prosecution offered: "Every conceivable kind of statement, rumor, report, at first, second, third or further hand, written, printed or oral, and one 'propaganda' film were allowed to come in." [13] The elementary evidentiary safeguards that are available to the meanest petty thief in our courts were thus denied to a vanquished enemy who, by surrendering to our forces, doubtless deemed himself protected as a prisoner of war by the rules of international law, which he himself was later charged with having violated.

And to what avail all this unseemly haste and disregard of the fundamentals of fair procedure? Though we may still technically have been at war with Japan, there was, after the surrender of the Japanese forces, no danger to our security that justified such drastic departure from the time-tested Anglo-American road of justice. Of course, those who commit war crimes should be subject to just punishment, and, as the case of the German saboteurs shows, such punishment can be meted out by a military tribunal. Except on the actual field of combat, all the same, there is no valid reason why guilt and sentence cannot be determined by a procedure consistent with the fundamentals of fair play. It is hard to see the necessity for the type of "judicial lynching" to which the Japanese generals were subjected (unless, of course, those responsible for the proceedings doubted their ability to win a verdict of "guilty" in other than a "kangaroo court"). We need have no sympathy for Yamashita and Homma if they were guilty of the atrocities for which they were executed. But we can sympathize with the need for justice administered according to law, even for enemies coming within our power. The natural desire for retribution does not, in Justice Murphy's phrase, "justify the abandonment of our devotion to jus-

tice in dealing with a fallen enemy commander. To conclude otherwise is to admit that the enemy has lost the battle but has destroyed
our ideals." [14] Stark retribution cannot be permitted to masquerade
in a cloak of false legality without impairing the great ideals to
which our Nation is dedicated.

In the case of General Yamashita, the Supreme Court expressly
rejected the Government's contention that it had no authority to
inquire into the legality of Yamashita's trial and conviction. For
the purpose of determining whether Yamashita was entitled to any
judicial review, his case was basically like that of the German saboteurs. At the time of his case, the Philippines were part of our
insular possessions; thus Yamashita's offenses were committed on our
territory, he was tried within the jurisdiction of our insular courts,
and imprisoned within American territory. Under conditions of
global war, at the same time, it may happen that our military authorities try and convict someone beyond the limits of our territory.
In such a case, do our courts have any competence to review the
legality of the trial and conviction?

This was the question presented to the Supreme Court in the 1950
case of *Johnson v. Eisentrager*.[15] The petitioners there were German nationals captured in China by our army and tried and convicted there by military commission for violations of the law of war;
they were serving their sentences in a prison in occupied Germany.
They sought review of the legality of their imprisonment in a habeas
corpus action in the federal courts, but the Supreme Court held that
such enemy aliens, resident, captured, and imprisoned abroad, had
no standing at all to demand access to our courts. A similar result
was reached in 1948 in *Hirota v. MacArthur*,[16] where the petitioners were Japanese who had been convicted in Japan of so-called war
crimes against humanity by the International Military Tribunal for
the Far East (the counterpart in Japan of the Nuremberg tribunal
which tried the German war criminals). Here, too, the Court held
there was no authority in American courts to review the trials and
convictions. In addition to the lack of territorial jurisdiction involved in *Johnson v. Eisentrager*, there was also the fact that the
convicting tribunal had been an international one, and hence one
which, in the Court's opinion, was not subject to the reviewing authority of the American courts.

Few may disagree with the Court's refusal to place the litigation
weapon in enemy hands in circumstances such as those present in
the *Eisentrager* and *Hirota* cases. But those cases have implications
beyond their fact patterns of enemies convicted of war crimes outside American territory. As Justice Douglas stated, in a concurring

Hirota opinion, "Today Japanese war lords appeal to the Court for application of American standards of justice. Tomorrow or next year an American citizen may stand condemned in Germany or Japan by a military court or commission." [17] The type of case referred to by Justice Douglas soon arose before the Supreme Court. In the 1952 case of *Madsen v. Kinsella*,[18] the Court had to deal with the conviction of the wife of an American serviceman who killed her husband while living with him in the American Zone of Germany. She had been tried and found guilty by the United States Court of the Allied High Commission for Germany, a tribunal which had been set up under the Presidential authority to govern areas occupied by our armed forces. Despite the contrary implications in the *Eisentrager* and *Hirota* cases, here the Court did review the legality of the conviction of the American citizen, even though her crime had been committed and she had been arrested outside American territorial jurisdiction. On the merits, nonetheless, the Court upheld the authority of the military government courts in Germany in such cases. It must be remembered that they were the only judicial tribunals then functioning in the defeated country. They took the place of the German courts that had previously existed and had the same jurisdiction over offenses committed on German soil which the German courts had had before the occupation and which those courts have since acquired on their reconstitution under the government of West Germany.

More recently, with the transfer of much of the jurisdiction of military government courts, like that involved in the *Madsen* case, to national courts in occupied areas, a new means of trying Americans accompanying the armed forces abroad has been provided. Under the Uniform Code of Military Justice enacted in 1950, the Congress provided that all persons accompanying the armed forces outside American territory should be subject to the Code, which means as a practical matter that they are subject to the jurisdiction of the same military tribunals that American servicemen are. In the 1956 case of *Kinsella v. Krueger*,[19] the wife of an American officer in Japan, who had been tried and convicted for the murder of her husband by a general court-martial in Tokyo, challenged the jurisdiction of such court-martial. The Court held, however, that Congress could authorize the trial of civilians accompanying our forces abroad under ordinary military law. The Constitution, said the Court, does not require trial before a court set up under Article III of the Constitution in a foreign country for offenses committed there by an American citizen, and Congress may provide for trial of such offenses by a legislatively created tribunal such as a court-martial.

Those accompanying the armed forces abroad can be deemed to have subjected themselves to the same jurisdiction as those whom they are accompanying. As the Court puts it in its opinion:

In all matters of substance, the lives of military and civilian personnel alike are geared to the local military organization which provides their living accommodations, medical facilities and transportation from and to the United States. We could not find it unreasonable for Congress to conclude that all should be governed by the same legal standard to the end that they receive equal treatment under the law.[20]

The principle of the *Krueger* case applies only to civilians who accompany American servicemen abroad. It has no application to other civilians, who can only be tried for crimes in our ordinary courts, with all the safeguards customarily associated with judicial proceedings. The Constitution distinguishes the military from the civilian class as separate communities; to try by court-martial a civilian entitled to trial in an Article III court is a violation of the Constitution. The prohibition against subjecting civilians to military justice applies even to ex-servicemen who are tried for crimes committed before their discharge. This was clearly settled in the high Court's 1955 decision in *Toth v. Quarles*.[21] * At issue there was the trial and conviction by court-martial of an ex-serviceman arrested after his discharge and charged with a murder allegedly committed while he had been an airman in Korea. His military trial had been based upon an act of Congress purporting to subject ex-servicemen to trial by courts-martial for offenses punishable by more than five-years' imprisonment committed by them while they were in the service, where they could not validly be tried for such offenses in an American court. The Court held that the Congress itself could not subject civilians to military jurisdiction and that an ex-serviceman, upon his discharge, became entitled to all the safeguards afforded other civilians under our Constitution. It is only those actually in the service or (under the *Krueger* case) those living with them in American bases abroad who are subject to court-martial jurisdiction; military jurisdiction cannot be extended to civilian ex-soldiers who have severed all relationship with the military and its institutions.

Martial Law

Despite the unequivocal language of the Court to the contrary in *Toth v. Quarles*, it is clear that there is one very important class of case where civilians can validly be subjected to the jurisdiction of

* *Supra*, p. 58.

military tribunals. Such is the case in areas governed by martial law. According to Chief Justice Stone, "martial law is the exercise of the power which resides in the executive branch of the Government to preserve order and insure the public safety in times of emergency, when other branches of the Government are unable to function, or their functioning would itself threaten the public safety. . . . It is a law of necessity to be prescribed and administered by the executive power." [22] When it is absolutely imperative for the preservation of the public safety and good order, ordinary legal processes can be superseded and military tribunals authorized to exercise the jurisdiction normally vested in the courts. Such may be the case in times of extreme emergency such as an invasion, insurrection, or catastrophic natural disaster.

The power of the executive to declare martial law, so necessary in true emergencies, is, however, one which is capable of great abuse. Both James I and Charles I authorized martial law for the purpose of more expeditiously punishing crimes committed by civilians, and, not so long ago in our own country, there were misuses of the doctrine of martial law by state governors attempting to intervene in industrial disputes through military authority exercised in the name of specious necessity.[23] To ensure against such abuses, the power to proclaim martial law must be confined within narrow limits. Our courts must say to our military authorities what Lord Chief Justice Hale stated to a military officer in seventeenth-century England: "You are the King's servants and intended for his defence against his enemies, and to preserve the peace of the Kingdom; not to exempt yourself from the authority of the laws. And indeed it were a vain thing to talk of Courts and laws, if military men shall thus give the law, and control legal proceedings." [24]

It was in its 1866 decision in the celebrated case of *Ex parte Milligan* [25] that the Supreme Court laid down the boundaries of martial-law power. Milligan, a leading Copperhead during the Civil War, had been arrested in Indiana during the war and tried, convicted, and sentenced to be hanged by a military commission convened at the order of the commanding general of the military district of Indiana. The Supreme Court held that a civilian like Milligan could not be tried by military tribunal in a part of the country remote from the actual theater of military operations and in which the ordinary courts were open and functioning. The *Milligan* case, explained a member of the highest Court in 1946, holds,

that the military lacks any constitutional power in war or in peace to substitute its tribunals for civil courts that are open and operating in the proper and unobstructed exercise of their jurisdiction. Only when a foreign invasion or civil war actually closes the courts and renders it impossible for them to administer criminal justice can martial law validly be invoked to suspend their functions.[26]

The so-called "open court" rule of the *Milligan* case (barring martial law when the courts are open and in the proper and unobstructed exercise of their jurisdiction) has been criticized as inadequate to meet the needs of modern warfare. Yet it was essentially the *Milligan* rule that was followed by the Supreme Court in dealing with the legal problems posed by the proclamation of martial law in Hawaii, following the attack on Pearl Harbor. Such proclamation was issued by the Governor of Hawaii immediately after the surprise Japanese attack on December 7, 1941. It suspended the writ of habeas corpus and authorized and requested the Commanding General of the Army in the area, "during the . . . emergency and until danger of invasion is removed, to exercise all the powers normally exercised" by the Governor and by the "judicial officers and employees of this territory."

There is little doubt that the attack on Pearl Harbor was an "invasion" justifying the proclamation of martial law and the taking over of the government of Hawaii (including the administration of justice) by the military authorities. But it is a fundamental rule that, just as necessity furnishes the occasion for martial rule, so it also limits its duration.[27] What was true of Hawaii when Pearl Harbor was bombed was not necessarily true of Hawaii after the danger of invasion had passed. Despite this, the regime established by the Governor's December 7, 1941 proclamation was continued in Hawaii, with certain modifications, until almost the end of 1944. Though the civil courts were permitted to function on January 27, 1942, they were forbidden to exercise criminal jurisdiction until 1943, and, even then, they were barred from trying criminal prosecutions for violations of military orders, which actually covered a wide range of civilian conduct. In August, 1942, a Honolulu stockbroker was tried and convicted by a military tribunal on a charge of embezzling stock. In February, 1944, a civilian shipfitter employed in the Honolulu Navy Yard engaged in a brawl with two Marine sentries at the yard. He, too, was tried and convicted by a military tribunal, the charge against him being that he violated a military order which prohibited assaults on military personnel. Both the stockbroker and the shipfitter challenged the power of the military courts to try them by petitions for writs of habeas corpus and the Supreme Court dealt with the legality of their convictions in its 1946 decision in *Duncan v. Kahanamoku*.[28]

The majority of the high tribunal decided that the military tri-

bunals in Hawaii had no authority to try civilians like the stockbroker and the shipfitter and ordered that they be set free.   Although
recognizing that the Congress had empowered the Governor of
Hawaii to declare martial law in a situation such as that presented
by the attack on Pearl Harbor, the Court denied that this gave the
armed forces the power to supplant all civilian laws and to substitute military for judicial trials under the conditions which existed in
Hawaii at the time the stockbroker and the shipfitter were tried. At
that time, the regular civil courts were both open and functioning;
they were perfectly capable of exercising their normal criminal jurisdiction had the military allowed them to do so.   In such a situation,
the courts could not be superseded by military tribunals in their enforcement of the ordinary criminal law.

The military action at issue in the *Duncan* case well illustrates
the truth of Madison's observation that "power is of an encroaching
nature."   As already pointed out, the situation on December 7, 1941,
clearly justified the declaration of martial law and the complete taking over by the military of government in Hawaii.   But the Japanese "invasion" of Hawaii began and ended long before the stockbroker and the shipfitter were tried and convicted by military
tribunals.   After the shock of the Japanese attack had been dissi-
pated, there was no need for the military to strip the civil courts of
their ordinary criminal jurisdiction.   The civil courts were then
fully capable of functioning and criminal trials in them no more endangered the public safety than the gathering of the populace in
saloons and places of amusement, which had been authorized by
military order.   It is hard to disagree with the Governor of Hawaii,
who testified in the *Duncan* case that the trial of civilians before
military tribunals for criminal offenses was unnecessary and unjustified by the conditions in Hawaii when the stockbroker and shipfitter were thus tried.   As a concurring member of the Supreme
Court pungently put it: "In short, the Bill of Rights disappeared by
military fiat rather than by military necessity." [29]

Yet, if *Duncan v. Kahanamoku* demonstrates anything, it is that
military fiat is not conclusive proof of the validity of martial-law
action.   The mere fact that a military commander, on the basis of
his conception of military necessity, requires civilians accused of
crime to be tried summarily before military tribunals, does not make
the Bill of Rights bow humbly to his judgment, despite the unquestioned ability of the civil courts to exercise their criminal jurisdiction.   On the contrary, as the *Duncan* decision shows, the high
Court will scrutinize such a case closely, to determine whether there
is, in fact, any real need for the supplanting of the ordinary courts

by a system of military justice. In the language of Chief Justice Stone's concurring *Duncan* opinion,

executive action is not proof of its own necessity, and the military's judgment here is not conclusive that every action taken pursuant to the declaration of martial law was justified by the exigency. In the substitution of martial law controls for the ordinary civil processes, "what are the allowable limits of military discretion, and whether or not they have been overstepped in a particular case, are judicial questions." [30]

Japanese Evacuation

The case of Toyosaburo Korematsu is one that is unique in American law:

Korematsu was born on our soil, of parents born in Japan. The Constitution makes him a citizen of the United States by nativity and a citizen of California by residence. No claim is made that he is not loyal to this country. There is no suggestion that apart from the matter involved here he is not law-abiding and well disposed. Korematsu, however, has been convicted of an act not commonly a crime. It consists merely of being present in the state whereof he is a citizen, near the place where he was born, and where all his life he has lived. [31]

Had Korematsu been of Italian, German, or English ancestry, his act would not have been a crime. His presence in California was made a crime solely because his parents were of Japanese birth. The difference between innocence and crime, so far as he was concerned, resulted not from anything he did, said, or even thought, but only from his particular racial stock. For Korematsu was a victim of what a *Harper's* article was to term "America's Greatest Wartime Mistake," namely, the evacuation of those of Japanese ancestry from the West Coast shortly after the Pearl Harbor attack.

Even those who agree with the *Harper's* characterization of the Japanese evacuation must concede the seriousness of the situation faced by our Government on the Pacific Coast at the outbreak of the last war. This situation has been well described by Justice Douglas:

After the disastrous bombing of Pearl Harbor the military had a grave problem on its hands. The threat of Japanese invasion of the west coast was not fanciful but real. The presence of many thousands of aliens and citizens of Japanese ancestry in or near to the key points along that coast line aroused special concern in those charged with the defense of the country. They believed that not only among aliens but also among citizens of Japanese ancestry there were those who would give aid and comfort to the Japanese invader and act as a fifth column before and during an invasion. If the military were right in their belief that among citizens of Japanese ancestry there was an actual or incipient fifth column, we were indeed faced with the imminent threat of a dire emergency.[32]

Acting upon their belief that those of Japanese ancestry thus posed a security threat, the military moved to eliminate the danger by a series of restrictive measures. Among these was a curfew applicable to all persons of Japanese ancestry on the West Coast. In its 1943 decision in *Hirabayashi v. United States*,[33] the Supreme Court upheld the validity of this curfew as an exercise of the power of the Government to take steps necessary to prevent espionage and sabotage in an area threatened by Japanese attack. The curfew was, nevertheless, but the beginning of the military program to deal with those of Japanese ancestry. The military commander of the Western Defense Command, early in 1942, issued a series of Civilian Exclusion Orders, excluding "all persons of Japanese ancestry, both alien and non-alien" from the westernmost part of the country. Those so excluded were gathered together in so-called Assembly Centers and then evacuated to what were euphemistically termed "Relocation Centers" in interior states, in which they were detained until almost the end of the war. Under this evacuation program, over 112,000 persons of Japanese ancestry were herded from their homes on the West Coast into the Relocation Centers, which, had they been set up in any other country, we would not hesitate to call by their true name of concentration camps.

The record of his Government in dealing with the West Coast Japanese during the war is hardly one which an American can contemplate with satisfaction. As the high Court eloquently declared in 1943, "Distinctions between citizens solely because of their ancestry are by their very nature odious to a free people whose institutions are founded upon the doctrine of equality." [34] Yet it cannot be gainsaid that those who, like Toyosaburo Korematsu, were forced into the Relocation Centers were deprived of their freedom merely because they were the children of parents as to whom they had no choice and belonged to a race from which there was no way to resign. Under the evacuation program, in the words of one member of the Supreme Court,

no less than 70,000 American citizens have been placed under a special ban and deprived of their liberty because of their particular racial inheritance. In this sense it bears a melancholy resemblance to the treatment accorded to members of the Jewish race in Germany and in other parts of Europe. The result is the creation in this country of two classes of citizens for the purposes of a critical and perilous hour—to sanction discrimination between groups of United States citizens on the basis of ancestry.[35]

Despite these disturbing aspects, the high Court upheld the evacuation of the Japanese (though with three strong dissents) in the 1944 case of *Korematsu v. United States*.[36] Korematsu had been convicted for remaining in a military area contrary to the Civilian Exclusion Order of the military commander. Such an order, said the Court, could validly be issued by the military authorities in the light of the particular situation confronting them on the West Coast after Pearl Harbor. In the face of a threatened Japanese attack, citizens of Japanese ancestry could rationally be set apart from those who had no particular associations with Japan; in time of war residents having ethnic affiliations with an invading enemy may be a greater source of danger than those of a different ancestry. That being the case, it could not be said that the exclusion order bore no reasonable relation to the demands of military necessity: "We are unable to conclude that it was beyond the war power of Congress and the Executive to exclude those of Japanese ancestry from the West Coast war area at the time they did. . . . exclusion from a threatened area, no less than curfew, has a definite and close relationship to the prevention of espionage and sabotage." [37]

It should be emphasized that the Court's decision in the *Korematsu* case was not at all a judicial seal of approval on the manner in which Korematsu had been treated. Here, as in other cases involving the exercise of its review authority, the high tribunal's role is not that of hierarchical superior of those whose act it is reviewing. The test in a case like this is not whether the Court feels that the action taken by the military was in fact necessary, but only whether there was a reasonable basis for such action. As the *Korematsu* opinion emphasizes, "We cannot—by availing ourselves of the calm perspective of hindsight—now say that at that time these actions were unjustified." [38]

Even if we agree with the *Korematsu* decision that the original exclusion and evacuation program was within the boundaries of the war power, that hardly justifies the continued detention of most of these evacuated for almost three years. It is one thing to place in "protective custody" particular individuals, whom there is good reason to suspect of disloyalty in wartime. It is quite another to detain en masse a section of the community, which is thus discriminated against solely because of its racial origins, regardless of the loyalty of the particular individuals affected. Even if original wholesale evacuation is justified by the practical impossibility of separating the loyal from the disloyal at the outset, that does not permit indefinite mass detention. On the contrary, those who are loyal citizens have the right to be released after sufficient time has elapsed for their loyalty to have been investigated and determined. After the lapse of such a period, there is no longer any excuse, military or otherwise, for compounding the loyal and disloyal into a single mass: "Obedience to the military orders is one thing. Whether an individual member of a group must be afforded at some stage an opportunity to show that, being loyal, he should be re-classified is a wholly different question." [39]

Just such a loyal citizen detained in a Relocation Center long after the original necessity had passed was Mitsuye Endo. Even the Government conceded that she was a loyal and law-abiding citizen. But, if that was true, said the Court in its 1944 decision in *Ex parte Endo*,[40] she was clearly entitled to her unconditional release from detention. The original evacuation program was justified by military necessity as a measure reasonably calculated to prevent espionage and sabotage by those affiliated ethnically with the enemy. But such justification cannot apply to a concededly loyal citizen after sufficient time has gone by to enable the Government to separate the loyal from the disloyal among those detained. In the words of the *Endo* decision: "A citizen who is concededly loyal presents no problem of espionage or sabotage. Loyalty is a matter of the heart and mind, not of race, creed, or color. He who is loyal is by definition not a spy or a saboteur. When the power to detain is derived from the power to protect the war effort against espionage and sabotage, detention which has no relationship to that objective is unauthorized." [41] In the case of Miss Endo, the authority to detain her as part of a program against espionage or sabotage was exhausted as soon as her loyalty was conceded. Consequently, said the Court, "Mitsuye Endo is entitled to an unconditional release by the War Relocation Authority." [42]

The *Endo* decision demonstrates both the strength and weakness of judicial review of exercises of the war power. Certainly, the Court's grant of habeas corpus to Miss Endo vindicates the rule of law even in wartime. It shows that, even though military authorities can take whatever measures may be demanded by the exigencies of war, the military's *ipse dixit* is not of itself conclusive of the necessity for the measures taken. The test of necessity is, with us, a judicial question, and the *Endo* case well illustrates how it can be applied by the Court to condemn measures that bear no reasonable relation to military needs. At the same time, the *Endo* case shows clearly the limitations of judicial power as a practical check on military arbitrariness. By its very nature, judicial justice is dispensed ever so slowly, though it may be dispensed exceedingly well. Mitsuye Endo was evacuated from her home and placed in a Relocation Center early in 1942. In July, 1942, she filed a petition for a writ of habeas corpus in a federal district court; yet it was not until December, 1944, that she was ordered released by the Supreme Court. But the high Court's decision did not and could not affect her three-year deprivation of liberty, illegal though such deprivation might have been. Despite the Supreme Court's decision, to quote from the concurring opinion of Justice Roberts, "An admittedly loyal citizen has been deprived of her liberty for a period of years. Under the Constitution she should be free to come and go as she pleases. Instead, her liberty of motion and other innocent activities have been prohibited and conditioned." [43] This is not, of course, to minimize the importance of judicial control in our system. Such control serves both to restrain improper exercise of authority and to correct abuses after they have arisen. In particular cases, it may even be the restraining aspect that is the more significant. To those affected, Supreme Court reversal of arbitrary action can never be as satisfactory as proper action in the first place would have been. Mitsuye Endo may have the satisfaction of being immortalized in the *Supreme Court Reports;* but she is most unlikely to consider that an adequate substitute for her loss of liberty during her illegal confinement in the Relocation Center.

Property Rights

Just as drastic as its impact upon personal rights and liberties is the impact of the war power upon the rights of property. Nor is it surprising that this should be so. At a time when it is the undoubted law of the land that a citizen may by conscription be compelled to give up his life for his country's cause, it should occasion no astonishment that he may similarly be required to yield his earthly possessions, if that be demanded of him. Both person and property are thus subject to the overriding guardianship of the State in wartime. We may resist a wholly planned economy and the coming of the omnipotent socialized State in peacetime; at the same time, complete control of both person and property (what Justice Jackson aptly termed "military socialization" [44]) is accepted by all as a patriotic necessity in time of war.

Despite what has just been said, in one important respect at least, the right of property in wartime appears better protected in our system than even the right of life itself. The individual may be compelled by conscription to serve in the armed forces even at the cost of his life, and neither he nor his next of kin have any legal claim if he is maimed or killed. On the other hand, the Fifth Amendment to the Constitution provides expressly that private property shall not be taken for public use without just compensation. The Supreme Court has held consistently that this prohibition applies even in wartime. Consequently, while it is recognized that, under the war power, private property may be requisitioned or otherwise impressed into public service without the consent of the owner, such taking implies a promise on the part of the Government to reimburse the owner in accordance with the requirement of the Fifth Amendment. In a number of cases decided during the last war, the Supreme Court assumed that the Fifth Amendment was applicable to property requisitioned for war purposes and that the owners of such property were consequently entitled to just compensation under the constitutional provision.[45]

The principle of just compensation has never given any difficulty when applied to ordinary property taken for the use of the armed forces or other war purposes. Very often, however, in war conditions, private property may not be literally taken for the use of our forces, but may instead be destroyed in order to prevent its falling into the hands of the enemy or to impede the enemy in his military operations. Does such destruction of property by our forces constitute a "taking" for public use under the Fifth Amendment, for which just compensation must be paid? This was the question presented to the Supreme Court in the 1952 case of *United States v. Caltex, Inc.*[46] At issue there were the claims of two oil companies which owned terminal facilities in Manila at the time of the Japanese invasion of the Philippines at the end of 1941. Just before the fall of Manila, our troops destroyed the companies' facilities in order to prevent their imminent capture and use by the Japanese. After the war, the companies demanded compensation for their property which had thus been destroyed. The Government refused to compensate them and they sued for the value of the facilities, claiming a constitutional right under the Fifth Amendment to just compensation. The Supreme Court rejected their claim, stating that the Fifth Amendment is no comprehensive promise that the United States will make whole all who suffer from every ravage and burden of war. In wartime, said the Court, "many losses must be attributed solely to the fortunes of war, and not to the sovereign." [47]

The Court's remark just quoted states but a truism. One wonders, nevertheless, whether it is really applicable to the case under discussion. Here, it was patently the act of the sovereign that was responsible for the oil companies' loss. It is true that the act in question was necessitated by the military situation. Yet that is also the case with regard to most property taken for public use under the war power. It is one thing to say that property taken in time of war should not be placed on a more preferential plane than the person of the individual drafted into the armed forces. But when we once admit (as we must under all the Supreme Court decisions) that the Fifth Amendment's demand of just compensation applies to property taken for war purposes, it is hard to see why we should discriminate against the property owner whose property is destroyed rather than used in the military interest. Such owner is certainly as drastically affected by the taking of his property for public use; his property was as clearly appropriated to help win the war as were animals, food, and supplies requisitioned for the war effort. It seems unjust to deprive him of the just compensation which other property owners are guaranteed, even in wartime, under the Fifth Amendment: "Whenever the Government determines that one person's property—whatever it may be—is essential to the war effort and appropriates it for the common good, the public purse, rather than the individual, should bear the loss." [48]

Important though these cases involving direct takings of private property for war purposes doubtless may be, they hardly begin to exhaust the effects of the war power upon rights of property. Most property owners in wartime are affected, not by direct takings by the Government, but by the all-pervasive types of economic regulation that have become a necessary concomitant of the modern war effort. Such economic regulation has come more and more to restrict the rights of private property in wartime; it is, in truth, no mere figure of speech to talk of the wholly "planned economy and galloping socialism of modern war." [49] Total mobilization of the economy has become a categorical imperative for national survival in an era of total war.

Total mobilization of both manpower and the economy reached its peak (in our system at least) during World War II. The authority exercised by the Federal Government under the war power was so vast that its extent can be only cursorily sketched. The President was given the power by the Selective Training and Service Act to make rules and regulations for the drafting of male citizens into the armed forces, and to terminate their periods of service. So-called "conscription of industry" was also provided for: Plants that refused to give preference to the United States in the execution of war orders or to manufacture necessary supplies or to furnish them at a reasonable price, as determined by the Secretaries of War or the Navy, could be taken over by the President.

In addition, broad requisitioning and priorities powers were conferred upon the President. He was authorized to requisition any property, equipment, machinery, tools, or supplies when he deemed such requisitioning was needed for the national defense. He could also, in his discretion, give priority, over all deliveries for private account or for export, to contracts or orders of the armed forces and all other contracts or orders which he deemed necessary or appropriate to promote the national defense. The President was also given the power to allocate any materials and facilities where necessary to the war effort. This power furnished the foundation for the extensive system of consumer rationing administered by the Office of Price Administration, as well as for the comprehensive control of industrial materials and output which was exercised by the War Production Board.

The broadest powers of price control and wage stabilization were likewise conferred. The Emergency Price Control Act of 1942 granted the power to regulate prices and rents in the most sweeping terms, and the Stabilization Act of the same year was similarly broad in its delegation of the authority to stabilize wages. Control of labor disputes affecting the war effort was provided for by the War Labor Disputes Act of 1943. The National War Labor Board was empowered to decide such labor disputes, and to provide by order the wages and hours and all other terms and conditions governing the relations between the parties. And, to enable the Board's orders to be enforced, the President was empowered to commandeer plants whose operations were impaired by labor disturbances.

Under these and other war statutes delegating authority to him, President Franklin D. Roosevelt can be said to have been vested with more arbitrary power over person and property than any English-speaking statesman since Oliver Cromwell. But such total power in the executive was deemed necessary to meet the demands of global war. And the Supreme Court was in the forefront of those recognizing this necessity. The power fully to mobilize manpower had been recognized in the Government during the First World War; [50] thus, as the high Court put it in 1948, "The constitutionality of the conscription of manpower for military service is beyond question." [51] The Court's decisions arising out of World War II recognized in the Government authority over property rights as extensive as that possessed by it over manpower. Said the Court, in the case just quoted from, with regard to the impact of "total global warfare" upon our system: "With the advent of such warfare, mobilized property in the form of equipment and supplies became as essential as mobilized manpower. Mobilization of effort extended not only to the uniformed armed services but to the entire population. . . . The language of the Constitution authorizing such measures is broad rather than restrictive." [52]   Under the Constitution, the Congress is given the power to "raise and support Armies," to "provide and maintain a Navy," and to make all laws necessary and proper to carry these powers into execution. Under this authority, as already noted, the Congress can clearly draft men for battle service. And, according to a 1942 opinion of the high tribunal, "Its power to draft business organizations to support the fighting men who risk their lives can be no less." [53]

Perhaps the most important decisions during World War II upholding governmental authority over property rights were those rendered in two 1944 cases which involved the validity of price and rent controls. In *Yakus v. United States,*[54] it was contended that the Emergency Price Control Act of 1942 unconstitutionally delegated to the Price Administrator the authority to control prices. Under the act in question, the Administrator was empowered to fix maximum prices for all commodities. It was under this law that there was carried out during the war the most extensive scheme of price-fixing ever attempted in our system. The prices of almost all goods and services were directly controlled from Washington in a manner which was unprecedented, at least judged by normal peacetime standards. Yet the high Court had no difficulty in sustaining the Congressional assertion of such broad authority under the war power. Indeed, the constitutional authority of the Congress to prescribe commodity prices as a war emergency measure was so apparent under modern conditions that even counsel attacking the Price Control Act in the *Yakus* case did not question its existence. And the same was true in *Bowles v. Willingham,*[55] where the rent control provisions of the same act, under which maximum rents were fixed throughout the country, were at issue. There, too, the substantive power of the Congress was hardly questioned. The relation of rents both to the general problem of controlling wartime inflation and to the special problems of housing created by war activities was seen to give adequate grounds for exercise of federal power.

In these two cases, the Court sustained under the war power governmental authority which enveloped the entire economy over the most important aspect of the right of property, namely, the right to dispose of property at the highest obtainable price. Just as important as the substantive powers of price and rent control recognized in the Congress was the manner in which such power was exercised through the Price Control Act. In the first place, it should be noted that that act involved a tremendous delegation of authority to the executive branch. It was left almost entirely up to the Price Administrator which prices and rents would be controlled and at what levels they should be regulated. His commission was, in reality, to take any action with respect to prices and rents which he believed would preserve what he deemed would be a sound economy during the war emergency. It is, in fact, not going too far to assert, as did a dissenting Justice with regard to the rent control features of the law:

Whether there shall be a law prescribing maximum rents anywhere in the United States depends solely on the Administrator's personal judgment. When that law shall take effect, how long it shall remain in force, whether it shall be modified, what territory it shall cover, whether the different areas shall be subject to different regulations, what is the nature of the activity that shall motivate the institution of the law,—all these matters are buried in the bosom of the Administrator and nowhere else.[56]

Despite the undoubted breadth of the delegation of power contained in it, the Price Control Act was, nonetheless, sustained under the war power.

As unprecedented as the extent of discretion delegated by the Price Control Act was the procedural machinery provided by it for giving effect to its provisions. Prices and rents were fixed administratively without the full notice and hearing normally required in our law. This failure to provide the normal procedural safeguards was justified by the Court on the ground that only through the more summary procedure could the administrative battle against runaway wartime inflation be won.

More difficult to deal with were the review and enforcement provisions of the law. The legislative scheme with regard to them was wholly unprecedented. Instead of the right of review in an ordinary court, those aggrieved by price or rent orders could challenge their legality only by filing suit within thirty days in a specially created Emergency Court of Appeals. All other courts, federal and state, were expressly barred from considering the validity of such orders and divested of jurisdiction to enjoin them or set them aside. At the same time, the ordinary courts were made available to the Government for the enforcement of price and rent orders in both civil and criminal proceedings. But, in these enforcement proceedings, too, the courts were barred from considering the validity of the orders they were enforcing. The statute thus afforded the individual, to question a price or rent order's validity, one route and that a very narrow one, and open only briefly. The Government, to enforce such order, had many routes. And, in the enforcement proceedings, the issues were so cut down that little more than the fact of whether there had been a violation of the order as written could be inquired into by the courts. We thus had the constant spectacle of criminal proceedings in which the defendant could not set up the defense that he had committed no crime because the order he was charged with violating was itself invalid. The criminal court could not, under the act, consider the validity of the price or rent orders upon which prosecutions before it were based. According to Justice Rutledge who dissented, such an enforcement pattern could not be reconciled with the constitutional guarantee of a full trial of all the issues essential to guilt in criminal cases. To the majority of the Court, on the other hand, the enforcement procedure, though perhaps unusual, was one which Congress could prescribe under the war power.

In the realities of a war economy, even more important to the Government, as a means of securing obedience to its orders, than the traditional methods of enforcement in the courts provided for in the Price Control Act were the sanctions available to it through the use of its power over priorities and allocations. Thus, the power given to the President to allocate materials during World War II was used extensively to withhold materials from those who disobeyed the economic control orders of governmental agencies. This was true, even though there was no statutory authority for such coercive use of the allocation power. A good example of the manner in which the power was so used is found in the 1944 case of *Steuart & Bros. v. Bowles*.[57] There a retail dealer in fuel oil had been found by the Office of Price Administration to have violated its rationing order by obtaining large quantities of fuel oil from its supplier without surrendering any ration coupons and by delivering many thousands of gallons of fuel oil to consumers without receiving ration coupons. As a punishment, the OPA suspended the right of the dealer to receive any fuel oil for resale for a year. This so-called suspension order was upheld by the Supreme Court as against the claim that it imposed a penalty not provided for by the Congress. The President's statutory power to allocate materials, said the Court, included the power to issue suspension orders against retailers and to withhold rationed materials from them where it was established they had violated the ration regulations. The extreme sanction thus utilized by the OPA (which amounted, in effect, to an economic death sentence against the dealer concerned, at least for the period of the suspension order) was sustained by the Court, although the power to impose such a sanction was nowhere conferred by the Congress. The normal reluctance of our courts to imply penal powers in the administration gave way in the face of what the Court felt to be the necessities inherent in a scheme of effective wartime rationing.

War and Peace

The cases just discussed show clearly that the Supreme Court has been second to none in acknowledging the need for full authority in the Government to meet the demands of total global war. "In total war," declared the Court in 1948, "it is necessary that a civilian make sacrifices of his property and profits with at least the same fortitude as that with which a drafted soldier makes his traditional sacrifices of comfort, security and life itself." [58] In line with this view, the Court has been willing to uphold ever-increasing federal regulation of civilian liberty and property in proportion to the ever-increasing demands of modern warfare. In time of war, both the raising and the support of the armed forces are essential. Both require mobilization and control under the authority of the Federal Government. And, while it may seem ironical to some that our Nation has had to move in the direction of the totalitarian State in order to preserve itself from totalitarian domination, the Supreme Court has found nothing in the Constitution to prohibit such transformation of our system in wartime. "In time of crisis," said the Court in the 1948 decision quoted above, "nothing could be more tragic and less expressive of the intent of the people than so to construe their Constitution that by its own terms it would substantially hinder rather than help them in defending their national safety." [59]

Few, today, would dispute the need to recognize in the Government whatever powers, both over person and property, that may be required to meet the demands of total war. At the same time, one may be permitted to express some doubt as to whether the high Court has not been overzealous in immolating the Constitution on the altar of the all-consuming modern Moloch. It is all very well for the Court to uphold the vast powers over liberty and the economy exercised by the Government during World War II. In so doing, however, the Court should be careful to confine its language and its reasoning to cases arising under a war emergency like that which gave rise to the powers before it. The validity of action under the war power must be judged wholly in the context of war. That action will be sustained under the war power is not, of itself, sufficient reason for holding that it should not be condemned when there is no war emergency. That extreme action in wartime is not to be stigmatized as lawless does not necessarily mean that similar action in time of peace must be held lawful.[60]

One of the disturbing features of many of the Supreme Court decisions during the war is the failure of the Court in them to distinguish adequately between war powers and similar powers exercised in time of peace. In the *Yakus* case,* the Court upheld a delegation of legislative power broader than any that had been before sustained. The authority to fix any and all prices and rents in the economy was conferred upon the relevant administrative official, who was given almost unfettered discretion with regard to when and how he should exercise his price- and rent-fixing powers. The Price Control Act set no limits of consequence upon the administrator's discretion and judgment; his judgment was made the final touchstone of the validity of his action. It is, of course, true that there may be valid reason for delegating much broader authority during war than in peacetime. In the words of a dissenting Justice in the *Yakus* case, as it is with the substantive authority of the Government under the war power, "so it is with delegating legislative power. War begets necessities for this, as for imposing substantive controls, not required by the lesser exigencies of more normal periods." [61]

But the Court in its *Yakus* opinion did not base the validity of the price control delegation upon the war power. Instead of holding that there is a difference between the delegation of wholesale discretion in wartime and that which may be conferred when peace prevails, the Court purported to treat the *Yakus* delegation just as it would ordinary peacetime grants of power. Thus, the Court upheld the Price Control Act, so far as the issue of delegation was concerned, by reliance upon the peacetime precedents. Actually, those precedents did not sustain the Court's decision, for the delegations in them were nowhere near as broad as that involved in *Yakus*. In truth, the only previous delegation comparable to that in *Yakus* was that made by the National Industrial Recovery Act of 1933, which had been held unconstitutional in the 1935 case of *Schechter Poultry Corp. v. United States*.[62] Even if the Court felt that a delegation comparable to that in *Schechter* should be upheld in wartime, there is no reason why it had to go beyond the actual case and indicate that such a delegation would be good in peacetime and in respect of peacetime administration. By its reasoning and the au-

* *Supra*, p. 297.

thorities cited by it, the Court in *Yakus* needlessly eliminated what many still feel to be a valuable safeguard where a war emergency does not render it inapplicable, namely, the rule restricting unlimited delegations by the Congress of its legislative power.

The same failure to distinguish between cases arising under the war power and peacetime cases is apparent in the Court's decision in *Bowles v. Willingham,* already dealt with in regard to the substantive power of the Congress to provide for a wartime system of rent control.* The landlord there did not really challenge the substantive authority of the Congress in this respect, but she did attack the procedural defects of the scheme of rent regulation as it had been administered with regard to her. The Price Administrator had issued an order reducing the rents charged by the landlord without giving her the full hearing that is normally required in our system before administrative action affecting the person or property of particular citizens may be taken. Once again, the Court could have justified its decision upholding the statute and administrative order in these circumstances by reliance upon the war power. It might well have held that the exigencies of rent control in wartime could not be met while affording to those affected the luxury of full compliance with the peacetime law of administrative procedure. The need to deal expeditiously with runaway inflation in wartime might be frustrated, if every landlord in the country were to be entitled to a full adjudicatory hearing before an order affecting the rents charged by him could be issued. But the Court did not base its decision entirely or even primarily on the war power. Its opinion was, rather, based mainly upon peacetime precedents and would seem to indicate that similar administrative action without full hearing would be valid even without a war emergency. Once again, as in *Yakus,* the Court went much further than the necessities of the case required. Instead of limiting its decision to the war situation before it, which alone would have justified the sustaining of the governmental action at issue, the Court gratuitously treated the case upon the same basis as cases not controlled by the war power. Its decision may thus serve as a precedent which may distort our normal law of administrative procedure. Perhaps some day, on the strength of *Bowles v. Willingham,* some court will have the hardihood to deprive an individual in peacetime of the right to a hearing to which he seems clearly entitled when there is no war emergency to justify the abrogation of that right.

Even though one does not disagree with the specific results reached by the Supreme Court in the cases on the extent of the war

* *Supra,* p. 297.

power decided during the last conflict, he may still be disturbed by the failure of the Court adequately to distinguish between war and peace and its tendency to treat the cases involving unprecedented powers granted and exercised by the Government in time of war as comparable, in both kind and degree, to cases involving peacetime powers. The Court's approach in decisions like those rendered in the *Yakus* and *Willingham* cases may become precedents to plague it, if similar broad powers are ever sought to be conferred upon the Government in peacetime.

Just as troublesome to one concerned with the war power is the question of the duration of that power. All will admit that the authority to wage war includes the power to prepare for it and the further power to deal with the problem of adjustment to peace after hostilities have ceased. As the Supreme Court said almost a century ago, the war power "is not limited to victories in the field. . . . It carries with it inherently the power to guard against the immediate renewal of the conflict, and to remedy the evils which have arisen from its rise and progress." [63] It was in reliance upon this principle that the Court, in its 1948 decision in *Woods v. Miller Co.*,[64] upheld the constitutionality of the Housing and Rent Act of 1947, fixing maximum rents two years after the actual war ended. The lower court had held that the authority of the Congress to regulate rents by virtue of the war power ended with the Presidential Proclamation terminating hostilities, but the Supreme Court rejected so restricted a view of the duration of the war power. The war power, said the high tribunal, does not necessarily end with the cessation of hostilities. It includes the authority to remedy the evils arising from war. Insofar as rent control (the precise power at issue in the *Miller Co.* case) was concerned, the Court pointed to the deficit in housing still existing in 1947 and asserted, "Since the war effort contributed heavily to that deficit, Congress has the power even after the cessation of hostilities to act to control the forces that a short supply of the needed article created." [65]

The Court's decision upholding rent control under the war power in 1947 is one with which few people would take issue. The law should not lag behind common sense. The effects of war do not cease with a cease-fire order; the war power is consequently not exhausted when the shooting stops. To hold otherwise would, as the Court pointed out in its *Woods v. Miller Co.* opinion, lead to a paralyzing result: "It would render Congress powerless to remedy conditions the creation of which necessarily followed from the mobilization of men and materials for successful prosecution of the war. So to read the Constitution would be to make it self-defeating." [66]

Even if we admit the soundness of this view in its application to the specific facts of the case before the Court, it is still one that should not be pressed too far. Under contemporary conditions, we are always either living in a state of war, preparation for war, or feeling the effects of war. If carried to its logical extreme, the *Woods v. Miller Co.* rationale may permit the war power all but to swallow up the Constitution. The effects of war under modern conditions may be felt in the economy for years and years and, if the war power can be used in days of peace to treat all the wounds which war inflicts on our society, the power is one which may abide with us forever. It is this indeterminate aspect of its duration that helps to make the war power the most dangerous one to constitutional government in the whole catalogue of powers. Even if we concede the scope of the power in time of war and shortly thereafter, we must still scrutinize with extreme care assertions of the war power to do things to the liberties of people or to their property years after the war emergency has receded. War powers may not be indefinitely prolonged merely because the Government has kept legally alive a state of war that had, in fact, long been ended. We must reject the view that the war power lasts as long as all the effects and consequences of war, for, if so, it is permanent—as permanent as the war debts.[67]

9

THE COLD WAR

"The healthy," says Carlyle, "know not of their health, but only the sick: this is the Physician's Aphorism; and applicable in a far wider sense than he gives it." [1] Certainly, it holds true no less in political than in merely corporeal therapeutics. It is only in a period of malaise that we can really appreciate what it was like when the State was in a wholly sound and healthy condition. It is not in the vigorous age of a secure polity that men realize most the blessings they are endowed with: "So long as the Commonwealth continues rightly athletic, it cares not to dabble in anatomy." [2] When the body politic is lusty and robust, men spend not their time in inquiring into the causes of civic decay. When, on the contrary, the vigor of the Commonwealth is impaired, then treatises on political pathology abound.

What is true of the body politic is also true of its legal system. In law, too, not the healthy, but only the sick know of their health. Not in periods of calm, when a government of laws operates in complete serenity, are we fully sensitive to the values of the constitutional structure set up by the Framers. It is only when our constitutional law is subject to severe stresses that we are apt to be wholly cognizant of its worth. By that time, however, has not the constitutional structure itself sunk from its former pristine condition? It is thus only when our public law is sick that we know of our former health: in law, as in the physical body, the Physician's Aphorism holds.

To the body politic, war and its stresses are the counterparts of grave illness in the animal body. It is when the Commonwealth is beset by the strains of external conflict that the Aphorism of the Physician has especial application. When the war power is exerted to control every aspect of the community's way of life, we are all too aware of our previous state of health, when the law was canalized within peacetime limits. During the past decade, nevertheless, we have come to realize that the Commonwealth, like the individual, can be subject to psychosomatic, as well as to purely physical, maladies.   The years since the last war have been, technically speaking, years of peace—or, at least, years during which this country has not been engaged in formally declared war.   At the same time, it is common knowledge that the decade has been one dominated by constant tensions which have had all-pervasive repercussions upon our life and law.   The period has been passed in a twilight zone between war and peace—in a penumbra labeled, appropriately enough, that of "cold war."

Almost needless to say, our old Aphorism holds true in a period of cold, as in a period of shooting, war.   In some ways, indeed, it is even more valid in such a time than it is when a formal conflict is raging.   In actual war, the law may, without much question, be compelled to remain silent; there are few who will, in wartime, urge that it speak with an all-commanding voice.   When the Commonwealth is engaged in the dire necessities of total war, none will gainsay the need for the most drastic measures.   Though men may recall the days when the body politic enjoyed normal health, they can hardly begrudge the steps taken to deal with the immediate perils besetting the State.   The same is not true of a period of cold war such as that in which we have been living.   The dangers at such a time are as much psychological as physical.   They may require the society to live under constant stresses and tensions; but these are not relieved by being directed against tangible corporeal objects.   The polity then may be subject to maladies similar to those that beset it in time of actual war; yet there will be wide disagreement about the remedies which may be needed, when the immediate clamor of arms does not still the normal discords that prevail in a free society.

It is in such a penumbral period of neither war nor peace that men tend to think most of the unimpaired health of the body politic in more normal periods.   Without any doubt, this is as true of the lawyer as it is of all others who are affected by the time's insecurities.   The cold war, in its impact upon the law, has meant predominance of governmental regulatory power such as that usually asserted only in time of actual conflict.   And even more important, perhaps, it has posed for our law, as almost never before, the problem of reconciling the antinomy between liberty and security.   Both are, to be sure, essential elements in the functioning of our polity, and their co-existence has always had to be reconciled by the law.   In an era of cold war, all the same, it is the element of security that has tended to take over the governmental field.   The response of our Government to the tensions of the postwar period has made our law security-conscious as it has never been before in our history, except in time of actual war. The legislative demand for security has been articulated in a number of laws restricting rights formerly deemed fundamental in our system of ordered liberty. It is in dealing with the validity of such laws and governmental action taken under them that the work of the Supreme Court has been directly affected by the impact of the cold war.

How has the Court reconciled recent restrictive legislation with the demands of the Bill of Rights, and especially those of the First Amendment? It is a common saying among lawyers that hard cases make bad law. What is not so generally realized is that cases decided under severe stress may make equally bad law. A Court overimbued with the dominant demand for security may tend to give effect to that demand, even if the cost be some distortion of accepted principles of constitutional law. Yet this can hardly be done without important consequences upon the general jurisprudence of that Court. A tribunal that molds its law only to fit the immediate demands of public sentiment is hardly fulfilling the role proper to the supreme bench in a system such as ours: "The Court has no reason for existence if it merely reflects the pressures of the day." [3] Of course, the Court should act in this field in a manner consistent with the doctrine of deference to the legislature that has dominated its work since 1937. But abnegation on the part of the Court hardly requires abdication by it of the judicial function. It is one thing to give way before a clearly expressed legislative policy in an area where men may reasonably differ as to the proper policy to be pursued. It is quite another to go out of the way to construe legislation as restricting rights normally granted in our law, where the legislature itself has not made such construction imperative.

Restrictions on Speech

Among the most important statutes enacted by the Congress in response to the need for national security has been the Smith Act of 1940. That law provides, in its two key sections:

SEC. 2 (a) It shall be unlawful for any person—
(1) to knowingly or willfully advocate, abet, advise, or teach the duty, necessity, desirability, or propriety of overthrowing or destroying any government in the United States by force or violence, or by the assassination of any officer of any such government;
(2) with intent to cause the overthrow or destruction of any government in the United States, to print, publish, edit, issue, circulate, sell, distribute, or publicly display any written or printed matter advocating,

advising, or teaching the duty, necessity, desirability, or propriety of over-throwing or destroying any government in the United States by force or violence;

(3) to organize or help to organize any society, group, or assembly of persons who teach, advocate, or encourage the overthrow or destruc-tion of any government in the United States by force or violence; or to be or become a member of, or affiliate with, any such society, group, or assembly of persons, knowing the purposes thereof. . . .

SEC. 3. It shall be unlawful for any person to attempt to commit, or to conspire to commit, any of the acts prohibited by the provisions of this title.

The Smith Act is a law which, at first glance at least, seems in-congruous in a country whose first article of faith is the principle of full and free discussion. None will deny the right of any govern-ment to outlaw acts of sedition. But the Smith Act is aimed, not so much at seditious acts, as at seditious teaching or advocacy. It restricts not so much deeds as words; as such, it constitutes a clear limitation upon the freedom of speech and of the press guaranteed by the First Amendment. Yet, to say this much is not necessarily to say that the Smith Act is unconstitutional. We have already seen that, except to a few extremists, it is clear that the unqualified language of the First Amendment cannot be taken literally.* The right of free speech, like other constitutional rights, must be recon-ciled with other rights safeguarded by the organic instrument; it can be restrained where necessary for the preservation of other freedoms essential to a democracy and guaranteed by our Consti-tution.

In wartime, as Justice Rutledge aptly put it, legal, as well as martial, tools adequate for the times' necessity must be invented: "Inevitably some will be strange, if also life-saving, instruments for a people accustomed to peace and the normal working of consti-tutional limitations."[4] Is the same necessarily true of a period of only cold war? In such a time, man may not unnaturally be more reluctant to countenance surrender of rights which, in more normal times, could not be impaired. Before the Smith Act was enacted, it was recognized that mere speech, though it taught or advocated seditious doctrine, could not be penalized if it were not accom-panied by overt action implementing the doctrine advocated. Un-der the 1940 act, on the other hand, men can be convicted of teach-ing and advocacy alone. How can such conviction be squared with the Bill of Rights? In many ways, this has been the most difficult question which the Supreme Court has been called upon to answer

* *Supra,* pp. 232-40.

in recent years. And it cannot be denied that there are many who are still not convinced that the Court did resolve it in a satisfactory manner. At the same time, to a tribunal imbued, as the post-1937 Court has been, with the doctrine of deference to the elected representatives of the people, the answer which the high Court gave to the question in the soon-to-be-discussed *Dennis* case * was easier for it than the resolution of a similar question might have been for its predecessors.

The starting point in the Court's answer to the legal problems presented by the Smith Act is the rejection, already referred to, of the absolute nature of the right of free speech provided for in the First Amendment. The Constitution does not allow absolute freedom of expression, any more than it provides for any other absolutes. Yet this, by itself, hardly tells us the circumstances under which government can restrict speech in the public interest. According to a famous opinion of Justice Holmes, delivered in a case which arose out of a conviction for violating the Espionage Act passed during World War I, "The question in every case is whether the words used are used in such circumstances and are of such a nature as to create a clear and present danger that they will bring about the substantive evils that Congress has a right to prevent." [5] Thus was enunciated the so-called "clear and present danger" test, upon which the validity of governmental restrictions upon speech turns.

It must be emphasized that the test articulated by Justice Holmes is above all a test of degree. "Clear and present" danger is a standard, not a mathematical absolute. "It is a question of proximity and degree," [6] said Justice Holmes, after the passage quoted above. As such, its application will vary from case to case and will depend upon the particular circumstances presented. Speech that would be innocuous if addressed to an audience of divines might produce an entirely different result in quarters where a light breath would be enough to kindle a flame. This was seen acutely by John Stuart Mill a century ago. In his essay *On Liberty*, he said:

Even opinions lose their immunity, when the circumstances in which they are expressed are such as to constitute their expression a positive instigation to some mischievous act. An opinion that corn-dealers are starvers of the poor, or that private property is robbery, ought to be unmolested when simply circulated through the press, but may justly incur punishment when delivered orally to an excited mob assembled before the house of a corn-dealer, or when handed about among the same mob in the form of a placard.

* *Infra*, pp. 312-19.

Under the Holmes test, legislative restrictions upon speech are justified if the speech and the circumstances in which it is delivered are such that there is created a "clear and present" danger that the speech in question will bring about some substantive evil that the legislature has a right to prevent. It is important to bear in mind that the danger referred to need not be one which clearly undermines the safety of the Republic. It is not imminent threats to the security of the country alone that authorize courts in sustaining legislation curtailing utterance.[7] On the contrary, speech can be abridged whenever it may lead to any substantive evil that the legislature has a right to prevent. "I do not doubt for a moment," declared Justice Holmes in another important case, "that by the same reasoning that would justify punishing persuasion to murder, the United States constitutionally may punish speech that produces or is intended to produce a clear and imminent danger that it will bring about forthwith certain substantive evils that the United States constitutionally may seek to prevent."[8] In other words, if speech will result in action that government can prohibit (even if the action is not necessarily one that may shake the State to its very foundations), then the speech itself can constitutionally be reached by governmental power, provided there is a clear and present danger that the action will result from the speech.

But whose conception of the clear and present danger is to prevail in a particular case? More specifically, is the judge to determine on his own independent judgment whether the required danger really exists, or is he to grant to the legislative judgment with regard to the existence of the peril the deference that he normally grants in other cases? The controversy that has arisen out of the present Court's application of the "clear and present" danger test has largely concerned itself with the manner in which this question has been answered by the Court.

In the normal case, we have constantly emphasized, the Supreme Court has, without any doubt, abandoned its pre-1937 role of Supreme Censor of all legislation. The Court today reviews only the *reasonableness*, not the *rightness*, of challenged laws. As we saw in Chapter 7,* however, there are those, both on and off the high bench, who feel that this doctrine of deference to the legislator is inapposite where First Amendment rights are concerned. They urge that laws restricting such rights should be scrutinized with a much more jealous judicial eye. In these cases, they say, it is not enough that the judge finds a rational connection between the law and the evil which the legislature may curb. He must himself

* *Supra,* pp. 231-36.

determine that the legislator was right in his judgment that there existed a "clear and present" danger that, if the particular right were not curbed, there would be brought about a substantive evil that the legislature has a right to prevent. Under this view, the legislative judgment is not to be upheld, merely if it is found to be reasonable, but only if the judge concurs in the opinion that it is right in the circumstances presented.

We have already dealt at some length * with the view that the rights guaranteed under the First Amendment are in a preferred position as compared with other constitutional rights, insofar as their enforcement by the courts is concerned. There are two basic objections to this view. The first arises from the fact that the "preferred position" doctrine requires the judge to impose his own standard of values upon the Constitution, despite the failure of the Founders thus to differentiate qualitatively among the different rights which they were safeguarding. We cannot, as Justice Jackson neatly put it, give some constitutional rights a preferred position without relegating others to a deferred position.[9] We cannot establish the firstness of the First Amendment without treating all other constitutional provisions as only seconds. Connected with this is the fact that the broadening of judicial review urged by critics of the high Court's First Amendment decisions is precisely the sort of thing that the constitutional revolution of 1937 was supposed to have ended. To be sure, the extreme review power asserted by the pre-1937 Court was exercised in an area entirely different from that with which present-day advocates of broadened review are concerned. Yet, this shift in emphasis aside, there is certainly a close resemblance between the approach to First Amendment cases urged by some today and the approach to cases of economic regulation followed by the majority of the Court before 1937. Of course, the old Court applied its theory of excessively broad review in cases involving economic interests, because interests of property held the first place in its members' table of values. It was, all the same, the substitution of its standard of values for that of the legislature that was objectionable in the pre-1937 Court's work. But that is exactly what the present exponents of broadened review are urging, though only in the area to which their personal table of values gives the primacy. In the field which they feel should be given first place, they are just as ready to assume the role of a super-legislature as were most of the members of the pre-1937 Court.

There is no more justification for a judicial tribunal to play the

* *Supra*, pp. 231-40.

part of a super-legislature in the field of First Amendment rights than there is where only rights of property are concerned. In both cases, the Supreme Court's function is to check, not to supplant, the judgment of the elected representatives of the people. Only if the legislature exceeds the bounds of constitutional reason is it the Court's prerogative to intervene, and then only with a constant sense of the gravity of its action. If the considerations militating against the pre-1937 extreme type of judicial review are sound in cases involving rights of property, they are also sound where rights given by the First Amendment are concerned. There is no constitutional basis for placing different rights upon different planes; there is only the yardstick of personal preferences of the particular judge. The judges of two decades ago erred by treating economic rights as absolutes, on a level which even the powers of the assembly in which the people vested legislative power could not touch. Are we to repeat their error today by giving a similar preference to rights under the First Amendment? If the Court was right in 1937 in rejecting the role of Supreme Censor of economic legislation, its more limited approach is correct as well in cases involving other kinds of legislation, including that impinging upon First Amendment rights. "Free-speech cases," in Justice Frankfurter's apt words, "are not an exception to the principle that we are not legislators, that direct policy-making is not our province. How best to reconcile competing interests is the business of legislatures, and the balance they strike is a judgment not to be displaced by ours, but to be respected unless outside the pale of fair judgment." [10]

Dennis Case

The 1951 decision of the highest Court in *Dennis v. United States* [11] is dominated by the same doctrine of deference to the Congress that has animated the Court in its post-1937 decisions involving other than First Amendment issues. The defendants in the *Dennis* case, ten of the principal leaders of the Communist Party in this country, were indicted for violating section 3 of the Smith Act by wilfully and knowingly conspiring (1) to organize as the Communist Party of the United States of America a society, group, and assembly of persons who teach and advocate the overthrow and destruction of the Government of the United States by force and violence, and (2) to advocate and teach the duty and necessity of overthrowing the Government of the United States by force and violence. The case was tried at great length. The trial extended over nine months, six of which were devoted to the taking of evidence, resulting in a record of 16,000 pages. The jury brought in a verdict against all the defendants, and they were sentenced in accordance with the criminal penalties provided in the Smith Act. The protracted trial before Judge Medina had, as is well known, been one of the most celebrated cases of recent federal court practice, and its repercussions in Supreme Court jurisprudence were not limited to the *Dennis* case.[12]

In evaluating the high Court's disposition of the appeals by Dennis *et al.* of their convictions under the Smith Act, it is important to bear in mind that the Court's reviewing function was limited to questions of law. For the purposes of the appeal, the Court had to assume the correctness of the findings of fact made by the two lower courts. These findings, based upon the lengthy record of the evidence presented at the trial, included the following basic propositions: the policies of the Communist Party, in the postwar period covered in the indictment, were changed from peaceful cooperation with the United States and its economic and political structure to a policy which had existed before the United States and the Soviet Union were fighting a common enemy, namely, a policy which worked for the overthrow of the American Government by force and violence; the Communist Party is a highly disciplined organization, adept at infiltration into strategic positions, uses of aliases, and double-meaning language; the party is rigidly controlled; the Communists, unlike other political parties, tolerate no dissension from the policy laid down by the guiding forces, and the approved program is slavishly followed by members of the party; the literature of the party and the statements and activities of its leaders advocated—and the general goal of the party was, during the period in question, to achieve—a successful overthrow of the existing order by force and violence.

On these findings, the jury could, without a doubt, return its verdict that defendants had violated the Smith Act. But the sufficiency of the evidence to support the jury's determination was not the matter with which the Supreme Court was concerned. At issue before that tribunal was the question whether the Smith Act, inherently or as construed and applied in the particular case, violated the First Amendment.

The majority of the *Dennis* Court answered this question in the negative. Its decision rests upon two propositions stated in Chief Justice Vinson's opinion. In the first place, says he, with regard to the Smith Act, "The obvious purpose of the statute is to protect existing Government, not from change by peaceable, lawful and constitutional means, but from change by violence, revolution and terrorism." [13] In the second place, states the Chief Justice, "That it is within the *power* of the Congress to protect the Government of the United States from armed rebellion is a proposition which requires little discussion." [14] Few will, it is believed, dispute these two statements from the *Dennis* opinion: "No one could conceive that it is not within the power of Congress to prohibit acts intended to overthrow the Government by force and violence." [15] Nor can it be denied that the Smith Act is aimed at preventing the ultimate overthrow of the Government by force and violence. The real question, however, is that of the closeness of the connection between the Congressional purpose in the particular case and its conceded authority to protect the Government from seditious acts. As has already been shown, the Smith Act does not aim to protect the Government directly against changes brought about by revolution; its provisions are not directed against overt acts of terror and violence. Instead, they seek to extend the prophylactic process one step further by suppressing the teaching or advocacy of the overthrow of the Government by force or violence. As such, they seek to restrict words rather than deeds. Yet, this raises directly the issue of the consistency of the Smith Act, as it was enforced against the *Dennis* defendants, with the "clear and present" danger test, which, we have seen, is the criterion by which the constitutionality of legislative restrictions on speech are to be judged.

"In this case," states the opinion of Chief Justice Vinson for the majority of the *Dennis* Court, "we are squarely presented with the application of the 'clear and present danger' test, and must decide what that phrase imports." [16] Under the test laid down by Justice Holmes, legislative limitations upon speech must be justified by direct danger from the proscribed speech of a substantive evil which the legislature has a right to prevent. In the case of the Smith Act, restriction of speech teaching or advocating the overthrow of the Government by force is valid only if there is some "clear and present" danger, from the speech in question, of a violent act against the Government—in this case, the substantive evil which all concede that the Congress has the power to prevent.

In the light of the findings made by the lower courts, could the Supreme Court reasonably be expected to conclude that the Congress had no basis for finding that Communist advocacy constituted a "clear and present" danger to the security of established government in this country? It may well be true that reasonable men might differ on the question of whether the Communist Party has really presented an imminent danger to American government. Yet, as the Court indicated in its *Dennis* opinion, the validity of restrictions upon advocacy of violent revolution do not depend upon the immediacy of revolt resulting from such advocacy. The "clear and present" danger test, states the Court,

obviously . . . cannot mean that before the Government may act, it must wait until the *putsch* is about to be executed, the plans have been laid and the signal is awaited. If Government is aware that a group aiming at its overthrow is attempting to indoctrinate its members and to commit them to a course whereby they will strike when the leaders feel the circumstances permit, action by the Government is required. The argument that there is no need for Government to concern itself, for Government is strong, it possesses ample powers to put down a rebellion, it may defeat the revolution with ease needs no answer. For that is not the question. Certainly an attempt to overthrow the Government by force, even though doomed from the outset because of inadequate numbers or power of the revolutionists, is a sufficient evil for Congress to prevent.[17]

In line with this reasoning, the *Dennis* Court rejects the contention that success or probability of success in revolutionary advocacy is the criterion upon which the "clear and present" danger test turns. On the contrary, states the Court, the correct interpretation of that test is that articulated by Judge Learned Hand in the court of appeals decision in the case: "In each case [courts] must ask whether the gravity of the 'evil,' discounted by its improbability, justifies such invasion of free speech as is necessary to avoid the danger." [18] Using this statement of the rule, the high Court concludes that the requisite danger existed for the Smith Act validly to be applied to Communist Party activities in this country. Nor, according to the *Dennis* opinion, does the fact that Communist activities did not, during the period covered by the indictment, actually result in an attempt to overthrow the Government by force and violence furnish an answer,

to the fact that there was a group that was ready to make the attempt. The formation by petitioners of such a highly organized conspiracy, with rigidly disciplined members subject to call when the leaders, these petitioners, felt that the time had come for action, coupled with the inflammable nature of world conditions, similar uprisings in other countries, and the touch-and-go nature of our relations with countries with whom petitioners were in the very least ideologically attuned, convince us that their convictions were justified on this score.[19]

Dennis and Deference

Critics of the *Dennis* decision have attacked the Supreme Court's refusal to determine for itself the reality of the Communist Party's threat to our established system of government. How, they ask, can such an inconsequential group, whose doctrines have been so utterly rejected by the American people, be seriously considered a "clear and present" danger to government in this country? In the words of a dissenting Justice in the *Dennis* case:

Communists in this country have never made a respectable or serious showing in any election. I would doubt that there is a village, let alone a city or county or state, which the Communists could carry. Communism in the world scene is no bogeyman; but Communism as a political faction or party in this country plainly is. Communism has been so thoroughly exposed in this country that it has been crippled as a political force. Free speech has destroyed it as an effective political party. . . . How it can be said that there is a clear and present danger that this advocacy will succeed is, therefore, a mystery.[20]

Of course, Communists in this country are miserable merchants of unwanted ideas, whose wares remain unsold.[21] But does that justify a judicial tribunal in substituting its judgment for that of the elected representatives of the people that the Communist Party constitutes a "clear and present" danger to our national security? To be sure, even under the doctrine of deference to the Congressional judgment, which, we have urged, applies in free-speech as in other constitutional cases, there must be a reasonable basis for the legislative judgment. Can anyone who looks realistically at contemporary history, nevertheless, deny that the Congressional judgment with regard to the Communist Party has, at the least, some rational basis? For a Court to base its decision on such denial would be for it to shut its eyes to what all other men see.

Any Court confronted with a case like *Dennis* must, if it is not to be blind to actualities, base its decision upon recognition of the true nature of the contemporary threat presented by world communism. That threat has been a very real one during the past decade. Those who gloss over this fundamental fact distort reality even more than those who may be so obsessed by it that they see nothing else of significance in the world today. It might well be more comforting to treat the Communist Party as just another political party, and to analogize restraints upon it to similar restraints imposed upon, let us say, the Democratic or Republican parties. Yet, disconcerting though it may be to some, the Communists are not and have not been a political party in any accepted sense of the term; to treat them as such would be to indulge in a patent legal fiction of the kind that has often brought the law and lawyers into popular disrepute. Justice Frankfurter aptly characterized the Communist Party in a concurring opinion in the *Dennis* case.

The Communist Party was not designed by these defendants as an ordinary political party. . . . the party rejects the basic premise of our political system—that change is to be brought about by nonviolent constitutional process. . . . the party advocates the theory that there is a duty and necessity to overthrow the Government by force and violence. . . . the party entertains and promotes this view, not as a prophetic insight or as a bit of unworldly speculation, but as a program for winning adherents and as a policy to be translated into action.[22]

Perhaps the most striking judicial statement of the actual character of the American Communist Party is to be found in a 1950 opinion of Justice Jackson, which is remarkable for the breadth of its language and its judicial notice of data not in evidence before the Court.[23]

From information before its several Committees [reads the opinion referred to], and from facts of general knowledge, Congress could rationally conclude that, behind its political party façade, the Communist Party is a conspiratorial and revolutionary junta, organized to reach ends and to use methods which are incompatible with our constitutional system. A rough and compressed grouping of this data would permit Congress to draw these important conclusions as to its distinguishing characteristics.

1. The goal of the Communist Party is to seize powers of government by and for a minority rather than to acquire power through the vote of a free electorate. . . .

2. The Communist Party alone among American parties past or present is dominated and controlled by a foreign government. . . .

3. Violent and undemocratic means are the calculated and indispensable methods to attain the Communist Party's goal. It would be incredible naïveté to expect the American branch of this movement to forego the only methods by which a Communist Party has anywhere come into power. . . .

4. The Communist Party has sought to gain this leverage and hold on the American population by acquiring control of the labor movement. . . .

5. Every member of the Communist Party is an agent to execute the Communist program.[24]

Although unsupported by the kind of evidence that would usually be required in a law court, the broad indictment of the Communist Party in Justice Jackson's opinion comports with the common sense of the subject. Unless Justice Jackson's analysis is rejected, it is hard to see how the Supreme Court can be condemned for deciding as it did in the *Dennis* case. In a democratic system, as has been emphasized, the primary responsibility for determining when there is danger that speech will induce the substantive evil that the Government has a right to prevent—in this case, attempts to overthrow government by force and violence—must surely lie with the elected representatives of the people. In this, as in other fields of judicial review, the Supreme Court's function is to serve as a brake upon arbitrary extremes. But its task is exhausted when there is found to be a rational basis for the particular exercise of Congressional judgment. It may well be true that the test of reasonableness makes it unlikely that most legislative acts will be declared unconstitutional. Yet that seems to be the necessary result of making the review power of the highest Court consistent with the postulates of representative democracy—unless, that is, we are to return to the concept of "government by judiciary" which dominated our constitutional law prior to 1937. The Court's basic duty is to abstain from confounding policy with constitutionality; this, in Justice Frankfurter's phrase, "demands perceptive humility as well as self-restraint in not declaring unconstitutional what in a judge's private judgment is deemed unwise and even dangerous." [25]

Can a tribunal like the Supreme Court affirm with any assurance that the teachings of the Communist Party have not constituted a "clear and present danger" to the American system? Judicial prescience in this respect could turn out to be as unreliable as would have been a similar judgment with regard to the Bolsheviks in pre-revolutionary Russia or the National Socialists in the early days of the Weimar Republic:

To make validity of legislation depend on judicial reading of events still in the womb of time—a forecast, that is, of the outcome of forces at best appreciated only with knowledge of the topmost secrets of nations—is to charge the judiciary with duties beyond its equipment. We do not expect courts to pronounce historic verdicts on bygone events. Even historians have conflicting views to this day on the origin and conduct of the French Revolution. . . . It is as absurd to be confident that we can measure the present clash of forces and their outcome as to ask us to read history still enveloped in clouds of controversy.[26]

It is important to bear in mind that the Supreme Court in the *Dennis* case was not at all concerned with the question of the desirability of the legislative restrictions upon speech contained in the Smith Act. The sole issue for the Court was that of the Congressional power to enact such a statute. "It is not for us," declared Justice Frankfurter, "to decide how we would adjust the clash of interests which this case presents were the primary responsibility for reconciling it ours. Congress has determined that the

danger created by advocacy of overthrow justifies the ensuing restriction on freedom of speech." [27] The desirability and wisdom
of the Smith Act may be quite another matter. But it is a matter
with which the high Court could not rightly concern itself in the
Dennis case.

Restrictions upon Aliens

The extent to which the Supreme Court has deferred to the Congressional judgment in the field of security legislation is well shown
by its treatment of laws imposing restrictions upon aliens. Such
laws have been an integral part of the Congressional program for
dealing with the tensions both of the war and the postwar period.
The Smith Act provisions themselves, discussed above in connection with the *Dennis* case, were part of a law passed in 1940 governing the conduct of aliens, and the postwar deterioration of relations
between the Communist and non-Communist countries has been
reflected in a further tightening up of the laws relating to aliens.
The foreigner has always been looked upon with some suspicion,
even in a country where, in Franklin Roosevelt's phrase, we are
all immigrants. In times of tension, his lack of full allegiance to
his new residence is felt to make him particularly prone to subversive activities. It is hardly surprising then that the past two
decades have seen the imposition, in the name of internal security,
of additional restrictions upon aliens, culminating in the McCarran
Immigration and Nationality Act of 1952, a complete revision and
codification of our laws relating to aliens.

Among the most important restrictions imposed was that in a
1940 law providing for the exclusion and deportation of aliens who
are members of, or affiliated with, an organization that advocates
the overthrow of the Government by force and violence. The deportation provisions of this law apply to aliens who, at any time
after entry, come within these provisions, and not only to those
who do so at the time of the deportation proceeding.

In *Harisiades v. Shaughnessy*,[28] decided in 1952, the high Court
held the deportation provisions of this law constitutional. Its decision started by conceding the power in the Congress to provide for
the deportation of aliens within our boundaries, drastic though deportation may prove to be for particular aliens, for whom, in Justice
Brandeis' eloquent words, it "may result . . . in loss of both property and life; or of all that makes life worth living." [29] Said the
Court in *Harisiades*: "That aliens remain vulnerable to expulsion
after long residence is a practice that bristles with severities. But

it is a weapon of defense and reprisal confirmed by international
law as a power inherent in every sovereign state. Such is the traditional power of the Nation over the alien and we leave the law on
the subject as we find it." [30]

The Court thus concedes that the power of the Congress over
aliens is necessarily very broad, touching as it does basic aspects
of national sovereignty. This concession really disposes of the
claim that the law authorizing the deportation of Communist aliens
is invalid. According to the Court, "any policy toward aliens is
vitally and intricately interwoven with contemporaneous policies
in regard to the conduct of foreign relations, the war power, and
the maintenance of a republican form of government. Such matters
are so exclusively entrusted to the political branches of government
as to be largely immune from judicial inquiry or interference." [31]
When this approach, peculiar to the law of aliens, is combined
with the doctrine of deference toward the Congress generally followed by the present Court, it makes the challenged law all but
unassailable. Can the high tribunal rightly hold that a law expelling
alien Communists does not constitute at least a reasonable exercise
of the traditional Congressional power over aliens?

Under the conditions which produced this Act, can we declare that
congressional alarm about a coalition of Communist power without and
Communist conspiracy within the United States is either a fantasy or a
pretense? . . . Certainly no responsible American would say that there
were then or are now no possible grounds on which Congress might
believe that Communists in our midst are inimical to our security.[32]

The 1940 law at issue in the *Harisiades* case made membership
in an organization which advocates the violent overthrow of the
Government a ground for deportation. Under that act, it was necessary in each case to prove that the organization to which the particular alien belonged did, in fact, advocate the overthrow by force
of the Government. In the Internal Security Act of 1950, the Congress dispensed with the need for such proof in the case of aliens
belonging to the Communist Party. In that law, the Congress itself
found that the Communist movement was aimed at establishing a
Communist dictatorship by any means deemed necessary and made
present or former membership, in and of itself, a ground for deportation. In its 1954 decision in *Galvan v. Press*,[33] the Supreme
Court held that the dispensation with proof of the character of the
Communist Party provided for in the 1950 Act was within the Congressional power, as applied to an alien who had been a willing
member of the Party. "Certainly," declares the Court, "we cannot

say that this classification by Congress is so baseless as to be violative of due process and therefore beyond the power of Congress." [34] Nor did it make any difference that the particular alien claimed that he was ignorant that the Communist Party was committed to violence. The Congress could order the deportation of all aliens who had willingly been Communists. To require the Government to prove in each case that the alien fully understood the Communist program would be to impose upon the Government a burden which might unduly hamper practical administration of the legislative program, or at least so the Congress might reasonably have thought.

Perhaps the most extreme statutory provision restricting the rights of aliens with which the Supreme Court has had to deal in the cold war period is the provision of the Internal Security Act at issue in the 1952 case of *Carlson v. Landon*.[35] It provides that the Attorney General may, in his discretion, hold in custody without bail, pending determination as to their deportability, aliens charged with being members of the Communist Party, when there is reasonable cause to believe that their release on bail would endanger the safety and welfare of the United States. This is, without any doubt, a most drastic power to confer upon a nonjudicial officer. It permits an administrative official to arrest aliens and hold them in custody pending determination of the charge that they are Communists. An alien can thus be imprisoned by administrative decree upon the bare allegation of the Attorney General that he is a Communist who cannot be left at large without danger to national security. To be sure, he can be held only while his deportation proceeding is pending. Yet such proceedings may drag on for many months, if not years; during that period, it is wholly up to the administration to determine whether the alien should be in custody. Certainly, this law represents a striking departure from our normal practice. Indeed, if there is one thing that differentiates our system from those we disparagingly describe as totalitarian, it is the absence in our system of administrative power to imprison for indefinite periods without judicial trials. Yet that is precisely the power vested in the Attorney General by the Internal Security Act, at least so far as aliens alleged by him to be Communists are concerned. It may be that such administrative authority is necessary in conditions of cold war. But its delegation is clearly one that goes to the very limits of Congressional constitutional authority. At the same time, the Court in *Carlson v. Landon* held that it did not pass those limits. The plenary power of the Congress over aliens was seen to justify the requirement by it that aliens charged with Communist membership, who were found to constitute a threat to national security, be kept in custody pending deportation. The exercise of this Congressional power in particular cases, the Court held, could be delegated to the Attorney General.

Carlson v. Landon illustrates how far the present Court is willing to go in adherence to its doctrine of deference to the Congress. The statute at issue there may, as the Court held, be properly fitted within the constitutional powers of the Congress; but it is surely true that it is in such a case that the constitutional shoe really pinches.

At the same time, it must be emphasized once again that, in these alien cases, as in the *Dennis* decision, the highest tribunal was not at all concerned with the question of the desirability or wisdom of challenged legislation. As the Court stated in the previously discussed *Harisiades* case, "We, in our private opinions, need not concur in Congress' policies to hold its enactments constitutional. Judicially we must tolerate what personally we may regard as a legislative mistake." [36] The question of the desirability of the restrictive laws upheld is, of course, quite another matter. In finding that Congress has acted within its power, the judge does not necessarily imply that he favors the implications that lie beneath the legal issues. On the question of wisdom, it can reasonably be urged that much of the Congressional reaction to the cold war has gone to unnecessary extremes: for a mouse of security, a mountain of undesirable security apparatus has been built up. Yet, even on this point, it is all too facile to assert doctrinaire condemnation. In the apt words of the late Justice Jackson, "It would be easy for those of us who do not have security responsibility to say that those who do are taking Communism too seriously and overestimating its danger." [37] That there have been abuses in Congressional assertions of its power to provide for national security can hardly be denied. But it smacks of the ludicrous to aver that the Congress has gone so far as itself to subvert the very system it professes to protect. True it is that the laws that have been discussed are symptomatic of the malaise that has persisted in contemporary society. Laws like the Smith Act are not needed in the wholly healthy Commonwealth. Loyalty, like the patriotism of which it is a form, becomes a concern of the State only after it has begun to decline. Once again, we may see the applicability of our old friend, the Physician's Aphorism, to law in the age we live in. Laws like the Internal Security Act and the Smith Act have made us all too aware of the present unhealthy state of our public law. We know all too well of our health, alas, now that we are among the sick.

Loyalty-Security Program

The statutes already discussed in this chapter have been but a part of the Government's response to the problems posed by the cold war. Even more important in their impact upon the community have been the various loyalty programs administered by both Federal and state governments. In their numerical effects, these programs are unique in our history. In 1956, the federal loyalty-security program alone covered nearly six million civilian employees in both government and private industry; and this figure does not include the millions who are affected by comparable state measures. It is true that the problems of loyalty and protection from subversion and espionage are not wholly new in this country. Almost at the outset of our history, in fact, the now notorious Alien and Sedition Laws of 1798 were enacted to meet the security threats seen to be posed by the French Revolution. Yet, these and later measures down to our own day were predominantly punitive rather than preventive in character. They outlawed specified offenses, and their prohibitions were enforced by the ordinary processes of the criminal law. The present-day loyalty-security programs, on the other hand, go far beyond this traditional type of criminal prohibition. Their aim is preventive, rather than merely punitive. The threats posed by the totalitarian movements of the present century have led to the adoption of an all-pervasive program designed to safeguard the Government against disloyalty and subversion. This program has sought to weed out from government positions those who are disloyal or who otherwise constitute security risks.

It may be argued that a loyalty program such as that inaugurated for the federal civil service by Executive Order 9835 (the so-called loyalty order promulgated by President Truman in March, 1947) attempts to achieve the impossible. During the first century and a half of the Republic, our people took it for granted that those whom they employed as government servants were loyal to the United States. So far as their loyalty was concerned, civil servants were asked only to take the oath to support and defend our Constitution. More recently, it has been felt that this was hardly enough to ensure the loyalty of government employees. Yet, paradoxically enough, is not this concern over loyalty itself an indication that loyalty in this country is not what it may have been in former days? While the Decii are rushing with devoted bodies on the enemies of Rome, what need is there of preaching patriotism? [38] When loyalty is made a principal object of the State's concern, it has already sunk from its pristine all-transcendent condition.

Be that as it may, however, President Truman's 1947 order instituted a broad loyalty program in the federal civil service, which has been continued (though with substantial modifications) under the Eisenhower Administration since that time. Under that program, the loyalty of all federal employees and would-be employees has been inquired into. Nor has there been any real doubt of the authority of the Government to dismiss or refuse to hire employees who are disloyal or who constitute security risks. The power of the Congress in this respect has not been directly passed upon by the Supreme Court, but its 1956 decision in the soon-to-be-discussed case of *Cole v. Young* * is clearly based upon the implicit assumption that the Congress can require disloyal civil servants to be discharged in the national interest. And the Court has expressly confirmed the authority of the states to institute programs designed to eliminate disloyal employees from their civil service systems. Thus, the Court has upheld the power of a state to require its employees to take an oath affirming that they did not advocate or teach the forcible overthrow of the Government, nor were they affiliated with an organization that did so, nor had they been so within the preceding five years.[39] And, in a similar fashion, the Court has sustained a state law barring from employment in any public school any member of any organization advocating the violent overthrow of the Government.[40] The rationale of these decisions was stated in the first of them by Justice Frankfurter:

The Constitution does not guarantee public employment. City, State and Nation are not confined to making provisions appropriate for securing competent professional discharge of the functions pertaining to diverse governmental jobs. They may also assure themselves of fidelity to the very presuppositions of our scheme of government on the part of those who seek to serve it. No unit of government can be denied the right to keep out of its employ those who seek to overthrow the government by force or violence, or are knowingly members of an organization engaged in such endeavor.[41]

But, if the authority of the Federal Government to bar disloyal employees from its service has not really been open to question, the same has not been true of the means used to implement the Govern-

* *Infra*, p. 329.

ment's conceded power in this connection. And this has been particularly true of the procedural aspects of the Government's loyalty-security program. In this respect, it is important to note that, despite the many criticisms that have been directed against that program, it is not fair to conclude that it has been administered in a manner wholly unconcerned with the adjective rights of civil servants. On the contrary, President Truman's 1947 order instituting the loyalty program sought to protect those rights by providing for an elaborate procedure of hearing, decision, and review, in order to safeguard individual civil servants charged with disloyalty.

At the same time, one must recognize that, despite the intent of the Government to provide fair procedures, it is almost impossible for a loyalty-security program effectively to be carried on with all the procedural safeguards that are deemed necessary in other fields of our law. Basic in American law have been the requirements of notice and opportunity for a full and fair hearing before administrative action is taken that adversely affects the private individual. "Notice and opportunity to be heard," in Justice Douglas' phrase, "are fundamental to due process of law." [42] Under the principles of administrative law developed by our courts, an administrative agency may not act in a manner which adversely affects an individual unless he is given a full, adversary hearing at which he can present his side of the case. At such hearing, he must be permitted to bring forward any oral or documentary evidence that he may have, must be fully apprised of the agency's case against him, and must be allowed to cross-examine the witnesses upon whom the agency's case rests. And the agency decision, when rendered, must be based solely upon evidence contained in the record of the hearing. These principles are all given express legislative articulation in the Federal Administrative Procedure Act of 1946.*

It can hardly be controverted that the administration of the Federal Government's loyalty-security program has not been consistent with all the procedural demands imposed by a law like the Administrative Procedure Act. This has not, indeed, been denied by those responsible for the program's execution. They have, all the same, asserted that the loyalty-security program could not, by its very nature, be effectively executed if hearings under it were required to comply fully with all the procedural demands imposed upon administrative agencies in other cases. The right of cross-examination can serve to illustrate their assertion. Every party to an administrative proceeding, reads the relevant section of the Ad-

* *Supra,* p. 120.

ministrative Procedure Act, "shall have the right . . . to conduct such cross-examination as may be required for a full and true disclosure of the facts." In cases involving the loyalty of civil servants, however, to allow those charged with disloyalty to confront and cross-examine those who have given the Federal Bureau of Investigation the information upon which the charge is based might impair the functioning of the investigative network which the Bureau has built up. As one federal court has said, "The Federal Bureau of Investigation has uniformly insisted that practically none of the evidential sources available will continue to be available to it if proper secrecy and confidence cannot at all times be maintained with respect to the original source of information." [43]

The point of view of the Federal Bureau of Investigation in these cases is not difficult to understand. It is hardly to be expected that the Bureau will think it worthwhile to impair the usefulness of its undercover operatives by disclosing their identity. Nevertheless, it cannot be gainsaid that the failure to accord the full rights of confrontation and cross-examination may make it most difficult for federal employees in individual cases to defend themselves against charges of disloyalty. What this can mean in practice is shown by the 1955 case of *Peters v. Hobby*.[44] Dr. Peters, a professor of medicine, had been employed as a Special Consultant in the United States Public Health Service. Though he had twice been cleared of charges of disloyalty by the employing agency's loyalty board, he was barred from federal employment by the Civil Service Commission's Loyalty Review Board, which determined that there was a reasonable doubt as to his loyalty. Dr. Peters had been given a hearing on charges relating to alleged membership in the Communist Party, sponsorship of certain petitions, affiliation with various organizations, and alleged association with Communists and Communist sympathizers. At the hearing, the sources of the information as to the facts bearing on the charges were not identified or made available to Dr. Peters' counsel for cross-examination. In truth, the Board itself did not even know the identity of all the informants against Dr. Peters. In these circumstances, the situation confronting one in Dr. Peters' position is an almost impossible one. Where the individual does not know the identity of his accusers and cannot confront or cross-examine them, his task in refuting their charges becomes all but insuperable. This was acutely noted by Justice Douglas in the *Peters* case:

Dr. Peters was condemned by faceless informers, some of whom were not known even to the Board that condemned him. Some of these informers were not even under oath. None of them had to submit to cross-examination. None had to face Dr. Peters. So far as we or the Board know, they may be psychopaths or venal people, like Titus Oates, who revel in being informers. They may bear old grudges. Under cross-examination their stories might disappear like bubbles. Their whispered confidences might turn out to be yarns conceived by twisted minds or by people who, though sincere, have poor faculties of observation and memory.[45]

Confrontation and cross-examination under oath are essential elements in the American ideal of due process. How can condemnation by "faceless informers" of the type involved in the *Peters* case be reconciled with this ideal? It must be stated, in all frankness, that the Supreme Court has never given anything like a satisfactory answer to this question. In fact, the Court has been most astute to avoid having to give a reasoned reply to it. In the *Peters* case itself, the Court was able to shun the constitutional question by deciding the case on other grounds. In the 1951 case of *Bailey v. Richardson*,[46] the Court did, it is true, uphold the kind of procedure which prevailed in *Peters*, but it did so only by affirming, four-to-four, the decision in favor of the Government of the lower court; and, as is customary in cases where there is an equal division in the highest tribunal, the Court did not deliver any opinion in the *Bailey* case.

If there is a legal justification for the type of procedure followed by the Loyalty Review Board in the *Peters* case, it is that relied upon by the lower court in *Bailey v. Richardson*. Its opinion turns upon the view that public employment is only a "privilege," not a "right." Where such a privilege is involved, the Government is not bound by the procedural requirements of due process. Full notice and hearing must be given only in cases involving personal or property rights. "Due process of law," declared the lower *Bailey* court, "is not applicable unless one is being deprived of something to which he has a right." [47] This reasoning of the lower court remains the only rationale we have of the *Bailey* decision, since the Supreme Court affirmed, four-to-four, without opinion.

To deny the rudiments of adjective justice to the civil servant because public employment is only a privilege is to employ the kind of legal reasoning that has all the beauty of abstract logic and all the ugliness of injustice. Its chief support in the law is the famous statement of Justice Holmes that "The petitioner may have a constitutional right to talk politics, but he has no constitutional right to be a policeman." [48] It is, to say the least, sardonic to make Justice Holmes the victim of a tendency which he fought all his life, whereby phrases are made to substitute for critical analysis by being turned into dogma.[49] "It is one of the misfortunes of the law," reads a characteristic passage by Holmes, "that ideas become encysted in phrases and thereafter . . . cease to provoke further analysis."[50] Yet this is precisely what has happened to the Holmes phrase on the absence of a constitutional right to public employment.

We need not disagree with the view that no one has a vested right to a government job. But this is only the beginning, not the end, of legal reasoning in cases like those growing out of the loyalty-security program. The fact that public employment may be termed a "privilege" does not answer the question of what procedures must be followed before the individual is barred from such employment. Calling civil-service status a "privilege" does not justify the administrative taking-away of government employment without affording to the individual affected a full right to be heard. If taking away the right to practice of a doctor or lawyer without a full opportunity of defense is unjust, depriving the civil servant of his position without a similar opportunity is equally unjust.

To describe public employment as a "privilege" is a convenient way of avoiding the problem of due process. Yet, that is a problem which the courts are under a duty to meet, particularly in an age when government employment so dominates the field of opportunity. It does not at all follow that, because the law does not guarantee to anyone a right to public employment, the Government can resort to any scheme for depriving people of their positions in the civil service. As Justice Jackson put it in a 1951 opinion, "The fact that one may not have a legal right to get or keep a government post does not mean that he can be adjudged ineligible illegally."[51] As far as the effect on the individual is concerned, the loyalty case, regardless of the tag used, involves a need for fair procedure just as great as any other administrative proceeding. The power of the State to deny a so-called "privilege" altogether should not mean that it can be taken away from particular individuals by administrative decision without full adherence to the fundamentals of fair play. It is procedure that spells much of the difference between rule by law and rule by arbitrary power. This is as true in cases involving "privileges" as it is in cases involving "rights."

As far as the Supreme Court has been concerned, this basic problem of fitting loyalty-security procedures into the mold of due process has been essentially a lost opportunity. The same has not, however, been true of what many have seen to be another grave defect of the Government's loyalty-security program, namely, its unduly wide scope. The Government's program has, since 1947, applied to all employees of the executive branch, including those of the independent agencies and commissions. The only federal employees exempt from the program have been the employees of the Congress and the courts. It was this all-pervasive scope that led a member of the highest Court to characterize the Government's program as a "dragnet system." [52]

The statute underlying the personnel security system of the Federal Government is a 1950 act, subjecting the employees of eleven named federal departments and agencies to a security program. These eleven are agencies which have a direct relationship to national security: eight are concerned with military operations or weapons development, and the other three with international relations, internal security, and the stock-piling of strategic materials. The relevant law also provides that it may be extended to "such other departments and agencies of the Government as the President may, from time to time, deem necessary in the best interests of national security." Acting under this authorization, the President in 1953 directed that the provisions of the 1950 statute be extended "to all other departments and agencies of the Government." The result has been that, as already pointed out, the federal personnel security program has applied to all employees in all agencies of the Government, instead of being limited to the sensitive departments and agencies listed in the 1950 law.

In the 1956 case of *Cole v. Young*,[53] the President's authority thus to extend the loyalty-security program to all federal employees was challenged. Kendrick M. Cole was a food and drug inspector employed by the Department of Health, Education and Welfare. He was discharged on loyalty grounds, his agency head having found that his employment was not "clearly consistent with the interests of national security." He claimed in the Supreme Court that he could not be discharged consistently with the 1950 act, urging that the Congress did not intend to authorize the President to extend the personnel security program to a position like his which had no direct connection with national security. The Court's decision agreed with this contention. The Court relied primarily upon the fact that the authority given to the President by the 1950 law was limited by the phrase "national security": the President could extend the act only to departments and agencies where such extension was deemed necessary in the best interests of national security. According to the Court, the term "national security," as used in the act, was intended to comprehend only those activities of the Government that are directly concerned with the protection of the Nation from internal subversion or foreign aggression, and not those which contribute to the strength of the Nation only through their impact on the general welfare. That being the case, an employee in a nonsensitive position like that held by Cole could not be dismissed for security reasons under the 1950 law: an employee can be dismissed "in the interest of the national security" under the act only if he occupies a "sensitive" position.

The result of the high Court's decision in the *Cole* case is to limit the Government's loyalty-security program to civil servants in sensitive positions. It is recognized that this judicial limitation of the scope of the Government's program has been severely criticized by some. The Court's order, they say, has stricken down the most effective weapon against subversive activity available to the Government. Yet, even if this view of the effect of the *Cole* decision be correct, it is difficult to see how the Court could have decided otherwise and still conformed to correct canons of statutory construction. Had the Congress used the term "national security" in a manner broad enough to include all activities of the Government, it would hardly have named eleven specific agencies to which the 1950 act should apply, nor would the agencies named have been those which are directly concerned with the national defense and which have custody over information the divulging of which might endanger the country's security. If the President were intended to be given a power to sweep all agencies into the security program, the Congress would have had little reason to make the act apply only to the named sensitive agencies and to condition the President's authority to extend the act's coverage by the standard of national security.

Aside from the purely legal issues involved, it may well be said that the Court's decision in *Cole v. Young* will make for administration of the Government's loyalty-security program in a manner that is both more equitable and more effective. A program as broad in its scope as that carried out prior to the *Cole* decision could not possibly be as adequate qualitatively as one more limited in scope. Investigative activity diffused upon six million persons might more effectively be concentrated where the interests of national security really require intensive scrutiny. From the security point of view, it is a waste of time and effort to investigate the loyalty of a food and drug inspector like Kendrick Cole. It is hard not to conclude that positions like his and those in a hundred other agencies wholly unconnected with national security were included in the loyalty-security program, not so much to safeguard the Government, as to punish Communists and their sympathizers who had secured government jobs. So far as security is concerned, it is difficult to think of a safer place to quarantine Cole than in his food and drug position. In this connection, it is pertinent to point to the conclusion of a special committee appointed by the eminently respectable Association of the Bar of the City of New York. Writing its report before the high Court's *Cole* decision, it recommended that clearance under the Government's personnel security program should be required for all in sensitive positions and no others. "By thus narrowing the scope of the programs to the areas where it is really needed," the committee declared, "we would both increase the efficiency of the programs and remove an unnecessary burden on positive security and on employees." [54] Such amelioration of the Government's personnel program is precisely what has been brought about by the Court's decision in *Cole v. Young*.

Administrative-Law Distortions

At the outset of this chapter,* it was pointed out that one of the distressing features of the Supreme Court's cold-war jurisprudence has been the distortion by the high tribunal in some cases of accepted principles of our public law in order to give full effect to the dominant demand for security. This more-than-occasional tendency of the Court is best illustrated in some of its recent administrative-law decisions in cases closely connected with security considerations. We have already seen how the normal rules governing the procedures of administrative agencies have given way in cases administered under the Government's loyalty-security program for its employees. While it may be true that the Court has never expressly approved the departures from the fundamentals of fair play in loyalty cases, neither has it taken the opportunities offered it to condemn such departures as alien to our law. Indeed, as a practical matter (at least so far as affected civil servants have been concerned), the Court's silence on the subject in the past decade has all but amounted to *de facto* condonation of the procedures followed in loyalty proceedings.

Condemnation without adherence to the rudiments of adjective justice as we normally know them has not, in the stresses of a cold-war period, been confined to cases instituted under the Government's loyalty-security program. On the contrary, confidential information furnished by faceless informers has become a common basis for administrative decision in areas affected by security considerations. Nor has the Supreme Court been quicker to censure these deformities in administrative justice than it was in the loyalty cases. In at least two recent cases, in fact, the Court has expressly

* *Supra*, p. 307.

approved the legality of such departures. And, in one of them, the
Court did so by going out of its way to construe an act of Congress
as restricting procedural rights, when the law itself might more
logically have been read in a more expansive manner.

The second case just referred to, *United States v. Nugent*,[55] decided in 1953, arose out of a conviction for violating the Selective
Service Act by willfully refusing to submit to induction into the
armed forces. Defendant claimed exemption from military service
as a conscientious objector. Under the act, if a conscientious objector's claim for relief is denied by his local draft board, he is entitled to further review by an "appropriate appeal board." All such
appeals are referred to the Department of Justice for an "appropriate inquiry" and a "hearing." The Department of Justice then
makes a recommendation to the appeal board, which may or may
not follow it in reviewing the local board's classification. In dealing
with cases referred to it by appeal boards, the Department has regu-
larly used the Federal Bureau of Investigation to investigate each
appealing registrant's background and reputation for sincerity. A
hearing is then held before a designated "hearing officer." The
registrant is allowed to appear. Upon request, he is entitled to be instructed "as to the general nature and character" of any "unfavorable" evidence developed by the Department's investigation. But
he is not permitted to see the FBI report, nor is he informed of the
names of persons interviewed by the investigators. It was the Department's refusal to disclose the FBI reports that precipitated the
issue before the Supreme Court. Defendant in *Nugent* claimed that
the failure to show him the FBI reports in his case rendered his
classification illegal.

The majority of the *Nugent* Court rejected this claim. According to it, the Department of Justice satisfied its duties under the
statute when it afforded the registrant an opportunity to speak his
piece before a hearing officer and supplied him with a fair résumé
of any adverse evidence in the investigator's report. The only
trouble with this holding is that, under the Selective Service Act,
the Department of Justice must hold a "hearing" when an appeal is
referred to it. "Hearing" is a term of art in our administrative law
which includes much more than a mere opportunity to speak one's
piece before the administrator. The right to a hearing is the right to
a full and fair hearing; it includes the right to be apprised of and to
refute the case on the other side and the right to have the decision
based exclusively upon the record of the evidence openly presented
at the hearing. It is wholly opposed to the concept of a decision
based upon secret evidence not revealed to the individual con-

cerned. Despite this accepted meaning of the term "hearing" in our law, the Court in *Nugent* held that "hearing" in the Selective Service Act meant something less.

"If there is no meaning in it," said Alice's King, "that saves a world of trouble, you know, as we needn't try to find any." It may be doubted whether this way of dealing with words should be the method of the judicial process. The Congress uses a recognized word like "hearing" in a statute presumably because it intends the word in the statute to have its accepted meaning in the law. It is one thing for the Court to accept a procedure devised by the Congress, out of deference to the legislative judgment, even though it be at the very boundaries of due process. In *Nugent,* however, the Court was not called upon to devise a just procedure, in opposition to that prescribed in the statute, but only to apply that clearly spelled out by the Congress. The very purpose of giving registrants a hearing is to give them the opportunity to meet adverse evidence normally associated with the requirement of a hearing in our law. It makes a mockery of the Congressional intent to suggest that such adverse evidence can be effectively met if it is not known. Nor is the situation changed because the Court asserts a right in the registrant to a "fair résumé" of the adverse evidence. A hearing includes the right to rebut all the evidence against him, not merely the right to rebut what an administrative officer is willing to divulge as a résumé of the evidence. How can the registrant and the Court be confident that a résumé is fair, when they do not even know what it is a résumé of? "A page of history is worth a volume of logic," according to a celebrated statement of Justice Holmes.[56] In *Nugent,* the Court rejects both the history and the logic of the term "hearing" in order to give effect to its conception of what is required for effective administration of a law calculated to function in times of peril.

A more recent case in which the high Court has approved the administrative use of information kept confidential despite the failure of the Congress to authorize such a departure from the principles of fair procedure is *Jay v. Boyd,*[57] decided in 1956. It arose under a section of the Immigration Act which provides that the Attorney General "may in his discretion" suspend deportation of any deportable alien who meets certain statutory requirements relating to moral character, hardship, and period of residence within the United States. If the Attorney General does suspend deportation under that provision, he must file, pursuant to the statute, "a complete and detailed statement of the facts and pertinent provisions of law in the case" with the Congress, giving "the reasons for such sus-

pension." It is true that there is, in these provisions, no specific requirement that the Attorney General hold a hearing before exercising the statutory power conferred upon him. On the other hand,
it is clear, as Chief Justice Warren pointed out in a dissenting opinion in the *Jay* case, that the Attorney General was not vested with
a wholly unfettered discretion. In the Chief Justice's phrase, "It
was an administrative discretion calling for a report to Congress on
the manner of its use." [58] The Attorney General, himself, recognized this, for he provided by regulation for hearings to be held in
cases calling for the exercise of his power to suspend deportations,
and a hearing had in fact been held in the *Jay* case. But the hearing
thus held did not, any more than the procedure followed in the
Nugent case, comply fully with the basic requirements for a fair administrative hearing in our law. For the relevant regulation of the
Attorney General provided that the determination in particular
cases of whether suspension of deportation should be granted might
"be predicated upon confidential information without the disclosure thereof to the applicant, if in the opinion of the officer or the
Board making the determination the disclosure of such information
would be prejudicial to the public interest, safety, or security." In
Jay v. Boyd, suspension of deportation had been denied on the
basis of certain confidential information. On appeal to the courts,
the alien urged that the regulation authorizing the reliance upon
such secret evidence was invalid.

As it had done in *Nugent,* the Supreme Court spurned the argument in favor of the fundamentals of fair play. To the Court majority, the statute was intended to give the Attorney General an uncontrolled discretion in these cases, which extended to procedural
as it did to substantive questions. In such circumstances, said the
Court, the exercise of administrative discretion could be based upon
confidential information where national security was deemed to require it. The Court's approach to the administrative power at issue
here is, however, the converse of that normally followed in our administrative law. Thus, here again, we have a bending of the
normal law to accommodate demands asserted in the name of security. If an administrative agency provides by regulation for a
hearing, the courts will ordinarily hold it to the terms of the regulation. This means that the hearing held must be a real hearing, not
one in which the adjective rights of the individual are ignored. The
administrator is not in such a case, any more than he is in a case
where a statute demands a hearing, permitted to keep the word of
promise to the ear and break it to the hope. In Justice Frankfurter's
expression in a dissent in *Jay v. Boyd,* if the Attorney General in-

vokes the aid of administrative law by establishing an adversary procedure he cannot then defy the presuppositions of a fair hearing. He "cannot shelter himself behind the appearance of legal procedure—a system of administrative law—and yet infuse it with a denial of what is basic to such a system." [59] The point is even more pithily put by the Chief Justice, when he declares, "Such a hearing is not an administrative hearing in the American sense of the term. It is no hearing. . . . To me, this is not due process." [60]

To a student of the high Court, distortions of the law of administrative procedure such as those countenanced in the name of national security by the Court in cases like *Nugent* and *Jay* are most disturbing. We have come in recent years to see that security, like the patriotism of Dr. Johnson, may also come to be the last refuge of a scoundrel; many are the things that can be done in security's name in a time of tension that would not be tolerated at other times. It is one thing for the Court to defer to the Congressional judgment in a period of cold war, even though individual adjective rights may be adversely affected. It is quite another for the Court itself to twist the statutory language to uphold unfair procedures, where the Congress has not made such restricted construction imperative. One of the most disquieting features of decisions like those in the *Nugent* and *Jay* cases is that they are not decided in a cold-war vacuum. The war-power cases dealt with in the last chapter have had effects upon our law that have persisted long after the close of hostilities. The same may well be true of the cold-war decisions of the high bench. As Chief Justice Warren put it in his *Jay* dissent, "If sanction of this use and effect of 'confidential' information is confirmed against this petitioner by a process of judicial reasoning, it may be recognized as a principle of law to be extended against American citizens in a myriad of ways." [61] To be sure, there has been a real problem of security in this country in the past decade and a half. One wonders, nonetheless, whether the highest Court should march in the forefront of those who emphasize security considerations at all costs. A tribunal fully cognizant of the procedural values inherent in due process will hesitate before construing the law so as to deny adjective justice. Certainly, whatever we may say about the strains and stresses of the period we are living in, the enemy is not yet so near the gates that we must abandon our respect for the traditions of fairness that have heretofore prevailed in our system.[62]

Fair Play for Those We Hate

Few legal proceedings have attracted as much world-wide attention in recent years as those involving the convicted atom spies

Julius and Ethel Rosenberg. From a legal point of view, the high
point of the *Rosenberg* case was the hearing held in the Supreme
Court Chamber on June 18, 1953, just the day before the Rosenbergs
were electrocuted. On that day, the highest tribunal heard argument upon an application of the Attorney General to review a stay
of execution which had been granted to the Rosenbergs by Justice
Douglas. The opinion of the Court on the Attorney General's application starts by stating that its action in this case was unusual. But,
says Chief Justice Vinson, who delivered the opinion, "So were the
circumstances which led to it. The Court's action should be considered in the context of the full history of the proceedings which
have marked this case." [63] Taking the Chief Justice at his own
words, what were the circumstances that led up to the Supreme
Court hearing of June 18? The Rosenbergs had been indicted on
August 17, 1950, for conspiring to commit espionage in wartime, in
violation of the Espionage Act of 1917. After a lengthy jury trial,
they were found guilty, and, on April 4, 1951, they were sentenced
to death. The next two years were filled with legal maneuverings
on the part of the Rosenbergs' attorneys seeking to have their convictions reversed. After the court of appeals affirmed the sentence,
they sought review by certiorari in the Supreme Court. That tribunal denied certiorari in October, 1952. Six times after that, the
Rosenbergs appeared before the high Court, attempting by one
means or another to have the execution of their sentence stayed.
In addition, individual applications were made to the Chief Justice,
as well as to other members of the Court, seeking to obtain various
forms of relief. Just such an application for a stay of execution was
made to Justice Douglas on June 15, 1953. But this time the Rosenberg counsel raised a legal issue which had not before been pressed,
that of the question of whether the 1917 Espionage Act, under
which the Rosenbergs had been sentenced, had not been superseded
by the Atomic Energy Act of 1946, which provides for the death
sentence in espionage cases only if the jury specifically so recommends. After two days of deliberation, Justice Douglas decided
that the new legal point was a substantial one which should be decided after full argument and deliberation, and he granted a stay
until it could be determined by the appropriate lower courts. It
was then that the Attorney General applied to the Chief Justice for
the full Court to vacate Justice Douglas' stay order. Although the
Court had by then recessed for its summer vacation, the Chief Justice convened a special term of the Court, which met the very next
day. As already mentioned, the Court heard argument on that day
(June 18); it considered the matter only one day, for, on June 19, it

announced its decision vacating the stay ordered by Justice Douglas, though without opinion. That very night the Rosenbergs were electrocuted. The opinion of the Court explaining why it had vacated the stay order was not filed until July 16, 1953, weeks after the protagonists in the drama themselves had been forced from the stage.

In a dissenting opinion which he, too, filed after the sentence on the Rosenbergs had been carried out, Justice Frankfurter meetly asserted, "To be writing an opinion in a case affecting two lives after the curtain has been rung down upon them has the appearance of pathetic futility." [64] The same may well be true of a commentary on the Supreme Court's handling of the *Rosenberg* case, particularly one like the present that is written some years after the case itself has become a page of legal history. Be that as it may, the high tribunal's treatment of the case certainly deserves consideration in an analysis of the impact of the cold war upon the Court's jurisprudence. For, in many ways, *Rosenberg v. United States* is the cold-war case par excellence, both because of the circumstances surrounding it (which made of it the *cause célèbre* it hardly deserved to be, from its legal aspects alone) and because of the effect which those circumstances may have had upon the manner in which the Supreme Court disposed of the case.

It is well known that the action of Justice Douglas, in granting his June 17 stay order, was the object of severe censure. One congressman, in fact, went so far as to introduce a resolution looking toward Justice Douglas' impeachment for granting the stay. From the legal point of view, all the same, there is no doubt whatsoever that Justice Douglas' action was wholly within his powers as a member of the Nation's highest tribunal. In the words of the high Court itself, "No one has disputed this, and we think the proposition is indisputable." [65] From the legal aspect alone, how could there be any doubt about a power that has existed uninterruptedly in individual Justices of the supreme bench since the very founding of the Republic? It is difficult, in truth, to see how Justice Douglas could have acted other than he did, believing, as he did, that the new legal issue raised before him for the first time was a substantial one which deserved full consideration from the judicial process. Unless a stay were granted, such consideration could hardly occur as a practical matter before the Rosenbergs themselves were executed.

More debatable than the question of Justice Douglas' power to issue his stay order is that of the propriety of the full Court's action in vacating the Douglas order. In making this statement, it is not the present writer's intention to cast doubts upon the legality of the

Rosenbergs' convictions or the fairness of the proceedings involving
them. So far as one not personally connected with the case can see
from the published materials, there was ample justification for the
jury's verdict and the sentence of the trial judge. And the appellate
proceedings were conducted throughout with meticulous fairness
and care. The court of appeals (the one appellate tribunal fully to
review all aspects of the case) was deeply conscious of its responsibility in such a case. As it stated in its opinion affirming the convictions, "Since two of the defendants must be put to death if the
judgments stand, it goes without saying that we have scrutinized
the record with extraordinary care to see whether it contains any
of the errors asserted on this appeal." [66] It may well be that in a
case like *Rosenberg,* where capital punishment was imposed, the
defendants should have a right to full review by the Supreme Court.
In Justice Frankfurter's words, "Petitioners are under death sentence, and it is not unreasonable to feel that before life is taken review should be open in the highest court of the society which has
condemned them." [67] Since 1911, nevertheless, there has been no
appeal as of right to the Supreme Court in capital cases. Appeals
from death sentences, since that time, have come to the Supreme
Court only under the same conditions that apply to any criminal
conviction in a federal court. The Rosenbergs were treated just as
any other convicted defendants in accordance with the accepted
practice of the Supreme Court. But this is precisely all they were
entitled to, despite the spectacular nature of their case. If no other
criminal defendants are entitled to review as of right in the high
tribunal, there was no reason for the Court to twist its settled jurisprudence in favor of these particular defendants.

Yet, even with the above conceded, one is still left with something of an uneasy feeling about the high Court's disposition of the
Rosenberg case at the Special Term convened to review Justice
Douglas' stay order. Nor does this feeling have anything to do with
the merits of the case. As has been intimated, few whose minds
are not already distorted by propaganda accounts of the case can
fail to conclude, after examining the available materials, that the
Rosenbergs were properly tried and justly convicted. At the same
time, there is little doubt that the legal issue which was raised before Justice Douglas was, in fact, a substantial one. Justice Douglas himself has stated his reaction to the argument raised before him
for the first time: "When the motion for a stay was before me, I was
deeply troubled by the legal question tendered. After twelve hours
of research and study I concluded, as my opinion indicated, that the
question was a substantial one, never presented to this Court and

never decided by any court. So I issued the stay order." [68]   The
Rosenbergs had been convicted under the Espionage Act of 1917 for
communicating to a foreign government, in wartime, secret atomic
and other military information. The overt acts relating to atomic
secrets occurred before enactment of the Atomic Energy Act of 1946;
but other aspects of the conspiracy continued until 1950. The
Rosenbergs' attorneys contended before Justice Douglas that, since
some of the criminal acts had occurred after the 1946 act went into
effect, it was only under that law that the Rosenbergs could be sentenced; and, as already stated, under the Atomic Energy Act of
1946, the death penalty cannot be imposed for espionage unless the
jury recommends it—a recommendation that was lacking in the
Rosenberg case. This argument may or may not be sound; but it
certainly raises a substantial legal point and one which deserves full
judicial consideration, since, as Justice Douglas pointed out, it was
never decided by any court. That the question was a substantial
one is shown by the fact that three members of the Court publicly
dissented from the Court's decision that it was not substantial
enough to justify further litigation of it. Justice Douglas went so
far as to assert the correctness of the Rosenbergs' argument on the
merits. Justices Black and Frankfurter did not go that far; but both
declared that the argument was weighty enough to require the
judicial process to deal with it fully.

What is particularly distasteful to one who believes that the law
is more than a system of societal retribution is the undue dispatch
with which the high Court acted to vacate Justice Douglas' stay
order. "Judicial haste," in the words of Justice Black, "is peculiarly
out of place where the death penalty has been imposed for conduct
part of which took place at a time when the Congress appears to
have barred the imposition of the death penalty by district judges
acting without a jury's recommendation." [69]   After Justice Douglas
had acted, as it was his clear duty to do once he felt that the legal
argument raised before him was a substantial one, the Court did not
wait more than a day to hear the Government's petition for review
of the stay. This left scarcely a working day for those concerned to
prepare to argue on the issue raised before Justice Douglas. Between argument and decision, also, the Court itself had all of one
day for the independent study and reflection that a conscientious
judge needs before deciding any case of consequence. It is almost
self-evident from the judicial chronology of events that the Court
had neither the time nor the opportunity for sufficient study to give
the kind of informed judgment that the case demanded. The basic
question raised before Justice Douglas was one of statutory con-

struction. In such a case, the judge will normally seek light from the legislative history and other materials in which the intent of the Congress might be revealed. Yet, as Justice Frankfurter plaintively points out, "It is almost mathematically demonstrable that there just was not time within twelve waking hours to dig out, to assess, to assemble, and to formulate the meaning of legislative materials." [70] In the time available, neither Court nor counsel could be expected to go below the surface of the legal question raised.

And why this unseemly haste? Would the national security really have been imperiled by delay in the departure from the scene of two miserable traitors? Was not, indeed, the greater injury done by the fostering of an impression that the judicial process had let itself be used as an instrument for the execution of the Government's retribution schedule?

The law knows no finer hour than when it cuts through transitory emotions to apply civilized standards of fair play even for those most repugnant to us as individuals. The goddess of Justice is portrayed with a blindfold, not because she must be hindered in seeing where the right lies, but that she may not discriminate against suitors before her, dispensing instead an even-handed justice to all. It is particularly important in cases involving those who are personally most distasteful to us that our law lean over backwards to ensure, not only that justice be done, but that it manifestly and undoubtedly seem to be done. For is it not in our adherence to justice according to law that we differ most from those like the Rosenbergs, who are partisans of faiths which relegate the law to a subordinate status as an instrument of governmental policy? As a member of the Supreme Court eloquently states:

Vishinsky wrote in 1938, in The Law of the Soviet State, "In our state, naturally, there is and can be no place for freedom of speech, press, and so on for the foes of socialism." Our concern should be that we accept no such standard for the United States. Our faith should be that our people will never give support to these advocates of revolution, so long as we remain loyal to the purposes for which our Nation was founded. [71]

To men like Vyshinsky, our whole conception of justice according to law is a pious fraud. The judicial process, says he, is not really an instrument for the dispensing of even-handed justice. Instead, he asserts, "It has always been an instrument in the hands of the dominant class, assuring the strengthening of its dominance and the protection of its interests." [72] If we are to remain true to our own faith, it must be our constant concern to give the lie to the Vyshinsky assertion, and especially in cases involving those who, like the Rosenbergs, seek only to be martyrs to the Vyshinsky view of our system. "If justice had a voice," declares a common saying, "she would speak like an English judge." Yet the only quality that the bench in England has to merit this tribute is that its members, each and every one of them, seek to be fair. Every judge in England will see to it that every man coming before him—even though he be a Klaus Fuchs or a Gerhart Eisler—has a fair trial. Let it be the perpetual care of our own high Court that a similar compliment can always be paid to it.

Perhaps we are being overcritical of the Court's action in the *Rosenberg* affair. The case itself and the judicial disposition of it are but symptoms of the period of tension through which we have been passing. To talk of the Commonwealth as endowed with life is more than a mere metaphor. The political, like the animal, body has its periods of sickness and vigor. The past decade and a half has, without any doubt, been one in which our body politic has been constantly afflicted. At such a time, it is to be expected that much of the vital spark goes out of the society, as it would out of an afflicted individual. This understood, let it not seem idle if we refer once again to the fact that our old Physician's Aphorism holds in politics and law, as it does in animal life. In a period of cold war, the law knows of its health, as it could never be expected to in less troubled times. It should, however, be recognized that, in the animal body, health is the natural, sickness the artificial, state. The same may well be the case of the body politic and the law. The cold-war jurisprudence of the highest Court may thus be characterized as an artificial jurisprudence. In all vital things, men distinguish between artificial and natural, with the artificial being considered as something inferior. Few students of the Supreme Court will deny that this is true as well of the recent "artificial" jurisprudence of the high tribunal. To be sure, the day will come when the body politic, like the animal body, will be restored to its pristine state of full vigor. We cannot, of course, know just when that will happen, just as no one at the bottom of an economic cycle can be sure just when prosperity will come around the corner. Yet happen it will, in our legal as in our political life. Then it will be that cases like some of those discussed in this chapter will be looked upon as the aberrations in the law that they really are.

10

ANATOMY AND
PATHOLOGY
OF THE COURT

The life of an institution such as the Nation's highest Court, like a piece of tapestry, is made up of many strands which, interwoven, make a pattern; to separate a single one and look at it alone not only destroys the whole but gives the strand itself a false value.[1] All too many studies of the Supreme Court, or of its individual members, tend to overlook the institutional nature of that governmental organ. They concentrate upon single strands of the Court's work, emphasizing, more often than not, those aspects which diverge most sharply from the over-all pattern. Such an approach is bound to give a distorted picture of the functioning of the high tribunal. Not infrequently, in truth, the reaction of writers about the Supreme Court to that august institution is akin to that of the blind men from Hindustan when first confronted with an elephant. The aspect of the Court's work emphasized by the particular author tends to dominate his conception of the Court as a whole; yet he almost never really comes to picture the Court as the institutional entity that it is. Small wonder, then, that the public, both legal and lay, has no clear picture of the working of our unique high judicial organ and of its proper place in a representative democracy.

The Supreme Court is the only continuing governmental institution in our constitutional structure;[2] individual Justices may come and go, but their arrivals and departures scarcely affect the unbroken functioning of the Court as a judicial organ. Neophytes on the high bench—even the strongest of them—are immediately aware of the overpowering institutional traditions of the tribunal to which they have been elevated. Such awareness continues through the Justices' professional life and, more than is generally realized, molds into the Court's pattern all but the most eccentric of its members. It has been said of one of the greatest of modern Justices, Louis D. Brandeis, that he had an almost mystic reverence for the Court, whose tradition seemed to him not only to consecrate its own members, but to impress its sacred mission upon all who shared in any measure in its work.[3] Few members of the high tribunal may be capable of penetrating into its *mystique* with the perception of a Brandeis; still, all of them become, to greater or lesser extents, strongly imbued with its institutional traditions.

The present work has been written upon the assumption that the pattern of the tapestry is more important than the single strands. Similarly, the Supreme Court as an institution is more significant than the individual Justices who make up its membership. Undoubtedly, the development of the Court's institutional traditions has been not dissimilar to the manner in which Topsy described her own developmental process. By 1957 A.D., nevertheless, the Court as an institution has all but fully "growed." And it is upon the Court as an institution that this and the prior chapters are concentrated.

To be sure, to treat the high Court as an institutional entity may seem outdated in an age when even the law has succumbed to our society's preoccupation with the behavioristic sciences. Judges are only men, we are told—which is, of course, an indisputable observation. All the same, it hardly follows from this that it is only studies of the psychological makeups of the individual men who compose the high Court that are now worthwhile. The state of a man's mind is as much a fact as the state of his digestion, according to the famous statement of a nineteenth-century English judge. Now, however, we are told that the two are intimately related and that the state of a judge's mind can hardly be known without some knowledge of the state of his stomach. To advocates of this sort of gastrological jurisprudence, all attempts to describe the Court as an institutional entity are fundamentally naive. This is particularly true, we are told, of the supreme bench since 1937, when the institutional ethos of the Court has often seemed at its lowest ebb. At such a time, it is said, it is only the makeup of the individual Justice that is important if we are to understand the decisions of a fragmented Court.

No one not blind to the facts of legal life can deny that the high Court in the past two decades has often presented a far from edifying spectacle of internal atomization. But even this has not prevented that tribunal from functioning as an institutional entity. The Supreme Court has been splintered before (dissents and five-to-four decisions are not recent inventions on the part of law professors);

still, the Court's work as a governmental organ has had to go on, as, indeed, it has had to during the past twenty years as well. This is, in fact, a basic difference between an ultimate judicial tribunal and commentaries upon its work. The Court cannot adopt an *either-or* approach—it *must* decide the case before it, even though such decision requires it to choose between two conflicting truths. The theorist need wholly reject neither, where neither states an exclusive verity; the Court *must* choose between them. Yet it is a mistake to assume that, because, in such cases, the individual members of the tribunal are sharply divided, the Court has ceased to function as an institution. On the contrary, even amidst a plethora of such cases, the institutional pattern continues to be woven. It may be harder to determine the boundary at which the post-1937 Court has balanced conflicting interests than it was to make a similar determination with regard to its predecessors. The Court in the past two decades has, nonetheless, been engaged in drawing such a boundary; while we may still not be able to determine it by a general formula, points in the line have been fixed by decisions that this or that concrete case falls on the nearer or farther side.

The present book has been based upon the view that, even in a splintered Supreme Court, there are certain broad principles that have dominated the Court's work. It is this which makes possible an analysis of the high tribunal's jurisprudence from an institutional point of view without more than passing reference to the individual personalities of the Justices. The Court as a whole (though not, it is true, all its members with the same consistency) has accepted the implications inherent in the constitutional revolution of 1937, which so drastically altered the judicial approach to questions of constitutional law. It is its adherence to the basic principles upon which its post-1937 jurisprudence has been built that has furnished more internal consistency to the work of the high tribunal than is often realized, and it is this consistency, in turn, that has made it possible for the new jurisprudence of the Court to be analyzed in logical fashion as it has been in the preceding pages of this book. In the present chapter, we shall be dealing not so much with the high bench's case law as with the Court itself as an institution. Particular attention will be paid, as it must, to the pathological aspects of the Court's institutional functioning—to those respects in which the Court's institutional ethos has seemed to be at its weakest.

Good for This Day and Train Only?

In a 1953 opinion, Justice Jackson gave voice to what has been the most frequently heard criticism of the post-1937 Supreme Court.

Rightly or wrongly, the belief is widely held by the practicing profession that this Court no longer respects impersonal rules of law but is guided in these matters by personal impressions which from time to time may be shared by a majority of Justices. Whatever has been intended, this Court also has generated an impression . . . that regard for precedents and authorities is obsolete, that words no longer mean what they have always meant to the profession, that the law knows no fixed principles.[4]

One of the essential requirements of any successfully functioning institution is that of internal consistency and adherence to established precedents. It is only thus that the institution can avoid functioning by whim and caprice alone. A business or governmental organ that constantly changes its policies and procedures can hardly hope to achieve as effective results as one that pursues a consistent path in furtherance of its aims. Adherence to precedent is a characteristic which is not limited to purely judicial institutions. The principle of *stare decisis* is, on the contrary, one which tends to guide all reasonable human action. Yet, important though consistency of conduct may be in other spheres, it is in the law that it attains its peak of perfection. The very basis of law in a civilized society is that it enables men in like circumstances to be dealt with in a similar manner. But this can be true only if the law itself is settled and applied consistently in specific cases. One can, perhaps, picture a satisfactory dispensation of justice by St. Louis under the oak at Vincennes; yet who would be willing to submit his case to the uncontrolled discretion of other than a saint? In a developed system of law, the individual will of the magistrate must be fettered by the doctrine of adherence to settled principles and precedents. In a judicial tribunal, *stare decisis* is not so much a virtue as a necessity.

If adherence to precedent were the only judicial virtue, it could hardly be gainsaid that the Supreme Court since 1937 has been among the least virtuous of modern judicial tribunals. For one of the outstanding features of the Court in the past twenty years has been the frequency with which it has declined to follow decisions handed down by its predecessors. So far in fact has the Court's tendency in this direction gone at times that it has seemed to many all but to eliminate that stability which is one of the prime justifications for any system of law. In most legal matters, it is even more important that the applicable rule of law be settled than that it be settled right.[5] Since 1937, on the other hand, the high bench has been so concerned with the correction of what it deemed erroneous jurisprudence that it has often unsettled previously settled rules of law. To such an extent, indeed, had this proneness of the Court to overrule precedents gone by 1944 that it led Justice Roberts, in dissent, to charge that it is "the present policy of the court freely to disregard and to overrule considered decisions and the rules of law announced in them." [6]   The result, said the learned judge, in one of the few bon mots he ever permitted himself while on the bench, is that adjudications of the Supreme Court are brought "into the same class as a restricted railroad ticket, good for this day and train only." [7]

It has been the fashion among writers on the high Court to deprecate these strictures of Justice Roberts. To be sure, they concede, adherence to precedent is basic as an abstract desideratum of the law. But it must not take precedence over the need for the law to be right, particularly on constitutional issues. These writers often quote a famous statement of Justice Brandeis on the need for adherence to precedent to give way when prior constitutional decisions are deemed erroneous. Though, according to him, *stare decisis* is usually the wise policy, "in cases involving the Federal Constitution, where correction through legislative action is practically impossible, this Court has often overruled its earlier decisions. The Court bows to the lessons of experience and the force of better reasoning, recognizing that the process of trial and error, so fruitful in the physical sciences, is appropriate also in the judicial function." [8]

We may admit that it would be most undesirable for the Supreme Court inexorably to follow prior precedents in every case. So interpreted, *stare decisis* would become the doctrine of the dead hand. As early as 1851, the high Court itself saw the need for flexibility in its application of the rule of adherence to precedent.[9] *Stare decisis* with us is, in Justice Brandeis' phrase, not "a universal, inexorable command." [10]   In truth, the worst thing that could happen in a legal system like ours, where the judge plays such a primordial part, would be to bind him rigidly to all the rules fashioned by his predecessors. Certainty and change—these are the essential needs of a legal system. Obviously, they both cannot be given full scope; in their pure forms they are antagonistic poles. Neither can be made the exclusive concern of the legal system: Without certainty, the law becomes not a chart to govern conduct, but a game of chance; with only certainty, the law is as the still waters in which there are only stagnation and death. Inherent in every system of law is the antinomy between certainty and change. The law must be stable and yet it cannot stand still; that is the great juristic paradox which no legal system has as yet been able to resolve in a wholly satisfactory manner.

From what has just been said, it follows that the Supreme Court is scarcely subject to criticism simply because it has not adhered slavishly to the rule of adherence to precedent. Constitutional law cannot be cast in a rigid mold; we must never forget, in John Marshall's celebrated phrase, that it is a *constitution* we are expounding —an instrument that could hardly have been intended to endure through the ages, if its provisions, once judicially construed, became fixed as irrevocably as the laws of the Medes and Persians. In fact the very subject of this book would have been impossible had the Supreme Court firmly followed the doctrine of *stare decisis*. The essence of the constitutional revolution of 1937 was the casting aside of the whole approach to questions of constitutional law which had dominated the pre-1937 high tribunal. Furthermore, it cannot reasonably be contended that much, at least, of the Court's rejection of the pre-1937 jurisprudence was not justified. Few today desire a return by the Court to its position of twenty years ago as the Supreme Censor of all legislation. It must not be forgotten that the jurisprudence of the 1890–1936 Court itself constituted a drastic departure from earlier, more restrained estimates by the high bench of the proper scope of its review authority. In this sense, the new position of the Court under the post-1937 case law has marked a return to the view held by the high tribunal itself during most of the nineteenth century and particularly by the Marshall Court. To Chief Justice Marshall (writer, as he was, of the classic opinion affirming a power in the judiciary to review the constitutionality of laws), the Supreme Court was, without a doubt, endowed with the authority to nullify invalid statutes; but such power was to be employed only as a last resort, when a patent conflict with the Constitution made its use unavoidable.* In rejecting the pre-1937 Court's assertion of a far wider power of review, the present Court has only reverted to the position originally laid down by John Marshall.

Insofar as the Court has given effect to the basic premises of the constitutional revolution of 1937, its action cannot be condemned, even though it has involved the overruling of decisions of the pre-1937 high tribunal. The Court's assertion of the widest possible review power in the pre-1937 period had placed it in an untenable position, bearing in mind the premises upon which its employment of that power had been based and the manner in which it had been used to prevent the assumption by government of authority that was clearly necessary to meet the time's changed needs. In such circumstances, is the Court to be blamed if it has remolded its jurisprudence to accord with the demands of the twentieth century? The tree that does not bend to the blast will be broken; for the high Court to have insisted upon remaining in the exposed position, in

* *Supra*, p. 13.

which its pre-1937 jurisprudence had left it, might have done untold
harm both to itself and the constitutional structure it had sworn to
defend. As Justice Roberts put it in 1951, in a passage already cited,
"An insistence by the Court on holding federal power to what
seemed its appropriate orbit when the Constitution was adopted
might have resulted in even more radical changes in our dual structure than those which have been gradually accomplished through
the extension of the limited jurisdiction conferred on the federal
government." *

Once the basic premises of the constitutional revolution were accepted, much of the jurisprudence of the pre-1937 Court became so
much deadwood to be cut off as soon as the opportunity presented
itself. But the high tribunal did not remain content with merely
pruning the constitutional tree. All too often in the years after 1937,
the Court has overruled prior decisions which were not based upon
premises that became outmoded in the post-1937 period. Especially significant in this respect have been cases overruling decisions
made in the post-1937 period itself. The most striking example, perhaps, was the Jehovah's Witness flag-salute case, where the Court
in 1943 overruled its own 1940 decision in a similar case. † It may
well be, in Justice Holmes's noted phrase, revolting to have no better
reason for a rule than that so it was laid down in the time of Henry
IV.[11] But a decision rendered by the same Court only a few years
back is hardly a derelict on the stream of the law. Such a decision
is scarcely an outmoded one eroded by time. Whatever else might
be said about *stare decisis,* it must require a judicial tribunal to follow its own recent jurisprudence. As Justice Frankfurter put it in
dissent, in a case where the Court discarded an important holding
made only two years earlier, "Especially ought the Court not reen-
force needlessly the instabilities of our day by giving fair ground for
the belief that Law is the expression of chance—for instance, of unexpected changes in the Court's composition and the contingencies
in the choice of successors." [12]

According to a recent calculation by Justice Douglas, in the
period from 1937 to 1955, the Supreme Court handed down some
twenty constitutional decisions expressly overruling prior cases.[13] It
is, however, important to note that, of these twenty decisions, only
five were rendered in the years since 1947. The reason for the preponderance of these decisions in the earlier period is not difficult to
determine. The old order changeth and giveth way to new; but
the period of transition is inevitably one of unsettlement and flux.

* *Supra,* p. 18.
† *Supra,* p. 236.

The unsettling effect is one which may last for some years. During that time, the deadwood is cut away and the new doctrinal positions consolidated. After a decade or so, the new constitutional position becomes more or less fixed. Then the endless legal cycle between stability and change begins again. Today's new decision becomes an anchorage for settled constitutional doctrine. The former proponents of change become partisans of the new order and adhere strongly to its basic principles and the decisions rendered in accordance with them. This tendency has manifested itself in the Supreme Court of the past twenty years (as it has in countless judicial tribunals of the past) and helps to explain the decline in the Court's propensity to overrule precedents, which was so disturbing in the 1937–47 period.

It is believed that what has just been said is now true of the Supreme Court, taken as an institutional entity. This does not, to be sure, mean that the high bench no longer overrules precedents. Even the most conservative tribunal will find some occasions to discard prior decisions. Yet it does indicate that the wholesale repudiation of established law, which caused such distress, to lawyers and laymen alike, in the early part of the post-1937 period, is now a thing of the past. Whatever may have been the case ten years ago, decisions of the Court today may no longer be classed with Justice Roberts' restricted railroad ticket—good for this day and train only. To the Court today, *stare decisis* embodies an important social policy. It represents an element of continuity in the law, and is rooted in the psychological need to satisfy men's reasonable expectations.

Activism and Stare Decisis

Though the Supreme Court as a whole has thus been moving more and more toward a policy of adherence, wherever possible, to the rule of *stare decisis*, this has not been true of all of its members. Resistance to what has been essentially a conservative trend in the Court has particularly characterized the so-called activists on the high bench—those Justices who believe that it is the judge's active duty to use his position to translate his personal policies and preferences into law (though, of course, they would strongly deny the validity of any such blunt characterization of their position). Before 1937, the majority were activists in this sense, though, doubtless, almost exclusively in favor of property rights. Today, our activists on the Court have been aptly termed "libertarian activists." [14] As already emphasized,* though their concern is with personal

* *Supra*, pp. 237-38.

rights, their approach in rejecting the doctrine of deference to the legislature is essentially similar to that followed by the pre-1937 Court majority. The activists of both the pre- and post-1937 variety appeal, not to the Constitution as a whole, but only to a mutilating selection of those parts which for the moment find favor with them.[15]

To the judicial activist, *stare decisis* is a harmless homily which can hardly be permitted to stand in the way of a policy which he happens to deem desirable. On the contrary, he exhibits a constant readiness to undo the work of his predecessors on the bench whenever he himself would not have made the initial determination. To him, the high Court's function is analogous to that of the Roman praetor who was ever disposed to suppress precedents deemed inconvenient. No wonder, then, that Justice Douglas (who, with Justice Black, is the most persistent advocate of the activist view) could declare as late as 1956, "Stare decisis has . . . little place in American constitutional law."[16]

What the Douglas-Black approach to *stare decisis* means in practice is shown in cases in which it has been applied by them. We have already dealt at some length with their espousal of the view that the Fourteenth Amendment incorporates all the provisions of the Bill of Rights,* as well as with their assertion that First Amendment freedoms should be given a preferred position,† despite the fact that, on both these points, all prior decisions of the Court had adopted the contrary view. There have been other cases, equally striking, of the Douglas-Black tendency to reject settled law in favor of the personal policy of the moment. In some ways, the most characteristic of these occurred in 1938, only three months after Justice Black was appointed to the bench. In a dissent delivered at that time, Justice Black asserted the view that the provision in the Fourteenth Amendment guaranteeing to all "persons" due process and the equal protection of the laws did not apply to corporations. "I do not believe," declared the learned judge, "the word 'person' in the Fourteenth Amendment includes corporations."[17] More recently, in a 1949 dissent, Justice Douglas expressed the same view, with Justice Black concurring.[18] Yet, whatever might be said of the Black-Douglas view on this point as a matter of abstract legal logic, it is surely relevant that history has gone the other way. In 1886, the Court declared its view that legal as well as natural persons were included within the protection of the Fourteenth Amendment.[19] Since that time, innumerable cases have been decided on the unquestioned assumption that corporations are entitled to the

* *Supra,* pp. 163-67.
† *Supra,* pp. 235-40.

constitutional protection. The mass of authority in support of the established law on the point did not deter Justices Black and Douglas. To them, the volume of history was not worth as much as their page of logic, based upon their personal belief that corporations should not be afforded the same constitutional protection as natural persons.

Two more recent decisions well illustrate the extent to which the Douglas-Black contingent is willing to go in discarding constitutional landmarks to attain their view of what the rule of law, which for the moment finds favor with them, should be. In *Harisiades v. Shaughnessy* and *Galvan v. Press,* already discussed in another connection,* the Court upheld the power of the Congress to order the deportation of aliens who were members of the Communist Party at any time after their entry into this country. To Justices Douglas and Black, this was to countenance a violation of the *ex post facto* clause of the Constitution, since it allowed deportation for an act that was entirely lawful when it was done. It is certainly true that the statutes at issue in these two cases had a retroactive effect. But, if there is one principle settled in our constitutional law, it is that a law does not violate the *ex post facto* clause merely because it may have retroactive aspects. As early as 1798, the Supreme Court decided that the *ex post facto* clause applied only to penal and criminal statutes.[20] This early holding has been consistently applied to limit the scope of the constitutional prohibition and, in a number of cases, the Court expressly held that it has no application to deportation, which, drastic though it may be to the alien concerned, is not a criminal punishment. Well could the Court, in its *Harisiades* opinion, state, with regard to the law challenged there, "even if the Act were found to be retroactive, to strike it down would require us to overrule the construction of the *ex post facto* provision which has been followed by this Court from earliest times." [21] To those who hold to the Douglas-Black view, this necessity is of slight moment, compared to the desirability of extending the *ex post facto* clause to a case like deportation.

The Douglas-Black readiness to remake our constitutional law in their own image is also shown in their dissents in the 1956 case of *Ullmann v. United States.*[22] That case dealt with the constitutionality of the Immunity Act of 1954, which authorizes the federal courts, in certain cases, to compel witnesses to testify despite their constitutional privilege against self-incrimination, but goes on to provide that no such witness shall be subject to prosecution on account of any transaction, matter, or thing concerning which he is

* *Supra,* pp. 319-21.

compelled to testify under the statute. It had been settled by the high Court as long ago as 1896 [23] that the constitutional prohibition against self-incrimination is not violated, even though a witness may be compelled to incriminate himself, where he is given complete immunity from prosecution which might be aided by his testimony. The Immunity Act of 1954 appears to give witnesses just such immunity, and the majority of the *Ullmann* Court consequently held it to be constitutional. To Justices Douglas and Black in their dissent, on the other hand, the 1954 Act did not go far enough in protecting the witness. The witness in *Ullmann* itself was ordered to testify concerning Communist activities and affiliations. In such a case, said the dissent, it is not enough only to immunize the witness against criminal prosecutions, for there are numerous other disabilities created by law that attach to a Communist: "These disabilities include ineligibility for employment in the Federal Government and in defense facilities, disqualification for a passport, the risk of internment, the risk of loss of employment as a longshoreman—to mention only a few." [24] To be valid, in the view of the dissenters, the Immunity Act must supply protection against these disabilities as well as criminal penalties. Once again, however, Justices Douglas and Black ignore the fact that it has long been established in Supreme Court jurisprudence that the privilege against self-incrimination applies only to testimony which may incriminate the witness of crimes. Well could the Court majority quote, in answer to the dissent, Justice Holmes's passage, already cited,* about a page of history being worth a volume of logic: "For the history of the privilege establishes not only that it is not to be interpreted literally, but also that its sole concern is, as its name indicates, with the danger to a witness forced to give testimony leading to the infliction of 'penalties affixed to the criminal acts. . . .' " [25]

There are, it must be admitted, those who express admiration for the boldness that characterizes the Douglas-Black approach to the question of precedent. Black's "mental boldness," says a commentator expressing this opinion, "was illustrated in an early dissent where he argued, brilliantly and alone, that, despite mountains of precedents running the other way, corporations should not be, and should never have been, judicially rated as 'persons' entitled to the protection of the Fourteenth Amendment." [26] One who does not subscribe to this laudatory view of the Douglas-Black readiness to repudiate the past may question whether mental boldness, of the type illustrated by rejection of the holding (wholly unchallenged from 1886 to 1938) that corporations are entitled to the protection

* *Supra,* p. 333.

of the Fourteenth Amendment, is really a desirable attribute in a member of the highest tribunal. Great judges can hardly be radical innovators and remain true to the demands imposed by society upon the judicial process. "I venture to suggest," states Justice Frankfurter, "that had they the mind of such originators, the bench is not the place for its employment. Transforming thought implies too great a break with the past, implies too much discontinuity, to be imposed upon society by one who is entrusted with enforcing its law." [27] Stability and change, we have seen, are the twin sisters of the law. The judge who yields only to the demands of change is scarcely serving the real progress of the law whose servant he professes to be.

It is not for the judge to repudiate a prior decision every time he would have decided the original case the other way. This is true even though, were the slate wiped clean, much could be said for the other view, which the judge might personally favor. In cases like those discussed, the slate is not clean. The judge who is prepared cavalierly to cast aside the repeated precedents of a century must necessarily assume that he is wiser or more sensitive to the needs of the law than his predecessors—certainly a precarious assumption on the part of one who sits on the bench once occupied by Holmes, Brandeis, Hughes, Stone, and Cardozo (to mention only the very greatest of living memory). The foremost duty of the judge is to preserve the internal consistency of the law, unless departure from established principles has become an overwhelming necessity. He must not treat constitutional law as carte blanche upon which he is free to scribble what he pleases. He is, on the contrary, bound to respect the accumulated experience contained in prior decisions of the Court. Such decisions, particularly when they have remained unquestioned in later cases in point, must be adhered to, in the absence of compelling reasons for repudiation. And the personal preference of the particular judge is not such a compelling reason. The judge who acts as though he can change constitutional law the way women change their fashions brings the very administration of justice into disrepute. Respect for courts must fall when the public and the profession come to understand that decisions are to have only contemporaneous value and that nothing that has been said in prior adjudication has force in a current controversy.[28] Despite Justice Douglas' contrary view,* *stare decisis* does have a vital place in our constitutional law. For *stare decisis* is the only real link which joins the high Court directly to its predecessors. Without such a link, there can be no real continuity in the law; each genera-

* *Supra*, p. 350.

tion of judges must decide in individual isolation, aided neither by the experience nor restraining influence of prior generations. If such is the case, the law itself has lost all perduring value—the work of the Court becomes as fleeting as the flies of a summer.

Dissentio ad Absurdum

Apart from the question of adherence to precedent, the most common complaint voiced against the Supreme Court in recent years has concerned the all too frequent tendency of that tribunal to render nonunanimous decisions. Constant division in the high Court all but destroys the feeling of certainty in the law which men may reasonably expect to have in their legal system. More than that, it has a direct adverse effect upon the respect in which the Court and the law are held. The supreme bench is identified in the public mind as the authoritative expounder of American law. What detracts from the esteem in which the highest tribunal is held cannot but reflect adversely upon the law throughout the land. In our system, the Supreme Court is clothed with much of the panoply and prestige that the ancients associated with their religious oracles. But even the Apollo at Delphi could not long retain the allegiance of men if it spoke with utterly inconsistent voices.

It is recognized, to be sure, that disagreement within the high Court is an inevitable occurrence. The history of all thought is a history of disagreements. "How amazing it is," declares Chief Justice Hughes, "that, in the midst of controversies on every conceivable subject, one should expect unanimity of opinion upon difficult legal questions!" [29] The questions which the Supreme Court is called upon to resolve are such that reasonable men may well differ in their answers; only the most difficult problems presented to the judicial process are now able to run the gauntlet of certiorari procedure and gain access to the high tribunal. It would be strange, indeed, if the Court could settle all of them without any disagreements among its members. In the recent words of Justice Frankfurter, "If the materials on which judicial judgments must be based could be fed into a machine so as to produce ineluctable answers, if such were the nature of the problems that come before the Supreme Court and such were the answers expected, we would have IBM machines doing the work instead of judges." [30]

We must thus acknowledge that disagreement within the Court must play a necessary part in its work. We may go further and concede that, whatever may be the situation in most other countries (where dissenting and concurring opinions are unknown), the prac-

tice of having Justices, who do not agree with the holding or reasoning in an opinion of the Court, express their individual views in
dissenting or concurring opinions has played a definite role in de-
veloping the jurisprudence of our high tribunal. This has, in fact,
been recognized from the very beginning of Supreme Court history.
As early as 1796, Chief Justice Ellsworth, in announcing the decision
of the Court, felt compelled to state, "This is the opinion of the
court; but not unanimously." [31] And Justice Wilson, who followed,
delivered a full-fledged dissenting opinion—the first in Supreme
Court history—saying, "I consider the rule established by the second
proposition to be of such magnitude, that being in the minority on
the decision, I am desirous of stating, as briefly as I can, the principles of my dissent." [32] In a case like this, unanimous opinion
would be but a mere façade; it may be better to bring the judicial
disagreement into the open than to convey a false sense of concord
by the rendering of a single opinion for the entire Court.

Yet, even with the dissent and the concurrence conceded to have
a proper place in our law, one may wonder whether members of the
high Court have not, in recent years, made too great a use of their
right to differ publicly from their colleagues. Every right can be
abused and the right of members of the Supreme Court to express
disagreement with the views of their colleagues is no exception.

Just after his elevation to the supreme bench, Justice Frankfurter
stated, in a concurring opinion, "The volume of the Court's business
has long since made impossible the early healthy practice whereby
the Justices gave expression to individual opinions." [33] The practice referred to by the learned judge has persisted to the present day
in other English-speaking countries. The American lawyer who
visits the Law Courts in London perceives this at once. Where he is
normally accustomed to the explanation of a judicial decision by an
opinion of the court, his English confrere is habituated to a *seriatim*
expression of views by each judge who is a member of the tribunal.
One by one, the judges rise and declare their opinions, when judgment is rendered by an English appellate court.

The American lawyer is bound to be somewhat perturbed by the
English practice. Notwithstanding Justice Frankfurter's already
quoted statement, he may doubt whether such a practice is a
"healthy" one. "What is the rule of the case?" is the lawyer's natural query upon the decision of an important case by an appellate
tribunal. It is a question which one may not be able to answer
with any degree of confidence after he has heard the opinions delivered by an English court. Instead of an authoritative opinion
by the tribunal, he has before him a number of opinions, of equally

binding force, each of which approaches the problems to be decided from the viewpoint of its individual author.

The weakness of the English practice of having opinions rendered *seriatim* by each of the judges of a court of last resort lies in its effects upon the certainty of the law. Unless each member of the court approaches the case in the same manner, the public is bound to be left to some extent in the dark on the true *ratio decidendi* of the decision. Even if the judges agree in the result, if they differ as to the grounds of decision, it is difficult to ascertain the doctrine of the case. It is only when there is an expression of opinion by the court as a whole, rather than by each of the individual judges, that this difficulty can be avoided. This was seen at an early time in American judicial history by John Marshall. When he was appointed Chief Justice of the Supreme Court, that tribunal followed the English custom of having opinions pronounced by each of the individual Justices. The advent of Marshall to the Chief Justiceship led to an immediate change in the Court's practice. As soon as he began to discharge his duties as head of the Court, states Beveridge's classic life of the great Chief Justice,

he quietly began to strengthen the Supreme Court. He did this by one of those acts of audacity that later marked the assumptions of power which rendered his career historic. For the first time the Chief Justice disregarded the custom of the delivery of opinions by the Justices *seriatim,* and, instead, calmly assumed the function of announcing, himself, the views of that tribunal.[34] Thus Marshall took the first step in impressing the country with the unity of the highest court of the Nation.[35]

The change from the individual to the Court opinion was admirably suited to strengthen the power and prestige of the fledgling Supreme Court. To John Marshall, the needed authority and dignity of the Court could be attained only if the principles it proclaimed were pronounced by a united tribunal. To win conclusiveness and fixity for its constructions, he strove for a Court with a single voice. How well he succeeded in this is shown by the reception accorded Justice Johnson, when the latter sought for the first time to express his own views, in a case where he disagreed with the decision of the Court. "During the rest of the Session," he plaintively affirmed in a letter to Thomas Jefferson, "I heard nothing but Lectures on the Indecency of Judges cutting at each other, and the Loss of Reputation which the Virginia appellate Court had sustained by pursuing such a course."[36]

If carried to its extreme, the right to concur or dissent leads back, in effect, to the practice of the pre-Marshall Court of *seriatim* opinions. Yet this is, in truth, what has seemed to be happening in the Supreme Court of the past two decades. That the Court has divided publicly more frequently in recent years than was formerly the case is common knowledge. What is not so generally realized is the extent to which dissents have come to dominate the work of the Court. In the past, the public expression of dissent was, even in sharply divided Courts, a comparatively rare thing; since 1937, it has become literally an everyday occurrence. In the 1934–36 period, when the high Court collided directly with the New Deal, and there was a basic cleavage between the majority and Justices Stone, Brandeis, and Cardozo on the proper scope of judicial review, the dissents annually delivered ranged from 13 to 19 per cent of the cases decided with opinion by the Court.[37] Since 1937, even though there has been no such fundamental split in philosophy on the bench, the percentage of cases in which dissenting opinions were filed has always been much higher. In the terms from 1943 to 1956, in fact, dissents were delivered in the majority of cases; in the 1951 and 1952 terms, dissents were filed in an almost incredible 80 and 71 per cent of the cases formally disposed of by the Court.[38]

Nor is this the whole picture. The phenomenal increase in dissents has been accompanied by a similar proliferation of concurring opinions. Justices of the present Supreme Court express disagreement with the reasoning of their colleagues, even though they concur in their decision, with a readiness that would have shocked earlier Courts. It is common today for opinions of the Court to be followed by one or more such concurrences. Indeed, in all too many cases now, the opinion formally delivered for the Court is but the starting point for one seeking to analyze the high Court's jurisprudence. More and more in recent years, the majority viewpoint of the Court has been represented by more than one opinion. Sometimes, this is carried to an almost ridiculous extreme. Thus, in the *Steel-Seizure* case, as already emphasized,* the six Justices who concurred in the decision each delivered a separate opinion approaching the issues in the case from his own individual viewpoint, and another opinion was rendered for the dissenting Justices. The observer could well feel that he was listening to the House of Lords in its most expansive moments, when he heard the profusion of opinions delivered in such a case.

The overabundance of opinions delivered by members of the Supreme Court in recent years means that that tribunal has forgotten the lesson taught by our early judicial history. As soon as he was appointed Chief Justice, John Marshall saw that a court of last re-

* *Supra,* p. 71.

sort could function effectively as the ultimate interpreter of the organic instrument and statute law, only if it spoke through opinions rendered by the tribunal as a whole. If it voiced merely the views of its individual members, its pronouncements would never have the authority needed to enable it to take the place intended for it under our constitutional system, as one of the three coordinate branches of government. Would-be concurring or dissenting Justices have the duty of exercising their right to disagree with their colleagues in such a way that the effectiveness and dignity of the Court itself as an authoritative expounder of the law will not be impaired.

It will, however, be objected that this approach is unfair to the individual judge, who happens to have his own strong views upon the issues involved in a case. "Angry, vindictive passions of men," sagely stated a Supreme Court Justice over a century and a half ago, "have too often made their way into judicial tribunals." [39] A judge, stalwart though he may be, is a human being, and is it not setting him too exacting a standard to expect him to be silent, for the sake of the tribunal upon which he sits, when he burns to speak out as an individual? The judge who feels strongly is more likely to say, as once did Justice Johnson, that it is better for him to express his own opinion, "to avoid having an ambiguous decision hereafter imputed to me, or an opinion which I would not wish to be understood to have given." [40]

The Justice who feels this way should, nevertheless, remember that he is primarily a member of a collegiate body. His greatest responsibility is to contribute what he can to the effective functioning of his tribunal as a team. It is only when such effective functioning is assured in the individual case that he may exercise his right to disagree publicly with his colleagues. If the Court is so divided that a free employment of the right to express individual views will lead, in effect, to *seriatim* opinions by the members of the tribunal, each judge has the duty of asking himself whether his first obligation is not to hold his peace, rather than to contribute to the atomization of the authority of the Court.

On this, as on so many other matters, the members of the contemporary high Court have much to learn from John Marshall. There have been few judges with stronger convictions than the great Chief Justice. Yet he was ever ready to stifle the expression of his own opinion, if it was necessary for the effective working of the Court as a whole. In the well-known case of *The Flying Fish*,[41] to take one example, there are clear indications in Chief Justice Marshall's opinion that his own convictions were at variance with the views enunciated by him in rendering the opinion of the Court.

The expression of his own opinion gave way here to the desirability of having a united Court speak through its Chief Justice, in an important case, which touched upon the relations of the United States with other countries.

The abuse which has occurred in recent years in the excessive use by individual Justices of their right to concur or dissent must, in large part, be laid at the door of Justice Holmes. It cannot be denied that the reputation of that jurist was to a considerable extent built upon the celebrated opinions in dissent which he rendered. Ever since his retirement, members of our Court of last resort have harbored the hope that the mantle of the "great dissenter" might descend upon their shoulders.

These would-be Yankees from Olympus have, all the same, forgotten that the greatness of Justice Holmes lay in the fact that he did not dissent merely for dissent's sake. This was acutely seen in a commemorative essay by Sir Frederick Pollock, Justice Holmes's famous English correspondent. "Some people seem to think that Mr. Justice Holmes is always dissenting," his comment reads. "Does he really dissent much oftener than his learned brethren, or is the impression due to the weight rather than the number of the dissents?" [42]

In actual fact, as students of Justice Holmes's life and character have concluded, he himself hated to dissent; he by no means desired to be known as fighter, reformer, or dissenter.[43] This is clear from his very first dissenting opinion, after his appointment to the Supreme Court. After stating, at the beginning of that opinion, that he was unable to agree with the judgment of the majority of the Court, he went on to assert, "I think it useless and undesirable, as a rule, to express dissent." [44]

Why, then, feeling as he did about the general undesirability of dissent, did Justice Holmes feel bound in this case to express dissent and to give his reasons for it? The answer is to be found in the very next sentence of his opinion: "Great cases like hard cases make bad law." [45] A judge is, in other words, justified in expressing his own views in dissent or concurrence, when the particular decision disposes of a "great case" or a "hard case." But, if the case is an ordinary one, which does not have real importance in shaping the law of the future, a separate statement of views is not justified, merely because the particular judge may happen to disagree with his colleagues.

That Justice Holmes, himself, tried to adhere to this principle is indicated by his record upon the supreme bench. It shows that his practice was far from that of publicly stating his views in every instance where they differed from those of other members of the Court. While he was on the bench in Washington, the Supreme Court disposed of just under six thousand cases with opinion. Yet the "great dissenter" saw the need to state his opinion in dissent only seventy times. The facts amply bear out the conclusion of a popular biographer that "the fact that Holmes's most famous opinions were dissenting opinions by no means sets him down as a rebel or a no-sayer. Holmes always regretted the necessity of dissenting, believing that too many dissents detract from the prestige of the Court." [46]

Members of the high Court who seek to emulate Justice Holmes tend all too often to overlook this. Mere disagreement with the opinion of the Court should not of itself lead to the expression of individual concurring or dissenting views. As Justice Holmes himself saw, nothing takes away more from the prestige of an appellate tribunal than constant public articulation of dissidence among its members.

"A dissent in a court of last resort," stated Chief Justice Hughes in an oft-quoted passage, "is an appeal to the brooding spirit of the law, to the intelligence of a future day, when a later decision may possibly correct the error into which the dissenting judge believes the court to have been betrayed." [47] Such appeals can surely be made more successfully by judges who have not exercised overfreely their right of speaking to the future. The most effective dissents are not those rendered by Justices who have established a reputation for consistently disagreeing with their colleagues.

In his lectures upon the nature of the judicial process, Justice Cardozo reminded us that the cases which come to courts of last resort for decision fall into three categories. The majority do not present any difficulty for the judge, for the law and its application are plain with regard to them. In another and considerable percentage, the rule of law is certain, and the application alone doubtful. Finally, there is a small percentage of cases "where a decision one way or the other, will count for the future, will advance or retard . . . the development of the law." [48]

It is only in cases of the last type that a member of a court of last resort is justified in expressing publicly his concurring or dissenting opinion. It is true that, in the second category also, differences of opinion are often provoked among judges. In those cases, all the same, lack of judicial unanimity should not be carried beyond the conference room. As Justice Cardozo puts it, they are the cases where jurisprudence remains untouched, regardless of the outcome. A public rupture of the unity of an appellate tribunal is warranted only where the outcome of the case will produce a positive effect upon jurisprudence. These are the cases where the creative element in the judicial process finds its opportunity and power.[49]

Here, we are back, in essence, to the test laid down by Justice Holmes in his first dissenting opinion on the supreme bench. Re-iteration of his principle, which is essentially that of Justice Cardozo as well, that dissent is undesirable except in what he terms "great cases" and "hard cases," is justified because it contains the key to the true function of concurring and dissenting opinions.

The purpose of such opinions is not to enable their authors publicly to state their views, whenever they happen to differ from those of their colleagues. It may well be, as Justice Johnson pointed out in 1816, that "Few minds are accustomed to the same habit of thinking, and our conclusions are most satisfactory to ourselves, when arrived at in our own way." [50] But this does not excuse a return to the pre-Marshall practice of *seriatim* opinions. Unless an expression of separate views will make a significant contribution to the development of the law, the would-be concurrer or dissenter would do better to guard his silence.

The concurring and dissenting opinion, like the majority opinion itself, thus should seek primarily to aid in the development of the law by a reasoned statement of the principles involved in the given affair. In the ordinary case, which leaves jurisprudence untouched, the articulation of individual opinions can serve only to confuse. The concurrence and dissent can then have little function other than to leave an impression of dissonance within the tribunal.

If the Justice who finds that his convictions are not in harmony with those of his colleagues can honestly say, as did the dissenting Justice in an early case, "I view this question as one of the most momentous importance," [51] then he is justified if he states an opinion in concurrence or dissent. Yet, even in such cases, the role of concurrer or dissenter should be exercised with restraint. In the first place, even in a case significant enough to warrant the enunciation of separate views, the right of the individual judge to differ should not be exercised outside the conference room, where the disagreement within the Court is so great that its expression in public would tend to destroy confidence in the authority and prestige of the tribunal. The members of the highest Court have no duty greater than that of preventing the spectacle of a separate opinion by each Justice, each of whom deals with the case from his own individualistic point of view.

And, when concurring or dissenting opinions are expressed, here, too, the judge should not overlook the need for self-restraint. Com-

paratively speaking, we are told, the dissenter tends to be irresponsible: "The spokesman of the court is cautious, timid, fearful of the
vivid word, the heightened phrase. He dreams of an unworthy
breed of scions, the spawn of careless dicta. . . . Not so, however,
the dissenter. . . . For the moment, he is a gladiator making a last
stand against the lions." [52]

The Justice who concurs or dissents often exercises a freedom of
expression which is not entirely becoming to a member of a tribunal
of last resort. He, indeed, is the first to recognize this when he de-
livers the opinion for the majority of the Court. At that time, the
realization that he is pronouncing the law in the given case restrains
the looseness of the language which he might otherwise utter. The
importance which concurring and dissenting opinions have assumed
in the jurisprudence of the Supreme Court should, nevertheless, lead
the judges who deliver such opinions to exercise the caution which
they show in pronouncing majority opinions. The peril of misun-
derstanding should put a warning finger to the lips of the concurring or dissenting Justice, as it does to the spokesman of the majority of the Court. Especially is this true insofar as expressions of
acerbity toward his colleagues who do not agree with him are concerned. The candor of a Cato is wholly out of place in a member
of the highest judicial tribunal.

"Liberals" versus "Conservatives"

It has become the common practice in recent years to classify
Justices of the Supreme Court according to their supposedly liberal
or conservative predilections. To those who engage in this sort of
pastime, Felix Frankfurter has always posed something of a problem. Before his appointment to the bench, he was known for his
interest in libertarian causes and particularly for his courageous
efforts on behalf of the anarchists Sacco and Vanzetti. He was also
closely connected in the public mind with the New Deal, and it was
generally expected that, once on the high Court, he would continue
along a more or less liberal path. Yet, if one thing is certain about
Supreme Court personnel, it is that it is extremely risky to make
dogmatic predictions in advance of how new appointees to the high
bench will behave after they don the robe. "One of the things,"
Justice Frankfurter has recently stated, "that laymen, even lawyers,
do not always understand is indicated by the question you hear so
often: 'Does a man become any different when he puts on a gown?'
I say, 'If he is any good, he does.' " [53] Certainly Felix Frankfurter
himself has seemed to many an altogether different man as a Justice

than he was off the bench. As a law professor, he was clearly characterized as one of the country's foremost liberals (to many, in fact, he was the Academic Eminence behind the New Deal); as a judge, he has, more often than not, been a leading spokesman of what is usually termed the "conservative wing" of the high Court.

If Justice Frankfurter has thus proved a puzzle to many of those who applauded his appointment, the same has not been true of Justice Douglas. Before his elevation to the Court, William O. Douglas was a prominent administrator in the Washington of the New Deal; as a Justice, he has (along with Justice Black) been the leading spokesman of the so-called "liberal wing" of the high tribunal. In recent years, in truth, it is Justice Douglas who has become identified in the public mind as the most articulate libertarian spokesman on the high bench. Whatever else might be said about Justice Douglas, it must be conceded that there is nothing of the Sancho Panza in his makeup. He it was who issued the stay order in the *Rosenberg* case,* and he it has been who has constantly tilted a lance against all restrictions upon civil liberties called forth by the cold-war tensions of the postwar decade. He has never allowed his judicial position to condition the freedom of his utterances off the bench on public issues. Whether his robe be donned or doffed, Justice Douglas has been, to the public, the personification of the ultra-liberal.

A propensity for tilting at windmills is, however, hardly a qualification for judicial office. It is necessary to probe more deeply into the work of Justices Frankfurter and Douglas before one can make an informed value judgment on their respective performances on the bench. The difference between the two Justices is, despite the popular conception, not so much a difference between their adherence to liberal or conservative viewpoints. So much must be clear to anyone who is at all familiar with Felix Frankfurter's lifelong record of partisanship for libertarian causes. Nor could it seriously be contended by one who knows either the man or his work that Justice Frankfurter on the bench has been less sympathetic toward such causes than he was prior to his judicial appointment. Yet Frankfurter, consciously liberal though his personal predilections may be, has been most careful throughout his career on the high Court to preserve a sharp distinction between his preferences as an individual and his work as a judge. Himself a lifelong student of the Supreme Court, he has always been keenly aware of the perils pregnant in a judicial tribunal which seeks to transform its private views of right into legal standards.

* *Supra,* p. 336.

In this respect, Justice Frankfurter has merely been trying to follow in the judicial footsteps of Oliver Wendell Holmes, whom he has always considered his mentor on the bench. This does not mean that the two Justices have been alike in their personal philosophies. On the contrary, Holmes was without a doubt extremely conservative, both in his economic and political views, while Frankfurter, so far as we can tell, has never personally departed from the liberal tenets that guided his career before his appointment to the Court. But this difference in personal beliefs has not prevented both Justices from reaching similar results with regard to the proper scope of the high tribunal's power to review the constitutionality of laws. Holmes, economic conservative though he was personally, did not allow his individual opinions to interfere with the scope which he felt the legislature possessed to enact regulatory laws that ran counter to many of the basic beliefs of conservatives like himself. The same has been true of Justice Frankfurter; libertarian though he has been personally, he has always been ready to defer to the legislative judgment, even on laws that restrict civil liberties.

In a biographical sketch written in 1944, Justice Frankfurter neatly summed up the relationship between the personal philosophy of Justice Holmes and his approach to the Supreme Court's reviewing function:

His personal views often ran counter to legislation that came before him for judgment. He privately distrusted attempts at improving society by what he deemed futile if not mischievous economic tinkering. But that was not his business. It was not for him to prescribe for society or to deny it the right of experimentation within very wide limits. That was to be left for contest by the political forces in the state. The duty of the Court was to keep the ring free.[54]

As is often the case with such writings, they are as much a mirror of their author as of their subject. Justice Frankfurter, too, has not allowed his personal libertarian views to prevent him from giving ample scope to the legislative judgment in civil liberties cases.

Rigorous employment of the Frankfurter approach and the emotional trials it may present to the sensitive judge are perhaps best seen in Justice Frankfurter's dissent in West Virginia Board of Education v. Barnette,[55] a case which caused as much soul searching on the Justice's part as any he has participated in. At issue in Barnette was the action of a state making it compulsory for children in its public schools to participate in a flag-salute ceremony. In the case itself, the compulsory flag-salute requirement had been applied to several of the Jehovah's Witness sect, whose religious

beliefs forbade them to salute the flag or any other "graven image."
As a private individual, Justice Frankfurter certainly found state
action such as that at issue repugnant. He began his dissent from
the Court's holding that the flag-salute requirement was invalid with
the following striking statement of where his personal preferences
lay: "One who belongs to the most vilified and persecuted minority
in history is not likely to be insensible to the freedoms guaranteed
by our Constitution. Were my purely personal attitude relevant I
should wholeheartedly associate myself with the general libertarian
views in the Court's opinion, representing as they do the thought
and action of a lifetime." [56] Yet the whole point about Justice
Frankfurter's position is that his private notions of policy were irrelevant, no matter how deeply he might cherish them. The sole
question for the judge in such a case was that of the reasonableness,
not that of the desirability, of challenged action. In Frankfurter's
own words, "It can never be emphasized too much that one's own
opinion about the wisdom or evil of a law should be excluded altogether when one is doing one's duty on the bench. The only opinion of our own even looking in that direction that is material is our
opinion whether legislators could in reason have enacted such a
law." [57] In a case like this, said Justice Frankfurter, "it would require more daring than I possess to deny that reasonable legislators
could have taken the action which is before us for review." [58] That
being the case, in the Frankfurter view, the challenged state action had to be upheld however much it conflicted with the Justice's
personal libertarian views. As was the case with Justice Holmes,
the individual preferences of the judge had to give way before the
legislative judgment where there was no absence of a rational
justification for such judgment.

It has, however, come to be denied by many that Justice Frankfurter is the true successor to Oliver Wendell Holmes on the high
bench. It is said that, while Holmes deferred to the legislative
judgment on economic issues, he would scarcely have done so on
the issues of civil liberty that have been coming before the Supreme
Court in the past two decades. To proponents of this view, the
Justices who approximate most closely to Holmes on the present
Court are those who, like Douglas, have been most militant in trans-
lating their personal libertarian preferences into the law which they
would make could they but speak for a majority of the Court.

It is probably irrelevant whether Douglas or Frankfurter is more
the Holmes brought up to date on the high bench. All the same,
it is difficult to see how men can presume to speak for one no
longer here in a manner which runs so counter to both his views and

actions. Certainly, if there is any Justice today who does violence
to the basic Holmes tenet of judicial self-restraint, it is Justice
Douglas. It is true that he does so in cases involving personal
rights, whereas the doctrine of deference was applied by Holmes
in cases where property rights were at issue. Yet, it is somewhat
presumptuous, at the very least, to assert that it follows from this
that Holmes would have limited his restrained approach to economic cases. On the contrary, there is no reason to assume that
he would have denied the ample scope to legislative judgment on
matters of personal right that he gave to it on matters of economic
policy.[59] There is no indication in his work that personal rights
were deemed worthy of preferential treatment as compared with
other constitutional rights. Indeed, if there is one thing clear about
the philosophy of Justice Holmes, it is that he eschewed absolutes;
even freedom of speech he did not erect into a dogma of absolute
validity, nor did he enforce it to doctrinaire limits.[60] A typical
Holmesian comment on his approach to the review power is contained in a passage already quoted: * "About seventy-five years
ago I learned that I was not God. And so, when the people of the
various states want to do something I can't find anything in the
Constitution expressly forbidding them to do, I say, whether I
like it or not, 'Goddammit, let 'em do it!' " [61] Would such a judge
really have presumed to play God vis-à-vis the legislature in civil
liberties cases?

It is inaccurate to state the differences between Justices Frankfurter and Douglas by labeling the one a conservative and the other
a liberal. It is not nearly as simple as that. The difference between
the two is primarily that of the extent to which they apply the
Holmes philosophy of judicial self-restraint to the issues of today.
Both Douglas and Frankfurter are united in agreement that that
philosophy should determine the judicial approach in cases similar
to those in which it was articulated by Justice Holmes—in those
involving matters of economic policy. They stand apart on the
question of whether the rule of self-restraint is the proper one in
the civil liberties cases that have arisen since Holmes left the
bench. But their difference on this score is not accurately described
in terms of the liberal-conservative dichotomy. If we are to use the
customary labels, in truth, which Justice are we to say is the more
"liberal," he who uses his position to promote his personal libertarian
philosophy in noneconomic cases or he who consistently exercises
his authority in accord with the Holmesian tenet that the primary

* Supra, p. 23.

responsibility of a liberal judge is to restrain undue assertions of judicial power?

Deference and Democracy

Speaking in 1954 in a House of Commons debate, Sir Winston Churchill referred to Her Majesty's judges in the following terms: "There is nothing like them at all in our Island. They are appointed for life. They cannot be dismissed by the executive Government. . . . They have to interpret the law according to their learning and conscience." [62]

Sir Winston's words are at least equally applicable to the Justices of our Supreme Court. Of them, too, it may be said that there is nothing like them in our country. If anything, in fact, the members of the highest American Court enjoy an even more exalted status than the judges in Britain. It is their unique function to serve as the guardians of the constitutional ark. To enable them to do so effectively, they are armed with the awesome authority to nullify any governmental act deemed by them to be in conflict with any provision of the organic instrument. It may be true, as has been emphasized throughout this book, that the Court's power in this respect has come to be exercised more circumspectly than was formerly the case. Yet this scarcely lessens the importance of the power itself or the essential part that it continues to play in our polity.

With the advent in the years following 1937 of an entirely reconstituted Supreme Court, whose philosophic bases were so different from those of the pre-1937 Court, there were many who thought that the high bench would cease to be the vital center of our constitutional system. As one commentator puts it, those of that opinion expected the Court to wither away, much as the State was supposed to do in Marxist theory.[63] Yet, if one thing is clear, it is that both the Soviet State and our high tribunal have anything but withered away in the past two decades. The Supreme Court has been as much in the headlines and controversy in recent years as it has ever been, and, while this may hardly be a criterion of its effectiveness, it surely shows the continued significance of the Court in our constitutional scheme of things. It is, in fact, difficult to see how the high bench could cease playing a crucial part while our system remained true to its constitutional foundations. The Court as a working institution must always remain indispensable to government under a written Constitution. "It is," Justice Jackson wrote shortly before his death in 1954, "difficult to see how the provisions of a 150-year-old written document can have much vitality if there is not some permanent institution to translate them into current commands and to see to their contemporary application." [64] Like the report of Mark Twain's death, the predicted demise of the Supreme Court has been grossly exaggerated.[65] The work of the Court may be different, but it is no less consequential today than it has always been in our system. It would, in Justice Jackson's words delivered in 1940 at ceremonies observing the 150th anniversary of the Supreme Court, "be a mistake to regard the work of the Court of our own time as either less important or less constructive than that of its earlier days." [66]

The work of the highest tribunal in the past two decades has been of particular importance, for the constitutional revolution of 1937 inaugurated, as has been constantly stressed, a drastic reversal in our constitutional jurisprudence. In a sense, then, the Justices of the post-1937 Court have been in the position of Founding Fathers to those who will follow them on the bench. To be sure, the latter will re-examine the work of this Court and will reject some of it. Time will certainly disclose that, when the post-1937 Court has thought it was correcting errors of its predecessors, it was at times only substituting some of its own. But the greater number of its judgments are bound to become a part of the basic philosophy upon which future Courts will act.

The analysis given in the prior chapters of the different facets of the work of the Supreme Court in the past two decades does, it is believed, demonstrate a consistent basic philosophy which has motivated the bulk of its decisions. That philosophy is essentially the doctrine of self-restraint or deference to the legislative will, of which Justice Frankfurter has been the most articulate advocate on the high bench. The constitutional revolution of 1937 and its consolidation in the years since that time have meant the abandonment by the Court of its position of predominance in the constitutional structure. The super-legislature has been replaced by the referee whose task is, it is true, to keep the ring free, but only from governmental action that passes the bounds of reason. Rational basis has plainly taken the place of the individual judicial judgment as the criterion in determining the validity of a law. It may well be true that the Court has not adhered in every case to the doctrine of deference to the legislator. Complete consistency is, however, no more to be found in a judicial tribunal than it is in any other human institution. All the same, to one who has read thus far, it should be clear that deference to the legislative judgment has been the basic theme in the high Court's work and the one that helps to explain most of its post-1937 decisions, and particularly those that might otherwise present puzzling problems of analysis, such as some of the cases dealt with in Chapter 9.

It cannot be denied that there are those, both on and off the bench, who look upon the doctrine of deference as essentially a hypocrite's tool to justify the rendering of illiberal decisions. To them, the rule of restraint may have been sound when preached by Holmes in protest against judicial interference with legislative attempts at economic regulation; but it is out of place when it hobbles the judiciary in its ability to check legislative restrictions upon civil liberties. To those of this belief, the notion of judicial detachment from partisan politics is, at best, a pious fiction; the judge, they frankly admit, should use his authority to promote the policies which he personally favors. The view of those who believe this way was well stated in a 1947 article by Arthur M. Schlesinger: "The Court cannot escape politics: therefore, let it use its political power for wholesome social purposes. Conservative majorities in past Courts have always legislated in the interests of the business community; why should a liberal majority tie its hands by a policy of self-denial . . . ?" [67]

This view is wholly inconsistent with the very bases of the constitutional revolution of 1937 and the bulk of the Supreme Court's jurisprudence since that time. More than that, as already shown, it involves a return to the pre-1937 approach to questions of constitutional law which, one would have thought, had been conclusively rejected by the post-1937 high tribunal. What is it essentially that the pre-1937 Court had done which the constitutional revolution of 1937 was supposed to end? It was the erection by the high Court of its own personal predilections into constitutional dogmas which could not be touched by the legislature. It is true that the old Court's action in that respect was almost entirely limited to the field of economic policies; yet that was so because it was in that field that legislative action was threatening to upset the Justices' preconceptions. Today, all the members of the Court would find the economic philosophy that prevailed on the pre-1937 tribunal anachronistic. None of the present Justices has difficulty in accepting a need for government regulation that would have seemed all but revolutionary to the old Court majority. In the area of economic legislation, then, self-restraint accords with the personal convictions of the present Court. The same is not true in the area of personal regulation. Here, legislative restrictions run counter to the libertarian predilections of at least a majority of the Court. But are these Justices any more justified in writing their private notions of policy into the Constitution than were their pre-1937 predecessors?

The great ordinances of the Constitution, declared Justice Holmes in a celebrated passage, do not establish and divide fields of black and white.[68] Nor does the organic instrument differentiate qualitatively between the different provisions that make up its text. As no constitutional guarantee enjoys preference, the members of the high Court are not justified in engaging in mutilating selection of the Constitution, giving full effect to those parts only which for the moment find personal favor with individual Justices. This, in the words of the Court itself in 1956,[69] is to disrespect the Constitution.

Nor is it enough to say, as do those who reject the limited judicial role, that we can safely allow the Supreme Court to intervene actively only in cases involving personal rights. That may well be the area that for the moment finds favor. But are we justified in assuming that the preponderance on the Court will always be with those who are of the present Justices' persuasion? "Yesterday," said Justice Frankfurter in a recent address, "the active area in this field was concerned with 'property.' Today it is 'civil liberties.' Tomorrow it may again be 'property.' Who can say that in a society with a mixed economy, like ours, these two areas are sharply separated, and that certain freedoms in relation to property may not again be deemed, as they were in the past, aspects of individual freedom?" [70] To allow judicial activism, today, on matters of civil liberty would be to open the door to similar activism, tomorrow, in areas which may happen then to find favor. Fundamentally, of course, this would mean an abandonment of the self-restraint which has dominated the Court's jurisprudence during the last two decades and a return to the essentials of the Court's role during the pre-1937 period.

It should not be forgotten that, no matter how we may gloss over it, judicial review is basically an undemocratic institution. Through the exercise of its review power the Supreme Court may enable the will even of the great majority of the people to be frustrated. That this is no mere theoretical possibility is shown by what actually happened in the pre-1937 period. The high bench then consistently set at naught policies which most of the country approved of, and it did so by resort to constitutional theories that we now see had clearly become outmoded. The Supreme Court is essentially a check of the past upon the present. But it is the present that represents the will of the people and it is that will that must ultimately be given effect in a democracy. If the democratic bases of our system are to be respected, the review power of the one non-democratic organ in our Government must be exercised with rigorous self-restraint. It is paradoxical that it is those who profess to be the preachers of present-day liberalism who now assert the need for the Court to assume a more active responsibility in reviewing the constitutionality of legislative action. For if there was one principle that nineteenth-century liberals agreed upon, it was that of the primacy of legislative power. To them, it was the elected representatives of the people, not an irresponsible judicial organ, who were endowed with primacy in the governmental structure. Yet, whatever else we may think of the tenets of nineteenth-century liberalism, is this not the proper distribution of governmental power in a representative democracy? Laws duly enacted by the people's representatives should not be aborted by judicial fiat unless the judges are presented with no other choice in the matter. For the Court to assert again the degree of power it exercised prior to 1937 would be for it to deflect responsibility from those on whom in a democratic society it must ultimately rest—the people.[71] As Chief Justice John Marshall aptly said, "The people made the Constitution, and the people can unmake it. It is the creature of their will, and lives only by their will." [72] It is the Supreme Court's responsibility to see that their will is faithfully executed in the determination of controversies.

There are those, however, who fear that the high Court's deferential attitude toward the legislature tends to leave us utterly unprotected against violations of constitutional right. To them, the Court is the only real bulwark of our liberties; if it removes itself from the center of the constitutional stage, they are afraid that our only substantial safeguard will be gone. The present writer would be the last to denigrate our highest tribunal and the cardinal task which it performs in a system such as ours. But to overmagnify the role of the Court is to perform neither it nor the country a service. It was with profound insight that one of the greatest of modern jurists, Judge Learned Hand, declared, in a passage that has become deservedly famous,

I often wonder whether we do not rest our hopes too much upon constitutions, upon laws and upon courts. These are false hopes, believe me, these are false hopes. Liberty lies in the hearts of men and women; when it dies there, no constitution, no law, no court can save it; no constitution, no law, no court can even do much to help it. While it lies there it needs no constitution, no law, no court to save it.[73]

Though Judge Hand's comment may seem to some too pessimistic a gospel of despair, it contains a fundamental truth to one concerned about the proper constitutional role of the Supreme Court. Courts are not the only instruments of government that can be relied upon to preserve us against harm. If they were, they would be largely inadequate for the purpose. Civil liberties can at best draw only limited strength from judicial guarantees. Courts can hardly be expected by themselves to preserve us against our own excesses. It is no idle speculation to inquire which comes first, judicial enforcement of constitutional rights or a free and tolerant society. Must we, in Justice Jackson's recent question, first maintain a system of free government to assure a free and independent judiciary, or can we rely upon an aggressive, activist judiciary to guarantee free government? [74] Americans not infrequently forget the answer to this question. Without a doubt, the Court is of basic importance, particularly in molding public opinion to accept fully the implications of the rule of law; the law enunciated by it may have a definite educative as well as a normative effect. But it is the attitude of the society and of its organized political forces, rather than of its purely legal machinery alone, that is the controlling force in the character of free institutions.

The true relationship between the Supreme Court and the society in which it functions was stated on the 150th anniversay of the Court by Justice Jackson: "However well the Court and its bar may discharge their tasks, the destiny of this Court is inseparably linked to the fate of our democratic system of representative government." [75] And is that not the way it should be in a system such as ours? Democracy without the rule of law is a contradiction in terms. At the same time, judicial functions, as we have evolved them in this country, can only be discharged in a democratic society; it is that kind of society alone that is really willing to submit its conflicts to adjudication and to subordinate power to reason. To be truly effective, nevertheless, the high Court must exercise its functions in harmony with the basic principles of our society. Answering a tribute from the bar of Philadelphia in 1831, John Marshall remarked that, if he might be permitted to claim for himself and his associates any part of the kind things that were said, it would be this, that they had "never sought to enlarge the judicial power beyond its proper bounds, nor feared to carry it to the fullest extent that duty requires." [76] This remains the safe twofold rule; nor is the first part of it any less important than the second. If anything, indeed, it is more so, for it is once again the part which most requires to be emphasized in answer to the criticism of those who would freely use the judicial brake on the democratic process by invalidating laws that go against their grain. Today, as in Marshall's day, proper deference toward the representatives of the people remains the judicial handmaiden of democracy.

NOTES

NOTES

Chapter 1

1. Edward S. Corwin, *The Constitution of the United States of America: Analysis and Interpretation* (Washington, D.C.: Government Printing Office, 1953), p. x.
2. *Ibid.*
3. Charles Warren, *The Supreme Court in United States History* (3 vols.; Boston: Little, Brown & Co., 1922), III, 470-71.
4. Fred Rodell, *Nine Men: A Political History of the Supreme Court from 1790 to 1955* (New York: Random House, Inc., 1955), p. 33.
5. *The Economist*, May 10, 1952, p. 371.
6. 3 Howell's State Trials 45 (1627).
7. Quoted in Corwin, *op. cit.*, p. xi.
8. Joseph Story, *Commentaries on the Constitution of the United States* (Boston: Hilliard, Gray, and Co., 1833), § 1570.
9. James A. Bayard in the House of Representatives, February 20, 1802, quoted in Charles Warren, *Congress, The Constitution and the Supreme Court* (Boston: Little, Brown & Co., 1925), p. 42.
10. Arthur T. Vanderbilt, *The Doctrine of the Separation of Powers and Its Present-Day Significance* (Lincoln: University of Nebraska Press, 1953), p. 140.
11. James Bryce, *The American Commonwealth* (2 vols.; New York: Macmillan Co., 1917), I, 274.
12. Robert H. Jackson, *The Struggle for Judicial Supremacy* (New York: Alfred A. Knopf, Inc., 1941), p. 315.
13. Quoted in *ibid.*, p. 314.
14. Paraphrasing Burnet v. Coronado Oil & Gas Co., 285 U.S. 393, 408 (1932).
15. The Genesee Chief, 12 How. 443 (U.S. 1851).
16. Smith v. Allwright, 321 U.S. 649, 665 (1944).
17. McCulloch v. Maryland, 4 Wheat. 316, 407 (U.S. 1819).
18. Jackson, *op. cit.*, p. 86.
19. *Ibid.*, p. xi.
20. *Ibid.*, p. 286.
21. 294 U.S. 240 (1935).
22. Charles E. Hughes, *The Supreme Court of the United States* (New York: Columbia University Press, 1928), p. 95.
23. See, e.g., Jackson, *op. cit.*, p. 174.

24. *Ibid.*, p. 175.
25. Schechter Poultry Corp. v. United States, 295 U.S. 495 (1935).
26. United States v. Butler, 297 U.S. 1 (1936).
27. Morehead v. New York *ex rel.* Tipaldo, 298 U.S. 587 (1936).
28. Jackson, *op. cit.*, p. 175.
29. 1 Cranch 137 (U.S. 1803).
30. *Id.* at 178.
31. 9 Wheat. 1, 197 (U.S. 1824).
32. 198 U.S. 45 (1905).
33. *Id.* at 56.
34. Brandeis, J., dissenting, in Burns Baking Co. v. Bryan, 264 U.S. 504, 534 (1924).
35. Harold J. Laski, *The American Democracy* (New York: Viking Press, Inc., 1948), p. 111.
36. Quoted in Edward S. Corwin, *Constitutional Revolution, Ltd.* (Claremont, Calif.: Pomona College, 1941), p. 38.
37. Dissenting, in Nebbia v. New York, 291 U.S. 502, 556 (1934).
38. Lochner v. New York, 198 U.S. at 75.
39. Paraphrasing Holmes, J., dissenting, in Baldwin v. Missouri, 281 U.S. 586, 595 (1930).
40. Sutherland, J., dissenting, in West Coast Hotel Co. v. Parrish, 300 U.S. 379, 401 (1937).
41. *Ibid.*
42. *Id.* at 402.
43. *Ibid.*
44. United States v. Butler, 297 U.S. 1, 78–79 (1936).
45. *Loc. cit.* in note 39.
46. Corwin, *Constitutional Revolution, Ltd.* (1941).
47. Quoted in Alpheus T. Mason, *The Supreme Court: Vehicle of Revealed Truth or Power Group* (Boston: Boston University Press, 1953), p. 57.
48. *Ibid.*
49. 198 U.S. at 75.
50. Owen J. Roberts, *The Court and the Constitution* (Cambridge: Harvard University Press, 1951), p. 61.
51. *Ibid.*, p. 62.
52. Benjamin N. Cardozo, *The Growth of the Law* (New Haven: Yale University Press, 1924), p. 72.
53. West Coast Hotel Co. v. Parrish, 300 U.S. 379, 402 (1937).
54. Powell, quoted in Mason, *op. cit.* in note 47, p. 39.
55. West Coast Hotel Co. v. Parrish, 300 U.S. 379 (1937).
56. Jackson, *op. cit.*, pp. 207–8.
57. Merlo J. Pusey, *Charles Evans Hughes* (2 vols.; New York: Macmillan Co., 1951), II, 757.
58. For a confirmation of this view, see Felix Frankfurter, *Of Law and Men* (New York: Harcourt, Brace & Co., Inc., 1956), pp. 208–10.
59. Adkins v. Children's Hospital, 261 U.S. 525 (1923).
60. Wright v. Vinton Branch, 300 U.S. 440 (1937).
61. Virginian Ry. v. Federation, 300 U.S. 515 (1937).
62. Sonzinsky v. United States, 300 U.S. 506 (1937).
63. Jackson, *op. cit.*, p. 213.
64. Corwin, *Constitutional Revolution, Ltd.*, p. 65.
65. Jackson, *op. cit.*, p. 214.

66. 301 U.S. at 41.
67. *Id.* at 99.
68. Helvering v. Davis, 301 U.S. 619 (1937).
69. Steward Machine Co. v. Davis, 301 U.S. 548 (1937); Carmichael v. Southern Coal Co., 301 U.S. 495 (1937).
70. Quoted in Charles P. Curtis, *Lions under the Throne* (Boston: Houghton Mifflin Co., 1947), p. 281.
71. Jackson, *op. cit.,* p. 323.
72. Lochner v. New York, 198 U.S. at 76.
73. Brandeis, J., dissenting, in Burns Baking Co. v. Bryan, 264 U.S. 504, 534 (1924).
74. Holmes, J., dissenting, in Meyer v. Nebraska, 262 U.S. 390, 412 (1923).
75. Dissenting, in West Virginia Board of Education v. Barnette, 319 U.S. 624, 647 (1943).
76. Jackson, *op. cit.,* pp. xv-xvi.

Chapter 2

1. Robert H. Jackson, *The Struggle for Judicial Supremacy* (New York: Alfred A. Knopf, Inc., 1941), p. 104.
2. Edouard Lambert, *Le Gouvernement des juges* (Paris: Giard et Cie., 1921).
3. Dissenting, in West Virginia Board of Education v. Barnette, 319 U.S. 624, 649 (1943).
4. J. B. Thayer, quoted *id.* at 669-70.
5. Andrew A. Bruce, *The American Judge* (New York: Macmillan Co., 1924), pp. 6, 8.
6. Compare Jackson, *op. cit.,* at p. 323.
7. William O. Douglas, *We the Judges* (Garden City, N.Y.: Doubleday & Co., Inc., 1956), p. 192.
8. Edward S. Corwin, *The Constitution of the United States of America: Analysis and Interpretation* (Washington, D.C.: Government Printing Office, 1953), p. 118.
9. Wickard v. Filburn, 317 U.S. 111, 121 (1942).
10. Corwin, *op. cit.,* p. 192.
11. Wickard v. Filburn, 317 U.S. 111, 120 (1942).
12. 9 Wheat. 1 (U.S. 1824).
13. *Id.* at 229-30.
14. *Id.* at 196-97.
15. *Id.* at 227.
16. The leading case is Kidd v. Pearson, 128 U.S. 1 (1888).
17. Oliver Iron Co. v. Lord, 262 U.S. 172 (1923).
18. United States v. Butler, 297 U.S. 1 (1936).
19. 298 U.S. 238 (1936).
20. *Id.* at 304.
21. *Id.* at 309.
22. Schechter Poultry Corp. v. United States, 295 U.S. 495 (1935).
23. United States v. Butler, 297 U.S. 1 (1936).
24. 247 U.S. 251 (1918).
25. *Id.* at 276,

26. Jackson, *op. cit.*, p. 163.
27. Quoted in Edward S. Corwin, *Constitutional Revolution, Ltd.* (Claremont, Calif.: Pomona College, 1941), p. 76.
28. Jackson, *op. cit.*, p. 197.
29. National Labor Relations Board v. Jones & Laughlin Steel Corp., 301 U.S. 1 (1937).
30. *Id.* at 38.
31. *Id.* at 41.
32. Sunshine Coal Co. v. Adkins, 310 U.S. 381, 393, 396 (1940).
33. Mulford v. Smith, 307 U.S. 38 (1939).
34. Waialua Agricultural Co. v. Maneja, 216 F.2d 466, 476 (9th Cir. 1954).
35. Maneja v. Waialua Agricultural Co., 349 U.S. 254, 259 (1955).
36. 301 U.S. at 37.
37. United States v. Carolene Products Co., 304 U.S. 144 (1938).
38. Mulford v. Smith, 307 U.S. 38 (1939).
39. 312 U.S. 100 (1941).
40. *Id.* at 116.
41. *Id.* at 115.
42. *Id.* at 113.
43. *Id.* at 115.
44. McCulloch v. Maryland, 4 Wheat. 316, 403 (U.S. 1819).
45. National Labor Relations Board v. Fainblatt, 306 U.S. 601 (1939).
46. Concurring, in Schechter Poultry Corp. v. United States, 295 U.S. 495, 554 (1935).
47. Paraphrasing Stone, C. J., dissenting, in Borden Co. v. Borella, 325 U.S. 679, 685 (1945).
48. United States v. Wrightwood Dairy Corp., 315 U.S. 110, 120 (1942).
49. 317 U.S. 111 (1942).
50. Douglas, *op. cit.*, p. 209.
51. 317 U.S. at 125, 129.
52. Kirschbaum Co. v. Walling, 316 U.S. 517 (1942).
53. Martino v. Mich. Window Cleaning Co., 327 U.S. 178 (1946).
54. Mabee v. White Plains Pub. Co., 327 U.S. 178 (1946).
55. Consolidated Edison Co. v. National Labor Relations Board, 305 U.S. 197 (1938).
56. Schechter Poultry Corp. v. United States, 295 U.S. 495, 546 (1935).
57. Pensacola Telegraph Co. v. Western Union Co., 96 U.S. 1, 9 (1878).
58. United States v. South-Eastern Underwriters Association, 322 U.S. 533 (1944).
59. Paul v. Virginia, 8 Wall. 168 (U.S. 1869).
60. Prudential Ins. Co. v. Benjamin, 328 U.S. 408, 415-16 (1946).
61. *Id.* at 429.
62. Jackson, J., 322 U.S. at 589.
63. Paraphrasing Stone, C. J., dissenting, *id.* at 583.
64. *Id.* at 595.
65. Douglas, *op. cit.*, p. 217.
66. 9 Wheat. 1 (U.S. 1824).
67. 311 U.S. 377 (1940).
68. *Id.* at 407.
69. Douglas, *op. cit.*, p. 218.
70. 311 U.S. at 426.
71. Oklahoma v. Atkinson Co., 313 U.S. 508, 525-26 (1941).

72. Douglas, *op. cit.*, p. 220.
73. 311 U.S. at 433.
74. Douglas, *op. cit.*, p. 220.
75. Walton H. Hamilton and Douglass Adair, *The Power to Govern; the Constitution—Then and Now* (New York: W. W. Norton & Co., 1937), pp. 62-63.
76. Douglas, *op. cit.*, p. 193.
77. Polish Alliance v. National Labor Relations Board, 322 U.S. 643, 650 (1944).
78. Joseph Story, *Commentaries on the Constitution of the United States* (Boston: Hilliard, Gray, and Co., 1833), § 906.
79. Quoted in Corwin, *The Constitution of the United States . . .* , pp. 112-13.
80. See *ibid.*, p. 113.
81. United States v. Butler, 297 U.S. 1, 66 (1936).
82. *Id.* at 75.
83. McCulloch v. Maryland, 4 Wheat. 316, 431 (U.S. 1819).
84. Mulford v. Smith, 307 U.S. 38, 48 (1939).
85. Sonzinsky v. United States, 300 U.S. 506, 513 (1937).
86. United States v. Sanchez, 340 U.S. 42, 44 (1950).
87. Helvering v. Davis, 301 U.S. 619, 640 (1937).
88. United States v. Sanchez, 340 U.S. 42, 44 (1950).
89. 345 U.S. 22 (1953).
90. Dissenting, in Lewis v. United States, 348 U.S. 419, 425 (1955).
91. Dissenting, 345 U.S. at 39.
92. Black, J., dissenting, *id.* at 36.
93. *Id.* at 28.
94. *Ibid.*
95. *Id.* at 38.
96. United States v. Rumely, 345 U.S. 41, 43 (1953).
97. 273 U.S. 135, 175 (1927).
98. Quinn v. United States, 349 U.S. 155, 160-61 (1955).
99. United States v. Rumely, 345 U.S. 41, 44 (1953).
100. Tenney v. Brandhove, 341 U.S. 367, 378 (1951).
101. Dissenting, in Eisler v. United States, 338 U.S. 189, 196 (1949).
102. 345 U.S. 41 (1953).
103. *Id.* at 47.
104. Douglas, *op. cit.*, p. 147.
105. 103 U.S. 168 (1880).
106. United States v. Rumely, 345 U.S. at 46.
107. Quoted, *id.* at 43.
108. United States v. Fleischman, 339 U.S. 349, 365 (1950).
109. 319 U.S. 463 (1943).
110. 328 U.S. 303 (1946).
111. 350 U.S. 11 (1955).
112. Frankfurter, J., concurring, in American Federation of Labor v. American Sash Co., 335 U.S. 538, 555 (1949).
113. *Ibid.*
114. J. B. Thayer, quoted in West Virginia Board of Education v. Barnette, 319 U.S. 624, 670 (1943).
115. Missouri, Kansas & Texas Ry. Co. v. May, 194 U.S. 267, 270 (1904).
116. Frankfurter, J., dissenting, in West Virginia Board of Education v. Barnette, 319 U.S. 624, 649 (1943).

Chapter 3

1. Rex v. Hampden, 3 Howell's State Trials 826, 1017, 1099 (1637).
2. Rex v. Hampden, 3 Howell's State Trials 826 (1637).
3. *Id.* at 1083.
4. Darnel's Case, 3 Howell's State Trials 1, 37 (1627).
5. Youngstown Sheet & Tube Co. v. Sawyer, 343 U.S. 579 (1952).
6. *Id.* at 641.
7. Compare *id.* at 593.
8. *Id.* at 594.
9. Henry Hallam, *The Constitutional History of England* (2 vols.; New York: A. G. Armstrong, 1897), I, 314.
10. Frankfurter, J., concurring, in United States v. United Mine Workers, 330 U.S. 258, 308 (1947).
11. Taney, C. J., letter of February 16, 1863, printed in 157 U.S. 701, 702.
12. Evans v. Gore, 253 U.S. 245, 253 (1920).
13. Robert H. Jackson, *The Supreme Court in the American System of Government* (Cambridge: Harvard University Press, 1955), p. 26.
14. *The Federalist,* No. 79.
15. *Loc. cit.* in note 10, above.
16. Paul L. Ford, *Writings of Thomas Jefferson* (10 vols.; New York: G. P. Putnam's Sons, 1892-99), IX, 60.
17. 4 Wall. 475 (U.S. 1866).
18. *Id.* at 501.
19. *Id.* at 500.
20. *Loc. cit.* in note 10, above.
21. Quoted in Charles H. McIlwain, *Constitutionalism Ancient and Modern* (Ithaca: Cornell University Press, 1940), pp. 135-36.
22. 332 U.S. 490 (1948).
23. 103 F. Supp. 569, 576 (D.C. 1952).
24. 343 U.S. at 677-78.
25. United States v. Lee, 106 U.S. 196, 220 (1882).
26. Murphy, J., concurring, in Duncan v. Kahanamoku, 327 U.S. 304, 329 (1946).
27. Paraphrasing Hughes, C. J., in Sterling v. Constantin, 287 U.S. 378, 397 (1932).
28. Samuel Rosenman (ed.), *The Public Papers and Addresses of Franklin D. Roosevelt, 1942* (New York: Harper & Brothers, 1950), p. 364.
29. Edward S. Corwin and Louis W. Koenig, *The Presidency Today* (New York: New York University Press, 1956), p. 59.
30. Theodore Roosevelt, *An Autobiography* (New York: The Macmillan Co., 1914), p. 372.
31. 343 U.S. at 589.
32. *Harvard Classics* (New York: Collier and Son), XLIII, 100.
33. 343 U.S. at 587, 589.
34. *Id.* at 587.
35. 103 F. Supp. at 573.
36. C. Herman Pritchett, *Civil Liberties and the Vinson Court* (Chicago: University of Chicago Press, 1954), p. 211.
37. 343 U.S. at 589.
38. Justice Clark.

39. 343 U.S. at 597.
40. *Id.* at 602.
41. *Id.* at 659.
42. *Id.* at 662.
43. *Ibid.*
44. Pritchett, *op. cit.,* p. 207.
45. 343 U.S. at 597.
46. 3 Howell's State Trials at 1125.
47. 343 U.S. at 633.
48. *Id.* at 659.
49. *Ibid.*
50. Compare Corwin and Koenig, *op. cit.,* p. 59.
51. 3 Howell's State Trials at 976.
52. *Id.* at 977.
53. 3 Howell's State Trials 193-94 (1628).
54. Mitchell v. Harmony, 13 How. 115, 134 (U.S. 1851).
55. *Ex parte* Milligan, 4 Wall. 2, 127 (U.S. 1866).
56. 3 Howell's State Trials at 1084.
57. Hirabayashi v. United States, 320 U.S. 81, 101 (1943).
58. 343 U.S. at 654.
59. Corwin and Koenig, *op. cit.,* p. 44.
60. 343 U.S. at 645.
61. Quoted in Edward S. Corwin, *The Constitution of the United States of America: Analysis and Interpretation* (Washington, D.C.: Government Printing Office, 1953), p. 464.
62. Edward S. Corwin, *The President: Office and Powers* (3d ed.; New York: New York University Press, 1948), p. 216.
63. Robert H. Jackson, *The Struggle for Judicial Supremacy* (New York: Alfred A. Knopf, Inc., 1941), p. 201.
64. United States v. Curtiss-Wright Export Corp., 299 U.S. 304, 319 (1936).
65. Ware v. Hylton, 3 Dall. 199, 260 (U.S. 1796).
66. Oetjen v. Central Leather Co., 246 U.S. 297, 302 (1918).
67. Chicago & Southern Air Lines v. Waterman S.S. Co., 333 U.S. 103, 111 (1948).
68. *Ex parte* Peru, 318 U.S. 578, 588-89 (1943).
69. Williams v. Suffolk Insurance Co., 13 Pet. 415, 420 (U.S. 1839).
70. 333 U.S. 103 (1948).
71. *Id.* at 111.
72. *Id.* at 118.
73. The term used, *id.* at 117.
74. 335 U.S. 160 (1948).
75. *Id.* at 170.
76. Black, J., *id.* at 174-75.
77. Ng Fung Ho v. White, 259 U.S. 276, 284 (1922).
78. Jackson, *The Supreme Court in the American System of Government,* p. 64.
79. Quoted in Harold J. Laski, *The American Presidency* (New York: Harper & Bros., 1940), p. 197.
80. Corwin, *The Constitution of the United States* . . . , p. 433.
81. McDougal and Lans, "Treaties and Congressional–Executive or Presidential Agreements: Interchangeable Instruments of National Policy," 54 *Yale Law Journal* 181, 290 (1945).

82. 301 U.S. 324 (1937).
83. *Id.* at 330.
84. *Id.* at 331.
85. 315 U.S. 203 (1942).
86. *Id.* at 230.
87. *Id.* at 231.
88. Ware v. Hylton, 3 Dall. 199, 236 (U.S. 1796). (Emphasis omitted.)
89. Foster v. Neilson, 2 Pet. 253, 314 (U.S. 1829).
90. Head Money Cases, 112 U.S. 580, 598 (1884).
91. 100 *Congressional Record* 1656 (February 15, 1954).
92. See Bernard Schwartz, *American Constitutional Law* (Cambridge: Cambridge University Press, 1955), pp. 187-206.
93. 2 Howell's State Trials 371 (1606).
94. Quoted in William S. Holdsworth, *A History of English Law* (6 vols.; Boston: Little, Brown & Co., 1924), VI, 47, n. 2.
95. 12 Co. Rep. 74 (1611).
96. United States v. Pink, 315 U.S. at 249.
97. 348 U.S. 296 (1955).
98. 204 F.2d 655 (4th Cir. 1953).
99. Youngstown Sheet & Tube Co. v. Sawyer, 343 U.S. at 655.
100. Quoted in Corwin and Koenig, *op. cit.,* p. 61.

Chapter 4

1. See Edward S. Corwin, *Constitutional Revolution, Ltd.* (Claremont, Calif.: Pomona College, 1941), p. 1.
2. Paschukanis (a leading Soviet jurist), quoted in Edgar Bodenheimer, *Jurisprudence* (New York: McGraw-Hill Book Co., Inc., 1940), p. 90.
3. Pound, "Fifty Years of Jurisprudence," 51 *Harvard Law Review* 781 (1938).
4. Youngstown Sheet & Tube Co. v. Sawyer, 343 U.S. 579, 593 (1952).
5. *Ibid.*
6. Cardozo, J., dissenting, in Panama Refining Co. v. Ryan, 293 U.S. 388, 440 (1935).
7. James M. Landis, *The Administrative Process* (New Haven: Yale University Press, 1938), p. 10.
8. Robert H. Jackson, *The Supreme Court in the American System of Government* (Cambridge: Harvard University Press, 1955), pp. 44-45.
9. William O. Douglas, *We the Judges* (Garden City, N. Y.: Doubleday & Co., Inc., 1956), p. 163.
10. Boyce Motor Lines v. United States, 342 U.S. 337 (1952).
11. According to United States v. Howard, 352 U.S. 212 (1957), such an administrative regulation *is* to be treated as a "law" under a statute making it unlawful to violate a "law of the State."
12. Panama Refining Co. v. Ryan, 293 U.S. 388, 421 (1935).
13. Douglas, *op. cit.,* p. 164.
14. *Loc. cit.* in note 12, above.
15. United States v. Chicago, M., St. P. and P. R.R., 282 U.S. 311, 324 (1931).
16. Panama Refining Co. v. Ryan, 293 U.S. 388 (1935); Schechter Poultry Corp. v. United States, 295 U.S. 495 (1935).

17. Panama Refining Co. v. Ryan, 293 U.S. at 430.
18. *Id.* at 553.
19. Fahey v. Mallonee, 332 U.S. 245, 250 (1947).
20. National Broadcasting Co. v. United States, 319 U.S. 190, 216 (1943).
21. *Id.* at 219.
22. Secretary of Agriculture v. Central Roig Refining Co., 338 U.S. 604, 611 (1950).
23. Kenneth C. Davis, *Administrative Law* (St. Paul: West Publishing Co., 1951), p. 46.
24. Humphrey's Executor v. United States, 295 U.S. 602 (1935).
25. Quoted in Arthur T. Vanderbilt's Introduction to Bernard Schwartz, *French Administrative Law and the Common-Law World* (New York: New York University Press, 1954), p. xv.
26. *In re* Larsen, 86 A.2d 430, 435 (N.J. 1952).
27. Wong Yang Sung v. McGrath, 339 U.S. 33, 41 (1950).
28. Jackson, *op. cit.*, p. 51.
29. 349 U.S. 302 (1955).
30. Wong Yang Sung v. McGrath, 339 U.S. 33, 45 (1950).
31. *Report of the Attorney General's Committee on Administrative Procedure* (Washington, D.C.: Government Printing Office, 1941), p. 204.
32. 333 U.S. 683 (1948).
33. *Id.* at 700.
34. *Id.* at 701.
35. Concurring, in Joint Anti-Fascist Refugee Committee v. McGrath, 341 U.S. 123, 178 (1951).
36. Davis, *op. cit.*, p. 330.
37. *Report of the Attorney General's Committee on Administrative Procedure,* p. 45.
38. Quoted in Davis, *op. cit.*, p. 357.
39. Morgan v. United States, 298 U.S. 468 (1936).
40. *Id.* at 480-81.
41. *Id.* at 481.
42. *Ibid.*
43. Federal Communications Commission v. WJR, 337 U.S. 265, 276 (1949).
44. Jones v. Securities and Exchange Commission, 298 U.S. 1, 28 (1936).
45. The term used by Cardozo, J., dissenting, *id.* at 33.
46. United States v. Morgan, 307 U.S. 183, 191 (1939).
47. United States v. Morgan, 313 U.S. 409, 422 (1941).
48. United States v. Morgan, 313 U.S. 409 (1941).
49. Morgan v. United States, 304 U.S. 1, 17-18 (1938).
50. *Id.* at 18.
51. Morgan v. United States, 23 F. Supp. 380, 384 (W.D. Mo. 1937).
52. 313 U.S. at 422.
53. Federal Communications Commission v. Pottsville Broadcasting Co., 309 U.S. 134, 144 (1940).
54. Davis, *op. cit.*, p. 364.
55. Wong Yang Sung v. McGrath, 339 U.S. 33, 36 (1950).
56. *Id.* at 37.
57. Universal Camera Corp. v. National Labor Relations Board, 340 U.S. 474, 487 (1951).
58. 339 U.S. 33 (1950).
59. *Id.* at 41.

60. *Id.* at 40-41.
61. Shaughnessy v. Pedreiro, 349 U.S. 48, 51 (1955).
62. National Labor Relations Board v. Cheney Lumber Co., 327 U.S. 385, 388 (1946).
63. United States v. Interstate Commerce Commission, 337 U.S. 426, 433-34 (1949).
64. Estep v. United States, 327 U.S. 114, 120 (1946).
65. 321 U.S. 288 (1944).
66. *Id.* at 309.
67. *Id.* at 309-10.
68. Brannan v. Stark, 342 U.S. 451 (1952).
69. 327 U.S. 114 (1946).
70. Concurring, *id.* at 136.
71. *Id.* at 120.
72. *Id.* at 122.
73. Shaughnessy v. Pedreiro, 349 U.S. 48, 51 (1955).
74. Fleming v. Moberley Milk Products Co., 160 F.2d 259, 265 (D.C. Cir. 1947).
75. Concurring, in Joint Anti-Fascist Refugee Committee v. McGrath, 341 U.S. 123, 151 (1951).
76. United States v. Storer Broadcasting Co., 351 U.S. 192 (1956).
77. The leading case is Federal Communications Commission v. Sanders Bros. Radio Station, 309 U.S. 470 (1940).
78. 308 U.S. 517 (1939).
79. Dissenting, in Federal Communications Commission v. National Broadcasting Co., 319 U.S. 239, 260 (1943).
80. Lord Hewart, *The New Despotism* (New York: Cosmopolitan Book Corp., 1929), p. 155.
81. Dissenting, in United States v. Storer Broadcasting Co., 351 U.S. 192, 214 (1956).
82. Rochester Telephone Corp. v. United States, 307 U.S. 125, 139-40 (1939).
83. Securities and Exchange Commission v. Chenery Corp., 318 U.S. 80, 94 (1943).
84. Landis, *op. cit.*, p. 152.
85. *Report of the Attorney General's Committee on Administrative Procedure*, p. 88.
86. St. Joseph Stock Yards Co. v. United States, 298 U.S. 38, 51 (1936).
87. Douglas, *op. cit.*, p. 175.
88. National Labor Relations Board v. Nevada Consolidated Copper Co., 316 U.S. 105, 107 (1942).
89. *Ibid.*
90. Universal Camera Corp. v. National Labor Relations Board, 340 U.S. 474, 478 (1951).
91. Quoted in Landis, *op. cit.*, p. 136.
92. 340 U.S. 474 (1951).
93. *Id.* at 487-88.
94. Jaffe, "Judicial Review: Substantial Evidence on the Whole Record," 64 *Harvard Law Review* 1233, 1239 (1951).
95. Matter of Stork Restaurant v. Boland, 282 N.Y. 256, 274 (1940).
96. 285 U.S. 22 (1932).
97. Concurring, in Estep v. United States, 327 U.S. 114, 142 (1946).

98. 314 U.S. 402 (1941).
99. 322 U.S. 111 (1944).
100. *Id.* at 136.
101. *Id.* at 131.
102. Board of Trade v. United States, 314 U.S. 534, 548 (1942).
103. Douglas, *op. cit.*, p. 445.
104. Compare Jaffe, "The Effective Limits of the Administrative Process: A Reevaluation," 67 *Harvard Law Review* 1105, 1107 (1954).
105. Vanderbilt's Introduction to Schwartz, *op. cit.*, p. xiii.
106. Concurring, in Schechter Poultry Corp. v. United States, 295 U.S. 495, 551 (1935).
107. Douglas, J., dissenting, in New York v. United States, 342 U.S. 882, 884 (1951).
108. Southern Railway Co. v. Virginia, 290 U.S. 190, 197 (1933).
109. Douglas, *op. cit.*, p. 179.
110. Peters v. Hobby, 349 U.S. 331, 345 (1955).
111. Securities and Exchange Commission v. Chenery Corp., 332 U.S. 194, 215 (1947).
112. Ellen Wilkinson, in Report of the Committee on Ministers' Powers (Cmd. No. 4060; London: H. M. Stationery Office, 1932), p. 138.

Chapter 5

1. Quoted in Robert H. Jackson, *The Supreme Court in the American System of Government* (Cambridge: Harvard University Press, 1955), p. 54.
2. *Ibid.*
3. Proceedings in memory of Mr. Justice Cardozo, 305 U.S. vi (1938).
4. Fred Rodell, *Nine Men: A Political History of the Supreme Court from 1790 to 1955* (New York: Random House, Inc., 1955), p. 179.
5. Jackson, *op. cit.*, p. 11.
6. Muskrat v. United States, 219 U.S. 346, 361 (1911).
7. C. Herman Pritchett, *Civil Liberties and the Vinson Court* (Chicago: University of Chicago Press, 1954), p. 220.
8. Concurring, in Joint Anti-Fascist Refugee Committee v. McGrath, 341 U.S. 123, 150 (1951).
9. See United States v. Congress of Industrial Organizations, 335 U.S. 106, 124 (1948).
10. Alabama Federation of Labor v. McAdory, 325 U.S. 450, 461 (1945).
11. Giles v. Harris, 189 U.S. 475, 486 (1903).
12. Frankfurter, J., concurring, in United States v. Congress of Industrial Organizations, 335 U.S. 106, 125 (1948).
13. Frankfurter, "A Note on Advisory Opinions," 37 *Harvard Law Review* 1002, 1006 (1924).
14. Cardozo, J., in Self Insurers Association v. Industrial Commission, 224 N.Y. 13, 17 (1918).
15. 306 U.S. 118 (1939).
16. Joint Anti-Fascist Refugee Committee v. McGrath, 341 U.S. 123, 153 (1951).

17. *Ibid.*
18. 330 U.S. 75 (1947).
19. John P. Frank in Edmond Cahn (ed.), *Supreme Court and Supreme Law* (Bloomington: Indiana University Press, 1954), p. 32.
20. Frothingham v. Mellon, 262 U.S. 447 (1923).
21. 342 U.S. 429 (1952).
22. Colegrove v. Green, 328 U.S. 549, 556 (1946).
23. 1 Cranch 137, 170 (U.S. 1803).
24. Ware v. Hylton, 3 Dall. 199 (U.S. 1796).
25. 328 U.S. 549 (1946).
26. *Id.* at 556.
27. 339 U.S. 276 (1950).
28. 328 U.S. at 553-54.
29. Quoted by Douglas, J., dissenting, in South v. Peters, 339 U.S. at 280.
30. Arthur T. Vanderbilt, *The Doctrine of the Separation of Powers and Its Present-Day Significance* (Lincoln: University of Nebraska Press, 1953), p. 138.
31. Dissenting, in *Ex parte* Peru, 318 U.S. 578, 592 (1943).
32. E.g., Harper and Pratt, "What the Supreme Court Did Not Do During the 1951 Term," 101 *University of Pennsylvania Law Review* 439 (1953); Harper and Leibowitz, "What the Supreme Court Did Not Do During the 1952 Term," 102 *id.* 427 (1954).
33. Robert H. Jackson, *The Struggle for Judicial Supremacy* (New York: Alfred A. Knopf, Inc., 1941), p. 281.
34. 304 U.S. 64 (1938).
35. Jackson, *The Supreme Court in the American System of Government,* pp. 34-35.
36. 16 Pet. 1 (U.S. 1842).
37. See Jackson, *The Struggle for Judicial Supremacy,* p. 275.
38. Jackson, *The Supreme Court . . . ,* p. 35.
39. Jackson, *The Struggle for Judicial Supremacy,* p. 274.
40. 304 U.S. at 77.
41. *Id.* at 78.
42. Edward S. Corwin, *The Constitution of the United States of America: Analysis and Interpretation* (Washington, D.C.: Government Printing Office, 1953), p. 605.
43. 304 U.S. at 66.
44. *Id.* at 69.
45. Jackson, *The Struggle for Judicial Supremacy,* p. 272.
46. *Ibid.,* p. 283.
47. See 304 U.S. at 72-73.
48. *Id.* at 74.
49. Fidelity Trust Co. v. Field, 311 U.S. 169, 180 (1940).
50. Jackson, *The Supreme Court . . . ,* p. 36.
51. *Ibid.*
52. West v. American Telephone and Telegraph Co., 311 U.S. 223, 236-37 (1940).
53. Fidelity Trust Co. v. Field, 311 U.S. 169 (1940).
54. King v. Order of Travelers, 333 U.S. 153 (1948).
55. William O. Douglas, *We the Judges* (Garden City, N.Y.: Doubleday & Co., Inc., 1956), p. 102.
56. Meredith v. Winter Haven, 320 U.S. 228 (1943).

57. Compare Frankfurter, J., concurring, in Bernhardt v. Polygraphic Co., 350 U.S. 198, 209 (1956).
58. Holmes, "The Path of the Law," 10 *Harvard Law Review* 457, 459 (1897).
59. Jackson, *The Supreme Court* . . . , p. 37.
60. Bernhardt v. Polygraphic Co., 350 U.S. 198, 208 (1956).
61. Jackson, *The Supreme Court* . . . , p. 36.
62. Frankfurter, J., concurring, in Lumbermen's Casualty Co. v. Elbert, 348 U.S. 48, 54-55 (1954).
63. *Id.* at 59.
64. Dissenting, in National Ins. Co. v. Tidewater Co., 337 U.S. 582, 651 (1949).
65. Bernhardt v. Polygraphic Co., 350 U.S. 198, 203 (1956).
66. Jackson, *The Supreme Court* . . . , p. 36.
67. Frankfurter, J., concurring, in Lumbermen's Casualty Co. v Elbert, 348 U.S. 48, 60 (1954).
68. Concurring, in St. Joseph Stock Yards Co. v. United States, 298 U.S. 38, 92 (1936).
69. McNabb v. United States, 318 U.S. 332, 340 (1943).
70. *Id.* at 340-41.
71. Dissenting, in Uveges v. Pennsylvania, 335 U.S. 437, 449 (1949).
72. Barron v. Mayor of Baltimore, 7 Pet. 243 (U.S. 1833).
73. Frankfurter, J., concurring, in Francis v. Resweber, 329 U.S. 459, 466 (1947).
74. Hurtado v. California, 110 U.S. 516 (1884).
75. 211 U.S. 78 (1908).
76. Hurtado v. California, 110 U.S. 516 (1884).
77. Maxwell v. Dow, 176 U.S. 581 (1900).
78. Twining v. New Jersey, 211 U.S. 78 (1908).
79. Palko v. Connecticut, 302 U.S. 319 (1937).
80. 332 U.S. 46 (1947).
81. *Id.* at 89.
82. Palko v. Connecticut, 302 U.S. at 329.
83. 332 U.S. at 71-72.
84. Morrison, "Does The Fourteenth Amendment Incorporate The Bill of Rights? The Judicial Interpretation," 2 *Stanford Law Review* 140, 161 (1949); Fairman, "Does the Fourteenth Amendment Incorporate the Bill of Rights? The Original Understanding," *id.* at 4.
85. Douglas, *op. cit.,* p. 264.
86. Malinski v. New York, 324 U.S. 401, 415 (1945).
87. Frankfurter, J., concurring, in Adamson v. California, 332 U.S. at 63.
88. *Id.* at 64.
89. Compare United States v. Public Utilities Commission, 345 U.S. 295, 319, 321 (1953).
90. 211 U.S. at 106.
91. Palko v. Connecticut, 302 U.S. at 325-26.
92. *Id.* at 325.
93. Frankfurter, J., concurring, in Francis v. Resweber, 329 U.S. 459, 468 (1947).
94. Rochin v. California, 342 U.S. 165, 169 (1952).
95. Quoted in Douglas, *op. cit.,* p. 272.

96. Frankfurter, J., concurring, in Fikes v. Alabama, 352 U.S. 191, 199 (1957).
97. Frankfurter, J., dissenting, in Irvine v. California, 347 U.S. 128, 145 (1954).
98. 332 U.S. at 69.
99. Concurring, in Rochin v. California, 342 U.S. 165, 177 (1952).
100. Concurring, in LeRoy Fibre Co. v. Chicago, Mil., & St. P. Ry., 232 U.S. 340, 354 (1914).
101. Rochin v. California, 342 U.S. 165, 170 (1952).
102. Edmond Cahn, *The Sense of Injustice* (New York: New York University Press, 1949).
103. Thomas Hobbes, in Jerome Hall, *Readings in Jurisprudence* (Indianapolis: The Bobbs-Merrill Co., 1938), p. 53.
104. Compare Frankfurter, J., concurring, in Haley v. Ohio, 332 U.S. 596, 602 (1948).
105. Rochin v. California, 342 U.S. 165, 171-72 (1952).
106. Cahn, "Authority and Responsibility," 51 *Columbia Law Review* 838, 850 (1951).
107. Galloway v. United States, 319 U.S. 372, 398 (1943).
108. District of Columbia v. Clawans, 300 U.S. 617 (1937).
109. Maxwell v. Dow, 176 U.S. 581 (1900); Jordan v. Massachusetts, 225 U.S. 167, 176 (1912).
110. Palko v. Connecticut, 302 U.S. at 325.
111. Glasser v. United States, 315 U.S. 60, 86 (1942).
112. Thiel v. Southern Pacific Co., 328 U.S. 217 (1946).
113. Ballard v. United States, 329 U.S. 187 (1946). Women can, however, be excluded from state juries according to Fay v. New York, 332 U.S. 261, 290 (1947).
114. Thiel v. Southern Pacific Co., 328 U.S. at 220.
115. Frazier v. United States, 335 U.S. 497 (1948).
116. Dennis v. United States, 339 U.S. 162 (1950).
117. Jackson, J., dissenting, in Frazier v. United States, 335 U.S. at 514.
118. Dissenting, in Dennis v. United States, 339 U.S. at 178.
119. *Loc. cit.* in note 114, above.
120. Smith v. Texas, 311 U.S. 128, 130 (1940).
121. Cassell v. Texas, 339 U.S. 282 (1950).
122. Hernandez v. Texas, 347 U.S. 475, 478 (1954).
123. Moore v. New York, 333 U.S. 565, 569 (1948).
124. 332 U.S. 261 (1947).
125. Murphy, J., dissenting, in Moore v. New York, 333 U.S. 565, 570 (1948).
126. Fay v. New York, 332 U.S. at 288.
127. 304 U.S. 458 (1938).
128. *Id.* at 463.
129. 287 U.S. 45 (1932).
130. 316 U.S. 455 (1942).
131. *Id.* at 473.
132. Palmer v. Asche, 342 U.S. 134, 135 (1951).
133. Dissenting, in Bute v. Illinois, 333 U.S. 640, 677 (1948).
134. 333 U.S. 640 (1948).
135. Uveges v. Pennsylvania, 335 U.S. 437 (1948); Haley v. Ohio, 332 U.S. 596 (1948).
136. Marino v. Ragen, 332 U.S. 561 (1947).

137. Massey v. Moore, 348 U.S. 105 (1954).
138. Gibbs v. Burke, 337 U.S. 773 (1949).
139. 335 U.S. 437 (1948).
140. *Id.* at 441.
141. 316 U.S. at 462.
142. Dissenting, in Bute v. Illinois, 333 U.S. at 678.
143. *Id.* at 681.
144. Chambers v. Florida, 309 U.S. 227, 237-38 (1940).
145. Watts v. Indiana, 338 U.S. 49, 55 (1949).
146. 318 U.S. 332 (1943).
147. Douglas, *op. cit.*, p. 364.
148. See, e.g., United States v. Carignan, 342 U.S. 36 (1951); United States v. Mitchell, 322 U.S. 65 (1944).
149. Upshaw v. United States, 335 U.S. 410 (1948).
150. 342 U.S. 55 (1951).
151. 322 U.S. 143 (1944).
152. *Id.* at 154.
153. Haley v. Ohio, 332 U.S. 596, 600-601 (1948).
154. Watts v. Indiana, 338 U.S. 49 (1949).
155. Turner v. Pennsylvania, 338 U.S. 62, 64 (1949).
156. Harris v. South Carolina, 338 U.S. 68 (1949). Fikes v. Alabama, 352 U.S. 191 (1957), is a more recent case of this type.
157. Watts v. Indiana, 338 U.S. 49, 53 (1949).
158. *Id.* at 58.
159. Gallegos v. Nebraska, 342 U.S. 55 (1951).
160. 346 U.S. 156 (1953).
161. *Id.* at 185.
162. *Id.* at 201.
163. *Id.* at 197.
164. *Id.* at 201.
165. Frankfurter, J., dissenting, in Harris v. United States, 331 U.S. 145, 163 (1947).
166. Weeks v. United States, 232 U.S. 383 (1914).
167. 338 U.S. 25 (1949).
168. *Id.* at 27-28.
169. *Id.* at 29.
170. See, e.g., Breithaupt v. Abram, 352 U.S. 432 (1957); Schwartz v. Texas, 344 U.S. 199 (1952).
171. Stefanelli v. Minard, 342 U.S. 117 (1951).
172. Rea v. United States, 350 U.S. 214 (1956).
173. Willard Hurst in Edmond Cahn (ed.), *Supreme Court and Supreme Law*, p. 59.
174. Yes, according to Francis v. Resweber, 329 U.S. 459 (1947).
175. Yes, according to Solesbee v. Balkcom, 339 U.S. 9 (1950).
176. Yes, according to Leland v. Oregon, 343 U.S. 790 (1952).
177. No, according to Rochin v. California, 342 U.S. 165 (1952). According to Breithaupt v. Abram, 352 U.S. 432 (1957), however, a state may allow the use in evidence of a blood sample taken from defendant's body while he was unconscious following an auto accident.
178. 351 U.S. 12 (1956).
179. Concurring, in Brown v. Allen, 344 U.S. 443, 540 (1953).

Chapter 6

1. Woodrow Wilson, *Constitutional Government in the United States* (New York: Columbia University Press, 1908), p. 173.
2. Quoted in American Communications Association v. Douds, 339 U.S. 382, 415 (1950).
3. Dissenting, in New York v. United States, 326 U.S. 572, 595 (1946).
4. Ableman v. Booth, 21 How. 506, 521 (U.S. 1859).
5. Robert H. Jackson, *The Supreme Court in the American System of Government* (Cambridge: Harvard University Press, 1955), p. 65.
6. United States v. Women's Sportswear Assn., 336 U.S. 460, 464 (1949).
7. Schechter Poultry Corp. v. United States, 295 U.S. 495, 546 (1935).
8. Hurtado v. California, 110 U.S. 516, 536 (1884).
9. 198 U.S. 45 (1905).
10. *Id.* at 56.
11. Concurring, in American Federation of Labor v. American Sash Co., 335 U.S. 538, 543 (1949).
12. Robert H. Jackson, *The Struggle for Judicial Supremacy* (New York: Alfred A. Knopf, Inc., 1941), p. 48.
13. Budd v. New York, 143 U.S. 517, 551 (1892).
14. *Loc. cit.* in note 11, above.
15. 198 U.S. at 53.
16. Dissenting, in Morehead v. New York *ex rel.* Tipaldo, 298 U.S. 587, 632 (1936).
17. Lochner v. New York, 198 U.S. 45 (1905).
18. Adkins v. Children's Hospital, 261 U.S. 525 (1923).
19. Coppage v. Kansas, 236 U.S. 1 (1915).
20. Truax v. Corrigan, 257 U.S. 312 (1921).
21. Morehead v. New York *ex rel.* Tipaldo, 298 N.Y. 587 (1936).
22. Tyson & Bros. v. Banton, 273 U.S. 418 (1927); Ribnik v. McBride, 277 U.S. 350 (1928).
23. Jackson, *The Struggle for Judicial Supremacy*, p. 50.
24. Felix Frankfurter, *Mr. Justice Holmes and the Supreme Court* (Cambridge: Harvard University Press, 1938) lists the cases in Appendix I.
25. Dissenting, in Baldwin v. Missouri, 281 U.S. 586, 595 (1930).
26. International Shoe Co. v. Washington, 326 U.S. 310, 325 (1945).
27. See *loc. cit.* in note 11, above.
28. Dissenting, in Morehead v. New York *ex rel.* Tipaldo, 298 U.S. 587, 636 (1936).
29. 198 U.S. at 75.
30. West Coast Hotel Co. v. Parrish, 300 U.S. 379, 391 (1937).
31. Day-Brite Lighting, Inc. v. Missouri, 342 U.S. 421, 424-25 (1952).
32. *Id.* at 423.
33. Ribnik v. McBride, 277 U.S. 350 (1928).
34. Olsen v. Nebraska, 313 U.S. 236 (1941).
35. Williamson v. Lee Optical Co., 348 U.S. 483, 488 (1955).
36. Lincoln Union v. Northwestern Co., 335 U.S. 525, 537 (1949). See similarly Railway Employees Department v. Hanson, 351 U.S. 225 (1956).
37. Jackson, *The Struggle for Judicial Supremacy*, p. 70.
38. Lincoln Union v. Northwestern Co., 335 U.S. at 536.

39. E.g., Kotch v. Pilot Commissioners, 330 U.S. 552 (1947).
40. E.g., Daniel v. Family Insurance Co., 336 U.S. 220 (1949).
41. Waite, C. J., quoted in *loc. cit.* in note 35, above.
42. Concurring, in Graves v. New York *ex rel.* O'Keefe, 306 U.S. 466, 488 (1939).
43. 4 Wheat. 316 (U.S. 1819).
44. New York v. United States, 326 U.S. 572, 576 (1946).
45. *Ibid.*
46. 11 Wall. 113 (U.S. 1870).
47. Helvering v. Gerhardt, 304 U.S. 405 (1938).
48. Graves v. New York *ex rel.* O'Keefe, 306 U.S. 466 (1939). See also O'Malley v. Woodrough, 307 U.S. 277 (1939), holding the salaries of federal judges subject to taxation.
49. Graves v. New York *ex rel.* O'Keefe, 306 U.S. at 480.
50. Jackson, *The Struggle for Judicial Supremacy,* p. 242.
51. O'Malley v. Woodrough, 307 U.S. 277, 282 (1939).
52. Panhandle Oil Co. v. Knox, 277 U.S. 218 (1928). The tax at issue was imposed upon sales to the Government.
53. James v. Dravo Contracting Co., 302 U.S. 134 (1937).
54. 314 U.S. 1 (1941).
55. Dissenting, in United States v. Allegheny County, 322 U.S. 174, 196 (1944).
56. 342 U.S. 232 (1952).
57. 347 U.S. 110 (1954).
58. Compare Douglas, J., dissenting, *id.* at 126.
59. 326 U.S. 572 (1946).
60. *Id.* at 582.
61. *Ibid.*
62. *Ibid.*
63. *Id.* at 590.
64. Federal Land Bank v. Bismarck Co., 314 U.S. 95, 102 (1941); Pittman v. Home Owners' Loan Corp., 308 U.S. 21, 32 (1939).
65. 326 U.S. at 584.
66. Douglas, J., dissenting, *id.* at 595.
67. *Id.* at 591.
68. *Id.* at 593-94.
69. William O. Douglas, *We the Judges* (Garden City, N.Y.: Doubleday & Co., Inc., 1956), p. 222.
70. License Cases, 5 How. 504, 574 (U.S. 1847).
71. Frankfurter, J., dissenting, in Panhandle Co. v. Michigan Commission, 341 U.S. 329, 339 (1951).
72. Baldwin v. Seelig, 294 U.S. 511, 523 (1935).
73. See *loc. cit.* in note 71, above.
74. Hood & Sons v. DuMond, 336 U.S. 525, 539 (1949).
75. Douglas, *op. cit.,* p. 233.
76. Hood & Sons v. DuMond, 336 U.S. 525, 534-35 (1949).
77. 12 How. 299 (U.S. 1851).
78. *Id.* at 319.
79. *Ibid.*
80. Kelly v. Washington, 302 U.S. 1, 15 (1937).
81. 325 U.S. 761 (1945).
82. *Id.* at 773.

83. Frankfurter, J., concurring, in Morgan v. Virginia, 328 U.S. 373, 388 (1946).
84. 325 U.S. at 773.
85. Compare Terminal Railroad Assn. v. Trainmen, 318 U.S. 1 (1943), where the burden on interstate commerce was so slight that the national interest in uniformity was outweighed by the state interest in enforcing its safety regulations.
86. 303 U.S. 177 (1938).
87. Southern Pacific Co. v. Arizona, 325 U.S. at 783.
88. Maurer v. Hamilton, 309 U.S. 598 (1940).
89. Welch Co. v. New Hampshire, 306 U.S. 72 (1939).
90. Railway Express v. New York, 336 U.S. 106, 111 (1949).
91. Fry Roofing Co. v. Wood, 344 U.S. 157 (1952).
92. California v. Thompson, 313 U.S. 109 (1941).
93. DiSanto v. Pennsylvania, 273 U.S. 34 (1927).
94. Dixie Ohio Co. v. Commission, 306 U.S. 72, 76 (1939).
95. Clark v. Paul Gray, Inc., 306 U.S. 583 (1939).
96. Bode v. Barrett, 344 U.S. 583 (1953). See also Capitol Greyhound Lines v. Brice, 339 U.S. 542 (1950), with an analysis of prior cases at 561.
97. Compare Edwards v. California, 314 U.S. 160 (1941), where the state "embargo" was on indigent nonresidents.
98. E.g., Mullaney v. Anderson, 342 U.S. 415 (1952); Hale v. Bimco Trading Co., 306 U.S. 375 (1939).
99. Buck v. Kuykendall, 267 U.S. 307 (1925).
100. Fry Roofing Co. v. Wood, 344 U.S. 157 (1952).
101. 348 U.S. 61 (1954).
102. Jackson, *The Supreme Court in the American System of Government,* p. 67.
103. Wisconsin v. J. C. Penney Co., 311 U.S. 435, 444 (1940).
104. Jackson, J., dissenting, in State Tax Comm'n v. Aldrich, 316 U.S. 174, 200 (1942).
105. Compare *id.* at 199.
106. Paul A. Freund in Edmond Cahn (ed.), *Supreme Court and Supreme Law* (Bloomington: Indiana University Press, 1954), p. 102.
107. 304 U.S. 307 (1938).
108. Gwin, White & Prince, Inc. v. Henneford, 305 U.S. 434, 439 (1939).
109. Department of Treasury v. Wood Corp., 313 U.S. 62 (1941).
110. Ford Motor Co. v. Beauchamp, 308 U.S. 331 (1939).
111. Butler Bros. v. McColgan, 315 U.S. 501 (1942). See similarly International Harvester Co. v. Evatt, 329 U.S. 416 (1947); International Harvester Co. v. Dept. of Taxation, 322 U.S. 435 (1944).
112. Nashville, C. & St. L. Ry. v. Browning, 310 U.S. 362 (1940). See similarly Canton R. Co. v. Rogan, 340 U.S. 511 (1951).
113. Greyhound Lines v. Mealey, 334 U.S. 653 (1948).
114. Ott v. Mississippi Barge Line, 336 U.S. 169 (1949).
115. International Harvester Co. v. Evatt, 329 U.S. 416, 422-23 (1947).
116. 322 U.S. 292 (1944).
117. Braniff Airways v. Nebraska Board, 347 U.S. 590 (1954).
118. The Court has so held, with regard to taxation of barge lines. Standard Oil Co. v. Peck, 342 U.S. 382 (1952).
119. 309 U.S. 33 (1940).

120. Miller Bros. Co. v. Maryland, 347 U.S. 340, 343 (1954).

121. 300 U.S. 577 (1937).

122. 322 U.S. 327 (1944).

123. Such a use tax was upheld in General Trading Co. v. Tax Comm'n, 322 U.S. 335 (1944).

124. 347 U.S. 340 (1954).

125. *Id.* at 357.

126. License Cases, 5 How. 504, 578-79 (U.S. 1847).

127. Adams Mfg. Co. v. Storen, 304 U.S. 307, 316 (1938).

128. Dissenting, in Gwin, White & Prince, Inc. v. Henneford, 305 U.S. 434, 454 (1939).

129. Concurring, in Morgan v. Virginia, 328 U.S. 373, 387 (1946).

130. Dissenting, in Southern Pacific Co. v. Arizona, 325 U.S. at 788. He repeated this charge in 1946. *Loc. cit.* in note 129, above.

131. Dissenting, in McCarroll v. Dixie Lines, 309 U.S. 176, 189 (1940).

132. Douglas, *op. cit.*, p. 254.

133. Illustrative cases of this type are Dean Milk Co. v. Madison, 340 U.S. 349 (1951); Hood & Sons v. DuMond, 336 U.S. 525 (1949); Toomer v. Witsell, 334 U.S. 385 (1948).

134. Douglas, *op. cit.*, p. 255.

135. Quoted in C. Herman Pritchett, *The Roosevelt Court; A Study in Judicial Politics and Values, 1937-1947* (New York: Macmillan Co., 1948), p. 82.

136. Dissenting, in Hill v. Florida, 325 U.S. 538, 547 (1945).

137. Allen-Bradley Local v. Board, 315 U.S. 740, 749 (1942).

138. Dissenting, in Cloverleaf Co. v. Patterson, 315 U.S. 148, 176-77 (1942).

139. Frankfurter, J., dissenting, *id.* at 178.

140. *Id.* at 179.

141. Rice v. Santa Fe Elevator Corp., 331 U.S. 218, 247 (1947).

142. 347 U.S. 672 (1954).

143. *Id.* at 691.

144. 330 U.S. 767 (1947).

145. Frankfurter, J., dissenting, *id.* at 778-79.

146. *Id.* at 782.

147. Hill v. Florida, 325 U.S. 538 (1945).

148. Automobile Workers v. O'Brien, 339 U.S. 454 (1950).

149. Bus Employees v. Wisconsin Board, 340 U.S. 383 (1951).

150. Garner v. Teamsters Union, 346 U.S. 485 (1953). But compare United Workers v. Laburnum Corp., 347 U.S. 656 (1954).

151. Railway Employees Department v. Hanson, 351 U.S. 262, 311 (1932).

152. Dissenting, in New State Ice Co. v. Liebmann, 285 U.S. 262, 311 (1932).

153. Dissenting, in Federal Power Commission v. East Ohio Gas Co., 338 U.S. 464, 489 (1950).

154. Dissenting, in Bethlehem Steel Co. v. State Labor Relations Board, 330 U.S. at 780.

155. Quoted, in Arthur T. Vanderbilt, *The Doctrine of the Separation of Powers and Its Present-Day Significance* (Lincoln: University of Nebraska Press, 1953), p. 56.

Chapter 7

1. 3 Howell's State Trials 1464-65 (1641).

2. *Id.* at 1464.

3. Robert H. Jackson, *The Supreme Court in the American System of Government* (Cambridge: Harvard University Press, 1955), p. 75.
4. *Id.* at 77.
5. *Loc. cit.* in note 2, above.
6. Meiklejohn, "What Does the First Amendment Mean?" 20 *University of Chicago Law Review* 461, 479 (1953).
7. William O. Douglas, *We the Judges* (Garden City, N.Y.: Doubleday & Co., Inc., 1956), p. 307.
8. Meiklejohn, in note 6, above, and his *Free Speech and Its Relation to Self-Government* (New York: Harper & Bros., 1948).
9. Schenck v. United States, 249 U.S. 47, 52 (1919).
10. Davis v. Beason, 133 U.S. 333, 345 (1890).
11. Frankfurter, J., concurring, in Pennekamp v. Florida, 328 U.S. 331, 352-55 (1946).
12. Frankfurter, J., concurring, in Dennis v. United States, 341 U.S. 494, 525 (1951).
13. Dissenting, in Poulos v. New Hampshire, 345 U.S. 395, 423 (1953).
14. 297 U.S. 1 (1936).
15. *Id.* at 87.
16. 304 U.S. 144 (1938).
17. Frankfurter, J., concurring, in Dennis v. United States, 341 U.S. 494, 526 (1951).
18. 304 U.S. at 152, n. 4.
19. Dissenting, in Milk Drivers Union v. Meadowmoor Co., 312 U.S. 275, 301-2 (1941).
20. Dissenting, in Dennis v. United States, 341 U.S. 494, 580 (1951).
21. Thomas v. Collins, 323 U.S. 516, 530 (1945).
22. See C. Herman Pritchett, *The Roosevelt Court; A Study in Judicial Politics and Values, 1937-1947* (New York: Macmillan Co., 1948), p. 92.
23. Thomas v. Collins, 323 U.S. 516, 526 (1945).
24. 310 U.S. 586 (1940).
25. 319 U.S. 624 (1943).
26. *Id.* at 639.
27. Concurring, in Kovacs v. Cooper, 336 U.S. 77, 95 (1949).
28. Dissenting, in Brinegar v. United States, 338 U.S. 160, 180 (1949).
29. Children's Hospital v. Adkins, 284 Fed. 613, 622 (D.C. Cir. 1922).
30. Dissenting, in West Virginia Board of Education v. Barnette, 319 U.S. at 666.
31. Quoted in Paul A. Freund, *On Understanding the Supreme Court* (Boston: Little, Brown & Co., 1949), p. 14.
32. Quoted, *id.* at 15.
33. Poulos v. New Hampshire, 345 U.S. 395, 405 (1953).
34. John Stuart Mill, *On Liberty* in *Harvard Classics* (New York: Collier and Son), XXV, 210.
35. Dissenting, in Falbo v. United States, 320 U.S. 549, 561 (1944).
36. 303 U.S. 433 (1938).
37. *Id.* at 452. See similarly Schneider v. State, 308 U.S. 147 (1939).
38. 310 U.S. 296 (1940).
39. *Id.* at 305.
40. Largent v. Texas, 318 U.S. 418, 422 (1943). Compare the fourth ordinance at issue in Schneider v. State, 308 U.S. 147, 163-64 (1939).
41. 340 U.S. 268 (1951).

42. 340 U.S. 290 (1951).
43. Fowler v. Rhode Island, 345 U.S. 67, 70 (1953).
44. Concurring, in Niemotko v. Maryland, 340 U.S. at 285.
45. Compare C. Herman Pritchett, *Civil Liberties and the Vinson Court* (Chicago: University of Chicago Press, 1954), p. 193.
46. Jackson, J., in Douglas v. Jeannette, 319 U.S. 157, 178 (1943).
47. Breard v. Alexandria, 341 U.S. 622, 642 (1951).
48. Cox v. New Hampshire, 312 U.S. 569, 574 (1941).
49. Breard v. Alexandria, 341 U.S. 622, 646 (1951).
50. 345 U.S. 395 (1953).
51. *Id.* at 405.
52. Frankfurter, J., concurring, in Niemotko v. Maryland, 340 U.S. at 284.
53. *Id.* at 284-85.
54. Dissenting, in Kunz v. New York, *id.* at 313.
55. 340 U.S. 315 (1951).
56. Pritchett, *Civil Liberties and the Vinson Court,* pp. 62-63.
57. Dissenting, in Kunz v. New York, 340 U.S. at 301.
58. It is perhaps paradoxical that Feiner's conviction was thus upheld while that at issue in Terminiello v. Chicago, 337 U.S. 1 (1949), where there had been a clear breach of the peace, was upset on technical grounds.
59. Saia v. New York, 334 U.S. 558, 561 (1948).
60. Dissenting, *id.* at 563.
61. *Id.* at 562.
62. Kovacs v. Cooper, 336 U.S. 77, 87 (1949).
63. 319 U.S. 141 (1943).
64. *Id.* at 149.
65. Frankfurter, J., dissenting, *id.* at 153.
66. Quoted in Breard v. Alexandria, 341 U.S. 622, 639, n. 27 (1951).
67. 341 U.S. 622 (1951).
68. *Id.* at 645. Though the Court tries to distinguish Martin v. Struthers, it is hard to disagree with the dissenting Justices who assert that the Breard holding is contrary to that of the earlier case.
69. Douglas v. Jeannette, 319 U.S. 157, 181 (1943).
70. Senn v. Tile Layers Union, 301 U.S. 468, 478 (1937).
71. 310 U.S. 88 (1940).
72. *Id.* at 104.
73. *Ibid.*
74. E.g., Cafeteria Union v. Angelos, 320 U.S. 293 (1943); Bakery Drivers Local v. Wohl, 315 U.S. 769 (1942); American Federation of Labor v. Swing, 312 U.S. 321 (1941).
75. Quoted by Frankfurter, J., concurring, in Kovacs v. Cooper, 336 U.S. 77, 96 (1949).
76. See Pritchett, *The Roosevelt Court,* p. 220.
77. See Freund, *On Understanding the Supreme Court,* p. 18.
78. Douglas, J., concurring, in Bakery Drivers Local v. Wohl, 315 U.S. 769, 776 (1942).
79. 336 U.S. 490 (1949).
80. Building Service Union v. Gazzam, 339 U.S. 532, 537 (1950).
81. Hughes v. Superior Court, 339 U.S. 460, 465 (1950).
82. Plumbers Union v. Graham, 345 U.S. 192 (1953); Building Service Union v. Gazzam, 339 U.S. 532 (1950).
83. Hughes v. Superior Court, 339 U.S. 460 (1950).

84. Teamsters Union v. Hanke, 339 U.S. 470 (1950).
85. *Id.* at 474.
86. James Bryce, *Modern Democracies* (2 vols.; New York: Macmillan Co., 1921), I, 109.
87. Douglas, *op. cit.,* p. 322.
88. Patterson v. Colorado, 205 U.S. 454, 462 (1907).
89. Hannegan v. Esquire, 327 U.S. 146, 151 (1946).
90. Douglas, *op cit.,* p. 327.
91. National Broadcasting Co. v. United States, 319 U.S. 190, 226 (1943).
92. *Id.* at 227.
93. Winters v. New York, 333 U.S. 507, 510 (1948).
94. 343 U.S. 495 (1952).
95. Mutual Film Corp. v. Industrial Commission, 236 U.S. 230, 244 (1915).
96. 343 U.S. at 501.
97. Douglas, J., concurring, in Gelling v. Texas, 343 U.S. 960, 961 (1952).
98. See Douglas and Black, J. J., concurring, in Superior Films v. Dept. of Education, 346 U.S. 587, 588 (1954).
99. 343 U.S. at 504-5.
100. 4 Blackstone's Commentaries 151.
101. Dissenting, in Zorach v. Clauson, 343 U.S. 306, 317 (1952).
102. *Id.* at 313.
103. Quoted by Rutledge, J., dissenting, in Everson v. Board of Education, 330 U.S. 1, 64 (1947).
104. See Kedroff v. St. Nicholas Cathedral, 344 U.S. 94 (1952), holding that a state may not intervene in the conflicts of religious sects.
105. See also Article VI, Section 3, of the Constitution, which expressly outlaws test oaths for holders of public office.
106. See Joseph Story, *Commentaries on the Constitution of the United States* (Boston: Hilliard, Gray, and Co., 1833), § 1879.
107. 325 U.S. 561 (1945).
108. 328 U.S. 61 (1946).
109. Dissenting, in West Virginia Board of Education v. Barnette, 319 U.S. at 654.
110. Concurring, in McCollum v. Board of Education, 333 U.S. 203, 213 (1948).
111. 330 U.S. 1 (1947).
112. *Id.* at 15-16.
113. *Loc. cit.* in note 110, above.
114. 330 U.S. at 17.
115. Zorach v. Clauson, 343 U.S. 306, 312 (1952).
116. Jacobson v. Massachusetts, 197 U.S. 11 (1905).
117. Prince v. Massachusetts, 321 U.S. 158 (1944).
118. Frankfurter, J., dissenting, in West Virginia Board of Education v. Barnette, 319 U.S. at 654.
119. *Id.* at 655.
120. 330 U.S. at 18.
121. *Ibid.*
122. 333 U.S. 203 (1948).
123. *Id.* at 210.
124. *Id.* at 212.
125. 343 U.S. 306 (1952).
126. *Id.* at 315.

127. *Id.* at 314.
128. Black, J., dissenting, *id.* at 318.
129. Jackson, J., *id.* at 324.
130. Concurring, in Everson v. Board of Education, 333 U.S. at 238.
131. Douglas, *op. cit.*, p. 413.
132. Nixon v. Herndon, 273 U.S. 536 (1927). See similarly Nixon v. Condon, 286 U.S. 73 (1932).
133. Grovey v. Townsend, 295 U.S. 45 (1935).
134. Paraphrasing Nixon v. Condon, 286 U.S. 73, 83 (1932).
135. 321 U.S. 649 (1944).
136. *Id.* at 664.
137. *To Secure these Rights, The Report of the President's Committee on Civil Rights* (New York: Simon & Schuster, Inc., 1947), p. 79.
138. Buchanan v. Warley, 245 U.S. 60 (1917).
139. Corrigan v. Buckley, 271 U.S. 323 (1926).
140. Shelley v. Kraemer, 334 U.S. 1, 13 (1948).
141. Corrigan v. Buckley, 271 U.S. at 330.
142. 334 U.S. 1 (1948).
143. *Id.* at 20.
144. Barrows v. Jackson, 346 U.S. 249 (1953).
145. 163 U.S. 537 (1896).
146. *Id.* at 551.
147. Brown v. Board of Education, 347 U.S. 483, 488 (1954).
148. 163 U.S. at 551.
149. Harlan, J., *id.* at 559.
150. Strauder v. West Virginia, 100 U.S. 303, 307 (1880).
151. Shelley v. Kraemer, 334 U.S. at 22.
152. 175 U.S. 528 (1899).
153. 275 U.S. 78 (1927).
154. Missouri *ex rel.* Gaines v. Canada, 305 U.S. 337 (1938); Sipuel v. Board of Regents, 332 U.S. 631 (1948); Sweatt v. Painter, 339 U.S. 629 (1950); McLaurin v. Oklahoma State Regents, 339 U.S. 637 (1950).
155. 347 U.S. 483 (1954).
156. *Id.* at 495.
157. *Id.* at 494.
158. 349 U.S. 294 (1955).
159. *Id.* at 301.
160. *Id.* at 300.
161. *Ibid.*
162. Marbury v. Madison, 1 Cranch 137, 176 (U.S. 1803).
163. Quoted, in Edward S. Corwin, *The Constitution of the United States of America: Analysis and Interpretation* (Washington, D.C.: Government Printing Office, 1953), p. xi.
164. Frankfurter, J., concurring in United States v. United Mine Workers, 330 U.S. 258, 312 (1947).

Chapter 8

1. Rutledge, J., dissenting, in Yakus v. United States, 321 U.S. 414, 461 (1944).
2. *Lincoln's Complete Works,* Gettysburg Edition (12 vols.; New York: Francis D. Tandy Co., 1905), X, 66.

3. Hirabayashi v. United States, 320 U.S. 81, 93 (1943).
4. Jackson, J., concurring, in Woods v. Miller, 333 U.S. 138, 146 (1948).
5. Robert H. Jackson, *The Supreme Court in the American System of Government* (Cambridge: Harvard University Press, 1955), p. 60.
6. *Ex parte* Merryman, 17 Fed. Cas. 144, 152 (1861).
7. Jackson, *The Supreme Court* . . . , p. 76.
8. *Ex parte* Merryman, 17 Fed. Cas. 144, 153 (1861).
9. *Ex parte* Quirin, 317 U.S. 1, 25 (1942).
10. *Id.* at 35.
11. *In re* Yamashita, 327 U.S. 1 (1946); Homma v. Patterson, 327 U.S. 759 (1946).
12. Quoted in Wesley McCune, *The Nine Young Men* (New York: Harper & Bros., 1947), p. 194.
13. Rutledge, J., dissenting, in *In re* Yamashita, 327 U.S. at 49.
14. *Id.* at 29.
15. 339 U.S. 763 (1950).
16. 338 U.S. 197 (1948).
17. *Id.* at 201.
18. 343 U.S. 341 (1952).
19. 351 U.S. 470 (1956).
20. *Id.* at 477.
21. 350 U.S. 11 (1955).
22. Concurring, in Duncan v. Kahanamoku, 327 U.S. 304, 335 (1946).
23. See Bernard Schwartz, *Law and the Executive in Britain* (New York: New York University Press, 1949), p. 309.
24. Quoted in William S. Holdsworth, *A History of English Law* (6 vols.; Boston: Little, Brown & Co., 1924), VI, 227.
25. 4 Wall. 2 (U.S., 1866).
26. Murphy, J., concurring, in Duncan v. Kahanamoku, 327 U.S. 304, 325-26 (1946).
27. *Ex parte* Milligan, 4 Wall. at 127.
28. 327 U.S. 304 (1946).
29. Murphy, J., *id.* at 328.
30. *Id.* at 336.
31. Jackson, J., dissenting, in Korematsu v. United States, 323 U.S. 214, 242-43 (1944).
32. Hirabayashi v. United States, 320 U.S. 81, 105-6 (1943).
33. 320 U.S. 81 (1943).
34. *Id.* at 100.
35. *Id.* at 111, per Murphy, J.
36. 323 U.S. 214 (1944).
37. *Id.* at 217-18.
38. *Id.* at 224.
39. Hirabayashi v. United States, 320 U.S. at 108.
40. 323 U.S. 283 (1944).
41. *Id.* at 302.
42. *Id.* at 304.
43. *Id.* at 310.
44. Jackson, *The Supreme Court* . . . , p. 60.
45. The cases are listed in Edward S. Corwin, *The Constitution of the United States of America: Analysis and Interpretation* (Washington, D.C.: Government Printing Office, 1953), p. 298, n. 6.

46. 344 U.S. 149 (1952).
47. *Id.* at 155-56.
48. *Id.* at 156, per Douglas, J.
49. Jackson, *loc. cit.* in note 5, above.
50. Selective Draft Law Cases, 245 U.S. 366 (1918).
51. Lichter v. United States, 334 U.S. 742, 756 (1948).
52. *Id.* at 755.
53. United States v. Bethlehem Steel Corp., 315 U.S. 289, 305 (1942).
54. 321 U.S. 414 (1944).
55. 321 U.S. 503 (1944).
56. *Id.* at 537, per Roberts, J.
57. 322 U.S. 398 (1944).
58. Lichter v. United States, 334 U.S. 742, 754 (1948).
59. *Id.* at 780.
60. Compare Frankfurter, J., concurring, in Korematsu v. United States, 323 U.S. at 224.
61. 321 U.S. at 462, per Rutledge, J.
62. 295 U.S. 495 (1935).
63. Stewart v. Kahn, 11 Wall. 493, 507 (1871).
64. 333 U.S. 138 (1948).
65. *Id.* at 142-43.
66. *Id.* at 143.
67. Compare Jackson, J., concurring, *id.* at 147.

Chapter 9

1. Thomas Carlyle, *Characteristics* in *Harvard Classics* (New York: Collier and Son), XXV, 333.
2. *Id.* at 345.
3. Frankfurter, J., dissenting, in West Virginia Board of Education v. Barnette, 319 U.S. 624, 665 (1943).
4. Dissenting, in Yakus v. United States, 321 U.S. 414, 461 (1944).
5. Schenck v. United States, 249 U.S. 47, 52 (1919).
6. *Ibid.*
7. Frankfurter, J., concurring, in Pennekamp v. Florida, 328 U.S. 331, 353 (1946).
8. Dissenting, in Abrams v. United States, 250 U.S. 616, 627 (1919).
9. Dissenting, in Brinegar v. United States, 338 U.S. 160, 180 (1949).
10. Concurring, in Dennis v. United States, 341 U.S. 494, 539-40 (1951).
11. 341 U.S. 494 (1951).
12. See Sacher v. Association of the Bar, 347 U.S. 388 (1954); Isserman v. Ethics Committee, 345 U.S. 927 (1953); Sacher v. United States, 343 U.S. 1 (1952).
13. 341 U.S. at 501.
14. *Ibid.*
15. *Ibid.*
16. *Id.* at 508.
17. *Id.* at 509.
18. *Id.* at 510.
19. *Id.* at 510-11.
20. Douglas, J., *id.* at 588.

21. *Id.* at 589.
22. *Id.* at 546-47.
23. See Alan Barth, *The Loyalty of Free Men* (New York: Viking Press, Inc., 1951), p. 21.
24. Concurring, in American Communications Assn. v. Douds, 339 U.S. 382, 424-31 (1950). (Emphasis omitted.)
25. Dennis v. United States, 341 U.S. at 552.
26. *Id.* at 551-52.
27. *Id.* at 550.
28. 342 U.S. 580 (1952).
29. Ng Fung Ho v. White, 259 U.S. 276, 284 (1922).
30. 342 U.S. at 587-88.
31. *Id.* at 588-89.
32. *Id.* at 590.
33. 347 U.S. 522 (1954).
34. *Id.* at 529.
35. 342 U.S. 524 (1952).
36. *Id.* at 590.
37. *Ibid.*
38. Carlyle, *Characteristics,* p. 345.
39. Garner v. Los Angeles Board, 341 U.S. 716 (1951).
40. Adler v. Board of Education, 342 U.S. 485 (1952).
41. 341 U.S. at 724-25.
42. Concurring, in Joint Anti-Fascist Refugee Committee v. McGrath, 341 U.S. 123, 178 (1951).
43. Parker v. Lester, 227 F.2d 708, 718 (9th Cir. 1955).
44. 349 U.S. 331 (1955).
45. Concurring, *id.* at 350-51.
46. 341 U.S. 918 (1951).
47. 182 F.2d 46, 58 (D.C. Cir. 1950).
48. McAuliffe v. Mayor of New Bedford, 155 Mass. 216, 220 (1892).
49. Compare Frankfurter, J., concurring, in Pennekamp v. Florida, 328 U.S. 331, 352 (1946).
50. Dissenting, in Hyde v. United States, 225 U.S. 347, 391 (1912).
51. Concurring, in Joint Anti-Fascist Refugee Committee v. McGrath, 341 U.S. 123, 185 (1951).
52. Douglas, J., concurring, *id.* at 182.
53. 351 U.S. 536 (1956).
54. Association of the Bar of the City of New York, *Report of the Special Committee on the Federal Loyalty-Security Program* (New York: Dodd, Mead & Co., Inc., 1956), p. 141.
55. 346 U.S. 1 (1953).
56. New York Trust Co. v. Eisner, 256 U.S. 345, 349 (1921).
57. 351 U.S. 345 (1956).
58. *Id.* at 361.
59. *Id.* at 372.
60. *Id.* at 362.
61. *Ibid.*
62. Compare Frankfurter, J., dissenting, in United States v. Nugent, 346 U.S. at 13.
63. Rosenberg v. United States, 346 U.S. 273, 277 (1953).
64. *Id.* at 310.

65. *Id.* at 285.
66. United States v. Rosenberg, 195 F.2d 583, 590 (2d Cir. 1952).
67. Rosenberg v. United States, 344 U.S. 889 (1952).
68. Dissenting, 346 U.S. at 310-11.
69. *Id.* at 299.
70. *Id.* at 307.
71. Douglas, J., dissenting, in Dennis v. United States, 341 U.S. at 591.
72. Andrei Y. Vyshinsky, *The Law of the Soviet State* (New York: Macmillan Co., 1948), p. 500.

Chapter 10

1. Compare Learned Hand, J., in 317 U.S. xi (1942).
2. It is often said that the Senate is a continuing body. This is, however, more form than fact; certainly, the Senate does not begin to approach the Supreme Court in this respect.
3. *Loc. cit.* in note 1, above.
4. Concurring, in Brown v. Allen, 344 U.S. 443, 535 (1953).
5. Brandeis, J., in Burnet v. Coronado Oil & Gas Co., 285 U.S. 393, 406 (1932).
6. Dissenting, in Smith v. Allwright, 321 U.S. 649, 666 (1944).
7. *Id.* at 669.
8. Dissenting, in Burnet v. Coronado Oil & Gas Co., 285 U.S. 393, 406-8 (1932).
9. The Genesee Chief, 12 How. 443 (U.S. 1851).
10. Dissenting, in Washington v. Dawson & Co., 264 U.S. 219, 238 (1924).
11. Oliver Wendell Holmes, *Collected Legal Papers* (New York: Harcourt, Brace & Co., Inc., 1920), p. 187.
12. Dissenting, in United States v. Rabinowitz, 339 U.S. 56, 86 (1950).
13. William O. Douglas, *We the Judges* (Garden City, N.Y.: Doubleday & Co., Inc., 1956), p. 431. C. Herman Pritchett, *The Roosevelt Court; A Study in Judicial Politics and Values* (New York: Macmillan Co., 1948), pp. 300-301 lists 32 cases as overruled during the 1937-47 period. The discrepancy between the two lists may perhaps be explained by the fact that a number of the decisions referred to by Douglas overrule more than one prior decision.
14. C. Herman Pritchett, *Civil Liberties and the Vinson Court* (Chicago: University of Chicago Press, 1954), chap. x.
15. Ullmann v. United States, 350 U.S. 422, 428 (1956).
16. Douglas, *op. cit.*, p. 429.
17. Connecticut General Life Ins. Co. v. Johnson, 303 U.S. 77, 85 (1938).
18. Wheeling Steel Corp. v. Glander, 337 U.S. 562, 576 (1949).
19. Santa Clara County v. Southern Pac. R. Co., 118 U.S. 394 (1886).
20. Calder v. Bull, 3 Dall. 386 (U.S. 1798).
21. 342 U.S. 580, 594 (1952).
22. 350 U.S. 422 (1956).
23. Brown v. Walker, 161 U.S. 591 (1896).
24. 350 U.S. at 440.
25. *Id.* at 438-39.
26. Fred Rodell, *Nine Men: A Political History of the Supreme Court from 1790 to 1955* (New York: Random House, Inc., 1955), p. 265.

27. Frankfurter, *Of Law and Men* (New York: Harcourt, Brace & Co., Inc., 1956), p. 6.
28. Roberts, J., dissenting, in Mahnich v. Southern S.S. Co., 321 U.S. 96, 112 (1944).
29. Quoted, in Frankfurter, *op. cit.*, p. 42.
30. *Ibid.*
31. Wiscart v. D'Auchy, 3 Dall. 321, 324 (U.S. 1796).
32. *Ibid.*
33. Graves v. New York *ex rel.* O'Keefe, 306 U.S. 466, 487 (1939).
34. In The Amelia, 1 Cranch 1 (U.S. 1801).
35. Albert J. Beveridge, *The Life of John Marshall* (4 vols.; Boston: Houghton Mifflin Co., 1919), III, 15.
36. Quoted in Morgan, "Mr. Justice William Johnson and the Constitution," 57 *Harvard Law Review* 328, 333 (1944).
37. See Pritchett, *The Roosevelt Court*, p. 25.
38. In the terms 1953-1955, the dissents receded somewhat, being recorded in 64, 60, and 58 per cent of the cases, respectively.
39. Johnson, J., dissenting, in Martin v. Hunter's Lessee, 1 Wheat. 304, 377 (U.S. 1816).
40. Marine Insurance Co. v. Young, 5 Cranch 187, 191 (U.S. 1809).
41. 2 Cranch 170, 179 (U.S. 1804).
42. Pollock, "Mr. Justice Holmes," 44 *Harvard Law Review* 693, 695 (1931).
43. Catherine D. Bowen, *Yankee from Olympus* (Boston: Little, Brown & Co., 1944), p. 375.
44. Northern Securities Co. v. United States, 193 U.S. 197, 400 (1904).
45. *Ibid.*
46. Bowen, *op. cit.*, p. 372.
47. Charles E. Hughes, *The Supreme Court of the United States* (New York: Columbia University Press, 1928), p. 68.
48. Benjamin N. Cardozo, *The Nature of the Judicial Process* (New Haven: Yale University Press, 1921), p. 165.
49. *Ibid.*
50. Martin v. Hunter's Lessee, 1 Wheat. 304, 362 (U.S. 1816).
51. *Id.* at 363.
52. Cardozo, "Law and Literature," 52 *Harvard Law Review* 472, 486 (1939).
53. Frankfurter, *op. cit.*, p. 133.
54. *Ibid.*, p. 175.
55. 319 U.S. 624 (1943).
56. *Id.* at 646-47.
57. *Id.* at 647.
58. *Ibid.*
59. See, e.g., Meyer v. Nebraska, 262 U.S. 390 (1923), where a Holmes dissent indicates that such was, in fact, his approach in civil liberties cases.
60. *Loc. cit.* in note 54, above.
61. Quoted in Charles P. Curtis, *Lions under the Throne* (Boston: Houghton Mifflin Co., 1947), p. 281.
62. Quoted in Alfred T. Denning, *The Road to Justice* (London: Stevens, 1955), p. 14.
63. Pritchett, *The Roosevelt Court*, p. 285.
64. Robert H. Jackson, *The Supreme Court in the American System of Government* (Cambridge: Harvard University Press, 1955), p. 26.

65. Freund, in Edmond Cahn (ed.), *Supreme Court and Supreme Law* (Bloomington: Indiana University Press, 1954), p. 91.
66. 309 U.S. vi (1940).
67. Quoted in Pritchett, *The Roosevelt Court*, p. 278.
68. Dissenting, in Springer v. Government of the Philippine Islands, 277 U.S. 189, 209 (1928).
69. Ullmann v. United States, 350 U.S. at 429.
70. Frankfurter, *op. cit.*, p. 19.
71. Compare Frankfurter, J., concurring, in American Federation of Labor v. American Sash Co., 335 U.S. 538, 553-55 (1949).
72. Quoted, 309 U.S. xv (1940).
73. Quoted in Pritchett, *Civil Liberties and the Vinson Court*, p. 251.
74. Jackson, *The Supreme Court* . . . , p. 81.
75. 309 U.S. vii (1940).
76. Quoted in Frankfurter, J., concurring, in West Virginia Board of Education v. Barnette, 319 U.S. at 668.

CASE INDEX

(The italic figures in parentheses, following the page reference, refer to notes.)

405

NAME INDEX

(The italic figures in parentheses, following the page reference, refer to notes.)

SUBJECT INDEX

(The italic figures in parentheses, following the page reference, refer to notes.)

M